The Tammany Regiment

THE TAMMANY REGIMENT

A History of the Forty-Second New York Volunteer Infantry, 1861–1864

FRED C. WEXLER

THE TAMMANY REGIMENT
A HISTORY OF THE FORTY-SECOND NEW YORK
VOLUNTEER INFANTRY, 1861–1864

iUniverse books may be ordered through booksellers or by contacting:

iUniverse
1663 Liberty Drive
Bloomington, IN 47403
www.iuniverse.com
1-800-Authors (1-800-288-4677)

ISBN: 978-1-4917-8770-0 (sc)
ISBN: 978-1-4917-8772-4 (hc)
ISBN: 978-1-4917-8771-7 (e)

Library of Congress Control Number: 2016900758

Print information available on the last page.

iUniverse rev. date: 01/19/2016

CONTENTS

Introduction ix

Chapter One: Formation of the Regiment 1
Tammany Hall responds to the start of the Civil War. William Kennedy appointed
Colonel. Officer ranks filled. Recruitment in New York and Boston. Acceptance by
the Union Defense League. Early desertions. Departure for the Seat of War.

Chapter Two: Washington D.c. to Ball's Bluff 15
Death of Colonel Kennedy. Milton Cogswell promoted to Colonel, James Mooney
to Lieut. Colonel. Michael Doheny and other high profile Fenians. Positions along
the Potomac River. Events at Mason's Island. Michael Madden awarded the Medal
of Honor. Lieut. George Hewitt Wallis, the first Tammany officer to be captured by
the enemy. Confrontation of Captain Timothy O'Meara and Lieut. Patrick Downing
at Conrad's Ferry. Resignation of the Downing brothers.

Chapter Three: The Battle of Ball's Bluff 31
General Stone's Corps of Observation. General McClellan orders a slight
demonstration. Recon by 15th Massachusetts. Movement of the Tammany regiment
to Harrison's Island and the Virginia shore. Disaster on the bluffs. Senator Baker
killed. Colonel Cogswell captured. Recovery of the bodies of Captains Alden and
Garretty. Feud between Major Bowe and Colonel Hinks, 19th Massachusetts.

Chapter Four: The Ball's Bluff Prisoners 67
Arrival in Richmond. Prison life. Capture of the privateer Savannah. Colonel
Cogswell and Captain O'Meara held hostage. Negotiations between Generals
McClellan and Robert E. Lee. Parole and exchange of hostages and prisoners.

Chapter Five: Winter 1861-2 81
Reassignment of Colonel Cogswell and Captain O'Meara. Command in chaos. Arrest of Lieut. Colonel Mooney. Edmund Charles appointed Colonel. Return of Patrick Downing. Tammany men serving with the signal service.

Chapter Six: Arrival on the Peninsula...........................105
Activities around Yorktown. Regimental band and musicians. Movement to the Chickahominy River. Sickness takes its toll. Officer ranks filled. Conflict in command. Resignation and reinstatement of Lieut. Colonel Mooney, Captain Tobin and Captain Lynch. Charges against Captain Tobin for abuse of authority by Quartermaster Garland. Arrest of First Lieut. Conroy. Arrest of First Lieut. Paine.

Chapter Seven: Fair Oaks-Seven Pines 125
Positions of the Army of the Potomac. Confederate attack. Union troops move to the Grapevine Bridge. Artillery cross the Chickahominy. Sumner and Sedgwick counterattack.

Chapter Eight: Seven Days Battles 137
Robert E. Lee takes command of Confederate forces. Jeb Stuart's ride around McClellan. Attack on Tunstall's Station. Capture of Captain McGrath and Lieut. Paine. McClellan's change of base to the James River. Movement of the Siege Train. Destruction of the Grapevine Bridge. Savage Station. Glendale, Colonel Charles wounded and captured. Regimental medical staff.

Chapter Nine: Harrison's Landing Withdrawal from the Peninsula... 159
Positions on the James River. Sick and wounded evacuated. Confederate attacks on Union positions. Lieut. Colonel Mooney and Major Bowe resign over political appointment of officers. Captain Bomford promoted to Lieut. Colonel. James Mallon named Major. Departure from Harrison's Landing.

Chapter Ten: Prelude to Antietam................................173
Arrival in Alexandria. Defenses of Washington. Lieut. Morgan Doheny captured. Movement to Sharpsburg.

Chapter Eleven: Antietam 181
Second Corps attacks. The Cornfield, Dunker Church and West Woods. 145 Tammany casualties.

Chapter Twelve: Movement to Fredericksburg..............................197
Reconnaissance to Charlestown, West Virginia. Burnside takes command. Changes to the officer ranks. Lieut. Morgan Doheny seeks appointment in regular army. Presentation of tattered colors to Tammany Hall.

Chapter Thirteen: Fredericksburg...207
Timeline of events. Crossing the Rappahannock. Fighting in the streets. Court martial and dismissal of Captain John Garland.

Chapter Fourteen: Winter 1863...227
Hooker takes command. Army of the Potomac General Orders: No. 18 and 27, Tammany regiment activities temporarily restricted for lack of readiness. Quartermaster and Commissary sergeants. Political controversies on officer appointments. James Mallon named Colonel. Resignation of Lieut. Colonel Bomford. Richard Halstead, aide to Gen. Sedgwick. Fenian leader Patrick Downing appointed Major. Tammany Hall supports Captain W. A. Lynch for promotion to Lieut. Colonel.

Chapter Fifteen: Chancellorsville Second Fredericksburg 245
Sedgwick's command and orders. Role of Tammany regiment in support of Sedgwick. Return to the streets of Fredericksburg. Picket duty, action in the graveyard and retreat across the Rappahannock.

Chapter Sixteen: Gettysburg 259
Movement to Gettysburg. Positions on Cemetery Ridge. July 2: Tammany men and 19th MA sent to reinforce General Sickles. July 3: Pickett's Charge. Counterattack at the Copse of Trees. 1891 Dedication of the Tammany Monument on Hancock Avenue.

Chapter Seventeen: Bristoe Station Mine Run...............................273
Federal Draft Act of 1863. Regimental reinforcements. Philip Kreis and John Vaze. Movements after Gettysburg. Position on the Brentsville Road. Confederate attack on the rail line. Union counterattack. Death and funeral of Colonel Mallon. Captain Poinsett Cooper.

Chapter Eighteen: Winter 1864..293
New recruits. Transfers to the Navy. Temporary duty assignments. War Department General Orders No. 92 and charges of desertion. Patrick Condon: from Lieut. to ambulance driver. Arrests and trials. Changes in the officer ranks.

Chapter Nineteen: Battle of the Wilderness.................................313
Grant takes command. Fighting under General Webb. Smoke and flames in the forest.

Chapter Twenty: Battle of Spotsylvania Court House....................321
Fighting on May 10. Arrest of Major Downing by General Webb. General Webb's family. May 12 attack on the "mule shoe". Captains Lennon, Tobin and O'Shea and Lieut. Coffey killed. Tammany regiment suffers 30% casualties.

Chapter Twenty-One: Battle of Cold Harbor 349
Union attacks. Trench warfare. Death of Sgt. James McNamara.

Chapter Twenty-Two: Jerusalem Plank Road Weldon Railroad......359
June 22, 1864, capture of the Tammany regiment. Deaths and survival at Andersonville. Families seek answers. Tammany men that served in the Confederacy. Mustering out. The Tammany colors.

Bibliography...391

INTRODUCTION

Whenever anyone sets out on a project like the writing of the history of a regiment of troops that fought in the Civil War, the author is plagued by many recurrent questions. Is there a good reason to write the book? Are there sufficient sources of information that will allow for an accurate account of the regiment's activities to be determined? Is the author capable of doing a suitable job of organizing the available data and putting it in front of readers in a way that will be clear, make sense and present something other than a list of facts?

These and other questions certainly were on my mind as I started this project. I was getting ready to retire after 33 years of corporate life and felt that I would have the time available to tackle the book. What was my inspiration? That is an easy question to answer. My wife Mary!

From the time we first met in the early eighties, I had visited Cape Cod and Mary's parents John and Eugenia O'Connell. In their home was a framed picture of a Civil War soldier. To be honest I had not really thought much about it. Although I had always been interested in military strategy and tactics, the Civil War was not of particular interest to me. I was more of a WWII man.

Captain Patrick Henry Lennon

I remember discussions about the picture that appears on the cover of this book and how members of the family had obtained some old military records of the man in the photo. I remember looking at the records and forming an image of the man and the time he'd served in high-echelon military organizations named "Army of the Potomac" and "II Corps" and the battles he had participated in. Some were names that stood out like Antietam and Gettysburg. Others I had never heard of like Ball's Bluff and Fair Oaks.

The man in the photo was Patrick Henry Lennon. Lennon was Mary's mother's maiden name. The regiment he belonged to was the Forty Second New York Voluntary Infantry, the Tammany Regiment. From the copies of the service and pension records in the file, I could tell that Patrick Henry Lennon had risen from the rank of Private to Captain and that he had been killed at the battle of Spotsylvania Court House on May 12, 1864 while commanding Company H of the regiment. He had previously been wounded at Gettysburg. The die was cast. I was hooked. I knew a little, I needed to know a lot more.

An opportunity presented itself. Mary and I were invited to a wedding in North Carolina and we decided to stop in Fredericksburg to see if we could shed some light on Captain Lennon's wartime experiences. Spotsylvania was nearby and we thought that we would make a side trip to see the place that he died as we headed for North Carolina. We flew to Washington, D.C., rented a car and drove to Fredericksburg. As we entered the town we saw signs with directions to the National Cemetery and decided that would be a good place to start. We expected that we might find an attendant that could help us locate some information on the battle at Spotsylvania Court House.

When we entered the headquarters building at the National Cemetery we went to the front desk and told the ranger our story including the name of Captain Lennon. He suggested that the best place to start was in the directory of the men that were buried in the cemetery. He cautioned us that many of the men were never identified and that large numbers of graves simply said unknown. We were all surprised when he quickly located Captain Lennon's grave and gave us directions to it. Within minutes we were standing in front of his grave, perhaps the first visitors to pay their respects in well over a hundred years. It was very moving. Both Mary and I had a tear in our eyes as we looked at the grave and thought our private thoughts.

Mary and Fred Wexler at grave of Captain Patrick Henry Lennon, Fredericksburg National Cemetery

We found our way to Spotsylvania Court House and followed the tour outline to the spot of the II Corps attack on Confederate positions in the early morning hours of May 12, 1864. We stood very close to the exact spot that Captain Lennon received a gunshot wound in the thigh that severed his femoral artery and resulted in his bleeding to death in the field that morning.

Mary and I made a number of other trips to other battlefields and I spent a sizable amount of time reading books about the Civil War, especially about the activities of the Army of the Potomac. I drew organization charts to see how the Forty Second New York fit into the overall picture. I wanted to know the names of all their brigade and division commanders. I wanted to know all there was to know about the Tammany Regiment.

I quickly found lots of information outlining the political formation of the regiment in New York City and the combat operations that it took part in. I was able to find out that it was virtually always aligned with several other regiments, the Nineteenth and Twentieth Massachusetts and the Seventh Michigan, during its three years of service. The more I learned the more convinced I became that the Forty Second New York played a significant role in the Civil War.

What amazed me was that I couldn't find a book with a title like: "The Regimental History of the Forty Second New York Volunteers". Many other regiments had their histories written and forever preserved for those that might want to revisit their exploits. Some were written by veterans of the regiments themselves following the war. Others were put together from groups of letters or diaries that had been compiled by an interested person.

It was at that time that I decided that I would do it. I would do it to honor a member of my wife's family, Captain Lennon, and all the men of the Tammany Regiment. I would do it to record the story of a group of men that fought for many different reasons. I would do it to honor the sacrifices of those who died and suffered wounds in combat. I would do it to honor those that were captured and imprisoned. I would do it to honor those that suffered from numerous diseases, which if not fatal, plagued them for most if not all of their lives. I would do it because it needed to be done!

Now that I had answered the first major question in the affirmative, I had the reason to write the book, would I be able to find the sources of information that would result in an accurate account of the regiment's service during the Civil War? There was no way to answer this question without doing the work, so I decided to set off on what I called the "Research Phase" of the project.

I located copies of the regiment's roster and sent off to Washington for the military records of all of the regiment's listed officers and a sizable sample of the enlisted men. I spent endless hours in various libraries viewing microfilm of newspapers from the Civil War era. I read and read and then read some more. I got copies of the histories of regiments that fought next to the Tammany Regiment to glean facts and background as best I could. I used the Internet for all it was worth. I visited the New York State Archives to see what I could find there. I drew battle maps and organization charts and tables to understand the role of the regiment in their many battles. I created a database of events to track when men joined and left the regiment so that I could somehow come up with figures for manpower strengths at key points in the conflict. I drew up lists of unanswered questions that required more research. I continually poured over the information I found to draw relationships among events and form theories for why things happened the way they did. I found that the story was going to be more than facts on what occurred on any given day. There were endless stories to be told. Some stories were quite simple but many were extremely complex and a few more bizarre than fiction.

At some point I declared the "Research Phase" complete. That didn't mean that I was not going to remain open to new inputs as the writing continued or that I wouldn't seek out some new piece of data. It simply meant that I believed that I had what I needed to write the book. The answer to question two was definitely yes!

Making that decision was not easy. There is always the thought that there is another document out there that will change a major part of the book. Perhaps there is a letter written by one of the officers describing a key battle. Perhaps there is another newspaper article that explains one of the lasting mysteries. What if I forgot something? This type of paranoia could have prevented me from moving ahead with the project. It almost did.

Then one day I was sitting at the beach on Cape Cod and I had a conversation with myself. I formulated the philosophy with which I was to write the book. Basically, I was going to do the best I could with what

I had put together. I was confident that I had done a pretty good job. Was it perfect? No way. Could I possibly get a fact wrong or a name misspelled? Guaranteed. In the end, that really didn't seem to matter to me. I would do the best that I could do and if something were missed or if someone out there had something that contradicted a position I took, so be it. I decided that it was better to do the job and get the history written. It could always be improved on either by others or me.

As I put things together, I quickly came to the realization that records in the mid 1800s were no different than records of any time. They are no better than the people that put them together using the techniques and technology of the time. There were no computers, data processing was a manual task performed under trying conditions and on a scale that was enormous. Conflicts in data were to be expected. What was needed was a way to sift through the data and come to a meaningful way to reach conclusions. I decided to use the "more likely than not" rule as I put the history together. What that means is that I did not require absolute certainty in developing a theory or presenting the actions of the regiment. I put all the data together and moved ahead with the project. As one reads this book it will be quite easy to see this rule in operation.

I am sure there are names misspelled or omitted. Certainly there are members of the regiment that were wounded or captured at various battles, or out of action sick from any number of diseases that I do not have records for. To their memory and any members of their families that might read this book, I sincerely apologize. I wish I had the resources to view the military and pension records of every one of the members of the regiment. I could not. I wish I had the ability to track down the final resting places and living relatives of all the Tammany men. I couldn't. Because of this the reading of this book will lead some to think that I have selected some men to research more than others. That is true certainly for Captain Lennon. I also concentrated on the officer and non-commissioned officers and those men that for one reason or another came to light in various ways during the research. In total I reviewed the military records of over four hundred Tammany men. I had to keep in mind that I was writing the history of the regiment and not the complete story of every soldier that served. I needed to describe the actions and events that shaped the contribution of the regiment using the specifics of individuals as building blocks in the construction of the total picture.

I first thought that I would include every event in each soldier's service that I had documented, every promotion, every trip to the infirmary, every leave to visit family. I thought I would document when each soldier mustered out and the reason his service had ended. That was not to be the case. I had to put some constraints on what I would include if for no other reason but to make reading easier. So what will the answer to the last question be? Have I put this book together in a way that readers will enjoy and find a rewarding investment of their time? I hope so but only time will tell.

In order to get this book published I had to make a number of compromises. I sent inquiries to several publishers but none of them were interested. So I decided that I would self-publish. Now that I am seventy-three years old I wanted to get this project completed so that I can move on with all the other projects I have in front of me. Choosing the self-publishing route allowed me to proceed in a way that made sense to me without the need for editorial critique. So if in reading this book you find that there are errors in grammar or spelling you can join Miss Perkins, my high school English teacher, in considering me grammatically challenged. If you wonder where the maps are, all I can say is that there are none. I was limited to a finite number of insertions and decided that the pictures included in the book were more important than maps. I certainly recommend that all who read this book consult maps of the areas discussed so that they will get a more complete experience.

There are extensive footnotes that should help a reader understand where the information for this book came from. In the footnotes you will find three generally accepted short citation forms: "Ibid", "Supra" and "Hereinafter". Ibid is used when a footnote refers back to the immediately preceding footnote. Supra refers the reader to another footnote other than the one immediately preceding, where the source document has been fully cited. Authors generally use Supra with a reference to where the full citation can be found such as "Author's name, supra, chapter 3, note 7". I have deviated from this form. When "Supra" is used it will always refer to a previous note in the same chapter. The reader will only have to look for the same author or work within the notes of the chapter being read. Hereinafter is used where a particular reference work is used repeatedly and has a title that is quite cumbersome. It simply means that in future notes that particular work will be referenced by a simpler form. For example the first reference to the Official Records will show the following citation: "U.S. War Department, The War of the Rebellion: A Compilation of the Official Records of the Union and Confederate Armies, 127 volumes, Washington, D.C., GPO, 1880-1901, hereinafter cited as OR". There is no index. The book is organized chronologically with a Table of Contents that provides some detail on what is covered in each chapter. For those readers that would like to pursue details on a specific Tammany soldier I suggest that they contact the New York State Military Museum and Veterans Research Center in Saratoga Springs, New York. All of the research materials, including the service records of hundreds of Tammany men used in putting this book together have been donated to the museum. If I had anything it is there.

I want to acknowledge the assistance that I received from the many libraries I used to search out information. Thanks to the members of the Cape Cod Civil War Roundtable and other students of the Civil War for the encouragement and assistance they provided to me over the years that I worked on the book. Thanks to the staffs at the National and the New York State Archives. Thanks to those who keep the historical battlefields and national cemeteries in good order so that interested citizens can walk the terrain and commune with those who fought some 150 years ago. Thanks to the New York Historical Society, Princeton University, The Abraham Lincoln Presidential Library and Museum, Sheila Vaughn, Martin Schoenfeld and Seward Osborne for allowing me to use materials and photographs from their collections. Thanks to Fred Kreiss a direct descendant of Philip Kreis and Ed Pearson a direct descendant of Captain Ed Cauvet. Most of all I want to thank my wife Mary. Without her there would be no book. I would never have heard of Captain Patrick Henry Lennon. Her ability to put up with all the stories and the ups and downs of this project deserve a medal for understanding and caring that has not yet been envisioned. It is to her that this book is dedicated.

Before I end this introduction there is one key issue I want to cover. I said that I was amazed that there was no book called: "The Regimental History of the Forty Second New York Infantry". That is not 100% accurate. In my research I came across an obscure library reference to a volume called: "Under Two Flags" by Philip Kreis. After some digging, I found a copy of the volume in the John Shaw Pierson Civil War Collection of the Rare Books Library at Princeton University. The call number is W6929.042.5. The full title of the work is "Under Two Flags, The Adventures of Philip Kreis, Story of the Tammany Regiment of New York". It has a sub-title that reads: "Experiences of one of the members who saw service first in the Southern Army, then in the 42d New York Volunteers". The work is a 17 page augmented reprint of an article written by Mr. Kreis and published in the February 18, 1891 issue of the New York Weekly Tribune. Mr. Kreis joined the Tammany Regiment on August 26, 1863. His work provides a brief outline of the regiment's history prior to that time and conveys some personal experiences of his around the time of the battle at Bristoe Station. There is no doubt that Philip Kreis was a Tammany man although it is my opinion that he served under the assumed name of John Vaze as described in Chapter 17. I tried to locate his records in Washington but was told they could not be found. His name is not listed in the regiment's roster published by the Adjutant General of New York. However, Mr. Kreis served as the Vice-President and Chairman of the Tammany Regiment Veterans Association and is listed, with the rank of Captain, as a participant in the dedication ceremony of the monument to the Forty-Second at Gettysburg on September 24, 1891 that was attended by over fifty survivors of the regiment. It is beyond imagination that Philip Kreis would have been accepted by the men of the Tammany Regiment as a leader of the Veteran's Association had he not served.

On page 11 of his work, Mr. Kreis mentions that Eugene Sullivan, another Tammany Regiment veteran, was in the process of preparing for publication a sketch of the regiment. I was able to locate three articles written by Eugene Sullivan and published in The National Tribune, a publication of the GAR, at the Library of Congress. The first article: "How the Battle was Fought and Lost: Part 1" appeared in Volume XIV, No. 23, March 21, 1895 and is a partial account of the action at Ball's Bluff. The second article is the completion of the account of the action at Ball's Bluff and appeared in Volume XIV, No. 24, March 28, 1895. The third article is titled "Bringing Up the Rear-Critical Times on the Peninsula of Virginia". It appeared in the January 7, 1904 edition of the National

Tribune, page 3 and details the actions of the Tammany Regiment from just after the Battle of Fair Oaks through the retreat of the Army of the Potomac to Savage Station.

Eugene Sullivan, who served with the rank of Sergeant, is also listed in the record of the dedication of the Tammany monument at Gettysburg with the rank of Captain and was the presiding officer of the Veteran's Association at that ceremony. Where did Eugene Sullivan and Philip Kreis obtain the rank of Captain? I have no answer to this question. Perhaps it was an honorary rank that was bestowed based on their service as senior members of the Veteran's Association. The dedication at Gettysburg is not the only time Philip Kreis was referred to as Captain. The New York Tribune of May 31, 1895 in an article describing the Line of March of the Decoration Day Parade says: "Among the battle flags carried in the parade were the four belonging to the Tammany Regiment … under command of Captain Philip Kreis". Philip Kreis died August 21, 1896.

I hope that all who read my book take away a feeling of what the men of the Tammany Regiment gave to their country. I have tried to add the flesh to the skeleton provided by Philip Kreis and Eugene Sullivan more than one hundred years ago. Perhaps someone will add to what I have done. Nothing would make me happier as the ultimate goal is that history has a better understanding of the role these men played and the contributions they made.

Chapter One

FORMATION OF THE REGIMENT

It was at a special meeting of the Democratic Republican General Committee in New York on Friday evening, April 26, 1861 that a committee of five men was appointed to draft resolutions expressing the sentiments of the city and Tammany Hall[1], relative to the troubled state of the country. In the resolutions they prepared they set the stage for the creation of the Tammany Regiment. The fifth resolution drafted read: "Resolved: That the democracy of this city are heartily united, with all of the citizens, as one man, to uphold the Constitution, enforce the laws, maintain the Union, defend the Flag and protect the Capitol of these United States in the full and firm belief that the preservation of our national unity is the only security for the rights, liberties and power of our own people, and the greatest hope of oppressed humanity throughout the world."

It is not the intent of this book to go deeply into the history or the individuals of Tammany Hall. Such an endeavor could fill volumes. Many works have been published outlining the good and the bad of Tammany Hall and all readers are urged to seek out sufficient information to satisfy their personal interests. On occasion, I will point out an issue or allude to an individual in New York politics, but I expect that there are endless

---

[1] The men appointed were: Nelson J. Waterbury, Claudius L. Monell, John T. Hoffman, Francis I. A. Boole and William Burns. Myers, Gustavus. The History of Tammany Hall, Second Edition, originally published 1917, reprinted 1968, Burt Franklin, New York, pages 1-30, 190-203. Also, Proceedings at the Dedication of the Monument to the Tammany Regiment erected on the battlefield of Gettysburg, September 24, 1891, Tammany Society, 1892, hereinafter cited as Proceedings.

scenarios that could be developed behind specific events well beyond those I might raise.

William Marcy "Boss" Tweed, Library of Congress

The beginnings of the Tammany Society, a forerunner of Tammany Hall, go back to the Columbian Order of New York City around 1789. Many of the customs of the society were based on Indian traditions and the name came from the Indian Chief Tamanend (there are many spellings) who on April 23, 1683 is reported to have struck a land deal with William Penn in Bucks County, PA. In 1776, Colonel George Morgan of New Jersey was sent by Congress to confer with the Delaware Indians. They gave him the name Tamanend in honor of their old chief. During the Revolutionary War he became known as "St. Tamany, the Patron Saint of America". The officers of the society were thirteen "Sachems", one from each of the thirteen tribes paired to each of the thirteen original colonies. From this group a "Grand Sachem" was selected as the head of the society. In the early days there was no love lost between the Irish and the members of Tammany. In 1791 Tammany announced that being a national body, it consisted of Americans, who would fill all offices though adopted Americans were eligible to fill honorary posts. It wasn't until 1809 that a Catholic would be allowed to have his name placed on a Tammany election ticket.

Another committee of three men was created at the April 26, 1861 meeting. William Miner, William D. Kennedy and Emanual B. Hart were charged with procuring a banner bearing the words of President Jackson: "The Union Must and Shall be Preserved", that would be suspended in front of Tammany Hall until the war was over.[2]

During the months of May through July of 1861 the Tammany Regiment, originally called The Jackson Guard, took the form it was to take to battle in the second half of the year. On May 4th and 5th recruiting ads were run in the New York Times reading: "Jackson Guards: The Union Must and Shall be Preserved: 550 Volunteers wanted to complete the Jackson Guard Regiment now forming to protect the Capital of our country. None but able bodied men will be accepted. Regimental Headquarters, Tammany Hall. Roll List now open. William D. Kennedy, Colonel, Commanding, Timothy O'Meara, Acting Adjutant".[3]

Why the regiment was originally known as the Jackson Guards is unknown to this author. One reason why it may have stopped using that designation is that there was a Confederate regiment, the First Arkansas Infantry, organized in May of 1861, which used the name Jackson Guards and had it embroidered in their battle flag.

An article in the May 5, 1861 New York Times read: "The Tammany Regiment … is to be a thoroughly drilled and fully equipped rifle regiment of skirmishers intended for outpost duty. It is to be drilled by an experienced Crimean Officer, in the modern system adopted by the French rifle regiments in the late war, and the drum and fife to be entirely replaced by the bugle … The arms are the minie rifle, swords, bayonets and revolver."[4] Inspection of the Tammany Regiment was ordered by the

---

2   The phrase: "Our Federal Union: It Must be Preserved" was a toast given by President Jackson at the Jefferson Day dinner on April 13, 1830. Grolier Multimedia Encyclopedia.

3   New York Times, May 3, 1861, page 5, column 6. Repeated on May 4. The ad also listed as sponsors many notable New Yorkers and Tammany men including Ely Smith, Jr., August Belmont, Elijah F. Purdy, Samuel J. Tilden, Daniel E. Delevan, Isaac Bell, N. J. Waterbury, Daniel Devlin, Michael Toomey, M. T. Brennan, Samuel Sloan, Charles Chipp, Edward Cooper, H.W. Ganet, John Kelly, Peter Sweeney, Francis Boole, Michael Connolly, E. B. Hart, William M. Tweed, William Miner, J. Y. Savage, James Nicholson, O. Ottendorfer and Horace Clark.

4   New York Times, May 5, 1861, page 8, column 4. The regimental band was not mustered in until late September 1861. Many of the musicians in the band were

Union Defense Committee for May 25 at 3PM on 14th Street between Sixth and Seventh Avenue.[5]

On May 26, 1861 the following announcement appeared in the New York Times: "The Tammany Regiment … appeared on the ground without uniforms or muskets but nevertheless making a very good appearance. They number 975."

The same article listed a group of acting staff officers including: Colonel: W.D. Kennedy, Lieut. Colonel: Michael Doherty, Major: George W. McLean, Adjutant: Timothy O'Meara, Quartermaster: William C. Rhodes, Assistant Quartermaster: J. F. Green, Paymaster: John Richardson. Company commanders and strengths were quoted as: A: ---- (122); B: Peter Bowe (46); C: J. Graham (62); D: H. E. Call (106); E: J. Lynch (85); F: C. R. Beneoic (62), G: John Quinn (43); H: John Mulligan (95); I: John Baker (26); K: William Vall (58); L: C. Fitzgerald (54); M: Wallace (101) and N: Farring Hall (106). Many of the names were incorrectly spelled and a number of the men were not to remain in their listed positions. Some were never to actually serve with the regiment.

Elijah F. Purdy, New York Public Library

On May 29, 1861 the following was printed in the New York Times: "The Tammany Regiment … raised under the auspices of the Old Wigwam, and of which Sachem William D. Kennedy is Colonel, was yesterday accepted by the Union Defence Committee, and will tomorrow proceed to

from upstate New York. Bugles were the main instrument of the band although fife and drum remained company level instruments.

5   New York Times, May 24, 1861, page 2, column 5.

the encampment selected for them, at Great Neck, opposite Flushing, Long Island. The regiment embarks from the foot of Tenth Street at 2 o'clock P.M. The Union Defence Committee has undertaken the equipment of the corps and guarantees its speedy call to active service."[6] The total cost of equipping the Tammany Regiment was $47,146.65 and included all clothing and equipment and rations for 1000 men for two months.[7]

The regiment was re-organized into the standard organizational framework of the time with 10 companies A-I and K. Each company was to be about one hundred strong and headed by a Captain with two additional officers, a First Sergeant and several other non-commissioned ranks as well as one or two musicians and a teamster or wagoner. The Regimental Staff was to be comprised of a Colonel commanding the Regiment, Lt. Colonel, Major, Adjutant, Quartermaster, Surgeon, Sergeant Major, Commissary Sergeant, Hospital Steward, Fife Major and Drum Major. All together the table of organization called for a little over 1000 men.

The regimental organizers were mostly successful in raising the required manpower from within the confines of New York State with the majority of men enlisting either in New York City or Great Neck, Long Island. On Sunday, June 16, 1861 the following notice appeared in the New York Times: "The Jackson Guard: This corps, under command of W. D. Kennedy, stationed at Great Neck, numbers 700 men, and are in good condition. They are doing their cooking in messes, in the open air. They have 125 wall tents, and 10 marquees. The regiment is nearly full, a good many being absent on leave. They will be inspected early this week."[8]

An exception to New York recruiting was Company H, which was partially staffed with a number of men that were recruited in Boston and signed on with the regiment on June 17 19, 1861 at that city. Plans were to recruit up to 50 men in Boston. Various records identify the names, using the "more likely than not criteria", of 49. All were originally recruited to be in Company C but were immediately transferred to Company H. This group is of special interest as Patrick Henry Lennon, the guy on the cover

---

6   New York Times, May 29, 1861, page 8, column 4.

7   New York Times, August 18, 1876, "Hewitt's Falsehoods".

8   New York Times, June 16, 1861, page 3, column 4.

and a relation of my wife Mary, was one of those that enlisted in Boston.[9] Why would men from Massachusetts join a New York regiment? Surely there were regiments being formed in Massachusetts. In fact, a number of regiments from Massachusetts had already been formed and the state was in the process of trying to form an additional ten regiments above their original quota. The process was slow in gaining the necessary political approvals. On the same day, June 17, 1861, that recruiting began in Boston an interesting article appeared in the same Boston Herald newspaper that ran the ad for recruits.[10] It said: "It seems unfortunate that Massachusetts men who desire to fight for the flag cannot go in Massachusetts regiments so that the old Commonwealth may have credit for their own. But we know that the anxious desire of some to get to the war will not allow them to wait the progress of events. It is well to remember that Massachusetts is a good state to hail from and that she will watch with tender care the interests of her children who go in her name."

---

[9] The 49 men I was able to identify as having enlisted in Boston were: John Anderson, James Boyce, William Byrne, James Byron, Patrick Conner, Phillip Cratton, Patrick Crosby, Thomas Delaney, Bernard Dolan, John Driscoll, William Elson, James Fallon, Leonard Fay, Patrick Flaherty, William Flynn, Andrew Galvin, William Hayley, Edward Kelly, John P. Kelly, James Kennedy, Patrick H. Lennon, Jeremiah Lynch, John Lynch, Michael Lynch, Timothy Manahan, Richard McAuliffe, Thomas McBay, Jeremiah McCarthy, Michael McCarthy, Bernard McGovern, Richard McGreal, Daniel Mears, James Merrick, Charles Michaels, Bernard Minturn, James Monahan, Patrick Moore, Andrew Mullen, Phineas B. Norris, John P. Nugent, Pete J. O'Connell, William O'Niel, Marcus M. Puffer, Michael Queenan, Nicholas Quinn, Bernard Reynolds, John G. Smith, John Southwick and Charles Thompson. Twenty-nine of these men would become casualties: killed, wounded or captured, before the war ended. Documents of the Assembly of the State of New York, 124th Session, 1901, Volume 6, No. 30, Part 3. Forty-Second Infantry, Albany, New York, hereinafter cited as Assembly Document. Also, National Archives Records Administration, Military Service Records of Individual Soldiers, Washington, DC, hereinafter cited as NARA. Also Roll of Honor, City of Chelsea, H. Mason & Son, 1880, pages 18 and 126. Phineus B. Norris and Daniel Mears are identified in this reference as being from Chelsea. Mears was discharged from the Tammany Regiment for disability on December 12, 1861. He enlisted in the First Massachusetts Infantry on December 28, 1861, was taken prisoner on the Peninsula in June 1862 and died in a Richmond prison on July 18, 1862.

[10] Boston Herald, Monday, June 17, 1861, page unknown, column 2.

The Tammany Regiment was not the only New York regiment recruiting in Massachusetts. The Bay State was the source of troops for many other units. Was the rush to sign up a sign of patriotism? Surely to some degree it was. But it was not patriotism alone that prompted enlistments. Units offered sign on bonuses of $100 or more. Other attractive inducements, real or not, most likely also appealed to potential recruits. The same newspaper of June 17 ran an article on page 1 called "The Pay and Pension of Our Volunteers". The article stated: "The following recapitulation affords useful information to volunteers and their families; 1. After being mustered into the service of the United States, volunteers are entitled to the same pay as regular troops. 2. If disabled by wounds received in service or by disease contracted in service, they are entitled to an invalid pension during life, or so long as the disability continues. 3. If any are killed or die in the service of the United States, leaving a widow, she is entitled to what pay was due her husband, and a pension. If there is no widow, the child or children of such volunteer is entitled to the pay and a pension until they are sixteen years of age. 4. If there is no widow or child under sixteen years of age, the other heirs of descendent are entitled to the pay due the volunteer at the time of his death-no pension. At this time neither the volunteers or any heir is entitled to land warrants, but there is no doubt an act of Congress will be passed early in July granting one hundred and sixty acres to every volunteer that shall serve fourteen days, or engage in battle and be honorably discharged-first to the widow, second to the children, third to the mother, fourth to the father: and if all of the foregoing heirs be dead, fifth the brothers and sisters of those who may serve and die without a warrant, in like manner as the volunteers who served in Mexico, are now rewarded ..."

It is not hard to imagine what went through the minds of the young men of Boston many of who were from poor, immigrant families. Here was a chance to serve your country, be paid for it, have security for your family and potentially emerge a landowner and all at the age of 19! Of course the land warrant bill never was passed but that didn't make a difference to the state of mind of the men of Boston on the morning of June 17, 1861. That day expectations were high.

The following advertisement also ran in the Boston Herald newspaper on Monday June 17, 1861. "NEW YORK REGIMENT: JACKSON

GUARD This regiment is now in camp at Great Neck Long Island, New York. About fifty able bodied men are required to complete Capt. S. Reete's Company. Capt. S. Reete is now recruiting over Little Brown & Co., 112 Washington Street. Apply early on Monday morning as the Regiment has full equipments and proceeds immediately to the seat of war."

Interestingly, the officer was Frederick Skeete who although referred to as a Captain was mustered in as a First Lt. in Company H on June 28, 1861. One possible explanation is that at the time of the Boston recruitment he had in fact been appointed as Captain of Company C but in the month that followed, before the regiment was mustered in, his position changed. This was not uncommon and there are several other examples of such changes. This would also be consistent with the fact that all of the Boston recruits were originally intended to be in Company C, and all were mustered into that company, but were immediately transferred to Company H where now First Lt. Skeete was second in command. The men had signed up to serve under the command of Frederick Skeete and they would serve with him. Captain Skeete was not the only member of the regiment that went to Boston to recruit. He was accompanied by First. Lt. S. M. Saunders a man that was appointed to the position of First Lt. of Company H and was so listed in an article in the New York Times dated July 7, 1861. There is no record of his being mustered in as a member of the regiment and as the troops left for war Frederick Skeete was the First Lt. of Company H.

Recruitment in Boston probably did not go as quickly as originally expected. On June 18, another ad was run: "VOLUNTEERS, ATTENTION! JACKSON GUARD: The First Squad of Capt. Skeete's Company left yesterday for the camp at New York. A few more able bodied men wanted. Apply early this morning over Little, Brown & Co., 112 Washington Street."

Elsewhere in the same paper was an article that read: "Jackson Guard. This is a New York Regiment, now in camp at Long Island, New York. Captain Skeete is now in this city recruiting at 112 Washington Street and he dispatched a fine body of men to New York last night. All who are desirous of getting quickly into active service should call at the recruiting office this day. Capt. Skeete or Lt. Saunders proceeds to New York this evening with another body of men."

On June 19 recruitment was still continuing with the following final ad being run: "VOLUNTEERS ATTENTION JACKSON GUARD: The Second Squad of Capt. Skeete's Company left yesterday for the camp at New York. A few more able bodied men wanted. Apply early this morning over Little, Brown & Co., 112 Washington Street."

Also in the June 19 paper was the following article: "The Jackson Guard: The second squad of Capt. Streeter's company went on to New York last evening. These men will join the Jackson Guard Regiment, which is to leave for the seat of war next week. Lieut. Saunders will leave with another squad this afternoon, at half past five o'clock." Once again Capt. Skeete's name was misspelled and the timing of the Regiment's departure for the seat of war was off by about a month. The official mustering in date for the Regiment was June 22, 1861 when over 900 men were officially taken into the service of the Union. On that date a notice appeared in the New York Times stating: "Tammany Regiment: Six companies of this regiment, Col. Kennedy, were sworn in yesterday. The remaining companies will be sworn in today or tomorrow."[11]

Over the next few weeks, additional men were mustered into the ranks so that by the time the unit was ready to leave for their first assignment near Washington DC on July 18, there had been 1176 men that had joined and been mustered in. That is not to say that there were 1176 men in the regiment on July 18. During the time between enlistment and leaving for Washington 140 men were lost to the regiment for one reason or another. The vast majority, 134 or 11.4% of the enrolled force, were men that chose not to stay with the regiment and deserted while waiting to leave Great Neck Long Island.[12] Five men were discharged for one reason or another

---

[11] New York Times, June 22, 1861, page 5, column 2.

[12] The word desertion creates a variety of feelings among readers, none of which are good. This is especially true when the term is used in relation to active duty in the military during war time. Over the years many individuals have paid with their lives upon conviction of war time desertion. Many Civil War soldiers shared that fate, but not the majority of those that were listed as having deserted. During the civil war there were "deserters" and there were "deserters". How does one tell the difference between the two? There is no answer to that question. It depended on the circumstances, the commander in the field at the time and numerous other factors that would lend themselves to a standalone volume. Many men left their regiments while recovering from wounds or sickness in

including Lt. Colonel Michael Doheny and one, Private Walter Smith from C Company, accidentally drowned. Another man, Private Edward Casey from F Company died as the result of an accident on July 19, 1861 as the regiment was on the way to Washington.[13]

Why men deserted is an interesting question. The most likely reason is to take the money and run. When joining up each recruit received a bounty. It was very common for men to join a regiment, collect the bounty and leave only to join another regiment and repeat the process. However there were other reasons as well. In some cases men were originally slated to be brought in as a First Sergeant or other non-commissioned rank but were brought in as privates. An example of this can be seen in Company G. George Thompson and Lewis Stone had originally been Sergeants and Edward McNally, John Kernan and Samuel Bragg were originally Corporals, however all five men were reduced in rank to Private and all five deserted prior to July 19, 1861. Jacob Ammen was originally the first

---

hospitals. Others left because they felt they had been misled as to the position they would hold in a newly formed unit or because the person that had recruited them had left. The government had trouble with the issue of desertion. After the war was over many veterans were denied pensions based on muster sheet entries of "deserted". On March 2, 1889 Congress passed a law titled: "Removal of Charge of Desertion: An act for the relief of certain volunteer and regular soldiers of the late war and the war with Mexico". That act stated in Section 1: "That the charge of desertion…against any soldier…shall be removed…where it shall be made to appear to the satisfaction of the Secretary of War…that such soldier served faithfully until the expiration of his term…having served six months or more, and by reason of absence from his command…failed to be mustered out and to receive an honorable discharge, or that such soldier absented himself from his command, or from hospital while suffering from wounds, injuries or disease received or contracted in the line of duty and was prevented from completing his term of enlistment by reason of such wounds, injuries or disease." The act continued on to detail the criteria for removal of the charge of desertion in nine sections. A number of amendments were made to the act through 1895. When reading this book it should always be remembered that when the term "deserted" is used it is based on what is written either in the individual record of a specific soldier or in a published regimental roster issued by the State of New York. It is quite possible that any charge of desertion made in those sources would have been reversed by the referenced act of Congress.

13 Private Casey slipped from a railroad platform near Baltimore and was instantly killed. National Republican, Washington DC, July 22, 1861, page 3.

Sergeant of Company K and William McCaffery was originally the First Sergeant of Company E. Both men were reduced in rank to Private and both deserted. Why were men reduced in rank? Was it justified? From the individual soldiers perspective it probably didn't matter. They had expected a certain position and they were not to get it. So they split. Desertions were not limited to the beginning of the regiment's history. Over the years the regiment was to lose men in this way with regularity. The Forty Second was not alone in suffering numbers of desertions. All regiments had to deal with this phenomenon. It was not uncommon at all. Not all companies were affected the same by desertions. Desertion rates averaged 11.5% and ran from a high of 21.8% in Company G to a low of 0.8% in Company C. It also appears that the process of recruitment anticipated the issue of men signing up and leaving as the strength after the initial round of desertions was what was sought from the beginning, a force of 1036. The strength of the companies varied a little but in general terms the regiment looked quite good, as it was ready to leave for battle. Strength levels averaged 102 and ran from a high of 123 in Company C to a low of 89 in Company H.

While the roster of the officers of the Regiment was generally filled out by the muster in date of June 22 there were to be some changes. On July 7 the New York Times reported the list of company officers to be: "A Company: Captain James Mooney, First Lieut. Henry Harrington and Second Lieut. Hugh McClusky; B Company: Captain Peter Bowe, First Lieut. James E. Boyle, Second Lieut. Thomas Abbott; C Company: Captain James Graham, First Lieut. Charles McPherson, Second Lieut. James Gillis; D Company: Captain Henry Call, First Lt. John P. Bendon, Second Lieut. Francis E. Town; E Company: Captain James B. Lynch, First Lieut. P. J. Downing, Second Lieut. Thomas W. Kelly; F Company: Captain Joseph Walter Tobin, First Lieut. Isaac Gotthold, Second Lieut. James Conroy; G Company: Captain John Quinn, First Lieut. Robert C. Wright, Second Lieut. Michael J. Lee; H Company: Captain Henry H. Alden, First Lieut. S. M. Saunders, Second Lieut. John Paine; I Company: Captain David Hogg, First Lieut. William A. Lynch, (no Second Lieut. Listed); K Company: Captain Michael Geraghty, First Lieut. Thos. Reynolds, Second Lieut. James McGrath."

Several of the names of the officers were misspelled, a common occurrence. Others were already or about to be replaced as the Regiment prepared for departing. As discussed earlier First Lieut. Skeete replaced S. M. Saunders in Company H. Captain Timothy O'Meara replaced Captain James Lynch in E Company. Second Lieut. Giberson filled the vacancy in Company I.

As the regiment left Great Neck the primary staff included: Colonel Kennedy, Lt. Colonel Cogswell, Adjutant Bomford, Surgeon Osborne, Asst. Surgeon Fossard, Quartermaster Rhodes and Sergeant Major Dennis Downing. There is no record of a major at that time. Michael Doheny, the regiment's original Lieut. Colonel was discharged on July 5. Lieut. Colonel Milton Cogswell replaced Doheny. Cogswell was a West Point graduate of the class of 1849 and the only graduate of West Point to serve in the regiment.

On July 18, 1861 the following notice appeared in the New York Times: "Local Military Departure of the Tammany Regiment: This Regiment was ordered to break camp at 3 o'clock this morning, and proceed at once to Washington. The steamer Kill Van Kull has been chartered to take the regiment direct from Great Neck, where it has been encamped for some time past, to Elizabethport, from thence it will take the cars for the Capital. Quartermaster Richardson (originally listed as Paymaster and not referred to as Quartermaster on any of the rolls of the Regiment) has already gone on to make arrangements for the regiment. Mr. George W. Rooke, keeper of the City Hall has presented Colonel Kennedy with a handsome revolver. Other friends of the Colonel have presented him with a sword, sash and belt. The Regimental standard is a very handsome affair, made of rich blue silk with heavy yellow fringe. The device is a combination of the National and State arms with a half globe and a spread eagle surmounting. Above is the name of the Tammany Regiment. Underneath is the motto: "Excelsior." Another article mentioned the blue Regimental Flag and added the "white guide colors marked "Jackson Guard" and embellished with the motto of New York "Excelsior". That same article mentioned yet another flag that was being prepared that would have on one side the temple of the Columbian Order, and on the other their motto, "The Union must and shall be preserved." The men were described as wearing grey jackets and pants trimmed with black and carrying Springfield muskets.[14]

---

[14] National Republican, Washington DC, July 22, 1861, page 3

On July 19 another similar notice was published in the New York Times: "Departure of the Tammany Regiment: The Tammany Regiment, otherwise known as the Jackson Guards, under command of Col. W. D. Kennedy, left yesterday for Washington. The steamer Kill Van Kull received the regiment on board at the encampment at Great Neck, in the afternoon, and they passed the City direct for Elizabethport about 7 o'clock. A baggage train of fourteen army wagons had previously been sent over, to go forward with the regiment, to be used for transporting their equipments after they reach Washington. A special train, with every convenience for the comfort of the men was placed at the Colonel's disposal, and the regiment was soon on its way to Washington, without accident or detention. The men appeared in excellent condition and expressed some fears that they might not be on hand in season to "assist" at the approaching battle at Manassas Junction. The Union Defense Committee furnished the regiments equipments."

During the time the regiment was preparing to leave for war many ceremonies took place during which weapons were given to individual officers other than Colonel Kennedy. Lieut. William Lynch received "a handsome and costly sword". Captain Hogg received a sword, sash and belt. Captain James Graham received "a complete set of officer's equipment". Captain Tobin and Lieut. Conroy were presented with "engraved swords, sash and belts.[15]

The July 20 edition of the New York Leader, the publication of the Tammany Society contained a tribute to Colonel Kennedy saying: "Our association with Colonel Kennedy sprung up in political life ... To a numerous class politics is a game in which one set of men are played off against another and in which tricks and cheating decide the contest ... True men ... will develop the faithful elements of their character ... and honesty in politics becomes the rule ... It was the mission of Father Kennedy and others to introduce this new element in the struggles of our party ... He will be loved by his men ... We trust he will soon be again among us ..."

---

15   Newspaper unknown, July 17, 1861, Military Museum, 61 Lake Street, Saratoga Springs, NY. Also, New York Leader, Saturday, July 20, page 5, column 7 and New York Irish American, July 20, 1861, page 2, column 2.

On July 21, 1864 a single sentence in the New York Times announced: "The Sixth Maine reached Washington last night and the Tammany Regiment this morning." The Tammany Regiment had indeed missed First Manassas but they were in Washington and ready to go to war. Their Colonel was at their head as they marched through the streets of Washington. Within twenty-four hours he would be dead from natural causes.

Chapter Two

WASHINGTON D.C. TO BALL'S BLUFF

The death of Colonel Kennedy, coming as it did at the same time as the Union defeat at Bull Run, hit the Tammany Regiment very hard. Equally hard hit were the folks back home, especially the political leaders of Tammany. Newspapers were full of articles reporting Kennedy's death and funeral. Tammany's newspaper, the Leader, on Saturday, July 27 had a long article saying first in reference to Bull Run: "The past week has been the gloomiest in the record of our National existence. From the proud eminence of assured victory to our Flag and Country, we were suddenly plunged almost to the depths of despairing apprehension for our existence", and then of Colonel Kennedy:" ... This death, sudden and startling as it was, came to us as a special grief touching a deeper chord than the general sorrow ... We knew the deceased intimately ... and therefore claim to speak of him with assured knowledge ... The quality of William D. Kennedy which we would advance in pronouncing his character, was that of vital earnestness ... On the March to Washington, although worn down by an attack of illness he was assiduous and unremitting ... for the welfare of his men. On arriving in Washington, he marched at the head of his regiment nearly five miles, under a burning sun, refusing to ride ... The next day, although nearly prostrate by sickness ... he was at camp ... and it was only when his nature fairly broke down, that he was induced to take to his bed, and this was literally to lay down and die. His system was too far exhausted by his insidious disease, cholera, to enable him to rally, and he sunk in death after a few hours".[1]

---

[1]　New York leader, Saturday, July 27, 1861, page 4, column 2-3

Meetings were held on Tuesday, July 23, at which the Tammany Society passed resolutions honoring Kennedy and declared that the front of the meeting hall be draped in mourning. The Colonel's body arrived back in New York City by railroad at 3:30 in the morning on July 24 accompanied by regimental Paymaster John Richardson and three soldiers. Kennedy's funeral was held in New York City on Friday, July 26 and was attended by numerous city politicians and other important people. Addresses were delivered by E. F. Purdy, John Vance and other Tammany members. Pall bearers included newspaperman Horace Greeley.[2] On July 31, a resolution was submitted in the Congress of the United States asking that the Committee on Invalid Pensions be instructed to inquire into "the expediency of reporting a bill granting ... a pension to the widow of the late William D. Kennedy".[3]

Between Colonel Kennedy's death and October 20, 1861, a number of high level promotions were made in the ranks of the 42NY. Milton Cogswell was promoted to Colonel from Lieut. Colonel, James Mooney moved up from Captain, Company A to Lieut. Colonel, his place being taken by the promotion of First Lieut. Henry Harrington. Captain Bowe, Co. B was promoted into the vacant position of Major. Thomas Abbott was promoted from Second Lieut. Co A to First Lieut. filling the spot vacated by Harrington. Sergeant Major Dennis Downing was promoted to Second Lieut. Co. F. Morgan Doheny, the son of former Lieut. Colonel Michael Doheny was promoted from Private to Second Lieut. Co. K. Other changes reduced the officer ranks. First Lieut. John Benden, Co. D resigned. Quartermaster William Rhodes and Paymaster Richardson were discharged and Second Lieut. Hugh McClusky deserted.[4]

This is a good time to acquaint the reader with some background on a number of the men mentioned in the preceding paragraph as this

---

2   New York Times, July 24, 1861, page 5 and New York Times, July 25, 1861, page 5.
3   Journal of the House of Representatives of the United States, July 4, 1861 to August 6, 1861. Colonel Kennedy's wife was Rachel Ann Gregg, born 1823 in Kentville, Nova Scotia. She died Dec. 28, 1895 in Pleasantville, New York. They had 3 children: William D. (1856-1891), Evelyn Elizabeth and Elmina W. (died 1887 London). Brooklyn Eagle, Nov. 19, 1887, page 3, Dec. 29, 1895, page 7 and Feb. 17, 1891, page 5.
4   NARA, individual soldier's records

knowledge will make the rest of this book clearer. Without understanding who these men were and who they were associated with, a significant part of the "ins and outs" of the politics of the Tammany Regiment will be lost. The detail required may seem a bit much, but it is necessary.

Let's start with Michael Doheny the first Lieut. Colonel of the regiment. He joined on May 21, 1861 and resigned on July 5, 1861 just two weeks after the regiment was mustered into service on June 22. He was born in Ireland May 22, 1805 and as a man in his mid fifties he had an agreement with Colonel Kennedy that allowed his name to be used to help recruit men for the regiment, but it was understood that as the regiment left for the seat of war the position of Lieut. Colonel would be filled by someone else.[5] What was so magical about the name of Michael Doheny? If you were of Irish descent you knew Michael Doheny! You knew that he was one of the men who had, in 1848, taken part in the uprising against the British Crown. He was a major player in the Fenian Brotherhood centered in New York and someone who most Irishmen held in extremely high esteem. He was well acquainted with Daniel O'Connell, perhaps the most famous of all Irish Catholics. Following the failure of the 1848 uprisings Doheny avoided capture and made his way first to London, then to Paris and ultimately to New York City arriving early in 1849.[6] Over the next ten years through associations with men like John O'Mahoney and other high profile Irishmen in New York, Doheny worked feverishly to achieve results for the Fenian goal of gaining Ireland's independence from Britain. With the outbreak of the Civil War the Fenian Brotherhood set two objectives that they felt would help their cause. The first was to have as many members of the Brotherhood fill positions in military units to gain experience that would be valuable in any future actions against the British. The second was to use the organized structure of the Union army to create a base for raising money needed to further the goals of the Brotherhood. Some readers may find it interesting to delve deeper into the Fenian movement both in the United States and in Europe and there are many works that could be useful in that regard. I recommend an article by Michael Ruddy called "An Irish Army in America", printed in The

---

[5]   New York Leader, July 13, 1861, page 5, column 7
[6]   Savage, John, Fenian Heroes and Martyrs, 1828-1888, pages 288-294, hereinafter cited as Fenian Heroes.

Civil War Times, April 2003. Following Doheny's resignation from the Tammany Regiment he continued to be active in Fenian affairs until his death on April 1, 1862. He is buried in Calvary Cemetery, New York.

Morgan Doheny was Michael Doheny's son. He was born in Ireland around 1840 and along with his mother joined his father in New York around 1850. At the age of 21 he was mustered into the Tammany Regiment as a private on June 22, 1861. Within a month he was promoted to Second Lieut., Co. K. Was his promotion in some way connected to his father? Morgan was well known in Fenian circles and it makes sense to assume that there were enough reasons to promote Morgan as could be found to appoint another to the vacant position. It certainly wouldn't hurt to continue to have a Doheny in the officer ranks of the regiment. Morgan's service with the regiment would be quite interesting with him holding a number of different positions. He would be captured and paroled in 1862, become the subject of correspondence with President Lincoln and would repeatedly be mentioned in accounts of the regiment's exploits by the Irish American press in New York City.

Michael and Morgan Doheny were not the only high profile Fenian Brotherhood members in the Tammany Regiment. Dennis Downing, his older brother Patrick and William O'Shea were among the group of Fenians sometimes referred to as the "Phoenix Prisoners" who on December 8, 1858 were arrested in Ireland. Trials were held, a number of the men were incarcerated for various periods of time and eventually an agreement was reached that allowed the Phoenix Prisoners to be released. Many of them made their way to the United States.[7] Dennis Downing's time with the Tammany Regiment would be quite short but Patrick Downing and William O'Shea would serve for years. Another member of the Fenian Brotherhood was Maurice Fitzharris whose role in the Tammany regiment would grow in 1863.

Between 1861 and 1864 quite a few officers served in the Tammany Regiment for short periods of time and while some of their stories might be quite interesting, my research has turned up little worth mentioning. They make their cameo appearance and leave. William Rhodes, John Richardson, John Benden, James Graham, George Moore and Hugh McClusky are men I have included in what I have termed the "Cameo

---

[7] Fenian Heroes, 346-357

Cadre". It is quite possible that I have missed some significant contribution they might have made to the regiment's history. If I have I am sincerely sorry for my error.

Colonel Milton Cogswell was not a member of the Cameo Cadre. Quite to the contrary he was a significant component of the history of the regiment from its conception through the early part of 1862. When the regiment left for the war it was Milton Cogswell that filled the position of Lieut. Colonel vacated by Michael Doheny as part of the agreement with Colonel Kennedy. Why was he chosen to fill that role? Just who was Milton Cogswell? He was born December 4, 1825 in Noblesville, Indiana. His father, Francis Beard Cogswell, was one of the earliest settlers of Hamilton County, Indiana. Francis held the rank of Colonel of Militia and served many years in the State Legislature of Indiana.

Colonel Milton Cogswell, post war image, USMHI

Milton graduated from West Point in 1849 and served in various positions in the regular army until the outbreak of the Civil War. In October of 1860 he married Susan Lane the daughter of a prominent New Yorker.[8] Given the shortage of trained, experienced and available professional soldiers it is not hard to see why Milton Cogswell, whose

---

[8]   Cogswell, 309, 404

family born in the United States could be traced back to 1651 in Ipswich, Massachusetts, was selected to be second in command to Colonel Kennedy as the regiment went to war. To say that Cogswell's time with the Tammany Regiment was significant, both on the unit and the man, would be a tremendous understatement.

James J. Mooney, age 29, mustered into the regiment June 22, 1861 as Captain, Co A. By convention that made him the senior Captain as it was customary to rank companies from A to K. Throughout his time with the regiment he repeatedly demonstrated his loyalty to the men that originally formed the regiment and his displeasure with the way officer promotions were handled by politicians. Peter Bowe, also age 29, mustered into the regiment June 22, 1861 as Captain, Co. B making him the second senior Captain. Bowe shared the views of Mooney and it would appear that they were quite close. Both men served through the Peninsula Campaign and resigned the same day.

The regiment remained in Washington until August 10 when they moved to Camp Lyons near Poolesville, MD arriving on the 15th and taking up positions along the Potomac. Between August 19-30, Company F was placed on picket duty near Monocacy.[9] While at Poolesville, a report was sent to the New York Leader by a correspondent operating under the name "Mazette". He described the regiment as: "in excellent health and spirits, though the death of Colonel Kennedy is still a matter of regret with many, Colonel Cogswell, however, becoming more popular every day, and winning the confidence of the men in his abilities to lead them to victory … The regiment while on its march from Washington, encountered a heavy rainstorm requiring it to halt at Rockville several days, until its wagons, ambulance and stores could overtake it. At Rockville the officers were given … the diet of the denizens in that benighted part consisting solely of new whiskey, cabbage variously cooked, and a composition called corn-bread, but not tasting like anything save what is known as "cripple's poultice" … A Minnesota regiment lies next to the Jackson Guard, and constant dress parade and company drill keep the men busy …"[10] Mazette's description of the conditions of the march is supported by a letter from

---

[9]   National Archives, Record Group 94, Records of the Adjutant General's Office

[10] New York Leader, Saturday, August 24, 1861, page 5, column 4. The Minnesota regiment was the 1MN.

General Stone dated August 13 in which he states: "Rockville ... I arrived here yesterday ... Found the Tammany Regiment ... The streams are swollen by the heavy rains and the roads are badly cut up. Inexperienced management of the trains has caused delay in the arrival of a large portion of the wagons of the Tammany Regiment, and it cannot advance until some of the delayed wagons arrive".[11]

A fuller picture of the troop deployment is provided by a letter to General McClellan from General Stone dated August 19 stating: "The troops of this command are now posted as follows, commencing on the right: Three companies of the Second NY Militia (82NY) are stationed at the mouth of the Monocacy, with pickets thrown out two miles above and the same distance below, connecting above with pickets ... of General Bank's command. This outpost is supported by the remainder of the Second Regiment, 300 strong only, stationed one-half mile from Poolesville, on the Monocacy Road. A picket of cavalry patrols the vicinity of the Monocacy. The Tammany Regiment (Cogswell) is stationed one mile from Poolesville, on the road to Conrad's Ferry, and has four companies detached to watch that ferry. The strength of this regiment is 532 in camp, besides the four companies on outpost. The outpost at Conrad's throws out pickets to meet those from Monocacy and those from Edward's Ferry below. The Minnesota regiment (Gorman) 788 strong is stationed 2 ½ miles from Poolesville on the road to Edward's Ferry furnishing an outpost of four companies to that ferry. This outpost throws out pickets to meet those from Conrad's on the right and those from Seneca on the left."[12]

Looking yet at the larger picture, General Stone's command was part of a hastily thrown together defense of Washington planned and implemented by General McClellan, who had, after his successes in western Virginia, been given command of the army by President Lincoln immediately after Bull Run.[13] McClellan's force was composed of independent brigades and

---

[11] OR, S1, V5, P560. U.S. War Department, The War of the Rebellion: A Compilation of the Official Records of the Union and Confederate Armies, 127 volumes, Washington, D.C., GPO, 1880-1901, hereinafter cited as OR, S, V. P.

[12] OR, S1, V5, P569

[13] Troops under the overall command of McClellan contained, disrupted and defeated Confederate troops in western Virginia at Phillippi, (June 3), Laurel Hill (July 9) and Rich Mountain (July 11). Although the magnitude of the Union victories were small compared to the defeat at Bull Run they were rare

regiments, each under a Brigadier General or Colonel, collectively called the Division of the Potomac.[14] The mission of this force was to observe the activity of Confederate troops nearby and protect the Capital until sufficient troops could be raised to take the fight to the enemy.

Most of the picket activity was routine with the men somewhat more concerned with what they were going to eat than any enemy action that might be on the horizon. Two reports published in the New York Times describe in detail how Ajax, a cook of African descent, went about the tasks associated with putting decent food on the officer's table at Conrad's Ferry.[15]

Ferry Landing at Mason's Island, Library of Congress

There were several exceptions to the quiet routine notably around the sizable piece of land in the Potomac River between Conrad and Noland Ferries named Mason's Island. By one account Mason's Island was thought to be the spot of an intended attack by the 27,000 rebels in the vicinity of Leesburg.[16] On September 3, 1861, Private Michael Madden, Co. K

---

examples of Union superiority and stood out in the minds of all politicians and common citizens to a degree much larger than their scope would otherwise have warranted.

[14] OR, S1, V5, P5-18

[15] New York Times, August 24 and September 10, 1861

[16] OR, S1, V5, P606 September 28, 1861 letter to General Stone from John W. Geary.

behaved in a manner that would see him awarded the only Medal of Honor to be won by a member of the Tammany Regiment in the Civil War. His citation reads: "Madden, Michael, Private, Company K, 42d New York Infantry. Place and date: At Mason's Island, Md., 3 September 1861. Entered service at: New York, NY. Born 28 September 1841, Ireland. Date of Issue: 22 March 1898. Citation: Assisted a wounded comrade to the riverbank, and, under heavy fire of the enemy, swam with him across a branch of the Potomac to the Union lines".[17]

More detail on the activities around Mason's Island is provided in a letter to Cogswell by Lieut. Doheny on September 18. Doheny had been asked by Cogswell to obtain details on the disappearance of First Lieut. George H. Wallis (sometimes spelled Wallace). Doheny had interviewed and obtained the following statement from Sergeant John Kelly, Co. K, who had been in command of the pickets on Mason's Island on September 17. "Lieut. Wallace called on me yesterday morning between the hours of 9 and 11 stating he would go over to the other side and bring back with him a boat which we tied there. I asked him not to go but it was of no use as he would. He got into the water just below the barn and took an oblique direction towards the Virginia shore. When he had attained a ... of about 100 yards he turned to me and said, "I see two men just over there", pointing across the river. I took no more notice until I saw him in the boat. Here I heard a voice saying, "come out of the boat or I will fire". I then heard Lieut. Wallace say, "don't fire, I am coming". I did not see him again but one of the men says he saw him pass in company with two others, but I have nothing further to say in regard to him."[18] Lieut.

---

[17] Michael Madden would continue to serve throughout the war and was mustered out with the regiment in July 1864. For approximately the last year of his service he was a teamster detached to the Brigade Quartermaster.

[18] NARA, Files of Lieut. G. H. Wallis and John Kelly. Sgt. John Kelly would be wounded at Glendale (arm) June 30, 1862. He arrived in DC on either the Vanderbilt or Louistana on July 4. New York Times, July 12, 1862, page 2 column 3 and New York Times July 6, 1862, page 8, column 4. He is listed on the rolls of Eckington Hospital for July and August 1862. The Muster Roll of U.S.A. General Hospital, York, PA for September and October 1862 lists a Private John Kelley, Co. K as having deserted on October 2. I have no way to know if this is the same man but the notice is in the NARA file for Sgt. John Kelly.

Wallace had been transferred to Co. K from Co. B the day before he swam the Potomac. Although originally listed on the regiment's rolls as having deserted, he had been captured and was taken to Richmond, arriving there on September 21.

Lieut. George H. Wallace, USMHI

Lieut. George Hewitt Wallis is an interesting member of the Tammany Regiment mainly because of his family connections. He was born in Canada, probably Toronto, to Thomas George Wallis and Mary Hewitt Wallis in the mid 1830's. Mary Hewitt was the second child of seven that were born to John Hewitt and Ann Gurnee. Mary's younger brother Abram Stevens Hewitt was a successful and powerful industrialist and politician who would become the Mayor of New York City in 1886. In 1855 Abram married Sarah Amelia Cooper, the daughter of Peter Cooper, whose metal working factories in Trenton, New Jersey supplied railroad rails, artillery carriages and gun metal for the Union during the Civil War. Lieut. Wallis was therefore the nephew of a leading industrialist with strong political ties to New York and was family connected to a major supplier of war materials needed by the Union. What is less clear is whether

Lieut. Wallis also had a family connection to Colonel Cogswell. Colonel Cogswell's father Francis Beard Cogswell had a younger brother John. John settled in Georgia and had a son named Levi Mangum Cogswell who on February 28, 1854 married Sarah Sallie Wallis in Mississippi.[19] L. M. Cogswell served as a private in the 22nd Texas Infantry during the Civil War. While no connection was found between Lieut. Wallis and the branch of the Wallis family Sarah belonged to it does seem interesting that Colonel Cogswell's first cousin was married to a Wallis.

Also listed as having deserted at Mason's Island in error was Private Bernard McIntire, Co. K. He had been captured while on picket duty.[20]

Major Patrick Downing and Sgt. Major Dennis Downing, USMHI

---

[19] Cogswell, page 405

[20] McIntire was sent to New Orleans and was paroled at Salisbury, N. C. May 28, 1862. He is listed by the War Department, Record and Pension Division in October 1892 as having deserted the Tammany Regiment and subsequently joining Co. B, 12 New Hampshire Infantry. NARA, record of Bernard McIntire.

Captain Timothy O'Meara, Lincoln Library
and Museum, Springfield, IL

An extremely significant event took place sometime around late August. While on picket duty at Conrad's Ferry, two Company E officers, Captain Timothy O'Meara and Lieut. Patrick Downing had what can best be referred to as an almost catastrophic confrontation. Lieut. Downing claimed that while he was under orders from Colonel Cogswell to improve some breastworks, Captain O'Meara countermanded the order and after a number of verbal exchanges pulled his pistol and threatened his life. Downing reported the event to Lt. Colonel Mooney and demanded that O'Meara be put under arrest. The events of the next few days are not that clear and can only be summarized as confused. Charges were made, at various times both O'Meara and Downing were placed in arrest and released, and both Patrick Downing and his brother Dennis tendered their resignations. Did the confrontation take place as Downing described it? In a September 3, 1861 letter by O'Meara to the Regimental Adjutant he said: " …I knew nothing of the charges prepared against me by Lt. Colonel Mooney and his friends. If I did through pressing the claims they should disappear when honor or my adopted country demands my presence". Nowhere in the words of O'Meara is there a denial of the event. Were there bad feelings between these men that predated the confrontation? There certainly were! O'Meara was listed as the first adjutant of the regiment when it was originally being formed. He was an experienced military officer having served in the Mexican Revolution as a Captain of Cavalry.

Downing was recruited by Michael Doheny as a fellow Fenian and was originally promised the position of adjutant but then was offered the position of Captain commanding a company. As the regiment took its final form several companies were consolidated and there was an issue as to who would command Company E between Downing and a James Lynch. Colonel Kennedy offered the job to Downing and Lynch agreed but Downing demanded that Lynch would have to leave the regiment before he would accept the captaincy. Lynch did leave but the command of Company E was given to O'Meara and Downing was given the position of First Lieut. The position of Regimental Adjutant was given to George N. Bomford, the son of a well known military man. To say that all of these events coupled with the pride of one of Ireland's Fenian heroes might have resulted in some hard feelings toward O'Meara is to state the obvious.[21]

---

[21]   NARA, Records of T. O'Meara and P. Downing. The full text of the letter sent by Downing on Jan. 21, 1862 to General Stone reads: "Allow me to have the honor of addressing you on a subject of very great import to myself. I have been informed by Colonel Charles that I was not recognized as an officer at your headquarters. I feel confident when I lay before you a statement of my claims that you will give them just and due consideration. I would have done so ere this but for having been in error as to the right of Colonel Mooney to reappoint me. From the many appointments made by Colonel Cogswell I was under the impression that the same right was vested in any commander, but Colonel Charles has informed me that the governor of New York had granted this privilege only to Colonel Cogswell. I might state briefly my present position with regard to those claims, but I know that I cannot show you any which are legal; therefore pardon my long statement. My reason for joining this regiment in particular before others was through the request of an acquaintance, Colonel Doheny, who offered in the name of Colonel Kennedy that I should have the position of adjutant without any bother with recruiting. Shortly after, when I had given up my business, and had been some time in camp, I was informed by Colonel Kennedy that he could do better for me; and if I could get forty men partially drilled he would fill up the company. I went around recruiting and in a short time, inside twelve days or there about, had enlisted thirty. At this time he began to amalgamate the several companies and I was sent into a company with a man named Lynch. The next day I had fifty men on the ground. At this time without any desire on my part Colonel Kennedy informed me that I should command the company; and Lynch in a meeting of the board of officers offered it to me but I refused as long as he remained. When about leaving for the seat of war he was bought off and the company handed over to a man who never recruited a man and who had no claim whatsoever upon me. The

The resignations of Patrick and Dennis Downing were accepted and they

men mutinied, but after a great amount of persuasion I had them to accept them. Colonel Cogswell is aware of this as well as all the officers who were then present. Immediately before leaving, at a meeting to decide the seniority of officers, I was put down junior First Lieutenant of the Regiment, although I was the fourth First Lt. who had any connection with it not taking into account the time I was in expectation of the position of adjutant. At camp near Washington a difficulty arose between some of the officers and Colonel Cogswell, who had been elected to the command after Colonel Kennedy's death, and gone to New York. In his absence these officers spoke in a unbecoming manner of him, for which he there declared that they would not remain in the regiment. It was in Captain O'Meara's tent that this occurred-he was my Captain and I was supposed to have been a party to it; but the contrary was proved, by Captain Tobin and my brother, then Sgt. Major-they were the two that defended Colonel Cogswell from this attack. After having arrived here my company was the first that went on picket service from the regiment to Conrad's Ferry. Major Bowe can testify how I performed my duty while there, and more particularly during the three days the enemy kept firing upon us. It is here that the cause of my resignation commenced. During one of those nights, Col. Cogswell ordered some repairs and alterations to be made in the sort of breast-work which was already there, and gave instructions for that purpose to Lt. Col. Mooney, who had me detailed to superintend it during the night. He informed Capt. O'Meara and desired him to send ten men as the detail from the company to report to me. While engaged in the work, and during the night, a sentry came in and informed me that the enemy was crossing on Harrison Island. I awakened Captain O'Meara and made him aware of the circumstances. He went and ascertained that it was a false alarm. When he returned and after looking at what I was doing, he took exception to it in the following terms-"Jesus Christ! This is not wanted here at all", and ordered me to go with him somewhere. I refused, by reminding him that I was ordered to perform this work when he made use of the observation- "If Colonel Mooney wants engineering done here, he must come and do it himself." I remarked that I hoped he would not prevent me from performing my duty, that I was placed in command of those men. He then turned around and said three times each time in a more threatening attitude until the last he pulled out his pistol. "God damn you, you have no command here". I expostulated with him upon his manner and assured him that he might accomplish this in a milder and less abusive manner, by commanding the men to cease. This he did. When I said that "if there were law in the US Army he should feel it". I saw Colonel Cogswell the next day, when he wished me to prefer charges against him, and complemented me for the manner in which the work was performed. I had no means of writing them until I returned to camp. Col. Mooney was ordered to place Captain O'Meara under arrest, (so he informed were mustered out on September 24, 1861.[22]

Two other officers: Henry Call, Captain, Co. D and Thomas Reynolds, First. Lieut. Co. K resigned in September, 1861. Both are men I consider to be "Cameo Cadre" although there is a small note in the file of Thomas Reynolds that reads: "Camp Lyon, August 29, 1861. Colonel Cogswell: Having incurred your displeasure, I hereby tender you my resignation as an officer in your command". What did Reynolds do that displeased Cogswell? I have no clue![23]

Two of the forty-eight Boston men, William Hayley and Pete O'Connell, deserted between August and September 1861. On October 10, Private William Maker, Co. G died of disease and on October 20,

---

me) but would not until I had written the charges. About seven days after, when arrived in camp, I did so, Col. Cogswell having them drawn up for me, and he was placed under arrest. About this time a document requesting Col. Cogswell to get our commissions was handed me to sign. I did so. Afterward I found another document, different to this, had been in circulation, but of which I knew nothing until I was accused of signing it. The next day I found one of the men of my company in the guard house and upon inquiry I found that it was because of his carrying this first document to the pickets. I went to the Colonel and begged that he release the man and informed him that it was I who sent him-he released him but place me under arrest and released Captain O'Meara. The next day I requested an interview and informed him that I should resign if the charges against Captain O'Meara were not investigated. He said that there was no help for me- that it was "un-military". I then requested liberty to see General Stone- he granted it. I went and saw you sir, but having informed you that I was under arrest, you would not listen to me, and moreover that you could not interfere in regimental affairs. The next day I was released from arrest and told by Colonel Cogswell to return to my company – but I tendered my resignation which will show that I could not trust Captain O'Meara. I do not want to accuse him now but the foregoing appears both on my charges and resignation- he said while under arrest "his enemies could not live". I have ever since joining the regiment been in trouble of some sort, and still I can say that there's nothing disreputable can be laid to me from then to now. I remain with respect, sir, your obedient servant, Patrick J. Downing."

22 Dennis Downing would join the 97th NY reaching the rank of Captain. He was wounded at Gettysburg, losing a leg. He would be transferred to the Invalid Corps. Patrick Downing would rejoin the Tammany Regiment. NARA, Records of Dennis and Patrick Downing.

23 Thomas Reynolds joined the 69th New York Infantry as First Lieut. Co. A, October 22, 1861. He was killed in action at Malvern Hill, July 1, 1862.

Private Charles Stewart, Co. F, died of an accidental poisoning at Camp Lyon, Pooleville, Md.

On October 10, First Lieut. Giberson was ordered by Cogswell to proceed to Washington with fifty men that were to be transferred to the Artillery and Cavalry. Giberson was to record the transfers and return to Camp Lyon in Poolesville. Records have been found for thirty men that were transferred to the U. S. Fifth Cavalry. One man, Andrew Cline returned to the Tammany Regiment. No records showing transfers to the artillery have been found.[24]

Company F recorded their activities, which were typical, on their muster rolls as follows: "Was ordered on picket September 14 by Col. Cogswell, marched from Camp Lyon near Poolesville Sept. 15 to Conrad's Ferry to report to Lieut. Colonel Mooney then in command of pickets stationed there, was posted one quarter of a mile northwest of Conrad's Ferry to the center of the small island east of Mason's Island to guard the Potomac, remained there until the 3d of October, was ordered back to camp near Poolesville on the above date. Remained there continually drilling until the 20th when we were ordered to support a section of the Rhode Island battery under command of Captain Vaughn. Remained there, posting sentinels on that night until the 21st when we were ordered to march to where our army was crossing the Potomac."[25] The crossing was being made at Ball's Bluff!

---

[24] The 29 men transferred to the Fifth U.S. Cavalry were: Co. B: George Reese, Co. C: Edward Connor, William Courtney, John Devereux, John Hanlon, Cpl. Richard Hanlon, Co. D: Francis Bogan, John Revel, Co. E: William Fitzgibbins, David Wilson, Co. F: John Connor, Philip Fagan, Jacob Housmann, James Kelly, John Taihen, Co: G:Patrick Fitzpatrick, Orris M. Sarle, James Williams, Co; H: Thomas Curley, Charles Michaels, Co. I: Henry Hayman, Ferdinand Heinman, August Kehrweider, Abram Levi, Co: K: Cpl. Bernard Cunningham, John Henchen, Thomas Mackey, Timothy Murphy, Peter Reilly. Andrew Cline was wounded slightly during the Battle of Chancellorsville (second Fredericksburg) and again in 1864 at the fight for the Weldon Railroad near Petersburg. He was promoted to Sergeant March 3, 1863 and was used extensively to travel back to New York to bring new recruits to the regiment. NARA: individual soldier records.

[25] NARA, Adjutant General's Office, Record Group 94, Muster Roll Tammany Regiment, Co. F, September–October 1861.

Chapter Three

THE BATTLE OF BALL'S BLUFF

On October 21, 1861 at a little known place in Virginia the Tammany Regiment met the enemy for the first time in battle.[1] That day on Ball's Bluff, overlooking the Potomac River and Harrison's Island, the members of the Forty-Second New York Infantry and those of several other regiments would suffer a terrible loss from which some might say they would never recover. Command would become confused, personalities would get in the way of decision-making, the lack of experience would prove costly and the inability to properly plan would create a disaster.

The war was not going well for the Union. Great losses of men and prestige were suffered at Bull Run exactly three months earlier and the Union was not prepared for what was about to happen just outside of Leesburg, Virginia. Although the number of men involved in the Battle of Ball's Bluff was not that great, only a few thousand on each side, the casualties suffered by the Union and the way the battle was fought left a deep wound on the men that fought it and the country as a whole.

After Bull Run little happened along the Potomac through the early part of October. The Union regrouped and established defensive positions. Priority was on gaining strength and preventing the Confederate Army from advancing on Washington. On October 15, General Bank's Division

---

[1] The Tammany regiment had been on picket duty from August through early October of 1861 and had encountered the enemy at Mason's Island, but Ball's Bluff was the first action where the entire regiment was ordered into action. Letter Lt. Doheny to Colonel Cogswell, NARA, Military Records File of Lt. G. H. Wallis.

was based at Darnestown, Maryland some fifteen miles east of Leesburg and General Stone's "Corps of Observation", of which the Tammany Regiment was assigned, was head-quartered at Poolesville, Maryland eight miles northeast of Leesburg. The Corps of Observation was actually a division strength unit composed of three brigades headed by generals Willis A. Gorman, Frederick W. Lander and Colonel Edward D. Baker with three batteries of artillery and six companies of cavalry. Both divisions were part of the command of General McClellan based in Washington.[2]

General Stone had been in command of a brigade consisting of the 34th New York, the Tammany regiment, the 2nd New York State Militia (later re-designated the 82nd New York), the 1st Minnesota Infantry and the 15th Massachusetts. Upon being given the command of the Corps of Observation, Stone turned over command of his brigade to General Gorman who had been Colonel of the 1st Minnesota. General Lander's Brigade consisted of the 7th Michigan and 19th and 20th Massachusetts plus Andrew's Company of Massachusetts Sharpshooters. Colonel Baker was in command of the 1st, 2nd, 3rd and 4th California regiments, later designated 71st, 69th, 72nd and 106th Pennsylvania Infantry. General Stone's command also included Kirby's Battery I, 1st US Artillery, Vaughn's Battery B, First Rhode Island Artillery and Bunting's 6th New York Militia Independent Battery and six companies of the 3rd New York cavalry under the command of Colonel Van Alen.[3]

On the Confederate side of the Potomac command was in the hands of Colonel Nathan (Shanks) G. Evans one of the standout officers from the battle of Bull Run exactly three months earlier.[4] Colonel Evans' orders were similar to those of General Stone. He was to watch the enemy activity and protect against a move by Union forces that might cut off Leesburg and interfere with movement along the roads that connected the important crossings of the Potomac.[5] Based in Leesburg, Evans had constructed a series of trenches some three miles to the southeast of the

[2]   Holien, Kim Bernard, Battle of Ball's Bluff, Publishers Press, 1985 page19-20.

[3]   Ibid

[4]   Colonel Evans' nickname, Shanks, was given to him at West Point because his legs were thin and knock-kneed. Farwell, Byron, Ball's Bluff, A Small Battle and Its Long Shadow, page 30.

[5]   Ibid, page 38

town called Fort Evans. The Confederate force had been designated the 7th Brigade of I Corps of the Army of the Potomac and reported to General Pierre Beauregard. Evan's Brigade consisted of the 8th VA, 13MS, 17MS, 18MS Infantry, 4 companies of Ball's Virginia Cavalry and Battery A, Richmond Howitzers.[6]

The land between Leesburg and the Maryland shore of the Potomac River was mainly part of thousand-acre farm owned by George Washington Ball, a nephew of the first president of the United States.[7] It varied between woods and open areas. A road connected Edward's and Conrad's Ferries with one to Leesburg. At the river edge was a bluff some 60-100 feet high with steep wooded slopes that took its name from the farm's owner. A few small houses and Smart's Mill accounted for the structures in the area. The area around Smart's Mill was not as severely sloped and the river could more easily be crossed at the mill to Harrison's Island than at the bluff.[8] Harrison Island, some 500 acres in size, was between the Maryland and Virginia shores of the Potomac. Little existed on the Island except for some old buildings and a few crude entrenchments, periodically occupied by several companies of the 15MA infantry. On the Maryland side of the river a road connected a landing with Poolesville and the Chesapeake and Ohio Canal towpath ran parallel to the river.

There are a number of excellent books written about the Battle of Ball's Bluff. It is not my intent to provide a complete account or definitive detail on the troop movements and actions of the battle. I do however want to convey sufficient detail to allow for the understanding of the role played by the 42nd New York and the effect that this relatively small action had on the regiment. The role was significant and the impact was enormous. By the end of this fateful day the Tammany regiment would have lost its Colonel, four company commanders, several other officers and almost 40% of the strength of the five companies that took part in the battle.

It all started when General Stone received a communication from General McClellan stating that it would be helpful if he made a "slight

---

[6]   Ibid, page 36
[7]   Ibid, page 75
[8]   Ibid, page 37

demonstration" in support of other movements of McClellan's army.[9] On October 20, Stone reacted and moved his troops concentrating Gorman's Brigade near Edward's Ferry supported by some cavalry and artillery. Other elements, including the 42nd New York were readied upstream at Conrad's Ferry. Gorman sent a small force across the river and then had them return completing the "slight demonstration".[10] At about the same time a reconnaissance had been ordered to move across Harrison Island to the Virginia shore with orders to scout the area between the river and Leesburg. This "recon" was conducted by Captain Chase Philbrick, commander of Company H, 15th Massachusetts with 21 of his men.[11] During the night of October 20, Captain Philbrick moved his small force within a mile of Leesburg and observed what he thought to be some tents but no campfires or sentries. Philbrick returned to Harrison Island about 10PM and reported back to General Stone who ordered a raid on the suspected camp. An order was given to Colonel Devens, commander of the 15MA to send a battalion (5 companies) of about 300 men across the river to destroy the camp. His return was to be covered by a force of 101 men from Companies E and I of the 20th MA under the personal command of Colonel Lee.[12] It was about 4 o'clock in the morning before the force had made the passage from Harrison Island to the Virginia shore using the three available boats that could carry a combined total of only 25-30 men

[9] Telegram A. V. Colburn, AAG to General Stone from Camp Griffin, October 20, 1861 stating: "General McClellan desires me to inform you that General McCall occupied Dranesville yesterday and is still there. Will send out heavy reconnaissance today in all directions from that point. The general desires that you keep a good lookout upon Leesburg, to see if this movement has the effect to drive them away. Perhaps a slight demonstration on your part would have the effect to move them." Holien, K. B., supra, page 22; McClellan, General McClellan's Reports and Campaigns, Shelden and Company, New York 1864, p.78.

[10] OR, S1, V5, 293-299

[11] Holien, K. B., supra, page 26

[12] Bruce, George A., The Twentieth Regiment of Massachusetts Volunteers, Houghton, Mifflin and Company, The Riverside Press, Cambridge, 1906 page 29-30, hereinafter cited as "Twentieth Massachusetts".

at a time.[13] The raiding force moved to the place where the camp had been reported and discovered that no camp existed and that what had actually been seen was a group of haystacks. A report was sent back to Stone who decided to take advantage of the situation and attempt to establish a presence on the Virginia side of the river. Whether the presence would be permanent would depend on what happened. Stone decided to put the command of the operation in the hands of Colonel Baker.[14]

Colonel Ed Baker was a Senator from Oregon before accepting his command and a personal friend of President Lincoln. He had been appointed to the rank of Brigadier General but he refused the appointment, as members of Congress were not allowed to jointly hold positions above the rank of Colonel.[15] He had accepted the position of Colonel of a larger than normal regiment of volunteers that had "ties" to California. Most of the men came from Pennsylvania and New York.[16]

Stone left Baker with discretion on how far to take his mission. According to Stone's report, Baker could decide to withdraw to the safety of the entrenchments on Harrison Island if he encountered a superior force of the enemy or if he felt confident, he could reinforce his position with additional troops under his command. In addition to his own brigade, Baker was given command of the 42nd New York, under the command of Colonel Milton Cogswell, and the 15th, 19th and 20th Massachusetts Infantry regiments supported by a few sections of artillery. Baker was a man of action and was not the sort of individual that would hesitate in

---

[13] The actual number of boats available for transport from the Maryland shore to Harrison's Island and from Harrison's Island to the Virginia shore varied during the day of the battle as additional boats were located and brought into service and as boats were moved from location to location on the island. While the actual number of boats available at any one time is hard to fix one thing is certain, there were too few and they were in poor condition.

[14] OR, S1, V5, 293-299

[15] Lash, Cary C., The History of Edward Baker's California Regiment, Butternut and Blue, Baltimore, MD, 2001, page 69

[16] Ibid page 30: although the California regiment had been authorized to have 15 companies it would be some time after the original organization was complete before full strength was achieved.

moving on the enemy. This part of his character would not work in his favor on this fateful day.[17]

Many of the reports describing what happened at Ball's Bluff make reference to the artillery that was brought to Virginia. These reports are confusing to most readers that try to follow the structure of the units because the actual pieces of artillery in the battle and their commanders were at times mixed due to the situation that developed. For those that would like a detailed account of the artillery organization see the footnotes.[18]

---

[17] Ibid, page 115

[18] OR, S1, V5, 293-299. On October 20, 1861, Battery B, First Rhode Island Artillery was split by sections of two pieces each: right section under Lt. Adams at Monocacy, center section under command of Lt. Bloodgood at Edward's Ferry and the left section under Battery Commander Captain Thomas F. Vaughn, along with all the battery's caissons, at camp in Poolesville, MD. On October 21, Captain Vaughn was ordered to Conrad's Ferry and took the left section to the river where the California Regiment was crossing to Harrison's Island under the command of Lt. Colonel Wistar. With the infantry backed up waiting to cross to the island in the few available boats, Captain Vaughn left the left section under the command of the battery Sergeant Major and went to Edward's Ferry to bring up the center section. While the Captain was gone most of the infantry crossed to Harrison's Island and Colonel Cogswell arrived with the 42nd New York Infantry. The left section of Battery B was occupying the landing and Colonel Cogswell ordered it to cross to the Island to make room for his infantry. Since no officer was with the RI artillery at the time, Colonel Cogswell ordered Lt. Walter M. Bramhall of the Sixth New York Battery to take command of the RI guns and cross as rapidly as possible. Using a large scow attached to a hawser that had been stretched across the river the two pieces of the left section were, along with their horses and limbers, taken to the island, moved across the island to the west shore and prepared for the trip to the Virginia shore. Lt. Bramhall crossed to Virginia with one James' rifled cannon, gun carriage and limber while a sergeant crossed with 7 horses and drivers in a second trip. Colonel Cogswell and Company C of the Tammany Regiment made the trip to Virginia with this artillery piece. The second piece of the left section reached the island about 30 minutes behind the first piece and never was transported to Virginia, as the need for additional infantry was more important. This piece took up a position overlooking the landing. The center section had returned with Captain Vaughn to the crossing in Maryland but never crossed to Harrison's Island and the right section remained at Monocacy. Rhodes, John H., The History of Battery B, 1st Regiment Rhode Island Artillery, pages 33-35. Also assigned to General Stone was Rickett's

What was the role of the Tammany Regiment in the Battle of Ball's Bluff? To be certain it was significant. Piecing together the available information paints a fairly detailed picture although there are numerous inconsistencies in the reports and gaps exist that may never be accurately filled. As was pointed out in previous chapters many changes had already taken place in the command structure of the regiment. It was also true that a number of other officers were not with the regiment as they moved into their first significant action. James Boyle, Captain of Company B was on medical leave suffering from residual effects of Typhoid Fever. Captain Graham of Company C and First Lt. Paine of Company K were on recruiting duty in New York City. First Lt. Robert Wright of Company G was on leave as well.

The best place to start putting together the pieces of the puzzle is with the Official Report of Lieut. Colonel James J. Mooney that was submitted on November 4, 1861 from Regimental Headquarters at Camp Lyon, near Poolesville, MD.[19] Interestingly, Mooney was not at Ball's Bluff. He was on leave settling the estate of his parents.[20] His report, which had to be based on accounts given to him by others, does however provide a framework from which other details can be added.

Mooney reports that on the morning of October 21, Colonel Cogswell received orders from General Stone to ready and subsequently move the regiment to a point two miles below Conrad's Ferry on the Maryland shore. The Mooney report simply states that upon arrival the entire regiment was transported to Harrison's Island "in good order and without accident". Reports of others would show that this representation was an over simplification.

Battery I, First US Artillery, a section of which, under Lt. Woodruff, was located on October 20 at Edward's Ferry. A section of the Sixth New York Independent (Bunting's) Battery under Lt. Bramhall located at Conrad's Ferry was also part of the command. This section, equipped with two mountain howitzers crossed to Virginia with the second battalion of the 20th MA under Major Revere. These two howitzers from the Sixth NY Battery, under the temporary command of Lt. French of the First US Artillery, were the two that were in the battle and lost to the enemy.

[19]   OR, S1, V5, 323-326
[20]   NARA, Personal records of Lt. Col Mooney

Mooney's report then states that the regiment started to move across to the Virginia shore using "inadequate means of transit provided, only about a company being able to cross at a time". Five companies were able to reach Virginia before "the boat used for transportation of troops to the battlefield was swamped on a return trip, laden with wounded and dead soldiers that had just fallen on the field of battle". The five Tammany companies that reached the Virginia shore were: A, Captain Harrington; C, Lt. McPherson; E, Captain O'Meara; H, Captain Alden and K, Captain Garretty.

The exact order followed by the five companies is not detailed in Mooney's report however he does state that Captain Alden "fell at almost the first volley from the enemy" and "though deprived of their commander thus early in the action, the company still continued to fight with commendable ardor" suggesting that Company H was one of the early arriving companies of the Tammany battalion that reached Virginia.[21] Captain Alden is not the only causality listed in Mooney's report. Colonel Cogswell is reported wounded slightly in the hand and likely captured. Captain Garretty was reported "killed pierced with several balls, and that his body was afterward terribly mutilated by passing cavalry of the enemy". Captain O'Meara is reported captured and is praised for his efforts in swimming from the Virginia shore to Harrison's Island seeking additional transport from Colonel Hinks of the 19th Massachusetts who was in command of forces on the island. Captain O'Meara, having failed in getting additional transport, then swam back to Virginia to assist his men. Sergeant Thomas Wright, one of the future bright stars of the Tammany Regiment, from Company G, who had been detailed to assist in transporting troops, was also reported as missing. Captain Harrington reached the safety of Harrison's Island after "he threw his sword in the river, divested himself of his wearing apparel, and swam".

There is virtually no detail in Mooney's report about the actual fighting on the bluff. He does mention that Colonel Cogswell assumed command

---

[21] Eugene Sullivan reported that companies C and H were the first of the Tammany troops to reach Virginia followed by companies E and K. Sullivan does not mention Company A, but the numerous casualties suffered by Co. A is sufficient to document the presence of that unit. "Ball's Bluff, How the Battle was Fought and Lost", National Tribune, Volume XIV, No. 24, March 28, 1895.

of the brigade following the death of Colonel Baker and "when retreat became inevitable, drew off the men in the best possible style, ordering them to cast their muskets and accouterments into the river rather than leave them as trophies for the rebels".

The remaining Tammany companies: B, Lt. McGrath; D, Captain Gotthold; F, Captain Tobin; G, Captain Quinn and I, Captain Hogg remained on Harrison's Island under the command of Major Peter Bowe who was assisted by Lt. Abbott of Company D in supervising the transportation of troops to and from the Virginia shore. Mooney reports that around noon on October 22 the 27th Indiana Infantry relieved the regiment and the Tammany men returned to Camp Lyon.

Colonel Cogswell had indeed been captured and taken to prison in Richmond.[22] He was paroled and arrived at Fortress Monroe by steamer on February 23, 1862 along with many other paroled prisoners.[23] It was not until September 22, 1862, almost seven months later, that Colonel Cogswell filed his report of the action at Ball's Bluff. Why such a delay? Colonel Cogswell had a lot on his mind. Although he had been paroled in February he was not finally exchanged until September 25, 1862.[24] Colonel Cogswell was also aware of the fate of General Stone who had been in prison until late August 1862. He also knew that General McClellan had sent a letter to Governor Morgan of New York just after he was paroled asking that he be given back the command of the Tammany Regiment and that no such order was forthcoming.[25] He was instead reassigned to command the 2nd New York Heavy Artillery on September 29, 1862 just one week after filing his report on Ball's Bluff.[26] In this author's opinion all these events are related. Colonel Cogswell was a political man with ambition and pride. At the time of his parole General Stone had already been arrested and confined. Those in power had made decisions. Cogswell was not going to rock the boat while his own future was up in the air.

---

[22] OR, SI, V5, 360-363
[23] New York Daily Tribune, February 26, 1862, page 6, column 1
[24] OR, S2, V4, 125
[25] OR, S2, V3, 335
[26] Almost from the date of appointment of Cogswell to 2d NY HA, he was placed in command of an artillery brigade within the defenses of Washington. In this capacity he was an acting Brig. General. NARA records, Cogswell, 2NYHA.

Cogswell took the course that protected his career and gave him the best chance to come out ahead. Was Colonel Cogswell required to file his report before he got his new command? Did Cogswell know about his appointment to the artillery as he wrote his report? Given his connections within the political structure of New York, I would think so. Did all of the above factor into Cogswell's thinking as he wrote his account of the battle at Ball's Bluff? I would think so. Nevertheless, his report[27] is a tremendous help in filling in the details about the conduct of the Tammany Regiment on October 21, 1861.

Colonel Cogswell reported that around noon on October 20 he had received verbal orders from General Stone's headquarters to move the Tammany Regiment to the vicinity of Conrad's Ferry and await orders. Four companies were on picket duty between Conrad's Ferry and the Monocacy River. Cogswell moved the other six companies and upon arrival at Conrad's Ferry reinforced the pickets there with four of the six companies keeping the last two in camp. At around 2 o'clock in the afternoon on October 21 he received orders to cross to Harrison's Island taking with him the artillery that was posted with his command. Cogswell reported, "I found the greatest confusion existing. No one seemed to be in charge or anyone superintending the passage of the troops, and no order was maintained in their crossing". Colonel Cogswell crossed to the island with a company of troops and two pieces of artillery and gave verbal orders to Major Bowe to remain in charge and have the remainder of the Tammany Regiment, that had been called in from picket duty, follow as soon as possible. Cogswell crossed the island and found further confusion. As he arrived at the landing Lt. Colonel Wistar, commanding the California Regiment, was just crossing to Virginia in the "life boat". Cogswell then crossed to Virginia "in a scow, taking with me Company C, Captain McPherson, of my regiment, and one piece of artillery, with its horses, under Lt. Bramhall, Sixth New York Battery". At the time of the action at Ball's Bluff Charles McPherson was a First Lieutenant. Colonel Cogswell calling him "Captain" is likely because of his promotion to that rank in March of 1862, following his release from captivity, and out of

---

[27]   OR, S1, V5, 320-323

deference to his recent, just a few days before the writing of Cogswell's report, death at Antietam on September 17, 1862.

Upon landing Company C was ordered to "the right and front" to clear away some enemy infantry who were firing on the boats. Cogswell reported to Colonel Baker at the top of the bluff, "on the edge of an open field of about eight or ten acres". With Baker, Cogswell found the California regiment and the 15th and 20th Massachusetts Infantry regiments and two howitzers of the U.S. Artillery under Lt. French. According to Cogswell, he discussed the position with Baker and advised the Brigade Commander to occupy some high ground beyond a nearby ravine. At the time the enemy did not occupy the high ground. The suggestion was not heeded and Colonel Cogswell was ordered to take charge of the artillery but was not given any specific assignment or mission. Some twenty minutes later the enemy opened fire from the high ground. Cogswell reports that he tried to bring artillery fire on the enemy positions but it was not effective and that the enemy quickly shot Lt. Bramhall and most of the artillerymen. At that time Colonels Cogswell and Baker and some other staff officers worked the guns themselves. Cogswell then moved to the area of the California regiment and found their commander, Lt. Colonel Wistar badly wounded. Cogswell then ordered Captain Markoe of the California regiment to reposition his company and hold a nearby hill. Some 20 minutes later Colonel Baker arrived from the right of the line and was shot and killed by the enemy.

At about that time, according to Cogswell, two companies of the Tammany regiment under Captain Alden arrived and took part in an attack "that pushed the enemy some 50 yards back". Cogswell states that: "Captain Harvey, assistant adjutant general, reported to me that Colonel Baker having been killed, I was in command of the field". Cogswell then conferred with Colonels Devens and Lee who were considering a retreat across the river to Harrison's Island and informed the two Massachusetts colonels that he was in command and that their planned retreat was not possible. Instead Cogswell ordered a move in the direction of Edward's Ferry, where he anticipated that General Gorman would be advancing, pressing the enemy's right. The two companies of the Tammany Regiment and portions of the California Regiment followed Cogswell but "for some reasons unknown to me, was not joined by either the Fifteenth or

Twentieth Massachusetts Regiments". Cogswell's force was overpowered and driven back to the riverbank. Upon reaching the river Cogswell observed Tammany companies K and E under Captains Garretty and O'Meara unloading from the large boat. These fresh companies were ordered up the slope to cover the retreat "and with their brave men held the bluff until long after nightfall, thus saving the command a long time from a murderous fire". As darkness fell Colonel Cogswell and some 20 men moved to check a ravine and were surrounded and captured.

From Colonel Cogswell's report some order can be placed on the timing of the arrival of the five companies of the Tammany Regiment that reached Virginia. Company C arrived in Virginia first with Cogswell. It is also clear that Company K and Company E arrived last on the same boat. Company H arrived under Captain Alden along with another company just about the time that Colonel Baker was killed. The other company must have been Company A. Cogswell made no mention of Captain Harrington, commander of Company A, probably because the two companies were under the command of Captain Alden who was senior to Harrington based on date of rank.[28]

Retreat from Ball's Bluff, Library of Congress

---

[28] Captain Alden was mustered in as Captain on June 28, 1861 while Captain Harrington was mustered in as Captain on July 23, 1861. Documents of the Assembly of the State of New York, 124th Session, 1901. Volume VI, No. 32, Part 3, pages 893 and 974, Albany, James B. Lyon, State Printer, 1901.

Cogswell also reported that Lt. Gillis, from Company E, who was acting as his adjutant and aide-de-camp during the battle "performed his duty most gallantly, and fell after the final repulse". Lt. Gillis had been promoted to First Lt. on September 14 and had tendered his resignation to Colonel Cogswell to accept a higher appointment in the California Regiment. He insisted on joining the Tammany Regiment in the battle and accompanied Colonel Cogswell as his aide.[29]

At the end of his Official Report, Colonel Cogswell commented on his opinions as to the reasons that the battle went the way it did. He laid most of the blame for the disaster at the feet of Baker referring to the lack of boats, the absence of artillery covering the crossing and the unwillingness of Baker to position the troops as he had suggested. It is important to remember that Colonel Cogswell was writing this report to General Stone just after Stone had been released from a long term confinement forced on him as a result of the political ramifications of Ball's Bluff.

While the reports of Colonel Cogswell and Lt. Colonel Mooney are the only ones from members of the Tammany Regiment there are many reports of other officers that comment or shed light on the activities of Tammany men during the battle.

General Stone's report dated October 29, 1861[30] provides the following detail. He confirms that the Tammany Regiment was ordered on Oct. 20 to Conrad's Ferry taking with it a section of Vaughan's Rhode Island Battery and that a section of Bunting's New York State Militia Battery, under Lt. Bramhall was already posted at Conrad's Ferry. Stone states that while other troops under his command were ordered back to their camps he held the Tammany Regiment at Conrad's Ferry awaiting the results of the scouting party commanded by Captain Philbrick of the 15th Massachusetts. Early in the morning, according to Stone, Colonel Baker was given command of a reinforced brigade that included the Tammany Regiment and ordered to cross to Virginia and develop the information gained by the scouting party. Stone reported that shortly after 3 o'clock in the afternoon "Colonel Cogswell, with a small portion of his regiment, succeeded in reaching the field in midst of the heaviest fire, and they came gallantly into action with a yell which wavered the enemy's line".

---

29 NARA, Letter from Lt. Gillis personal file
30 OR, S1, V5, 293-299

It is likely that the "small portion of his regiment" refers to Company C, under Lt. McPherson as the two companies under Captain Alden (H and A) did not appear on the battlefield until around the time of the death of Colonel Baker, reported by Stone to have been around 4 P.M. Stone's report confirms the transfer of command to Colonel Cogswell following the death of Baker and the orders given by Cogswell to attempt to cut through to Edward's Ferry. Stone's report states: "an officer of the enemy rode rapidly in front of the Tammany Regiment and beckoned them toward the enemy". Stone suggests that the Tammany men may have thought the mounted officer to be one of their own. Who was the mounted officer? In Colonel Cogswell's report there is no mention of a mounted officer urging the attack following Cogswell's assumption of command. Cogswell says that he ordered the advance. Was the mounted officer Colonel Cogswell? Did Colonel Cogswell have his horse with him during the battle? We do know that he crossed the Potomac to Virginia taking the horses of the artillery piece commanded by Lt. Bramhall. In the opinion of this author, given Cogswell's status as a regular army officer, a graduate of West Point and a man that was very proud of his position, it is more likely than not that he would have taken his horse as well.

Captain Francis G. Young, Quartermaster of Colonel Baker's Staff, in his report dated October 28, 1861[31] stated that "When Colonel Cogswell crossed the river he brought a second order in writing with him from General Stone, to the effect that Colonel Baker should, if he could, advance in the direction of Leesburg, and that he might count upon meeting the enemy in force of about 4000. These orders I found in Colonel Baker's hat, after he had fallen, stained with his blood". While Colonel Cogswell did not mention such an order in his report, his actions upon taking command after Colonel Baker's death are consistent with Captain Young's statement. Young also confirms that Cogswell was wounded in the arm. Young reported that Cogswell arrived in Virginia at 2 P.M. bringing with him "artillery, horses and men". This would have been Company C and Lt. Bramhall's artillery piece. Captain Young's report establishes that horses were with the Union troops. He states: "Colonel Baker and all the officers were on foot throughout the engagement, leaving their horses tied to trees, and they all fell into the hands of the enemy". The fact that

---

[31]   OR, S1, V5, 327-329

the enemy captured Union horses was confirmed in the Official Report of Lt. Colonel McGuirk of the 17th Mississippi Infantry.[32] McGuirk also reported that he loaned his horse to the wounded Colonel Cogswell after his surrender. Was Young referring to the officers of his regiment or all the officers of the brigade? It seems unlikely that Colonel Cogswell would be riding around the battlefield while all the other officers were on foot. Young also reported that at the time of Baker's death an enemy mounted officer was seen riding nearby.

General Stone did not think much of Captain Young or give much credibility to what he had to report. In forwarding Young's report on October 31, Stone said: "This extraordinary production of a fertile imagination is respectfully forwarded. I have no time to notice its misstatements, but would simply call attention to the last clause in the communication, which I am informed is true: "There was no regularity or order in the movement of the boats." Had there been, there would have been no disaster, and Mr. Young, the author of the within, was Colonel Baker's Quartermaster".[33] A court martial, headed by Colonel Devens of the 15th Massachusetts, tried and found Captain Young guilty of being absent without leave at a time not related to Ball's Bluff. He was dismissed from the army on January 2, 1862.[34]

The report of Colonel Devens, 15th Massachusetts dated October 23[35] adds very little. He confirms the appearance of the "officer of the enemy in front of the Tammany Regiment, who called on them to charge on the enemy". Devens states that "the Tammany Regiment, probably mistaking this for an order from their own officers, rushed forward to the charge, and the Fifteenth Massachusetts, supposing that an order had been given for the advance of the whole line, rushed with eagerness, but was promptly recalled by their officers, who had received no such order. The detachment of the Tammany Regiment was received with a shower of bullets and suffered severely".

---

[32]   OR, S1, V5, 360-363
[33]   OR, S1, V5, 330
[34]   Lash, Cary C., supra, page 157
[35]   OR, S1, V5, 308-312

Captain William Bartlett of the 20[36] Massachusetts reported[36] that following the retreat to the river he "ordered those of the regiment that could not swim to follow up the river … About 20 of the Twentieth, 20 of the Fifteenth, and 40 of the Tammany and California regiments followed us. I went up as far as the old mill, where I found, by means of a Negro there, a small sunken skiff in the millway, and induced him to get it out of water and down to the river. It was capable of holding 5 men … In an hour we were all across".

Confederate officers made a number of reports. Captain W. L. Duff, commanding Company K, Seventeenth Mississippi regiment, reported that sometime between noon and dusk a man who proved to be an officer in the Tammany Regiment stopped one of his skirmishers. Lt. Stephens shot the officer.[37] Who was the officer? Captain Duff had been sent to prevent the crossing of Union artillery. The only artillery that came across with Tammany men was with Company C. Lt. McPherson was captured but there is no record of him being wounded nor was any other officer of Company C known to be wounded or killed during the battle. If accurate the report must be talking about either Lt. Gillis or Captain Alden, as the only other officer killed in the battle was Captain Garretty who arrived at the very end of the action with Company K.

Elijah White, a volunteer rebel cavalryman, who later went on to head his own unit known as White's Cavalry, the 35th Battalion Virginia Cavalry Comanches, identified the officer that caused the Tammany Regiment to attack as Lt. Charles B. Wildman, a staff officer of General Evans.[38] What the true story is will likely never be known.

Information from many other sources helps tremendously in filling out the story of the Tammany Regiment at Ball's Bluff. In some cases however, conflicts in accounts add to the complexity of what actually happened and force one to make conclusions that may not necessarily be 100% accurate.

---

[36] OR, S1, V5, 318-320
[37] OR, S1, V5, 363-365
[38] Farwell, Byron, supra, page 107

Bodies of the slain in the Potomac River, Library of Congress

In a letter dated November 12, 1861 sent from the camp of the 9th Massachusetts near Falls Church, VA, Hard Scrabble reported that around the beginning of November the bodies of fourteen Tammany men were removed from the Potomac River in Georgetown and interred.[39] Who might these men have been? Were they all from the Tammany Regiment? It is impossible to know for sure as the bodies were not identified in the letter. If one looks at the list of the missing provided by Lt. Colonel Mooney and compares it to the list of the prisoners that were released and those who were known to have died, the following names are more likely than not among those found in the river: Company A: Privates James Cannon, James Douglas, George McClelland and John Wilson; Company C: Private James Fitzgerald; Company H: Private William Mooney and Company K: Sergeant M. Ryan, Privates F. Bopp, T. Draddy, A. A. Odwell, G. Blake, James Connor and James Gifford. These 13 men were originally reported as missing but ultimately found to have died.

The Richmond Examiner listed the names of many of the prisoners captured at Ball's Bluff including that of Lewis A. Bell a free black from Washington DC. The paper lists Bell as a member of the 20th Massachusetts but other sources identify him as a servant of Colonel

---

[39] Letter from Hard Scrabble, 9th MA, November 12, 1861, Boston Saturday Evening Gazette, November 23, 1861, page 1, column 5

Cogswell.[40] No mention of Bell is made in the Regimental History of the 20th Massachusetts.[41] Bell was released from prison along with other the troops captured at Ball's Bluff in February 1862.[42]

According to the Regimental History of the 20th Massachusetts, the third and fourth companies of the Tammany Regiment landed in Virginia at 5:45 P.M. and the last company (E), under Captain O'Meara arrived just as the retreating Union troops reached the river. O'Meara is described as "a very heroic and capable officer" and is given credit for providing a skirmish line that protected the disorganized men rushing to the river.[43] This same source reports that a rowboat was brought from the Maryland side of Harrison Island by men of the 20th Massachusetts and sent to Captain O'Meara. O'Meara took charge of the boat and sent it back to the island with a cargo of wounded men. All together the boat made several trips saving between thirty and forty men before the rebels captured the remaining troops waiting to be ferried across around 10 P.M.[44]

Also reported in the history of the 20th Massachusetts is the crossing of a number of New York officers under a flag of truce on November 6, 1861. These officers retrieved the body of Captain Alden of Company H and returned his body to his family.[45] Details on the recovery of Captain's Alden's body are provided in a New York Times newspaper article saying in part: " ...it has been my pleasure to visit the scene of the recent battle, and under the protection of what is technically known as a flag of truce but which, in reality, was nothing but a pocket handkerchief tied to a stick ... The object ... was to disinter and bring home the body of Captain Alden ... party consisted of Lieut. Colonel Palfrey ... flag officer of the day, Quartermaster Garland of the Tammany, Wm. K. Comstock, an undertaker with two assistants and a coffin and several soldiers as escort ... An after examination of Captain Alden's body disclosed a bullet hole through his neck, a similar one at his right breast, with an exit at his left

---

[40]   Farwell, Byron, supra, page 60
[41]   Twentieth Massachusetts
[42]   New York Daily Tribune, Saturday, February 22, 1862, page 6, columns 1-3, reports the release of Lewis Bell, a Negro from Ohio
[43]   Twentieth Massachusetts, page 52
[44]   Ibid, page 56
[45]   Ibid, page 71

hip, and three bayonet wounds in the left side and hip. An impressive funeral ceremony was performed at the Tammany camp, and the body, in charge of Mr. Comstock, was sent to Washington … and from thence to be sent to New York".[46]

Captain Henry Alden, USMHI, collection of Martin Schoenfeld

Who was Captain Henry H. Alden? He was born in Middleboro, Massachusetts. As a child he moved to New Hampshire and then as a young man to New York to pursue a career in the dry goods business owned by Elijah J. Brown whose roots can be traced back to mid-seventeenth century Ipswich, Massachusetts, the same town that Colonel Cogswell's family came from. Captain Alden's great, great, great, great, grandfather was Joseph Alden born 1624 in Massachusetts. Joseph was the second son of John Alden, perhaps the most famous passenger on the Mayflower. Was this connection to the early history of the United States a factor in granting permission to his family to retrieve his body for burial? Was his connection

---

[46] New York Times, November 13, 1861, Special Correspondent. Mr. Comstock was a family friend.

to Massachusetts a reason for his being given command of Company H, composed of a large number of men that had enrolled from Boston?[47]

The recovery of Captain Alden's body was well publicized in New York and prompted numerous requests from other families to visit Ball's Bluff for the purpose of recovering fallen family members. General Stone refused to allow other visits to the battle ground. One of the requests came from the wife of Captain Garretty. When her request, made first through a family friend and then in person to General Stone was refused she returned to New York. On January 9, 1862 a letter written on December 20, titled "A Woman's Story" appeared in the New York Tribune. It was signed "A Soldier's Mother". Was the letter designed to add fuel to the questions already being asked about the conduct of General Stone during the battle or was it merely meant to express the grief and frustration felt by Captain Garretty's family? Decide for yourself. The letter read:

"To the editor:

Sir: Having seen by the papers that an investigation into the causes of the disaster at Ball's Bluff was stifled in the House of Representatives, I give the following facts which have come to my knowledge, and which may give a clue to the spirit which prevails in the management in some portion of our army on the Potomac. The news and detailed accounts of that fearful event filled us with indignation. From day to day, contradictory statements of the killed and missing reached the relatives of those who participated in the engagement. Mrs. _____, wife of Captain _____, a brave and high-toned and respected officer in the Tammany Regiment of this city, received a letter from a brother officer stating that it was his painful duty to inform her that her husband had fallen at Ball's Bluff. For a time nothing could console her, but friends made some particular inquiry, and there seemed reason

---

[47] Alden, Ebenezer, Memorial of the Descendants of the Honorable John Alden, page 141. Also, Shea, John Gilmary, The Fallen Brave, Charles B. Richardson Co., New York, 1861, page 211.

to believe that he was only wounded, and a prisoner. She immediately sent a friend to Poolesville to make an investigation and discover the truth. She awaited his return in an agony of suspense. He came but brought no tidings. General Stone had refused him a flag of truce, although his letters gave ample proof that his mission was simply one of charity to relieve the heart of a disconsolate wife. Providing herself with influential letters, Mrs. _____, proceeded to Washington, and from thence to Poolesville. Stopping with a private family, she naturally made known her sad errand. The family assured her that there would be no difficulty in obtaining a flag of truce, for Gen. Stone had granted one to the wife of a Rebel officer to go to New York and remain three weeks; only a few days ago she had returned home again through Gen. Stone's kindness. Sanguine of success, and hopefully trusting that her husband still lived, Mrs. _____, presented her letter to Gen. Stone with an earnestness that should have touched any heart, however hardened, she told her grief, and asked the favor of a flag of truce to go and find her husband. "Madam", he replied, "your husband is dead. Capt. _____ was buried by the rebels." "Buried by the rebels", she answered, "How can that be?" When Captain Vaughn was sent to bury our dead, why should the rebels bury him? "The account they give," said he, is "that Captain Vaughn left him on the field and they buried him. He was lying about two yards from Captain Alden." "It is strange that they should so soon bury him." "They did it for my sake", said the General. "It is not likely, general", said Mrs. _____, "that Capt. Vaughn would bury one officer and leave another unburied within two yards of him. This is not to be believed. If the rebel is the only source from which you have gained the account of my husband's death, I do not credit it for they are not to be believed or relied upon at all." "Madam", said the General with sternness, "you surprise me. What better

51

Fred C. Wexler

source could you wish? The Rebels are gentlemen and are to be believed and relied upon. I wish you to know that many of them are my intimate friends, and I believe everything they say respecting your husband. You are very much mistaken in your ideas Madam." "I am sorry we differ so far in opinion respecting them, General. If they are what you represent them to be, there was no occasion to go to war with them. I do not believe my husband is dead and if he is, you will not refuse me a flag of truce to see the spot where he is buried and to obtain his body." "I cannot grant it, Madam." "Cannot grant it, General?" "No Madam, it cannot be done." "Am I not entitled to the favor as well as Mrs. Col. _____, the wife of a Rebel officer to whom you granted a flag of truce to go and come on a less important errand?" General Stone turned pale, and changed his stern manner but persisted in his refusal. Mrs._____ became much excited, and spoke to him of the Ball's Bluff affair as it would be well if those in power had eloquence and heart to speak. Just before leaving she said, "Had my husband died on the field of battle, and in so doing had he benefited his country, I could be resigned, but he was not led to battle but to slaughter." "Madam, do you intend that remark for me, said the General." "The blame rests upon someone, and whoever the cap fits may put it on!" she replied. "When we get to Virginia, I will make every investigation you desire." "When we get to Virginia? That does not look likely to happen soon. You, General, may be in Virginia before we can be." Leaving him, Mrs. _____ returned to Washington, distressed and disappointed. Here are the facts Sir, and how do they strike every reader? Can it be that the Rebel officers opposed to General Stone's Division are his "intimate friends"? Can it be that he considers them "gentlemen and to be relied upon?" How many more such intimate friends have the Rebels on the line of the Potomac? God only knows; and while our homes are made desolate, and our country bleeding at every pore, who will be the first to rise in their might and arouse our leaders to an effort worthy of the Sons of Freedom? Men of America! Are you men and stand in thousands and in hundreds of thousands, in the face of an insolent and rebellious foe and dare not strike the blow! There you stand, buffeted by the South on one cheek and by England on the other, and still you remain unmoved. You should have gone forth with half your numbers, not with strength of your own but with confidence in God, for your cause is just and with but an arrow and a sling, felt that you could have brought down the enemy. We, mothers, have sent forth our sons cheerfully. We have given them to the cause of Liberty, but we cannot see them sacrificed- we cannot see incompetent or traitorous leaders destroying brave and loyal men without mercy- see them led like sheep to the slaughter, and not raise our voice against it. We demand an investigation at once. When the leaves fell, we were to see justice done. The blow was then to be given effectually. It is now nearly mid-winter, and the fine weather almost gone. Our army is sleeping on the Potomac in sight of the enemy. The only general willing to trust to the strength of will and patriotism of his soldiers, rather than his numbers, is recalled on the eve of a battle! Our fleet when forth with flying colors and a "gods speed" from anxious hearts, but alas, there too, we find no noble deeds of daring and success to report. Why, is it sir? Why is this? We have a right to ask. I hope the facts related above will only apply to an isolated case, but it is the sacred duty of our government to know why we have not subdued the enemy. If we cannot, let us know it, and we will acknowledge to the world that we have no men among us, and like the women of old, we will fight our own battles. I speak not alone for myself, and from one aching heart, but for many, and from thousands who are mourning and waiting. A SOLDIER'S MOTHER. New York Dec. 20, 1861."[48]

The next day a letter was published in the New York Times defending the actions and honor of General Stone adding details to what took place at the meeting between Mrs. Garretty and general Stone. The author of the letter is not identified by name but states that he was on the staff of the New York Times serving with General Stone's command.

The letter read: "To the Editor of the New-York Times: The Tribune of yesterday contained a letter headed "A Woman's Story," which, if allowed to remain uncorrected, cannot fail to unfairly prejudice the minds of people against Gen. STONE. The letter asserts that in an ungentleman -- like and haughty manner the General abruptly refused "Mrs. -----, wife of Capt. ----, (a brave, high-toned and respected officer in the Tammany Regiment of this City,") a flag of truce, with which she might recover the body of her husband, who was killed at Ball's Bluff and buried by the rebels. This assertion is coupled with gratuitous insults to Gen. STONE, intimating very broadly that he is in sympathy with the rebels, and enjoys their intimacy. The writer of this paragraph was, on the occasion alluded to in the letter, the Special Correspondent of the TIMES, with Gen. STONE's Division, and is able, of personal knowledge, to state the following facts: Gen. STONE granted to the friends of Capt. ALDEN a flag of truce, and they obtained the body of their deceased relative by that means. The fact having become publicly known, Gen. STONE received scores of letters and telegrams from widows, brothers and friends, all over the country, asking the same favor, and so great became the demand that he peremptorily refused one and all, for obvious reasons. About this time, Mrs. GARRETTY, widow of Capt. GARRETTY, went to Poolesville and boarded with the family of Dr. POOLE. With the Doctor she visited the General, and desired permission to seek her husband's body. He told her of the numerous applications made and of his invariable reply; and then, alluding to the circumstances of her husband's death, said that he had died as any soldier might desire to die -- gallantly fighting at the head of his company, and so conducting himself as to win the admiration of foe and friend. His manner was peculiarly courteous and kind, and it seems

---

[48] New York Tribune, December 27, 1861

54

most strange to me, that one so eminently gentle as he, should be publicly accused of roughly treating a sorrowing woman. The parting between Gen. STONE, Mrs. GARRETTY, and Dr. POOLE, was devoid of anything like annoyance on her side, or incivility on his. In regard to Gen. STONE's intimacy with the rebel leaders, I will say a word. It seems rather hard that a man who has spent twenty years of his life in the service of his country should be so assailed behind his back, that comparative strangers feel it their duty to defend him, but, in spite of that, I will mention that Gen. EVANS, who commands the rebel forces at Leesburgh, was a pupil of Gen. STONE at West Point, and between them, as is the case with many officers on either side of this contest, there had always existed a warm friendship until the beginning of the rebellion, and when Gen. STONE, in reply to a question of Mrs. GARRETTY, replied that the officers at Leesburgh were gentlemen, and could be believed in their statements concerning the burial of her husband, he intended, as every reasonable person must see, to convince her that he believed they had carefully interred the Captain's remains, and that on that point she might be satisfied. NEW-YORK, Dec. 27, 1861."[49]

In a newspaper account of the battle written by Correspondent Carleton that was printed in The Boston Journal on October 26, 1861, when Colonel Cogswell ordered the final retreat Colonel Devens said: "Sir, I do not wish to retreat. Do you issue it as an order"? Cogswell replied: "Yes sir". Devens then said: "I would like to have you repeat it in the presence of my major, then". "I order you to retreat" was the response by Cogswell. Accounts of the battle were not always accurate. The same report in the Boston Journal reported Colonel Cogswell as having been killed.[50]

The Democratic Mirror reported on November 6, 1861 that a personal difficulty had arisen between Colonel Hinks of the 19th Massachusetts and Major Bowe of the Tammany Regiment. Reportedly, a challenge had been issued by Major Bowe based on comments made by Colonel Hinks regarding the conduct of some Tammany men under the command of Major Bowe on Harrison's Island. Representing the Colonel were the Lt. Colonel and Major of the 19th Massachusetts while two Tammany officers

---

49 New York Times, December 28, 1861
50 Boston Journal, Saturday Evening edition October 26, 1861

were representing Major Bowe. While this account sounds like a potential duel was in the offering the report stated: "there was no fear of a fight".[51]

What caused this feud were the comments made by Colonel Hinks in his Official Report to General Lander of October 23, 1861.[52] In his report, Colonel Hinks said: "I arrived at 1:30 p.m. and found among the troops at the point of crossing great confusion, no competent officer seeming to have been left in charge of the transportation". Colonel Cogswell had left Major Bowe in charge of the landing and of transporting the remainder of the troops then on Harrison's Island to Virginia. Colonel Hinks went on to state that: "I at once took command … restored order … I sent the 19th MA to the front … placed gun(s) in position … supported by 2 companies of the 20th MA and so much of the Tammany Regiment as was upon the island and could be induced to remain … No field officer was on duty on the island, with the exception of Major Bowe, of the Tammany Regiment." As if these remarks by Colonel Hinks were not enough to make Major Bowe angry, the Colonel went on in his report to comment on activities of the Tammany Regiment on October 22. He said: "I have to report that the remnant of the Tammany regiment, under command of Major Bowe, deserted its post in the entrenchments on the island at an early hour in the forenoon of the 22nd, and passed to the Maryland shore in disobedience of orders, while I was engaged in arranging for the removal of the wounded and the burial of the dead". In a special post script note, Colonel Hinks went on to say: "The fact that the remaining fragment of the Tammany regiment had left the island without orders was construed by the Confederate commandant as a violation of the stipulation that no movement of troops should be made from the island to the Maryland shore while the burying party was employed." Colonel Hinks was referring to a party of men sent to Ball's Bluff under a flag of truce to bury the dead. The party was under the command of Captain Vaughn of the Rhode Island Artillery. Permission had been granted with the proviso that no attempt would be made by any of the troops on Harrison's Island to try and reach the Maryland shore. When confederate officers saw activity by Union troops they threatened to take Captain Vaughn prisoner. What actually

---

[51]   Patch, Joseph D., The Battle at Ball's Bluff, page 113-14. The Democratic Mirror was a Loudoun County, VA newspaper published during the Civil War.

[52]   OR, S1, V5, 312-314

was the activity that caused the threat against Captain Vaughn and his burial party? According to Colonel Hinks report it was the movement of the Tammany regiment across the Potomac to the Maryland shore. Other reports, from the 19th Massachusetts and that of Colonel W. H. Jenifer, commander of the Confederate Cavalry, say that it was the shooting of a rebel mounted soldier that was attacking a Union survivor trying to get to safety. Perhaps most accurate in its detail is the report of Lt. Colonel John McGuirk of the 17th Mississippi which reads: "On the next day Captain Vaughn of the Federal Army, asked permission, under flag of truce, to come to the river bank and bury the dead. This was granted … during the time Captain Vaughn was on this side, I discovered the enemy moving off the island and towards Edward's Ferry. I notified Captain Vaughn of the fact, and told him if the two boats loaded were not brought back I would hold him as prisoner of war on account of violating the treaty. He had them brought back."[53] Taking Lt. Colonel McGuirk's version as accurate, since he was the one who actually talked to Captain Vaughn, there were troops moving off the island. It is likely that the troops were the battalion of the Tammany regiment under Major Bowe mentioned by Colonel Hinks. It appears though that the Tammany men came back when ordered to, which was not included in Colonel Hink's report. Did they leave without orders? Did they have orders from someone other than Colonel Hinks authorizing them to cross to Maryland?

On November 4, General Stone's headquarters issued Special Order No. 24 which stated that: "The general commanding has, with deep regret, observed in a report by Colonel E. W. Hinks … a statement reflecting severely on the conduct of the gallant Tammany regiment. Colonel Hinks reports that a portion of the Tammany regiment deserted the island … The commanding general deems it proper to give publicity to the fact that he himself requested Major General Banks to relieve the companies of the Tammany regiment early on that morning … Commanding officers are cautioned against making unnecessary and rash statements in their reports,

---

[53] Waitt, Ernest Linden, History of the Nineteenth Regiment Massachusetts Volunteers, Salem Press 1906, page 28, OR, S1, V5, 368-372 and OR, S1, V5, 360-363

especially in cases where the honor and reputation of other regiments may be involved ... By order of Brigadier General Stone." [54]

Upon receiving General Order 24, Colonel Hinks responded immediately defending his statements.[55] He restated his charges against Major Bowe in more specific language saying: "I directed Major Bowe to place the companies under his command behind the breastworks ... I received no orders for the relief of these companies, neither were they relieved by any other troops ... I was informed ... that the companies of the Tammany regiment had taken possession of the boats and were passing to the Maryland shore. I ... found that a portion had already crossed; others were preparing to cross. I ... inquired by whose authority they left the island? Several voices replied that no orders had been given for them to do so ... I replaced them with companies ... of the 19th MA." Colonel Hinks does not state in his report that he had the discussion with Major Bowe or any specific member of the Tammany regiment. He only states that "voices" responded to his questions.

Colonel Hinks summarized his position saying: "A remnant of the Tammany regiment was ... subject to my command ... was placed in position ... deserted ... to the Maryland shore in disobedience of orders. Twelve hours after it had deserted ... fresh troops arrived." The troops that arrived were three companies of the 2nd MA regiment which had been sent by General Hamilton apparently in response to General Stone's request to General Banks.[56]

Colonel Hinks, feeling personally attacked by Special Order 24 continued by saying: "It became my duty, however disagreeable to report the fact in precisely the terms that I used. For this report ... I have been censured in orders. I ... request a court of inquiry ... I beg further to state that I had and now have no desire to cast any dispersion upon any regiment or body of men in the service of their country, much less upon the gallant spirits who rallied to the call of Cogswell, or dashed upon the foe with O'Meara; but truth compels me to state that had the men of the

---

[54] Special Order 24, Headquarters, Corps of Observation, Poolesville, MD, November 4, 1861, signed by C. Stewart, Assistant Adjutant General.

[55] OR, S1, V5, 315

[56] Ibid, Enclosure A, message to Colonel Hinks, from Major L. H. D. Crane, 3rd Wisconsin, Acting Assistant Adjutant General for General Hamilton.

Tammany regiment upon the island put forth but a single response to my directions to bring a boat from the Maryland to the Virginia side of the island, many, if not all, of O'Meara's men now in imprisonment would have been rescued ... the act of desertion ... seemed to me to be more reprehensible ... they were the freshest troops ... were called on to do less than others on the island ..."

Interestingly, the discussion of the moving of boats was not presented in Colonel Hinks original report. The subject was discussed in the report of Lt. Colonel Mooney, also issued on November 4, where he stated that Captain O'Meara had "implored" Colonel Hinks for use of a boat to rescue his men, but was refused. What actually happened? We're likely to never know. Just two days later Major Bowe issued his challenge to Colonel Hinks.

The regimental history of the 19th Massachusetts says that on the night of October 21, Colonel Hinks deployed the portion of the Tammany regiment on Harrison's Island along with other troops to hold the island against a counter attack thought to be coming. By dawn no attack had come, probably due to the rain that had set in.[57] There is no discussion of the issues between Colonel Hinks and Major Bowe.

The New York Times of October 25, 1861 reported that: "The Tammany Regiment covered itself with glory. Captain O'Meara often rallied his command, throwing defiance into the very teeth of the enemy, and showing the rebels that he could scream equal to the worse of them. Capt. O'Meara took charge of the landing, and refused to let any but wounded men enter the boat, ordering the sound troops to go back and pepper the rebels. His conduct was very gallant throughout, evincing a true and lofty courage".[58]

The New York Times of October 29, 1861 published a detailed list of the casualties of the Tammany Regiment by company indicating rank, whether an individual was killed, wounded, missing or captured. In some cases the type of wound was reported. The list is reportedly that put together at the order of Lt. Colonel Mooney for his report to General Stone. In Company A, Sergeant Mills and Corporal Stapleton were both listed as

---

[57] Waitt, Ernesr Linden, supra, page 25

[58] New York Times, Friday, October 25, 1861, The Battle at Edwards Ferry, page 1, column 3

having been wounded in the foot. Privates Terry and Gilligan were listed as having been wounded in the back and hip respectively. Private Gallagher of Company K was reported to have had his right arm amputated. The report listed as killed: Company A: Private T. Bailey, Company C: Corporal D. McPhail (drowned), Company E: Private D. Graham, Company H: Captain Alden and Company K: Captain Garretty, and Privates J. Danver, J. Sullivan, J. Cahill and Edward Sullivan. Additionally, Private T. Dugan was reported as "supposed killed". He was not; he lived until his death at Glendale less than a year later. 120 men were listed as missing with the note that those listed as missing "are many killed and taken prisoner".

Other reports and descriptions of the actual battle and its disastrous aftermath mention the men of the Tammany Regiment frequently. These include:

"The Southerners were concealed by the dense forest and could be detected only by the smoke of their musket and rifle discharges. One coatless rebel who wore a red handkerchief tied around his head, stepped out from the timber and deliberately loaded and fired until a member of the Tammany Regiment who had just gained the top of the bluff brought him down."[59]

"Lieutenant Bramhall's gunners, too, were falling ... Colonels Baker, Cogswell and Lee, Lieutenant Colonel Wistar ... and several other officers ... fired six rounds before they returned to their respective commands."[60]

"Milton Cogswell worked at holding the left flank of the Union position. Now two companies of his Tammany Regiment panted up behind the Californians cheering most heartily. The New Yorkers charged into the fray pushing the Rebels back ..."[61]

A member of the 8th VA reported finding the body of "a gray haired private of the First California whose head had been mashed between two rocks by a ponderous Tammany man who had broken his own neck by the fall."[62]

---

[59] Lash, Cary C., supra, page 122.
[60] Ibid, page 123
[61] Ibid, page 126. The companies referred to were most likely A and H.
[62] Patch, Joseph Dorst, supra, page 17 quoting Shotwell, Randolph Abbott, Three Years in Battle, an autobiography of a member of the 8th Virginia.

"Milton Cogswell tried to bring some order to the great disorder ... He ordered the survivors of the 15th MA deployed as skirmishers to protect the river crossing. Two companies of the Tammany Regiment scrambled out of a large boat and up the riverbank. Cogswell posted them with the Massachusetts boys that were firing at Rebels."[63]

"A Californian and two members of the Tammany Regiment were at the oars of the boat as it steered toward Harrison's Island. Near the mid-point of the channel, one of the oarsmen was hit. Within moments, the others were struck down."[64]

"It was every man for himself at the river's edge. One ... member of the California battalion ... began divesting himself of his surplus clothing ... Just then a burly member of the Tammany Regiment ... drove the Californian into the mud."[65]

"A Federal officer ... neared the top of the escarpment, he turned to his command, waved his sword over his head and shouted: "Come on, ye brave Irishmen, come on! Where are ye, Americans? Where are ye?" A rebel volley toppled the officer."[66] Although not named, this officer could very well have been Captain Garretty in command of Company K as he was the only officer killed in the two companies of the Tammany Regiment that arrived last and were sent up the hill to protect the retreat of the others.

Captain Bartlett of the 20th Massachusetts told of his leading a group of about 80 men from all the Union regiments in the battle away from the bluff and trying to seek a way to escape to Harrison's Island. He said: I started up the river followed by about twenty men of the Twentieth Regiment, twenty of the Fifteenth and forty of the Tammany and California regiments ... We followed up the edge of the river, and came to an old mill ... I went up there and found a skiff under water ... it was capable of holding five persons ... When the boat was put in the water, the whole crowd made a rush for it. I had to use a little persuasion by stepping in front of it, drew my pistol ... and swore to God that I would shoot the first man who moved without my order ... I selected five men from my own company and sent them across first, with a man to bring

---

63   Lash, Cary C., supra, page 128. These were companies K and E.
64   Ibid, page 129
65   Ibid
66   Ibid, 131-2.

back the boat. So by degrees, I got those of the Twentieth, next those of the Fifteenth … and lastly those of the Tammany and California regiments … We saved eighty men."[67]

E. V. White, the local cavalryman, and eventual Colonel of the 35th Virginia Cavalry, who aided the rebel forces and performed so well during the day said in describing the scene at the water's edge: "Approaching the landing … and making the best investigation I could, I reported … the boat rapidly approaching the Virginia shore … that there were 1,500 of them … The Lieutenant said: "Don't you think we can capture them?" … It was agreed that I should … ride to the Eighth Virginia and ask them to come over to help us. In all fifty-two came … not a man among us knew the ground … they made me leader … the party descended the bluff … we heard the boat returning from the island. How many trips it had made in my absence I do not know, but the number of men … had diminished … All their officers … had left … except one, a gallant Irish Captain of the California (actually Tammany) regiment, who had swam over to the island to try for some way to get his men over, but failing that had swam the river back again to share the fate of his company. I think his name was O'Meara, and he deserves the Medal of Honor. This brave gentleman called out, as a last resort in the wreck and confusion, "We surrender, who is in command?" Captain W. N. Berkeley replied, "General White," and Captain O'Meara asked: "General White, what terms will you give us?" My unofficial promotions this day had been too rapid for my scant military knowledge … I replied: "The terms of war" … his clear voice called, "Men, General White gives us the terms of war; come out of the river and surrender" … he marched them up the bluff … and handed over … three hundred and twenty five prisoners."[68]

When Colonel Cogswell appeared on the battlefield Colonel Baker is reported to have said: "One blast on your bugle horn is worth a thousand men."[69]

---

[67]   Palfray, Francis W. Memoir of William Francis Bartlett, Houghton, Osgood and Company, Boston 1878 page 27-9

[68]   White, Colonel E. V., History of the Battle of Ball's Bluff, The Washington Print, Leesburg, 1904 page 6 as quoted in Holien, K. B. Battle of Ball's Bluff page 77-9.

[69]   Farwell, Byron, supra, page 93

Sergeant Compass of the 20th Massachusetts criticized the Tammany troops. He said: "I have talked to over 200 men and they all say the Tammany run back to their boats, before the order came, and they didn't support the advance at all … The three boats they had were filled with wounded, who were crossed over to the island by the Tammany men, as also many cowards of the Tammany crossed with them all the time."[70]

When Captain Vaughn crossed to Virginia to bury the dead he found and buried forty-seven bodies and had to leave with still around another twenty-four in view. One of the bodies that were buried had stitched to the trousers the name of "Captain Henry H. Alden, Company H, Tammany Regiment". Under another body was an envelope with the name James Douglass, a private in A Company.[71]

An interesting fact is that Colonel Cogswell and Lt. Oliver Wendell Holmes Jr. of the 20th Massachusetts Infantry and the future Supreme Court Justice, although they probably did not know it, were blood relatives. Distant relatives to be sure but related nevertheless. To find the connection it is necessary to go back many generations. O. W. Holmes' great, great, great, great grandfather was William Cogswell (1619-1700). William Cogswell had a brother named John Cogswell (1622-1653) who was Colonel Cogswell's great, great, great, great, great grandfather. Like I said, distant relatives but still related by blood.[72]

Summing up the Battle at Ball's Bluff is not easy to do but taking a close look at the casualties of the Tammany Regiment should help. Twenty-six Tammany men lost their lives at Ball's Bluff. Eleven were wounded and managed to escape to the Maryland shore. One hundred and twenty-three were captured including thirteen that had been wounded. In total one hundred and sixty men were casualties that I have been able to identify. The actual number is likely somewhat higher. What should stand out in these numbers is the lopsided ratio of killed versus wounded men. While I haven't done the research I would expect that it is quite rare for the number of wounded and killed in a battle to be equal!

---

[70] Ibid, page 126

[71] Ibid, page 145

[72] Cogswell, Donald James, Descendants of John Cogswell, 1635-1996, Family Line Publications, Westminster, Maryland, 1998, pages 215,404. Hereinafter cited as "Cogswell".

Looking closer at the casualties, the numbers by company are equally telling. If we assume for ease of calculation that all five companies that reached the Virginia shore were at full strength of one-hundred men, Company A lost 18% and Companies C, E, H and K lost 51%, 29%, 16% and 44% respectively. Company K, arriving quite late in the battle, lost fifteen men killed while the other companies suffered between two and four fatalities. It would appear that Company K came ashore right under the guns of Confederate troops on the bluff and suffered the consequences of being in the wrong place at the wrong time![73]

At the Battle of Ball's Bluff, Patrick Henry Lennon (the guy on the cover and hereinafter referred to as Uncle Pat) was First Sergeant of Company H having been promoted to that rank on June 28. In addition to the death of his company commander Captain Alden, Sgt. McCarthy and Private Mooney, two of Uncle Pat's comrades were wounded and taken prisoner along with ten others. All ten non-wounded men captured were Boston men![74]

If in reading this chapter you come away a bit confused as to what actually happened you are feeling what was felt by everyone at the time. To say that there was more information being reported than could be digested would be an understatement, to say that newspapers published information that was sometimes more inaccurate than accurate would be fair. Perhaps it is best to look at the words of Henry Livermore Abbott, an officer from the 20th Massachusetts who said: "Now look at the absurdity of the thing. To cross the river we had two rowboats that together carried over 30 men at a

---

[73] The Tammany KIA: Co. A: Privates James Cannon, James Douglas, George McClelland and John Wilson, Co. C: Corporal Duncan McPhail and Private James Fitzgerald, Co. E: First Lieut. James Gillis and Private Daniel Graham, Co. H: Captain Henry Alden, Sgt. Owen McCarthy and Private William Mooney, Co. K: Captain Michael Garretty, Sgt. Martin Ryan, Privates Frederick Bopp, Terrence Draddy, Andrew Odwell, George Blake, James Connor, James Gifford, John Cahill, Patrick Collins, James Danver, James Dennan, John Sanders, Edward Sullivan and John Sullivan.

[74] Company H men that had enrolled in Boston that were taken prisoner at Ball's Bluff were: Corporals Thomas McBay and John G. Smith, Privates Patrick Moore, James Monahan, James Byron, Bernard Dolan, Patrick Flattery, Michael Lynch, Michael Queennan and Nicholas Quinn. The two wounded men that were captured were Corporal Michael Doran and Private Augustus Bauer.

time. We landed on the hill, which was almost perpendicular and thickly wooded. When we got on the top, we are drawn up on the only open space there is, about wide enough for a front of two regiments, and about a short rifle shot in length, surrounded on every side by large, unexplored woods. It was in fact one of the most complete slaughter pens ever devised." [75]

---

[75] Scott, Robert Garth, Fallen Leaves, The Civil War Letters of Major Henry Livermore Abbott, Kent State University Press, Kent Ohio, 1991, page 60

Chapter Four

THE BALL'S BLUFF PRISONERS

Fortunately, at the time of Ball's Bluff, a policy was about to be put in place that allowed for relatively quick parole and exchange of prisoners by both sides. In fact, within four months the vast majority of the men captured would be paroled and back safely in Union hands. That is not to say that the companies to which the prisoners belonged immediately got their services returned. That was certainly not the case. Many were sick from their imprisonment and would never see action again, being discharged for various disabilities. However, many of the men from Companies A, C, E, H and K would rejoin their comrades in time to fight on the Peninsula in the spring and summer 1862.

A published account of what the men went through following their capture describes their ordeal in detail. "About 400 (actually the number was quite higher) of us were marched to Leesburg that night and from there to Manassas, a distance of about thirty-five miles, during which we received only a piece of corn bread, each about the size of a man's hand, which was the first morsel we had received for the previous thirty-six hours. At Manassas they took a list of the names ... they then marched us into some yards enclosed by board fences, about 15 feet in height ... and there we slept on the cold, wet ground, with not even a blanket for covering, or a fire for warmth and the supper provided consisted of raw ham. On the following morning, breakfast was served up, each man receiving half a small loaf of bread, after which we were formed in squads of 50 each and proceeded to Richmond by cars."[1]

The Richmond Dispatch reported that the train arrived in Richmond just before 10:30 AM on the October 24. The prisoners were escorted to Richmond by a detail of 84 men under the command of Lieutenant Colonel T. C. Johnson, 19GA, and Captain J. B. Andrews, 4NC State Troops. There were a total of 525 prisoners including 22 officers. In the group were 93 Tammany men (4 officers and 89 enlisted ranks), 149 from the 15MA, 184 from the 1CA, 72 from the 20MA and several others. After unloading, the men were marched down Broad Street enroute to their prison at Mayo's Factory on the corner of Cay and 25th Street. The next day a second trainload of Ball's Bluff prisoners arrived numbering a total of 132. The number of Tammany men in this second group is not known but Lieutenant McPherson is named as one of the two officers in the group.[2] The other four Tammany officers captured at Ball's Bluff were: Colonel Cogswell, Captain O'Meara and Lieutenants Giberson and Van Voast who had also been wounded. Upon arriving at the prison they were reunited with Lieutenant George H. Wallis, who had been captured at Mason's Island in September.

Prison life was described as "quite monotonous". There were two meals a day mostly consisting of bread and soup containing meat. There was no coffee and only a little tea. The officers ate a bit better; they had three meals a day. There was little opportunity for outdoor exercise. If you had some money you could get some vegetables or potatoes. Money usually took the form of "shinplasters" which were various types of circulating script that found varying degrees of acceptability among the prisoners, guards and the people of Richmond. Union currency, either coin or bank notes could be exchanged at a premium for quantities of shinplasters.[3]

New York newspapers frequently ran notices of the delivery of money to prisoners in Richmond by "Flag of Truce". Tammany prisoners that

[1]   New York Daily Tribune, Thursday, March 6, 1862, Return of Released Union Prisoners from Richmond, Statements of Thomas Pousland, First Sgt. Co. H, 20th MA and Thomas Ross, Corporal, Co. A, 15th MA.
[2]   Richmond Dispatch, October, 2 1861.
[3]   New York Times, Thursday, February 27, 1862, page 8, columns 3-4. Prison Life in Richmond

received cash included: Captain O'Meara: $5 gold, W. Wallace, $1 gold, M. Cunningham, $2.5 gold, T. Carney, $2.5 gold, B. Pegram, $2.5 gold, D. Mahoney, $2.5 gold, H. Adams, $1 gold, A. Donnelly, $1 gold, P. West $5 banknote, W. Jamison, $1 gold, T. Dunigan, $2.5 gold, J. Nagle, $3 gold, W. Byrne, $1 gold, E. McNally, $5 banknote, E. Lindsay, $2.5 gold, P. Reily, $2.5 gold.[4]

Captain O'Meara sent a letter to his brother John in New York dated: "Richmond Prison, November 5, 1861". In it he listed names and addresses of all of the Tammany men that were captured by company. The text of the letter gives a great insight to the character of Timothy O'Meara. "My Dear Brother: I forward to you a list of the men's names that were taken prisoner with me … who belonged to my own company … I wish you would go in person and report to their friends or write to them. The names of the others you can hand in to some of the papers for publication. It will be a satisfaction to their friends to know that they are all well. We expect to be sent to South Carolina in a few days. I hope you are all in good health. Tell my mother and Mary not to sorrow for me. God, who rules the destiny of all men, will, I hope, continue to bestow his blessings on me, and in His own good time deliver me out of this bondage … The people down here are not so cruel as people in the North would make them. We are treated well as we could expect under the circumstances".[5]

John Sullivan and Francis Campbell, both from Co. C and convalescents from the prison hospital in Richmond, were released in January, 1862.[6] The four Lieutenants were paroled with the majority of the enlisted men in February 1862.[7] Giberson was exchanged for James Cooper, 1LA, McPherson for A. W. Essell, NC State Troops, Van Voast for W. B. Wise, NC State Troops and Wallis for a Confederate naval officer.[8] Wallis would leave the Tammany Regiment within a month to join the

---

4   New York Herald, Dec. 26, 1861, New York Tribune, January 3, 1862, page 8, column 1-2, New York Daily Tribune, January 13, 1862, page 6, column 5.
5   Irish American, December 7, 1861, page 4.
6   New York Daily Tribune, January 20, 1862, page 6, column 1-2. "Names of Released Prisoners".
7   Numerous reports appeared in the newspapers listing the names of all the released prisoners. Not all the reports were consistent. Irish American, March 8, 1862, New York Times, February, 22, 1862, page 2, column 6
8   Richmond Enquirer, February 19, 1862.

80NY. Van Voast would be wounded again at Antietam and be discharged for disability in February 1863. Both Giberson and McPherson would be promoted to Captain in March 1862. McPherson would be killed at Antietam and Giberson's ill health resulted in his being placed in charge of the Ambulance Trains of II Corps and his discharge for disability in September 1862.[9]

The fates of Colonel Cogswell and Captain O'Meara, while ultimately ending with their safe parole and return, were not routine by any measure. Each would be held hostage and threatened with death as part of separate, but related, politically motivated maneuvers between the North and the South. Ultimately, both officers would return to the war effort but never again would either see action with the Tammany Regiment.

The three events that created the special circumstances to be faced by Colonel Cogswell and Captain O'Meara centered on a whether or not certain individuals, serving in various capacities for the Confederate States, were to be considered prisoners of war upon their capture and therefore subject to certain rules on their treatment. While each event can be viewed separately, a broader look more clearly shows the impact they had on Cogswell and O'Meara.

It all started in May 1861 when the 53-ton schooner Savannah, mounting a pivot gun, was fitted out as a privateer, in Charleston. The Savannah, commanded by Captain Thomas Baker, sailed under orders, signed by Jefferson Davis, with the mission of intercepting and capturing or destroying shipping of the United States. The Savannah's orders were considered by the South to be "Letters of Marque and Reprisal"; a common technique used by nations throughout history as a means of enlisting the naval services of those that would otherwise be considered pirates. On Monday, June 3, 1861 the Savannah captured the brig Joseph, carrying a load of sugar, and was in turn captured by the U. S. brig-of war Perry. The crew was eventually transported to New York and on July 16, 1861, indicted on a number of charges including that of piracy. Conviction would carry the death penalty. The United States refused to accept the papers issued to the Savannah as Letters of Marque as that would amount to the recognition of the Confederacy as a "nation". Due to issues related to the non-availability of judges, the trial was put off until October 23,

---

9   NARA, individual soldier records.

1861, just two days after the Battle of Ball's Bluff. The trial lasted about a week and ended on October 31, 1861, with the jury not being able to reach a verdict.[10]

After the indictment of the crew of the Savannah but before the start of their trial, on July 22, 1861, just about the time that the Tammany Regiment was reaching the seat of war, the U. S. Navy re-captured the 378-ton schooner Enchantress. The Enchantress had been captured by the Confederate privateer, Jeff Davis, and placed under a five-man crew commanded by Walter W. Smith. The small crew had the task of bringing the captured prize to a Confederate port quickly so that it could be placed into service for the South. Smith was put on trial in Philadelphia and after five days convicted of piracy. He was sentenced to death by hanging.

Smith's sentence was not immediately carried out, no doubt due in part to the events related to the larger profile case surrounding the Savannah in New York. Smith did however remain a condemned man, a fact that did not go un-noticed in the South. On November 9, 1861, following the non-verdict in the Savannah case, J. P. Benjamin, Acting Secretary of War for the Confederacy issued an order requiring the selection of hostages to be held and treated according to the treatment, by the United States, of Smith and the Savannah crew. Brig. General J. H. Winder, Department of Henrico, Richmond, VA, responded on November 11 stating:

"Sir: In obedience to instructions contained in your letter of the 9th instant one prisoner of war of the highest rank in our possession was chosen by lot to be held for execution in the same manner as may be adopted by the enemy for the execution of Smith, recently condemned to death in Philadelphia. The names of the six colonels were placed in a can. The first name drawn was that of Col. M. Corcoran, Sixty-ninth Regiment New York State Militia, who is the hostage chosen to answer for Smith. In choosing the thirteen from the highest rank to be held to answer for a like number of prisoners of war captured by the enemy at sea, there being only ten field officers it was necessary to draw by lot three captains. The first names drawn were Capts. J. B. Rickets, H. McQuaide and G. W. Rockwood. The list of thirteen will therefore stand-Colonels Lee,

10 Dershowitz, A. M., Trial of the Officers and Crew of the Schooner Savannah, The Notable Trials Library, Special Edition 1997, New York. This volume is a complete record of the trial.

Cogswell, Willcox, Woodruff and Wood; Lieutenant Colonels Bowman and Neff; Majors Potter, Revere and Vogdes; Captains Rickets, McQuaide and Rockwood." [11]

Of the selected men, four had been captured at Ball's Bluff: Cogswell, Lee and Revere from the 20MA and Rockwood from the 15MA. Colonel Cogswell sent a note to General L. Thomas, Attorney General of the Army on November 12, describing the selection process and pointing out that Captain Cox, 1KY offered to take the place of Captain Ricketts but was refused. However, since Captains Ricketts and McQuaide were seriously wounded they were withdrawn from the list and replaced, by drawing of lots, by Captain Bowman, 15MA and Captain Keifer, 1CA, both having been captured at Ball's Bluff.[12]

Colonel Corcoran was not in Richmond. He was at Castle Pinckney, near Charleston, South Carolina. His selection as the hostage to be placed in the most serious situation, to be treated as a condemned felon, was made by drawing of his name from a covered box by the Hon. Alfred Ely, of Rochester, New York, a congressman that had been captured at Bull Run. First Lieutenant John Whyte of the 79NY witnessed the selection process. Lieut. Whyte also mentions that Captain McQuaide was not expected to survive his wounds and that Captain Ricketts was in critical condition being attended to by his wife in a Richmond hospital and that the selection of captains Keifer and Bowman was made from among the eleven remaining captains then in prison.[13]

The officers, in Richmond, selected as hostages were all transferred from the Tobacco Warehouse to the Henrico County Jail. Cogswell, Lee, Wood, Revere, Keifer, Rockwood and Bowman were housed in a single 11 by 17 room.[14]

The other officers being held hostage were not in Richmond. Corcoran, Woodruff, Wilcox, Neff and Potter were initially housed in the tower of the Charleston Jail and kept separated from other prisoners. Following a

---

[11] OR, S2, V3, 739
[12] OR:S2, V3, 130-131
[13] OR:S2, V3, 131-132
[14] Letter by Captain Bowman to the Massachusetts State House, November 27, 1861 and OR:S2, V3, 136

fire in December they were transferred to Columbia Jail, South Carolina.[15] Another officer, Captain George Austin 2KY, was also with this group. While not a hostage for a member of the Savannah, Captain Austin would become a part of the unfolding events in a short time.[16]

Major Vogdes had been captured near Fort Pickens in Florida in early October. He was confined in Montgomery, Alabama until around April 1862, at which time he was transferred to Richmond.[17] Exactly where Lt. Colonel Bowman was held hostage is unclear, although it was not in Richmond. Eventually he joined the other, non-Richmond hostages as they were being paroled in the fall of 1862.

On December 16, 1861, Samuel Barlow, an influential New York lawyer whose firm had defended the crew of the Savannah and who was a close friend of Colonel Cogswell, sent a letter to J. P. Benjamin, through Secretary of State William Seward and Maj. General John Wool at Ft. Monroe. He stated that he was under the impression that Colonel Cogswell and the others were not being treated well, and he stressed his strong relationship with Colonel Cogswell.[18] The response by Mr. Benjamin, CSA Secretary of War shows clearly how the fates of the hostages were in the hands of the highest levels of political power in both the North and the South. He said: "I had noticed and appreciated the generous spirit with which your firm … had volunteered their services in defense of the prisoners taken by your government from the privateer Savannah … I accept at once … all that you say on the subject … yet … you cannot deny that they are in jail as felons, that men captured at sea in time of open war with national commissions in their possession are on trial for life as pirates … In this state of facts you make to me an appeal in behalf of Colonels Lee and Cogswell and other prisoners … The question, permit me to say, is not whether felons are well or ill treated in New York or Richmond … it is whether prisoners of war are to be treated as felons at all? It is whether this war is to be conducted as between civilized nations or savages. God knows … that I would prefer the former and … I would gladly hail the news that your Government, by abandoning its pretensions

---

[15]   OR:S2, V3, 324
[16]   OR:S2, V3, 193
[17]   OR:S1, V6, 439, OR: S2, V3, 754
[18]   OR:S2, V3, 162

that prisoners of war are pirates, left me at liberty to loosen the bonds of your friends … [19]

The fate of the hostages rested squarely with the politicians. In February 1862 all the men tried for piracy were declared to be prisoners of war and the threat of death was removed from them. In return, all the hostages were returned to prisoner of war status. Additionally, an agreement was reached allowing for the parole of all prisoners of war held in Richmond for the parole of a like number of rebel prisoners held by the North. On February 20 and 22 approximately 800 men were loaded on steamers and sent north to freedom. The group included all the Richmond held hostages and all the Tammany men captured at Ball's Bluff except for Captain T. O'Meara. The first group of released men were sent up the James River on the Confederate ship William Allison and were met by Union ships Express and George Washington. They arrived at Fortress Monroe at around 10 AM on Thursday, Feb. 20, 1862. Included in that group were Lieutenants Giberson, McPherson and Van Voast and many enlisted Tammany men. The second group arrived at Fortress Monroe and was sent to Baltimore. In this group were Colonel Cogswell, many Tammany enlisted men, the other six Richmond hostages and Lt. Wallis. The other hostages were not covered by the agreement, since they were not in Richmond; they had several additional months of prison time ahead before their parole in August. [20]

But why was Captain O'Meara not released in February? On November 25, Captain O'Meara and 19 other officers were transferred from Richmond to Tuscaloosa, Alabama. [21] He was most likely kept in either the Washington Hall Hotel or the Drish Building in Tuscaloosa. Since he was not in Richmond he was not covered by the agreement that resulted in the release of all the prisoners held in the Confederate capital.

---

[19]   OR: S2, V3, 780

[20]   New York Times, February 22, 1862, page 2, column 6, New York Times, February 25, 1862, page 1, column 4, New York Daily Tribune, February 26, 1862, page 6, column 1-2. OR: S1, V9, 17.

[21]   NARA, record of T. O'Meara and letter from Bernard Vassall to Samuel Barton, December 4, 1861. Siegel Auctions, 1977, Lot 4371. "…We officers are confined in one of the TobaccoWarehouses on Main Street. There are now about 40 of us, 20 having been sent to Tuscaloosa and 7 being in jail as hostages for the crew of the privateer Savannah."

In March 1862, events started to unfold that would lead to the final issue related to Captain O'Meara's time as a prisoner. On March 27, the South authorized the Virginia State Rangers. Captains John L. Spriggs and Marshall Triplett commanded two of the nine companies raised. Both Captains were captured in Greenbrier County, West Virginia in May 1862. Because of the tactics used by the Rangers, Union officials considered them to be guerrillas and threatened them with death by hanging. In a series of events, similar in nature to what had happened with the crew of the Savannah, the South selected two captains that were prisoners of war and held them as hostages, threatening them with the same fate as Captains Spriggs and Triplett. The selected Captains were T. O'Meara and George Austin, both of whom had been transferred to Salisbury, North Carolina from Tuscaloosa and Columbia, sometime around March 1, 1862.

Some very important generals and top-level politicians were to be intimately involved with the communications and decisions that were made regarding this situation. On June 6, Major A. C. Godwin wrote to General John H. Wildner, Commander of Department of Henrico, Richmond, VA telling him that in compliance with orders he had selected Captains O'Meara and Austin as the hostages.[22] On June 19, from his headquarters in Richmond, General Robert E. Lee, less than three weeks after he assumed command following the Battle of Fair Oaks on May 30, wrote to General George B. McClellan, Commander of the Army of the Potomac, telling him: "General: I am directed by the Secretary of War to state that having been informed of the capture of Captains Spriggs and Triplett, of the Ranger service of the State of Virginia, and of their intended execution by order of the United States Government, he has caused lots to be drawn from among the U. S. officers detained as prisoners of war for the purpose of selecting subjects for retaliation, and that the lots have fallen upon Capt. George Austin, Company B, Second Kentucky Regiment of Infantry, and Capt. Timothy O'Meara, Tammany Regiment, New York Volunteers. It is the desire of the Confederate Government to conduct this war in conformity to the usages of Christian and civilized nations, but should he have been correctly informed and should Captains Spriggs and Triplett be executed retaliation will be made on Captains Austin and O'Meara. This course will be determined by a due regard for

---

22 OR:S2, V3, 892

the citizens of the Confederate States and will be unhesitatingly though reluctantly pursued. I am most respectfully, your obedient servant, R. E. Lee, General"[23]

If there was ever an example of the efficiency of communications during the Civil War, this is it. Following the receipt of Robert E. Lee's letter, General McClellan, also on June 19, sent the following return message: "General R. E. Lee, Commanding Military Forces, Richmond, VA: I have the honor to acknowledge the receipt of your letter of today relative to a reported intention on the part of the United States Government to order the execution of two prisoners, Captains Spriggs and Triplett, of the Virginia Ranger Service. I know nothing of any such persons. If they were taken by this army the report is without foundation. I have telegraphed upon the subject to the Secretary of War and I will communicate the facts to you as soon as I learn them. I shall much regret any commencement of retaliatory executions. I have the honor to be, very respectfully, your obedient servant, George B. McClellan, Major General, Commanding."[24]

General McClellan's telegram to the Secretary of War prompted a flurry of communications on June 20 that included one from President Lincoln. McClellan received a single sentence communication from the President stating: "War Department, Washington, DC, Major General McClellan: In regard to a contemplated execution of Captains Spriggs and Triplett the Government has no information whatever, but will inquire and advise you. A. Lincoln."[25]

He also received a short note from Secretary of War Stanton which said: "War Department, Washington, DC, June 20, 1862: Major General McClellan: Your dispatch in relation to Captains Spriggs and Triplett has been received. This Department has no information of any proceedings against them, but will take immediate measures to ascertain the facts and inform you of them. Edwin M. Stanton, Secretary of War."[26]

Secretary Stanton immediately sent the following message to Major General Fremont in the west. "War Department, Washington DC, June 20, 1862. Major General Fremont: The President directs that if you have

---

[23] OR:S2, V4, 46
[24] Ibid
[25] OR:S1, V14, 236
[26] OR:S1, V4, 43

in your custody the rebel Captains Spriggs and Triplett who are reported to be under sentence of death as guerillas you shall suspend proceedings against them and make report to this Department of the facts of their cases. Please answer immediately. Edwin M. Stanton, Secretary of War."[27]

General Fremont did respond immediately: "Strasburg, June 20, 1862. Hon. Edwin M. Stanton: Dispatch just received. I have not yet received any report in cases of rebel Captains Spriggs and Triplett. Have probably been tried by military commission under General Kelley. I will immediately inquire and report. J.C. Fremont, Major-General Commanding."[28]

Secretary Stanton had no intention of waiting for a further report. He sent a message directly to General Kelley stating: "War Department, Washington DC, June 20, 1862. Brigadier General Kelley, Cumberland: Suspend proceedings against Captains Spriggs and Triplett and report by telegraph to this Department the facts in their cases. Edwin M. Stanton, Secretary of War."[29]

Secretary Stanton received a response from General Kelley and included it in a communication back to General McClellan saying: "War Department, Washington, June 20, 1862. Major General McClellan: A telegram is just received from General Kelley as follows: "Captains Triplett and Spriggs were captured by Colonel Crook's troops in Greenbrier County and I think are in Camp Chase. They have not been tried by court-martial or military commission. Major Dart, Provost Marshall at Wheeling, can give all information in regard to them. B.F.Kelley, Brigadier General". It appears from the foregoing that Captain Spriggs and Triplett are held as prisoners of war. This Department has no other information on the subject. Edwin M. Stanton, Secretary of War."[30]

All of the information received by General McClellan was sent to General Robert E. Lee on June 20 and 21. Additionally, General Order No. 71 was issued by the War Department on June 21, 1862 stating: "In every case of prisoners taken in arms against the United States who may be tried and sentenced to death the record of the tribunal before which the trial was had will be forwarded for the action of the President of the

---

[27] Ibid
[28] Ibid
[29] OR:S1, V4, 44
[30] Ibid

United States, without whose orders no such sentence in such cases will be executed. By order of the Secretary of War."[31]

The flurry of communications had succeeded in preventing any harsh treatment of either the Confederate or Union men concerned but it did not result in their immediate release. On July 22, Captain Austin, from his prison at Salisbury, N. C., sent a letter to J. A. Cravens, Member of Congress, stating that he had been told that he and Captain O'Meara would remain in prison, despite a general exchange that was about to take place, until Captains Spriggs and Triplett had been officially declared prisoners of war. Congressman Cravens forwarded the letter to Secretary Stanton asking him to intervene.[32]

By mid August everything was in place to affect the final parole and exchange of all the remaining hostages including Colonel Corcoran, the remaining Savannah hostages and Captains Austin and O'Meara. On August 17, Captain O'Meara was paroled at Aiken's Landing and was exchanged for Captain James Vance, 37VA on September 21. Captain Austin was exchanged for Capt. S. M. Sommers of the CSA, Quartermaster Corps.[33]

Tammany men that were captured at Ball's Bluff and subsequently released were (privates-if no rank is shown):[34]

Staff (1): Colonel M. Cogswell

Company A (10): E. Cleary, D. Devlin, T. Dugan, E. Flood, First Lieut. S. Giberson, Corporal F. Hughes, J. Thomas, J. McCarty, G. Sykes, and J. Wilson.

---

[31] OR:S1, V4, 46-49

[32] OR:S1, V4, 411

[33] OR:S1, V4, 577-584

[34] This list is compiled from cross referencing and using the best estimates of names listed in: New York Times, Feb. 22, 1862, page 2 column 6, Irish American of New York, March 8, 1862, New York Leader, November 30, 1861 and Daily Tribune, Feb. 26, 1862 as well as NARA, individual soldier's records and a letter written by Captain O'Meara to his brother, Irish American, December 7, 1861. It would not be surprising if this list is incomplete or somewhat inaccurate as to the spelling of names as there is tremendous variation within the cited accounts.

Company C (48): D. Barrett, C. Becker, C. Bower, P. Cahill, J. Calhoun, F. Campbell, W. Church, Corporal J. Craig, R. Crawford, A. Cronier, W. Dickelman, A. Donnelly, M. Donovan, J. Dougherty, T. Dunegan, M. Eagan, Sgt. F. Fagan, H. Gilchrist, J. Gorill, J. Greeble, M. Hawkins, J. Hecker, E. Hicks, G. Hyde, W. Jamieson, E. Lindsay, W. May, C. McCarty, J. McKenna, J. McLaughlin, R. McMonagle, First Lieut. C. McPherson, J. Moore, J. Moriarty, J. Nichols, Corporal G. O'Dell, H. Pardy, L. Peters, P. Riley, F. Schultz, C. Smith, T. Sommerville, Sergeant C. Sparrows, W. Stripp, J. Sullivan, D. Thompson, J. Walsh and C. Wiegard.

Company E (26): M. Brennan, M. Collins, F. Crilly, M. Cunningham, C. Dillman, Sergeant T. Dubbins, W. Dunham, J. Gearin, Corporal J. Joyce, Corporal J. Kean, F. Kiernan, Sergeant P. Lynch, W. Mahoney, O. McCabe, Orderly Sergeant J. McConvill, M. McDonogh, O. McLaughlin, P. McMorrow, Corporal E. McNally, T. Murphy, Captain T. O'Meara, D. O'Neill, T. O'Neill, J. Quinn, L. Souvey and E. Tief.

Company G (1): S. T. Wright

Company H (13): H. Adams, A. Bauer, J. Byron, B. Dolan, M. Doran, P. Flattery, M. Lynch, Corporal T. McBay, J. Monahan, P. Moore, M. Queenan, N. Quinn, J and Corporal J. Smith.

Company K (24): Corporal W. Byrne, D. Callaghan, T. Carney, M. Clancy, C. Dinneer, T. W. Early, W. Harding, R. Heany, A. Hydenoff, C. Landers, D. Mahoney, J. McCabe, J. McGeever, P. McManus, Orderly Sergeant J. Monaghan, T. Murray, J. Nagle, B. Pegram, A. Schlessinger, Corporal D. Sullivan, E. Sullivan, W. Wallace, W. Walsh and P. West.

Chapter Five

WINTER 1861-2

As 1861 faded away the Tammany Regiment was in what could kindly be called a mess. Ball's Bluff had thinned out or decimated roughly half of the regiment's companies, the commanding officer was in a Richmond prison being held as a hostage under a possible threat of death, the regimental major was in a feud that almost led to a duel over the alleged cowardice of his men, two company commanders had been killed with a third being made a prisoner and the regiment was under the command of a Lieut. Colonel who had missed it all while he was on leave to take care of personal business! One would think that things had to get better. They would not, at least not immediately. Understanding the complex series of events that impacted the Tammany Regiment during January through March of 1862 is best done by looking at three different components of events: external administrative, internal administrative and military activities.

Two significant external administrative events took place. The first was the investigation into the battle at Ball's Bluff conducted by the Committee on the Conduct of the War that ultimately resulted in the arrest of General Stone on February 9. As the Tammany Regiment was part of Stone's command his arrest left a void and made communications up the line more difficult. The second event was the creation of Second Army Corps on March 13, 1862 by General Order No. 101, Army of the Potomac. Command of Second Corps was given to Brigadier General Edwin V. Sumner a Boston native and a long time veteran soldier. The Tammany Regiment was assigned to the third brigade along with the 7th Michigan, 19th Massachusetts and the 20th Massachusetts. Brigadier

General Napoleon J. T. Dana commanded the brigade and reported to Brigadier General John Sedgwick commander of the third division of the corps. Sedgwick was a West Point graduate and until his promotion to General, Dana had been the colonel of the 1st MN.[1] Both Dana and Sedgwick assumed their command on February 22, three weeks before the official creation of the Second Corps.[2] Sedgwick was very nervous about his ability to command. In a letter to his sister Emily on February 18, he said: "I am very proud to think that General McClellan should think me worthy of such a command. But I enter upon the duties with a great deal of diffidence. It is a large command (thirteen thousand men), occupying an important position, and I fear, above my capacity; however, I shall do my best."[3]

At least on paper the organizational structure within which the Tammany Regiment was to fight for the foreseeable future was fixed. Internally, lots had to happen before the regiment would once again be ready to take the field. Highest in priority was to decide on who would command the regiment. Whose decision would that be? Would it be General Dana, or the Governor of New York or someone else? After all Colonel Cogswell was not dead. He was a prisoner held hostage in Richmond, but what exactly did that mean? Could he continue to command the regiment, on paper, while Lieut. Colonel Mooney took the troops to the field?

To see how things were decided it is necessary to look at a number of events. Taken together they define a kind of "soap opera" script. You may have to re-read these next sections a few times as they are somewhat complex, especially in the fixing of important dates.

Between October 1861 and March 1862 Lieut. Colonel Mooney had a number of run-ins with his senior commanders that had resulted in him being under arrest and subsequently released. The record is not exactly clear on the circumstances that landed Mooney in his predicament but it is for certain that he did not score many points with his superiors. On October 10, when Mooney requested a leave, General Stone attached

[1] Walker, Francis A., History of the Second Army Corps, Charles Scribner's Sons, New York, 1887, 3-9, hereinafter cited as Second Army Corps.
[2] Twentieth Massachusetts, 79.
[3] Correspondence of John Sedgwick, Butternut and Blue, Baltimore, MD, 1999, volume 2, page 38

an endorsement recommending that the leave be approved, "after Col. Mooney has complied with the order to appear before the Military Board in Washington". Mooney did get his leave. However, on December 19, General Stone received a letter telling him that Colonel Mooney had failed to comply with the order of the President of the Board of Examiners to appear before the board. A second letter sent on December 21, says: "I am directed by the President of the Board of Examiners, to request that you order Lt. Col. Mooney ... together with such officers of the regiment as have not yet been examined to appear before the board today, at Col. Deven's quarters, say by 2 O'clock, P.M". It is not really important to know the subject matter of the inquiry. Most likely the Board of Examiners was charged with determining whether the officers of the regiment complied with the requirements of General Order No. 78. That order in sections 16-17 stated in relevant part: "The commander in chief will appoint ... a board of examiners to examine into the qualifications of ... officers ... When an officer shall be found not qualified ... another nomination shall be made".[4]

What is important is that Mooney had not complied with requests made of him from higher headquarters. Attached to the second letter in Mooney's file is an endorsement, also dated Dec. 21, that reads: "Lt. Col. Mooney will comply immediately with the requirement of the board. By order of Brig. General Stone." The words "will comply immediately" are underlined. A second endorsement on the same letter, also dated Dec. 21 simply reads: "Contents noted. J. J. Mooney". On December 24, Mooney sent a letter to General Stone which in part reads, " ...As I am now under arrest by your order ..." Yet another letter dated December 24 reads, " ... you are consequently relieved from arrest".

Jumping ahead to February 15, Mooney made a request for a "parole" of fifteen days so that he could visit a family member that was "at the

---

4   General Orders No. 78, General Headquarters, State of New York, Albany, July 30, 1861. OR:S3, V1, 369-71. It appears that the examination that was originally intended to take place prior to a unit leaving for the seat of war actually was delayed and that examinations did not take place for some time. On August 15, 1861 the Governor of New York informed Simon Cameron, Secretary of War that no regiments were ready to send to the front and that none could be promised citing as the reason, "fearing their inability to pass the required examination before a board of examiners yet to be appointed". OR: S3, V1, 415.

point of death" in New York. Who the family member was is unknown but his parents were no longer alive.[5] This is clear as in his request for the leave that resulted in his not being at Ball's Bluff he listed the reason for the leave as "the purpose of settling the estate of my late parents left to me in New York". His use of the word "parole" is significant as he states in the letter that he was "placed in arrest by General Stone on a trivial charge" and that he is "awaiting the decision of the Courts Martial". The request for leave was denied on February 19, 1862. Mooney immediately sent a letter, also dated February 19, up the line to General Seth Williams, Assistant Adjutant General, Army of the Potomac, asking that the decision refusing the leave be reversed. Williams received the request on February 21. Consider how Mooney's request would have fit into the scheme of things being considered by the generals involved? Did his request really get looked at seriously? General Stone was out of the picture having been arrested on February 9 and sent to Fort Lafayette in New York, a prison usually reserved for traitors. Williams was helping McClellan create the structure of Second Corps and plan the campaign to be launched in April on the Peninsula. Generals Dana and Sedgwick had just assumed their commands as Mooney's request to Williams was forwarded to them for action on February 24. On February 25, Dana sent a response to Williams saying: "In reply to your dispatch to General Sedgwick … relative to Lieut. Colonel Mooney, the case is not a meritorious one and the leave is not recommended".[6] It would be reasonable to assume that Mooney was not happy at the rejection of his request. Actually, considering what was on the mind of the generals he was lucky he got a response at all.

Was there another reason that Mooney wanted to go to New York in mid February? Did Mooney think he was in line for a promotion to the colonelcy of the Tammany Regiment? Not likely as the Governor of New York had on December 18, 1861 appointed Edmund C. Charles to the rank of Colonel taking the roster spot of "Milton Cogswell, prisoner of war." The appointment was released from the Adjutant General's office on January 2, 1862 and notice of it appeared in the New York Times on January 6. Charles was mustered into the Tammany Regiment on January

5   Mooney was the grandson of William Mooney the first Grand Sachem of the Columbian Order (Tammany Hall).
6   NARA, record of Lieut. Colonel Mooney

7.[7] Milton Cogswell was transferred on December 31 to what was called a "skeleton regiment".[8]

Why had the command of the regiment not been reserved for Cogswell? There is no answer to this question but it can be assumed that the Governor of New York had his reasons. Interestingly, the Governor of Massachusetts had the same situation as Colonel Lee of the 20th MA was also a hostage in Richmond. He however, chose to hold the position open until Colonel Lee could return.[9]

Colonel Edmund C. Charles, USMHI, Collections
of Seward Osborne and Martin Schoenfeld

So who was Edmund C. Charles? In May 1861 Charles was the Lieut. Colonel of the 25th NY under the command of Colonel Kerrigan, a serving

---

7   NARA, record of Colonel Charles
8   Official Army Register of the Volunteer Force of the United States Army, Volume 2.
9   Twentieth Massachusetts, 67-68

New York Congressman who would eventually be dismissed from the army for unacceptable conduct.[10] Charles resigned from the 25th NY on October 4, 1861. His reason for resigning was because of ill health. Sometime around early September, Charles had returned to New York and had an operation. His doctor considered him unfit to resume his duties and recommended that he be discharged. Three months later he was ready to assume command of the Tammany Regiment and go back to the war!

How would Charles be received by the largely Irish rank and file of the Tammany Regiment? Certainly, they would know of his prior short service in the 25th NY and his association with Colonel Kerrigan, a well known Fenian. Charles was ordered to appear at Kerrigan's Courts Martial as a witness for the defense in mid January 1862, just as he was on his way to join the Tammany Regiment.[11] They might also know about his association with Company A, 71st Regiment NYSM, also known as the "Light Guards".[12] This unit was formed in 1850, founded by men with links to the "Know Nothing Party", an organization that was not fond of foreigners.

Any negative feelings that were created by the appointment of Colonel Charles might well have been erased based on Charles accepting the re-appointment of Patrick Downing as an officer in the regiment. As discussed in an earlier chapter, Downing, one of the most famous of the Fenians, had resigned his commission prior to Ball's Bluff after a confrontation with Captain O'Meara. On December 17, 1861, Downing wrote to Mooney from his home at 6 Center Street in New York requesting that he be re-instated saying: " …since having forwarded my resignation … to bring about an inquiry into the affair which prompted this action … under the impression that it was in accordance with military usage, knowing of no other, through inexperience in such matters … I find that it was not the proper course, therefore, I beg leave to express my regret for not having

---

[10] Kerrigan had been charged with much more serious offenses but was found guilty of "inefficiency and of conduct unbecoming an officer in the gross neglect of his military duty". New York Daily Tribune, February 27, 1862, page 6, column 5 and New York Daily Tribune, March 7, 1862, page 6, column 5. Kerrigan was one of the leaders in the ill fated Fenian invasion of Canada in 1866.

[11] NARA, File of Edmund C. Charles.

[12] New York Times, April 30, 1863, "Obsequies of Col. Edmund C. Charles".

abided more patiently in my position; and hereby tender my services to the government …". Two days later, December 19, Mooney signed Regimental Order No. 61: "Patrick J. Downing is hereby appointed First Lieut. in Co. E, Tammany Regiment, N.Y. Vols., appointment to date from the 1st of December 1861". The same day Mooney sent a request to General Williams requesting that the resignation papers of Downing filed in September be returned to him and stated that: "My knowledge leads me to recommend the applicant as an efficient officer who during his former connection with the Regiment, was remarkable for military knowledge as well as gentleman like conduct on all occasions …". On December 26, a letter was received by Mooney from Headquarters, Army of the Potomac informing him that he had no authority to re-appoint Downing. The letter was quite clear saying: "I am directed by the Commanding General to state in reply that the resignation of Lieut. Downing was accepted … and that it cannot be now reconsidered. As the power of filling vacant commissions are vested in the Governor … the only course open to Mr. Downing … is to make an application to the Governor of the State of New York". It was that letter that prompted Downing's letter to General Stone dated Camp Cogswell, Poolesville, January 21, in which Downing said that he had been informed by Colonel Charles that the Governor of New York had granted the authority to promote men to officer ranks to Colonel Cogswell but that no such authority had been given to him or any other officer in the Tammany Regiment.[13]

Where was Colonel Charles during the period between mid-January and mid-February when Mooney was so busy writing and receiving letters while in and out of arrest? Was he in Poolesville when Downing sent his letter to Stone? There is no solid answer to this question but there are some facts that give us hints on his whereabouts. As mentioned earlier Charles was called to be a witness at the trial of Colonel Kerrigan and on Saturday, January 11 he wrote a letter from Washington to General Stone saying that he would "remain until examined … when I shall immediately proceed and will report."[14] The prosecution ended its presentation against Kerrigan on January 13 and the defense started on January 14.[15] The trial had

---

13 NARA, File of Patrick Downing
14 NARA, file of Edmund C. Charles
15 New York Times, January 13, 1862

started in early December, so taking into account probable delays around the holiday season, the prosecution took around four weeks to complete. Considering that there were nine charges, some having a potential death sentence associated with them, it would not be unreasonable to expect that the defense would take some time. The decision in the case was reported on February 21, 1862 with Kerrigan being acquitted of all of the most serious charges but being found guilty of enough wrongdoing to be dismissed from the service.[16] We know that on January 16, Mooney sent a letter from Camp Lyons to General Seth Williams, reporting the strength of the Tammany Regiment and requesting that a number of men currently on recruiting duty in New York be recalled. Mooney signed the letter "James J. Mooney, Lt. Col. Commanding".[17] If Charles had been present would Mooney have signed as the commanding officer? So was Charles in Washington between January 17 and February 21? If he had been with the Tammany Regiment wouldn't his authority be the basis for Patrick Downing being brought back into the regiment? Wouldn't he have been the man Mooney would have made the request for a leave to? Wouldn't the letters from the Army of the Potomac been sent to him rather than directly to Mooney? Military protocol would have required at least an endorsement by Mooney's commanding officer on a request that went up the line for consideration. In all of the Mooney correspondence there is not a single endorsement from Colonel Charles. However, Colonel Charles did endorse the resignations of Lieut. Michael Lee and Lieut. Steven Botts on January 28 and 29. Additional endorsements dated February 3, 4 and 10, are on resignation requests of Lieut. Joseph Hogan, Lieut. Thomas Kelly, Captain John Quinn and Captain James Graham. Charles was at regimental

---

[16] New York Daily Tribune, March 7, 1862, page 6, column 5
[17] New York State Archives, Series B04-62-84, Adjutant general Correspondence and Petitions, Boxes 33, 39- 43, 45 New York State Archives, Albany, New York. Hereinafter cited as "New York State Archives". In this report the strength of the Tammany Regiment, present and absent was put at "807 rank and file". The men on recruiting duty were listed as Captain David Hogg, Sgt. Patrick Condon, Co. K, Sgt. Hugh Mills, Co. A, Private David Terry, Co. A and Private Cornelius Smith, Co. E. The report was forwarded to the Governor of New York and the men in New York were recalled.

headquarters, near Poolesville when he endorsed these six requests.[18] Therefore, the most likely explanation as to the whereabouts of Colonel Charles is that he arrived at regimental headquarters sometime between January 16 and 20 and that he was with Patrick Downing in Poolesville on January 21. What remains a mystery is why Charles was not included in any of the correspondence relating to Mooney's communications with higher authorities during February. Could it have been because all of the events leading up to the legal issues of Mooney predated Charles?

The appointment of Patrick Downing as an officer in Co. E created a number of issues. Captain O'Meara, the very man that Downing had said threatened him with a revolver, was the Captain of Co. E and as such would be Downing's commanding officer if he were returned to that position upon his parole and exchange. Clearly, Colonel Charles could not allow that to occur.

Three of the resignations referred to above had the return of Downing as a reason for resigning. Second Lieut. Thomas Kelly, Co. E cited the cause of his resignation as: "On being outranked by Patrick Downing who had to resign under charges on or about the 1st September and who is now reappointed as First Lieut. by Lieut. Colonel Mooney." The exact same language is contained on the resignation of Second Lieut. Joseph Hogan, Co. A. Second Lieut. Michael Lee, Co. G said: "That I have been outranked by P. J. Downing who has been permanently appointed a First Lieut.".[19]

---

[18] NARA, files of Lieut. Joseph Hogan, Lieut. Stephen Botts, Lieut. Michael Lee, Lieut. Thomas Kelly, Captain James Graham and Captain John Quinn

[19] NARA, files of individual officers. Lieut. Hogan had previously resigned his commission but rejoined following Ball's Bluff. Lieut. Lee sent a letter to the governor of New York on June 23, 1862 requesting an appointment in "a regiment likely to be active in the war". In his letter he stated that he had resigned from the Tammany regiment because "he was outranked by one whom I considered my inferior", an obvious reference to Patrick Downing. Lee also stated that "he passed, and was highly complimented by the Board of Examiners for my efficiency". New York State Archives, document 1826. Lee subsequently served as a Lieut. in the 4th NY Heavy Artillery. He was wounded at Spotsylvania Court House in May 1864 and died of his wounds on June 9, 1864 at Seminary Hospital, Georgetown.

Lieut. Botts had a problem with another officer. His resignation letter cited two reasons; the first was: "I have very little hope of passing the Board of Examination and would rather resign than be discharged from the service". The second reason was, "I could never stay in Co. F with First Lieut. Conroy". The issue with Lieut. Conroy is not specified in Botts resignation but in the file of Captain John Quinn, who also resigned, there is a hint as to what had happened. Quinn resigned citing important legal business in Wisconsin that required his attention. However, he had been brought up on charges of "Conduct prejudicial to good order and military discipline" from an incident that occurred on January 1, 1862. The specification reads: " ...between taps and revile was so riotous as to call the attention of the guard and when said officer of the guard did remark to said Capt. John Quinn that his conduct was decidedly improper said Captain John Quinn did reply that the suckers do not like it, and made an attempt to strike said officer of the guard and did also remark you may kiss my ass. I can lick you and your sword ... or words to that effect". The officer preferring the charge was Lieut. Conroy. Four other officers were listed as witnesses. Lieut. Botts was one of them.[20]

Captain James Graham had been shot in the knee while in Washington on July 26 and was carried on the rolls for some time while he recovered from his wound. Unable to return to active service he resigned. Discharged for disability was Captain James Boyle who had suffered for some time from the effects of Typhoid Fever.[21]

The loss of these officers coupled with those killed and captured at Ball's Bluff created large holes in the officer ranks that needed to be filled. Uncle Pat Lennon, William O'Shea, of Fenian fame, and Samuel Dexter were promoted to Second Lieut. from the enlisted ranks. James McGrath, Thomas Abbott and George N. Bomford were promoted from First Lieut. to Captain. Morgan Doheny and Edward Cauvet were moved up to First Lieut. from Second Lieut. Newly enrolled officers Henry Twiggs, Septimus

---

[20] NARA, file of Lieut. Steven Botts. Subsequent service Lieut. 11NY Cavalry. He had been ordered to appear before the board by Colonel Cogswell: Special Order No. 4, Tammany Regiment, October 10, 1861. Also file of Captain John Quinn. The other three officers listed as witnesses were Lieut. John Paine, Lieut. Michael Lee and Lieut. M. Doheny.

[21] NARA, files of individual soldiers

Cobb, Cornelius McLean and George W. Shaw arrived to begin their service. First Lieut. Charles McPherson, First Lieut. Sam Giberson, First Lieut. George Wallis and Second Lieut. Henry Van Voast were paroled and exchanged. Upon their exchange McPherson was promoted to Captain, Co. C and Giberson to Captain Co. H.[22]

The above changes filled out the officer ranks. The rank and file was thinned out by twenty eight discharges for medical reasons, several enlisted men deserted during the first three months of 1862 and Private Dennis Murphy, Co. A died of disease while in camp on February 3. The men that had been released on parole in February were, for the most part, anxious to return to their companies as soon as they could be sure of their exchange.[23] Unlike officers, enlisted men were not individually listed on exchange orders. Instead enlisted men were exchanged by group, sometimes numbering in the hundreds or thousands. What actually happened to the men that were paroled in February? A letter written in June, during the Peninsula Campaign, provides some insight into what was in the minds of the troops. On June 17 from camp near Fair Oaks, Va., First Sergeant James J. Monaghan, Co. K, wrote a letter to the Governor of New York that reads: "On behalf of a recently released prisoner of war on parole of honor by name James McGeever belonging to this Company K, 42d N.Y.S.V. who has been ordered to bear arms against the Southern Confederacy again will you be so kind as to let him know through me or direct to himself if you think it more proper, whether he has been exchanged yet or not as he is afraid it might bring him into a rather "bad fix" if again taken in arms without being duly exchanged and having enjoyed "Southern Hospitality" myself from the 21st of October till the 20th of February I am strongly inclined to agree ... as some of the First California Regiment ... were ordered back to duty in a "prisoners" regiment in Philadelphia, I would wish it no trouble you would send a letter advice for the benefit of myself and other "returned to regiment" prisoners ... if all the 42nd who were paroled are exchanged there is quite a number in New York who are not aware of it ... who would be overjoyed to hear of being released so as

---

[22] Ibid
[23] The released Ball's Bluff prisoners were sent to Camp Parole to await exchange. In some ways life there was not all that different then being in a prison camp. NARA, individual files.

to be again … in the Army of the Potomac ready to avenge "Ball's Bluff" at first opportunity".[24]

There is no way to know if the letter written by Monaghan was ever answered by the Governor's Office. However, a lot is made clear by the letter. It appears that the paroled men were ordered back to their units and that most made it to the Peninsula Campaign. A question has to be asked. Why would a First Sergeant have to write to the Governor to get an answer to the question of whether McGeever was paroled? Wouldn't he just have to ask his company officers? Surely, the regimental adjutant would have that answer. Was there some distrust in the answer that might have been provided by the regimental officers? Did Monaghan actually believe he would get a direct reply from the Governor without notice going through command channels? There has to be more to this letter than appears obvious.[25]

It was not uncommon for the process of parole and exchange for officers to be unclear. Although most Tammany officers simply were notified of their exchange by written orders the case of Colonel Cogswell demonstrates how frustrating the process could be. Cogswell was paroled and released in February, 1862. It is fair to assume that Cogswell, a West Point career officer, would look to be exchanged as rapidly as possible so that he could return to his command. As mentioned earlier that was not going to happen as command of the Tammany Regiment had already been given to Colonel Charles. So what was Cogswell to do for the rest of the war? Certainly he would not want to sit it out. Not while there were opportunities for a career officer to make his way through the ranks to greater glory. He had to be exchanged before a new command could be given to him.

On February 28, General George McClellan sent a letter to the Governor of New York saying: "Colonel Cogswell has returned and will

---

[24] New York State Archives: Document 2074

[25] First Sergeant James J. Monaghan would die from disease at Frederick, MD hospital on September 29, 1862. Private McGeever would spend almost ten months during 1863 sick in hospitals and on May 12, 1864 he would be wounded at the Battle of Spotsylvania Courthouse, gunshot wound of the left foot. He would recover at Emory Hospital in Washington and be mustered out with the regiment in July 1864. NARA: individual soldier's records.

I hope be exchanged in a day or two. Can you arrange to give Cogswell his old regiment back again? He is fairly entitled to it. Please reply to this".[26] There is no record of a response from the governor but the facts as they played out demonstrate that the command did not go back to Cogswell. Did McClellan actually believe that he would be able to get command back for Cogswell? Did he think that the governor would take command away from Charles? Was McClellan simply hoping that another appointment would come quicker if he showed support for Cogswell? Had McClellan been asked to intervene on Cogswell's behalf by those in political circles from the Midwest where both Cogswell and McClellan had roots? Regardless of what was behind McClellan's request it fell on deaf ears. McClellan was way off in his estimate of when Cogswell would be exchanged.

It wasn't until March 31 that steps started to be taken to gain Cogswell's exchange. A directive was sent to the commander of Fort Warren in Boston to release a colonel on parole who would travel to Fort Monroe. If an exchange could be not be effected the colonel would return to Fort Warren.[27] Colonel Joseph Drake, Fourth Mississippi was released on parole April 7. He travelled to Baltimore and then to Fort Monroe but because no copy of an order authorizing Drake's movements were received in Fort Monroe he was ordered back to Baltimore. On April 11, Secretary of War, Stanton authorized Colonel Drake to pass from Baltimore to Fort Monroe.[28] What happened next is a bit of a blur as no exchange was obtained. Was it because of all the commotion around Fort Monroe during the time of the encounter of the Monitor and Merrimac? Did the command structure have other things on their mind they considered more important than the exchange of Milton Cogswell? Whatever the reason Colonel Cogswell's exchange did not come until September 21, 1862, it had taken seven months and it was for Colonel J. M. Gee, Fifteenth Arkansas, not Colonel Drake.[29]

It is hard to imagine what must have been going through Cogswell's mind those seven months. How hard it must have been for a West Point

---

[26] OR: S2, V3, 335
[27] OR: S2, V3, 412
[28] OR: S2, V3, 441-442
[29] OR: S2, V4, 555

graduate that had served in the regular army up until the start of the Civil War, who had fought in a battle that had terrible results for his command, who had been in prison for several months awaiting a decision on whether he might be executed, who had learned that the command of his regiment had been given to another, to just sit around and do nothing. From the time Cogswell returned to New York he worked hard at gaining another position. On March 3 at a meeting of Tammany Hall a reception was held for Colonel Cogswell. Upon his arrival at the reception he was greeted with "nine tremendous cheers". Grand Sachem Nelson Waterbury introduced Cogswell saying "that he was happy to announce that a movement had been started for the purpose of procuring for him an appointment as General". Cogswell said: "he had done no more than his duty; that he had endeavored to do honor to the flag of Tammany; that, although there were few honors higher than that of Colonel of the Tammany Regiment, yet he could not forego the desire to be a General. When he resumed his position at the head of his regiment, he would then, as before, do no dishonor to the flag and the insignia of Tammany".[30] The movement referred to might have been based on General McClellan's letter to the governor of New York but whatever it was it did not succeed. But it did come close.

Cogswell was mustered in as Colonel, Second New York Heavy Artillery, serving as part of the defenses of Washington, following his exchange in September. He assumed command of the artillery brigade in October 1862 and held that position through April 1863. One might expect that such a command would have resulted in a promotion to Brigadier General but that was not to be the case. Apparently, the stress of the events of the past year was too much for Cogswell. In April 1863 he was brought up on charges of: "drunk on duty and conduct unbecoming an officer and a gentleman". Rather than stand trial Cogswell resigned his commission in the volunteer services and returned to his rank of Captain in the regular army.[31] In November 1863 he was on the staff of General

---

[30] New York Daily Tribune, March 4, 1862, page 8, column 6.

[31] Cogswell was presented with a sword, sash and belt by the City of New York on April 16, 1863. The sword was in a rosewood case and bore the inscription: "The City of New York to Col. Milton Cogswell...recognition of his love for, and zealous devotion to the cause of the Union..." New York Times, April 17, 1863.

Benjamin Butler, as Commissary of Musters.[32] In the early part of 1864 he was in command of the detachment of the 8th US Infantry at Fort Columbus, New York. From May to September 1864 he served as Provost Marshal of Ninth Corps around Petersburg, VA. He continued to serve in the army after the Civil War ended holding positions in the Department of South Carolina, California and Arizona. While enroute west Cogswell commanded the detachment of troops present at the driving of the golden spike linking the railroads of the east and west. He achieved the rank of Brevet Colonel in the regular army.[33]

Cogswell came very close to achieving his goal of being a general. In February 1869 he was nominated by President Johnson to the rank of Brevet Brigadier General "for gallant and meritorious services at the battle of Ball's Bluff" and to the rank of Brevet Major General "for gallant and meritorious service in defense of Washington". There is no record that the Senate ever approved these nominations.[34] Colonel Milton Cogswell died on November 20, 1882 in his quarters at the Soldiers Home in Washington. His wife Susan M. Cogswell died July 28, 1892. Both are buried in Arlington National Cemetery.[35]

Interestingly, there is a Civil War general named Cogswell. William Cogswell, a distant fifth cousin of Milton, served as Colonel of the Second Massachusetts Infantry. He was brevetted a Brigadier General with a date of rank of December 15, 1864. The Senate confirmed the appointment in

---

[32] OR: S1, V29, 494-5

[33] NARA: files of Milton Cogswell. Also Microfilm: M1064 roll 466.

[34] Journal of the executive proceedings of the Senate of the United States of America, February 17 and 19, 1869.

[35] Milton Cogswell had one child Susan Wiley Cogswell, born in New York, August 13, 1861, just after Milton left for the war. Susan married Amos Blanchard Shattuck, a member of the West Point class of 1886. He was the son of Amos B. Shattuck, a graduate of the Harvard Class of 1856 who died from wounds received at the battle of Fredericksburg in 1862 while a Captain in the Eleventh, NH. Susan's husband rose to the rank of Major, and died in the Philippine Islands after falling off his horse in 1913. They had two sons that were military men. Captain Amos Blanchard Shattuck, Jr. was serving in the Office of Chief of Engineers, Washington when he died in 1934. Susan, Amos and Amos Jr. are also buried at Arlington. The other son was Colonel Milton Cogswell Shattuck, born in Manila, P.I. in 1901. In World War II, he commanded the 318th Infantry Regiment in France. He died in 1984.

February 1865.[36] Another relative of Cogswell, through his marriage to Susan Lane, achieved the rank of Brevet Brigadier General for service in the Civil War. George D. Ruggles, Susan's second cousin, received his brevet promotion to Brigadier General dated to 1865, "for gallant and meritorious service during the operations resulting in the fall of Richmond". Ruggles continued his service after the war achieving the position of Adjutant of the Army in 1893. Also worth noting is the Cogswell connection to Major General Henry Halleck. In 1859, about the same time that Milton married Susan, George Cogswell, Milton's second cousin, married Ellen Mills Halleck, the general's sister. Given all of the "connections" of the Cogswell and Lane families it is both easy to see how Milton Cogswell would have been afforded the opportunity to command and how the lack of his achieving greater success would have weighed heavily on his ability to cope with what some might have considered less than what was expected of him.[37]

The same day that Colonel Milton Cogswell was exchanged, September 21, 1862, Captain Timothy O'Meara was exchanged for Captain James Vance of the Thirtieth Virginia. It had only been about a month since O'Meara had been paroled at Aiken's Landing on August 17. Like Cogswell, O'Meara was not to return to his command in the Tammany Regiment but unlike Cogswell he was to immediately receive a new assignment based on his close association with Colonel Corcoran while in captivity. On September 23 he was appointed Lieut. Colonel of the 90th IL, the Irish Legion of Illinois. Two months later he was named the Colonel.

About a year later while camped near Chattanooga, O'Meara wrote a letter to his brother John on November 23, 1863 that reads: " …Tomorrow we meet the enemy to fight the great battle of the war. Tonight we cross to the East bank of the Tenn … If it is my lot to fall I cannot have avoided

---

[36] General William Cogswell attended Dartmouth College and Harvard University Law School. After the Civil War he served as Mayor of Salem, Massachusetts as well as in the Massachusetts Senate and House. He died in 1895.

[37] New York Times, November 7, 1893 and Cogswell Family. George D. Ruggles was a graduate of West point in 1855. His parents died before he was 20 and he was raised under the guidance of Charles H. Ruggles, first cousin to Milton Cogswell's father-in- law, William Jared Lane. Charles H. Ruggles was a U. S. Congressman from New York, 1821- 1823 and Chief Judge of the New York Court of Appeals from 1851-1853.

it. If I am spared it will be another proof of Almighty God's goodness and mercy to me. If the former should take place I appoint you in behalf of my family to look after my affairs. Tell mother and Mary to pray for me. If I am killed I want at least a dozen masses offered up for the welfare of my soul. Poor mother will feel worried over this … To all my friends and acquaintances I send kind regards. If I have any enemies I send the defiance in life, forgiveness in death only."[38]

On November 25, 1863 at the Battle of Chattanooga, Colonel O'Meara was mortally wounded. He died shortly thereafter. An account of O'Meara's death said: " …the recklessly gallant Colonel Timothy O'Meara had acted as though he was on some Napoleonic field of glory. He went into the battle dressed in his best uniform, his famous sword at his side, his crimson sash across his breast, a foreign medal won in some other war above it, and last but not least a little amulet or charm hung by a cord around his neck. This, he said, would keep him from all harm. But the bright sash was his undoing. Some sharpshooter's ball pierced his body, and after a few hours of suffering, while faithfully attended by the Catholic chaplain of his regiment, he gave his life for the country he called his own."[39] The "foreign medal" was likely from O'Meara's service in the Mexican War of Reform.[40] It was said that as O'Meara lay dying his last command to his troops was "Go, do your duty."[41] His body was returned to New York. The Governor's Room at City Hall was given to the family "for the reception of his remains preparatory to internment". Following a private ceremony O'Meara was buried in First Cavalry Cemetery in New York City.[42]

---

[38] Swan, James B, Chicago's Irish Legion, the 90th Ill. Volunteers in the Civil War, SIU Press 2009, 95-6.

[39] Cozzens, Peter, The Shipwreck of Their Hopes, The Battles for Chattanooga, University of Illinois Press, Chicago, 1957, page 222.

[40] O'Meara came to the United States from King's County, Ireland around 1852. He joined the U. S. Cavalry serving 5 years in New Mexico and on the frontier. On his discharge he joined the "liberal" army of Mexico and served as a cavalry officer with the forces that overthrew Santa Anna. Irish American, December 19, 1863, page 2, column 3.

[41] Irish American, February 6, 1864, page 1, column 8.

[42] New York Times, December 10, 1863, page 11, column 5.

On April 27, 1864, General Order No. 63, Army of the Cumberland named one of Chattanooga's defenses in the main line of Fort Sherman Lunette O'Meara in honor of Colonel O'Meara.[43] Perhaps the greatest tribute to Timothy O'Meara was the action of General U. S. Grant, who upon hearing of O'Meara's death said: "Gone! A braver man never filled a saddle! I knew him well ... I shall never forget his noble defense of the trestle work at Holly Springs. He saved us all from starvation." Grant went to the river bank where O'Meara's coffin, covered with an American flag, was awaiting transport and had the coffin opened saying "I want to see him". Grant bent over the coffin and spent some time in private thoughts of the man who had come to America from Ireland and who had given his life for his adopted homeland.[44]

I feel compelled to add a personal note here. In writing this book I was privileged to become deeply familiar with many of the lives of the men of the Tammany Regiment. Without a doubt I have to say that it was Timothy O'Meara that had the most profound effect on me. Exactly why he had the effect he did is not all that clear but I can say that many a tear filled my eyes as I wrote about this man that came from a far off land to fall in love with a new nation he adopted with pride. His service in the Civil War, whether it be at Ball's Bluff with the Tammany Regiment, in various Confederate prisons or while he served with the 90th IL, his valor and dedication to his men and country, his love of his family and the land of his heritage all coupled with a strong religious belief simply left me overwhelmed.

Colonel Charles had two officer vacancies within the regiment that were inherited from Cogswell that he had no ability to fill. They were not actual vacancies but positions that were filled by officers that were on the books of the regiment but were serving as signal officers elsewhere. On August 14, 1861, Special Order, No. 26, Department of Virginia ordered Albert J. Myer to establish what would become the signal corps of the Army of the Potomac. Officers and men needed for the corps were to be collected from various regiments located in the area. The location of one of the signal camps of instruction was Poolesville, MD where the Tammany

---

[43] OR: S1, V32, 520
[44] Penniman, The Tanner Boy and How he Became Lieutenant General, Robert Brothers, Publishers, Boston, 1864, page 249-50.

Regiment and other units were encamped. On September 12, the initial group of officers and men selected to be assigned to signal duty were moved to a central camp of instruction in Gerogetown.[45]

Captain Franklin E. Towne, Signal Officer, USMHI

Colonel Cogswell selected Second Lieut. Franklin E. Towne, Co. D and Second Lieut. Franklin Ellis, Co. F to be assigned to signal service. Several enlisted men were also assigned. Privates Thomas Armstrong, William Elson, William Ross and Robert Skellin are known to have served with the signal service. There may have been others.[46]

---

[45] OR. S1, V5, 69. Report of Major Albert J. Meyer, Chief Signal Officer, U.S. Army, October 21, 1862.

[46] It was customary for each signal officer to have two enlisted men assigned to him to operate signal flags and fire rockets. Records establish that Robert Skellin was assigned to Franklin Ellis and Armstrong and Elson were assigned to Franklin E. Towne. Skellin, Ross and Armstrong enrolled in the Tammany Regiment in mid August 1861 and were immediately assigned to the signal service. On August 16, 1863 Skellin was transferred to the Signal Corps. Ross was transferred to the Signal Corps on August 22, 1863. No record of where he actually served was found. Armstrong served in South Carolina and was discharged for disability at Hilton Head on December 23, 1862. Elson, AKA Elston, was born in Louisville, Kentucky and enrolled in the regiment at Boston in June 1861. He was appointed

Franklin Ellis received his appointment as Lieut. on August 29, 1861 and was immediately assigned to the signal service. After completing his training he was assigned to IV Corps under General Keyes and saw service in the Peninsula Campaign. At the time of the Battle of Fair Oaks, on June 3, Ellis led a team of signal men to the James River to determine the practicality of using flag signals to communicate with the naval vessels on the river.[47] He served in various locations with the signal service through October 1863. He decided not to seek appointment in the Army Signal Corps and was returned to the Tammany Regiment. On January 5, 1864 Ellis wrote a letter requesting to be discharged saying: "…by continued use of the telescope my eye sight had become so impaired that I was obliged to ask relief from signal duty … and thus after more than twenty-eight months of involuntary absence I am returned to my regiment although I have never done regimental duty for a single day and am consequently as ignorant of it in every particular as on the day I entered the service." On January 19, 1864 Ellis was discharged by Special Order No. 20, Headquarters, II Army Corps.[48]

Franklin E. Towne's assignment to signal service does not fit the pattern of the others. It seems quite clear that Colonel Cogswell selected men for signal duty that for one reason or another did not fit cleanly into the Tammany regiment. Most were recent arrivals and could simply be assigned without disrupting the existing organization and one man had been a problem. Towne (sometimes referred to as Town) had been with the regiment from the beginning. There is nothing in his file that would suggest that he would be an officer that Cogswell would want out of the regiment. So why was Towne selected for signal service? There is no clear answer. Perhaps it was just a random selection to meet the need to comply with a directive from higher headquarters. Perhaps Towne requested the assignment although there is nothing in the file that confirms that. There

---

to first corporal, Company H on June 27 and to fourth sergeant on July 22. On September 1, 1861 he was reduced to the rank of private and detached to the signal service for the rest of his enlistment. He was restored to the rank of sergeant while with the signal service. Brown, Joseph Willard, The Signal Corps in the War of the Rebellion, U. S. Veteran Signal Corps Association, Boston, 1896, page 245, 293. NARA, individual soldier's records.

[47] OR: S1, V11, 999

[48] NARA, record of Franklin Ellis.

are several interesting facts that might provide a clue to what actually happened. Towne was one of the original officers assigned to be trained for signal duty. On October 9, Major Myer issued Special Order No. 9 listing the field assignments for seven officers and fourteen enlisted men. Two of the officers were Towne and First Lieut. William S. Cogswell. Is it a coincidence that an officer named Cogswell was also in the first group of men selected for signal service? Did William S. Cogswell and Towne know each other and decide to volunteer for the signal service together? Did Colonel Cogswell know William S. Cogswell? William Sterling Cogswell was born in Jamaica, Long Island, New York, December 1840. His family included a number of prominent military men and judges. He was a distant sixth cousin of Milton Cogswell.[49] No direct connection could be found between Towne and either Cogswell however, Towne joined the Tammany regiment at Bethpage, Long Island quite close to Jamaica and there are definite connections between the Towne and Cogswell families going back to the late seventeenth century and the Salem Witch Trials.[50]

Franklin E. Town served with distinction throughout the war with the signal service and never returned to the Tammany Regiment. He was officially transferred to the United States Army Signal Service with the rank of Captain on October 20, 1863. He served mainly in South Carolina and West Virginia resigning his commission in November 1864.

---

[49] William Sterling Cogswell was the son of Hon. William Johnson Cogswell a lawyer and judge in Jamaica, New York. His mother Alma Canfield Sterling was the daughter of Major General Elisha Sterling of the Connecticut Militia. At the start of the Civil War William S. Cogswell was appointed a First Lieut. in Company I, 5CT Volunteers, assigned to General Banks command on the Potomac. After serving in the signal service he returned to the 5CT reaching the rank of Lieut. Colonel in October 1864. Brown, Joseph Willard, The Signal Corps, U. S. A, in the War of the Rebellion, U. S. Veteran Signal Corps Association, Boston, 1896, page 245 and "Cogswell Family".

[50] Mary Estey and Rebecca Nurse, two daughters of William Towne were hanged as a result of the Salem Witch trials of 1692 and can be tied to the Cogswell family through their aunt Mrs. Abigail Peabody Towne, the wife of Lt. Thomas Perley and mother in law of Margaret Cogswell a second cousin, 5x removed of Milton. A third woman tried as a witch, Sarah Cole, was convicted in part on the testimony of Abraham and Elizabeth Wellman. Elizabeth's maiden name was Cogswell a fourth great grand aunt of Milton Cogswell. "Cogswell Family".

Military activity during the first three months of 1862 was quite limited. Soldiers spent their days doing what soldiers have done for centuries: training, parading, standing inspection and then repeating the process over and over. Life around Poolesville centered on trying to stay ready for what eventually would happen. Poolesville was described by James Fennessy, the imbedded reporter for the Irish American, as "remarkable for the abominable appearance of its dilapidated old houses, displaying their rotten timbers, no doubt relics of better days. Its only street might ... be compared to a farm yard. It contains two stores ..."[51] However, in late February movement of Confederate forces toward the Shenandoah Valley prompted McClellan to order General Banks to position his division to be able to advance on Winchester, VA. On March 4, Banks sent a message to Sedgwick confirming that his troops were in position and asking that Sedgwick place his troops "within supporting distance of Berryville" about ten miles east of Winchester.[52] The Tammany Regiment, along with the rest of Sedgwick's troops reached Berryville on March 13, travelling by foot and canal boat on the Monocacy River. Later that day Sedgwick issued Special Order No. 30, directing the division to move to Harper's Ferry. Banks was informed by McClellan that Sedgwick's troops were being detached from his command and would "probably be sent by rail to Annapolis".[53] Sedgwick summarized the actions of his division in a letter to his sister sent from Harper's Ferry on March 16 saying: " ...I ... expected to march on Winchester ... After making the arrangements to attack the place, the enemy evacuated, and our troops marched in without firing scarcely a gun ... My division was ordered to return to this place ... I presume by tomorrow we shall be on our way to Washington or Annapolis."[54]

Sedgwick was correct. His division did leave Harper's Ferry for Annapolis but he was not alone. The time had come for the Union to move against the Confederacy in the east. McClellan's grand plan to take Richmond was in motion. John Tucker, Assistant Secretary of War, had the responsibility to pull together the shipping required to move the Army of

---

[51] Irish American, January 4, 1862, page 1, column 8.
[52] OR: S1, V5, 733
[53] OR: S1, V5, 748, 750 also "Twentieth Massachusetts" 78-79.
[54] Correspondence of John Sedgwick, supra, volume 2, page 40

the Potomac to the Peninsula. In about 20 days almost 400 vessels moved more than 120,000 men, 44 artillery batteries, over 14,000 animals and 1,200 wagons to the area around Fortress Monroe.[55]

The Tammany Regiment accounted for less than one percent of the force sent to the Peninsula but it is likely that they were the only regiment that took with them a pet pigeon. There is in the literature a reference to a pigeon that had been captured by one of the teamsters of the Tammany Regiment while encamped by the Potomac. It is said that the pigeon would fly away and return each day and that the men of the regiment adopted it. Supposedly, the pigeon sailed with the regiment and remained with it throughout a significant part of the war.[56]

There is a record of a Matron that served with the Tammany regiment, most likely caring for men in the regimental hospital. Her name was Elizabeth Brennan. Details about where she served and for what period she served are unclear.[57]

---

[55] Sears, Stephen W., To the Gates of Richmond, page 24

[56] A Pigeon with a War Record, The Magazine of History, Vol. X, No. 3, page 178. In the article the name of the teamster that captured the pigeon is Mr. Tinker. No man named Tinker is listed in any of the rosters of the Tammany Regiment however; it is possible that "Tinker" was a nick name of one of the teamsters.

[57] NARA microfilm M551, roll 15: Card index to the compiled service records of Union soldiers belonging to units from the State of New York. There were 4 men named Brennan that served with the regiment: Francis T. Brennan, 21, mustered in June 22, 1861 and was discharged for disability November 4, 1861, John Brennan, 21, mustered in June 22, 1861 and was discharged for disability March 29, 1863, Michael Brennan, 22, mustered in as a wagoner June 22, 1861 and was killed in action at Gettysburg, Michael Brennan, 24, mustered in June 22, 1864, was at times a non-commissioned officer and was discharged for disability April 10, 1863. It is unknown whether Elizabeth Brennan was related to any of these men.

Chapter Six

ARRIVAL ON THE PENINSULA

The Tammany regiment arrived near Fort Monroe on March 31 having left Washington on March 27. On April 4 they marched up the Peninsula camping near Yorktown on April 5.[1] For certain, somewhere, there is a record of the ship or ships that carried the regiment but for some reason that record could not be found. It is known that the 20th and 19th Massachusetts, two regiments in the same brigade, sailed on the steamers Catskill and North America respectively. These two ships were part of a thirteen ship fleet that sailed from Alexandria on March 17 carrying the lead units of the Army of the Potomac. The fleet arrived on March 21. Other ships in the fleet were: Elm City, John A. Werner, William Kent, Canonicus, Arrowsmith, Kennebec, Pioneer, Naushon, C. Vanderbilt, Champion and John Brooks. Taking into account time required to ready the fleet for a return trip and adding the four days for the trip itself, it would certainly be possible that the Tammany men sailed on one or more of the ships named above. Of course new ships were being added to the fleet all the time so nothing is for certain.[2]

On March 28, Private Robert Trimble, Co. D, a teamster detailed to the regimental Quartermaster, drowned in the Potomac River after falling overboard. Whether Trimble was aboard the same vessel as the main body

---

[1]   National Archives, Record Group 94, Records of the Adjutant General's Office, Company Muster Roll, March and April 1862. Co. I, 42NY Inf.

[2]   Letter from a soldier in 38th NY written March 21, 1861 from Old Point Comfort, VA. Irish American, April 5, 1861.

of troops or was travelling on a towed schooner with the wagons and horses is not known.[3]

James Fennessy wrote a description of the regiment's activities for the Irish American newspaper on April 16 in which he describes the way the men spent their time and what they saw as they prepared for the attack on Yorktown. He said: " ...Having reconnoitered the several strongholds ... on the skirts of Yorktown ... the regiment bivouacked for the night on the plain where the whole division lay. That night ... waters came pouring down in torrents ... The rebels are in great force in Yorktown ... Great preparations are therefore, being made for a great advance ... The whole of Sedgwick's division, together with large trains of artillery, and cavalry in proportion, are encamped on a level plain, surrounded with woods thickly set with heavy pine ... The view of all the camp fires at night is beautiful in the extreme, and the pitch of the fife, the roll of the drum, and the sound of the bugle, mingled with the heavy boom of the distant gun, but cannot but awaked the sensitive mind to the glories of the battlefield ... The Tammany boys are armed with the new and excellent Springfield rifles ... The farther we advance the more conspicuous are the horrors of this fiendish rebellion. Here is a neat dwelling house once the home of some happy family ... now deserted, and its owners are probably in a rebel fortress. There is a schoolhouse in whose hall not a murmur is heard, nor cap nor bonnet hanging ..."[4]

Fennessy's mention of the sounds of the fife, drum and bugle make this the perfect time to present in some depth the musicians of the Tammany regiment. Naturally, there is some complexity to the subject as there was an official band and there were individual musicians assigned to each of the ten companies of troops. Authorization for musicians was part of an act of the Thirty-seventh Congress approved July 22, 1861 titled "An Act to authorize the employment of volunteers to aid in enforcing the laws and protecting public property". This act was far reaching and set the groundwork for the organization of the Union Army. Section 2 provided that: "Each regiment of infantry shall have ... twenty-four musicians for a

3 NARA, file of Robert Trimble.
4 The regiment had originally been armed with Enfield rifles. "Fourth Annual Report of the Bureau of Military Statistics, State of New York, Albany, 1867" and "Camp near Yorktown", April 16, 1862. Irish American, April 26, 1862.

band; and ... each company ... two musicians". Section 7 of the same act provided that one fourth of the band members would receive the pay of sergeants, one fourth the pay of corporals and the rest the pay of privates. Leaders of the band were to be paid as second lieutenants.[5]

Research has identified only fourteen original members the Tammany regiment band. All were mustered in between September 21 and October 3, 1861. There was a fifteenth member, Henry Muller, who had originally been a private in Co. H but was transferred to the band on an unknown date. Abraham B. Whitlock, age 30, was the band leader.[6] Horace B. Adams, age 26, was the lead musician.[7] The youngest was William Whitlock, age 19, a younger brother of the band leader[8]. The oldest member was Blosins Hipsey, age 46. Michael Troysl is listed as having deserted sometime in October. Two men were discharged for disability: Michael Angelo Castaldi just before the regiment left for the Peninsula and Nicholas Grobe in New York City on June 18.[9]

---

[5]   OR: S3, V1, 380-383

[6]   NARA: record of A. H. Whitlock. Abraham Benner Whitlock was the oldest child of William and Catherine Whitlock. Born in PA in 1831. He died on March 26, 1887 and is buried in Ithaca City Cemetery, Ithaca, New York. He studied music in New York and Philadelphia and was the leader of a number of bands in the Troy and Ithaca, New York area prior to the Civil War.

[7]   Horace B. Adams was mustered into the 21st NY Cavalry on July 20, 1863. He was appointed Chief Bugler November 29, 1863. He transferred to the 1st NY Veteran Cavalry January 19, 1865 where he served as First Lieut. and Regimental Commissary. Rosters of New York Volunteers, Annual Reports of the State of New York.

[8]   William Kasc Whitlock was born November 30, 1841 in Ithaca, NY. He died October 26, 1917 in Toledo, OH. Following the mustering out of the Tammany band, William enrolled in the 15th New York Cavalry, serving from August to December 1863 with the rank of Second Lieut. Another brother, who did not see service with the Tammany regiment, was John Ralston Whitlock, born January 1836. He served as Captain, Co. I, 32nd New York Infantry. Rosters of New York Volunteers, Annual Reports of the State of New York.

[9]   Other members of the band were: Christopher Love, George Keifner, Stephen Corbin and William H. Metcalf. Corbin became ill on the Peninsula and was sent north on the steamer Knickerbocker arriving in NY July 6. He was sent to a hospital in Brooklyn. New York Times, July 7, page 2, column 3 and New York Times July 14, page 8, column 4.

Three Stebbins brothers were in the band. George Janes, age 26, Dewitt Clinton, age 20 and Dwight Preston, age 22 were the sons of Augustine Holman and Mary Ann Stebbins. George was born in Painted Post, New York and his brothers were born in Masonville. Both towns are in western New York very close to the Pennsylvania border.[10]

On August 8, 1862, at Harrison's Landing on the Peninsula the Tammany band was mustered out of the service pursuant to Adjutant General Order No. 91 dated July, 19, 1862 that implemented an act of Congress. Section 5 of the act repealed the earlier act authorizing the formation of regimental bands and ordered "men composing such bands shall be mustered out of the service within thirty days".[11]

The loss of the band did not mean that there were no longer any musicians within the regiment. Each company was authorized a drummer and a fifer. Leading these men on the regimental staff were a Drum Major and Fife Major who were responsible for training of musicians in the musical techniques used for signaling on the battlefield, overall

---

[10] The Stebbins family can be traced back to Massachusetts in the mid seventeenth century. Dwight enlisted in the 5th NY Heavy Artillery on January 4, 1864 and was appointed Band Leader on March 18, 1865. William H. Metcalf also enlisted in the 5th NY HA the same day. Dewitt enlisted in the 1st NY Veteran Cavalry on July 14, 1863 serving as a trumpeter, Co. H through July 1865. "Rosters of New York Volunteers, Annual Reports of the State of New York". After the war the Stebbins brothers moved to Cleveland, Ohio. "Stebbins Descendants, genealogy, rootsweb. Ancestary.com". George Stebbins must have been ill while he was on the Peninsula. He is listed as having arrived in New York City on the transport Kennebec. New York Times May 25, 1862, page 8. That day he was issued an authorization for stage transport from Deposit, New York to Masonville, New York by the Assistant Quartermaster General's Office in New York City. Additional vouchers must have been issued covering transportation from New York City to Deposit, New York. Document in author's collection.

[11] OR: S3, V2, 278. Additional provisions of GO 91 stipulated that only men that were originally mustered in as members of the band were to be mustered out and that any men that had been detached from companies into the band were to be returned to their companies. Henry Muller was covered by this provision and in July 1862 he was transferred to Company I. He was discharged for disability in February 1863. Section 6 of the order established brigade level bands with each brigade allowed to have a band with sixteen members.

maintenance of the instruments and discipline within the ranks of the musicians.

The original Fife Major was London born William Darley, a professional musician in his mid thirties. He had blue eyes and stood five foot nine inches tall. He served until October 11, 1862 when he was discharged for disability at Harper's Ferry due to a partial loss of vision.[12] In January of 1863 James C. Brady filled the vacancy created by Darley's discharge. Brady, also in his mid thirties was born in Ireland and looked a lot like Darley as he stood five foot eight and had blue eyes. He had joined the regiment in December 1861 and served as the fifer in Company K until his promotion. Except for a time between May and August 1863 Brady served with the regiment throughout the rest of the war.[13]

The original Drum Major was 26 year old William A. Jackson. He served until September 19, 1862 when he was discharged for disability, caused by diarrhea, while in the General Hospital, Newark, New Jersey. On January 1, 1863 Washington Ryer, an original member of the regiment was promoted to Drum Major and was transferred from Company K to the regimental staff filling the vacancy left by Jackson's discharge. On July 13, 1864 Drum Major Ryer was mustered out in New York City.[14] Interestingly, when a promotion was forthcoming a musician from

---

12 NARA: File of W. Darley

13 NARA: File of J. Brady. The muster roll entries in Brady's file are somewhat confusing. He is listed as being "absent sick in hospital" for a period between May and August 1863. At that time there is also a notation that reads: "This man was transferred to Drum Major against orders and is therefore returned to his company again." Was that notation made because of a clerical error that promoted Brady to Drum Major instead of Fife Major or was Brady not to have been promoted at all? Subsequent muster sheets list Brady as "Fifer, Co. K" and his 1864 re-enlistment papers make no mention of the rank of Fife-Major. No record of another Fife Major was found so it is unclear whether Brady served in that position officially or unofficially or if there simply was no Fife Major for some period of the war.

14 NARA: Files of W. A. Jackson and Washington Ryer. In Ryer's file there are notations that have him in hospital in New York in the summer of 1862. Did he get ill on the Peninsula? There also are notes that state that he was promoted to Drum Major in early 1864 and that the earlier promotion had been in error. Although these notes make the record a bit fuzzy it is clear that Ryer was the last person to hold the rank of Regimental Drum Major.

Company K was selected for both the Drum Major and Fife Major raising the question of whether Company K was particularly fortunate to have the best musicians in the regiment.

As a group the more than thirty company musicians, not unexpectedly, tended to be young. Twenty-eight were teenagers with the youngest, Henry Bird a drummer in Co I, being fourteen. A number were mustered in and for one reason or another left the regiment before Ball's Bluff in November 1861.[15] Four drummers joined in March 1864 and served until the regiment was mustered out.[16]

As the troops settled in around Yorktown twelve drummers, five fifers and two other musicians, whose instruments are unclear from the records, were among them. Company A had Ernst Bauer[17], fifer and Bernard Hanlon, whose instrument is not known. Both were sixteen[18]. Company B had two sixteen year old drummers, John J. Heller and Charles Carr. Company C was served by fifteen year old fifer Daniel Donovan[19] and sixteen year old drummer William Cheeseman. With them was Michael Donovan, age thirty five, probably Daniels father.

---

[15]   Drummers Julius Newman, age 16, Co. D, Joseph Gwyer, age 15, Co. A, Francis Kenney, age 16, Co. A, Valentine Lutz, age 16, Co. A, Francis Hart, age 15, Co. A, Thomas McDonald, age 16, Co. A, John Nugent, age 18, Co. G. Musicians (instrument not known): Peter McGovern, age 15, Co K, George Dapper, age 17, Co. B. Edward F. Clarke, age 16, Co. K.

[16]   Owen McManus, age 18, Co. K, James H. Jolly, age 18, Co. H, Walter Flannagan, age 19, unassigned and James Hart, age 18, Co. D. Is it possible that Francis Hart, age 15, who was mustered into Co. D as a drummer and deserted in July 1861 and James Hart, age 18, who was mustered into Co. D as a drummer in 1864 are the same man? The only other Hart listed in the regimental roster is also named James Hart. He enlisted at age 23 as a wagoner, Co. D. He also deserted in July 1861. Was he the brother of Francis Hart?

[17]   Ernst Bauer is listed as being born in Erfurt, Prussia on one form in his record and in Switzerland on another.

[18]   The ages in this paragraph are those listed on the muster in documents of the individual musicians. By the time they were at Yorktown almost ten months had passed since they enlisted so many would have been a year older.

[19]   On September 15, 1862 Daniel Donovan was admitted to U.S.A. General Hospital, Frederick, Maryland and is listed as sick there through June 1863. His regimental records show him absent sick through August 1863 and present thereafter. In early 1864 he was charged $2.10 for a drum snare head.

While his instrument is not recorded in the records it would be likely that he also was a fifer. There were three drummers in Company D, fifteen year old Peter Mackey, Michael Gallagher[20], age eighteen and William Walsh, age nineteen. Sixteen year old drummer Francis Curry was the lone musician with Company E. Drummer John Hamilton, age seventeen, and fifer Edward Blake[21], age eighteen were with Company F. Drummer Eugene Mazzochi[22], age seventeen and fifer Richard McGreal, age nineteen, a Boston enlistee, were the lone musicians in Company G and H respectively. Drummers Thomas Ryan, age thirty and fourteen year old Henry Bird were with Company I. Company K was served by the future Drum and Fife Majors Washington Ryer and James Brady.

Several of the musicians listed in the preceding paragraph spent significant portions of their time performing other jobs. Charles Carr served as a cook and a nurse in the regimental hospital from April 30, 1862. John J. Heller served as a nurse at Brigade Headquarters from June 1863[23]. William Cheeseman performed the job of regimental mail carrier from August 1863.

The record of the youngest musician, German born Henry Bird, fourteen at the time of his joining the regiment simply shows him as present for most of the war except for being charged $1.50 for a drum head in 1862. Like many Tammany men he re-enlisted as a veteran in early

---

20   Michael Gallagher's NARA record lists him only as "present" in May-June 1862. He is listed as having been charged $3.00 for two drum heads. His file is silent on his status after June 1862.

21   The Hospital Muster Roll of U. S. A. General Hospital, Newark, New Jersey lists Edward Blake present there through August 1862. His regimental records show he was in the hospital from August 20, 1862 through sometime in November or December 1862. He again is listed as in the hospital from around May through August 1863.

22   NARA record shows Mazzochi to have been sent from Harrison's Landing on August 15, 1862 (sick). He is carried as "sick or wounded in hospital" on the July 1863 muster roll and as present on October 30, 1863.

23   The record of Joseph J. Heller shows that there was drummer named John J. Heller that was mustered into Co. B in June 1861 and discharged for disability (diarrhea) soon thereafter. John J. Heller and Joseph J. Heller were the same man. A note in the record says that J. J. Heller went to New York with a wounded officer in July 1863. The name of the officer and whether he was a Tammany man wounded at Gettysburg is not known.

1864 and was given a leave from which he returned April 16, 1864. On May 31 he was admitted to Third Division General Hospital, Alexandria, VA suffering from Chronic Diarrhea and was treated with "astringents and opiates". His record shows him listed as "Deserted" from the hospital on June 16 and apprehended in civilian clothes, without a pass in the Washington railroad depot with a ticket to New York City. On July 30 a letter was sent to the "Commanding Officer, 42nd N. Y. Volunteers" from the Provost Marshall, Washington, D.C. stating that Bird had been arrested and delivered to him as a deserter, asking confirmation of his status at the regiment. If he was carried as a deserter by the regiment the $30 paid by the government for his apprehension could be recovered as a fine. Since the Tammany regiment had been mustered out in mid-July with all the remaining men transferred to the 59th New York the letter was responded to by the commanding officer of the 59th. He stated: "Musician Henry Bird, of my command (late of 42nd NY) was dropped from the rolls July 24, 1864 as a deserter and is in my mind guilty. Was at the time of desertion, absent detached in hospital."[24]

A most interesting set of circumstances surround Owen McManus one of the four musicians that joined the regiment in 1864. His record says only that he was born in New York City and was eighteen when he enlisted as a drummer on March 15, 1864. He had grey eyes, dark hair and stood five foot three and had worked as a butcher. However, McManus is mentioned quite extensively in the record of First Lieut. Emmet Faye. Faye enrolled in the regiment on March 31, 1864 as a private in Company A. He received a commission as First Lieut. Company H, filling the spot created by Uncle Pat's promotion to Captain. Like the famous quote "truth is stranger than fiction" what happened next is really bizarre.

On April 30, Major Patrick Downing wrote a letter, as senior officer of the regiment in the field[25], to Brigade Headquarters that read: "I deem it my duty to state some facts in regard to a certain Mr. Fay, a recruit in the regiment … Previously to his enlistment he was employed as a clerk for recruiting purposes … Shortly after his arrival notice was received of

---

[24] NARA, record of Henry Bird. Listed as Henry's nearest relative on his hospital record is his sister Mary living at 127 Ridge Street, New York City.

[25] The commanding officer of the regiment was Lieut. Colonel Lynch, who at the time was in New York City on recruiting duty.

his appointment as First Lieut ... The enclosed statement contains facts, which came to my attention only accidently last night. A boy came to me and complained of being swindled out of $100 by the same Mr. Fay, and wished if possible, to recover the money exacted from him under false pretences. I deemed the statement to be of sufficient importance to act upon it, thinking that it might be possible to recover the money for the boy, who is at present a musician in this regiment."

The statement referred to by Downing dated April 29 read: "I Owen McManus, Musician in the 42nd NY do hereby declare that I saw Mr. Fay for the first time in Tammany Hall, New York on the 15th of March 1864. He addressed me, asking me if I desired to enlist and I answered that I should wish to enlist as a drummer boy. Mr. Fay, then said, that it would be very difficult to enlist me as a drummer boy but if I would agree to pay one hundred dollars to him, Mr. Fay, he would enlist me ... Immediately after receiving my bounty, Mr. Fay addressed me in these words: "Give me my money now." I handed him a 100 dollar bill. He then went away and I did not see him again until after I had joined the regiment ... I asked him whether he was the same Mr. Fay that had enlisted me and with whom I had made the agreement, but he affected not to know me and said: I am not, I am Lieut. Fay of this regiment". Signed Owen McManus" The statement was sworn to and countersigned by J. Ellendorf, Adjutant, 42nd NY. Was Lieut. Faye the same man McManus had given $100 to?

Exactly what happened will probably never be known but there is a piece of evidence that supports what McManus said. On February 26, 1864 Daniel E. Delavan, a top Tammany politician wrote to Major General John A. Dix, Commanding Eastern Department,[26] telling him that Emmet E. Faye was interested in joining the Tammany regiment and that Faye had much service in recruiting for the regiment. Delavan also indicated that Faye would like to be assigned to recruiting duty after being mustered. On February 27, Delavan's letter was forwarded with a recommendation that read: "for action as may be fit ... Mr. Delavan is a citizen of loyalty and worth."

So what happened as a result of the letter written by Downing? On April 30, Brig. General Alexander Webb endorsed the letter from Brigade

---

[26] General Dix was a pall bearer at the funeral of Daniel E. Delavan in April 1870. New York Times, April 5, 1870.

Headquarters to Division saying: "I have ordered that he (Fay) be placed in the ranks until after the next fight. I request that his muster as First. Lieut. in which rank he is commissioned be withheld for the present." On May 1, General Gibbons, Division Commander returned the endorsement saying: "If General Webb is satisfied that the complaint is well grounded he will have formal charges made out and forwarded. The General commanding the division has no control over the muster but, if it is desired to have this man's commission revoked and such an application is forwarded to these headquarters it will receive a favorable endorsement." Faye was mustered in as First Lieut. on May 2, 1864.

Ten days later, May 12, 1864, Faye was captured during the battle of Spotsylvania Court House. His name appears on a list of sick and convalescent prisoners at Columbia, South Carolina. Faye was paroled on December 10, 1864 at Charleston, South Carolina and reported to Camp parole on December 15 where he remained through February 1865[27].

Playing their instruments was their primary function but musicians performed other duties when needed. In the words of J. Fennessy: "The musicians have, for the present, slung their instruments on the holly trees, and have taken up in lieu thereof the stretchers on which the wounded are to be taken from the stage of the theatre. They follow us in all cases, thereby making themselves useful actors in the different scenes of the programme, the most solemn act of which may at any moment commence." On April 24, while with a group of men on picket duty, musician William Walsh was shot and killed. He was buried near the encampment of the regiment near Yorktown.[28]

The reference to stretchers by Fennessy was in anticipation of the large scale attack on Yorktown that was anticipated. To the surprise of the Union command the Confederate force in Yorktown withdrew from the fort and abandoned most of their heavy equipment. At 9 A.M. on May 4, General McClellan sent a dispatch to Secretary of War Stanton saying: "We have the ramparts, guns, ammunition and camp equipage. We hold the entire line of his works … I have thrown all my cavalry and horse artillery in

---

[27] On April 3, 1865 Faye was discharged by War Department, Special order No. 171, Paragraph 46, dated April 13.

[28] Irish American, May 24, 1862, page 2, column 8. "The Tammany Regiment: Camp Near Yorktown, May 5, 1862". Fennessy.

pursuit supported by infantry. I move Franklin's division and as much more as I can transport by water, up to West Point."[29]

Fennessy described the fall of Yorktown and the days immediately after saying: "The evacuation of Yorktown was the occasion of a great day among the troops of Sedgwick's division. The musicians sprung to their long silent pieces and very quickly struck up "Dixie". Nor were they laid by until many more favorite airs floated on the breeze to the great amusement of the men, who were at the time marching in brigades to their camps with colors flying … On Tuesday, the 5th, we struck tents, and advanced under a drenching rain to Yorktown, where we remained till next day … From its ramparts there was a magnificent view of the surrounding country, and of the thousand boats and war steamers lying in the broad river" … Wednesday, the 6th, we embarked on board one of the transports … up the York River … On Thursday morning, as the regiment was landed by means of pontoons, it formed in line of battle on the beach … the banners of some fifteen regiments were unfurled, the batteries were posted in their proper positions … ready for action".[30] Some fighting around West Point occurred between retreating rebels and the troops of Franklin's division but the men of the Tammany regiment were not actively engaged.

On May 9, the entire brigade moved several miles up the southern bank of the Pamunkey River to Eltham's Landing, remaining there in bivouac until May 15. The last 2 weeks of May were spent moving up the Peninsula toward the banks of the Chickahominy River through Cumberland and Trunstal Station. The weather was very hot with lots of rain. Bugs, snakes and mosquitoes were close companions of the soldiers and disease took its toll.

An accurate account of how many Tammany men got sick on the Peninsula is impossible. The number has to be in the hundreds. Some specifics however, can be documented. When George Stebbins, the band member discussed earlier, arrived in New York in late May from the Peninsula on the Kennebec thirteen other sick Tammany men were with him. The article in the New York Times of May 25 list the men on the Kennebec as "sick and wounded" but because of the date and the fact

---

[29] New York Times, May 5, 1862
[30] Irish American, May 24, 1862, page 2, column 8. West Point, VA, May 8, 1862. Fennessy

that the regiment had not seen any action resulting in casualties, other than the man lost at Yorktown, it is a safe assumption that the Tammany men on board were sick.[31] Captain David Hogg, Co. I, also arrived in New York in late May on the steamer Spaulding. Hogg was discharged for disability August 2, suffering from "Chronic Rheumatism and great debility following Typhoid Fever".[32] Captain Isaac Gotthold, Co. D, resigned his commission and was discharged in November 1862. He had been ill with typhoid since late May.[33] Ruben Bangs, Co. A died of disease on April 16 and was buried at Fort Monroe.[34] Thomas Woods, Co. E, Patrick Smith, Co. D and Edward Cleary, Co. A died at Harrison's Landing in July. William Smith, Sgt. Co. C and James Downey, Co. E died at Newport News in September. The regimental roster lists thirteen additional men that died from disease between April and December 1862 and forty five that were discharged at various locations for disability of some kind between April 15 and June 1, 1862.[35] Certainly, a sizable

---

[31] The thirteen additional men on the Kennebec were: Tomas Doras, Co. F, Benedict Fletcher, Co. I, James Hearn, Sgt. Co. D, John Miley (aka Wiley), Co. D, James Courtney, Co. F, Joseph Edwards, Co. B, William Murray, Co. B, Dennis Collins, Co. D, Ed Teafe, Co. E, John Gibson, Co. F, Dennis O'Neil, Co. E, William Burns, Co. F and Barnard Lavery, Co. A. Murray died from his illness in September 62. Six men: Fletcher, Hearn, Miley, Gibson, Burns and Lavery were discharged for disability between October 62 and September 63. Four: Edwards, Gibson, O'Neil, and Teafe are known to have returned to the regiment and saw further action.

[32] NARA:Hogg the original Captain of Co. I, was 38 when he was mustered into the regiment. He served as a recruiting officer in New York City from November-December 1861. His records are a bit confusing as he was sometimes referred to as Isaac Hogg.

[33] NARA: File of I. Gotthold. Letter from surgeon dated June 26, 1862 in New York City stating that Captain Gotthold "was recovering from typhoid fever of about a month's duration". Gotthold had been First Lieut. Co. F before being promoted to Captain Co. D on September 12, 1861.

[34] New York Times, "Men Buried at Fort Monroe", August 19, 1862, page 3, column 4-5.

[35] Michael Trainor died in June at Brandy Station. Henry Ruben, Co. I and George Devoe, Co. F died at Fairfax, VA in September. Benjamin Dowe died in November at Bolivar Heights, VA. George W. O'Dell, Cpl, Co. C died in Warrenton, VA in November. James Carroll, Co. G, Edward Connelly, Co. D, Harrison Ellis, Sgt. Co C, William Russell, Co. D, James J. Monaghan, Sgt. Co.

proportion of these soldiers developed illnesses that could be traced to the Peninsula. Add the men that got ill between June and August and the numbers can only be imagined.

To be sure Colonel Charles had his hands full dealing with disease and the constant movement through difficult terrain under adverse weather conditions all the while wondering when contact with the enemy would occur. By the end of May, Charles also had to deal with a number of the administrative issues that would further tax the command structure of the regiment as it moved up the Peninsula.

On April 23, Lieut. Colonel Mooney was dismissed from the service.[36] His dismissal was reversed on May 16.[37] What was the cause of Mooney's dismissal? The record is silent on this. The fact that it was reversed almost immediately could lead to the conclusion that the reason is moot, however it can be safely said that the confusion caused by these events within the regiment would do little to improve command unity and troop morale. What is known is that in addition to Mooney three of the regiment's captains, Henry Harrington, Co. A, Walter J. Tobin, Co. F and William A. Lynch, Co. K were also dismissed by the same Special Order. On May 3, a telegram was sent to the Governor of New York signed by George Ruggles, Asst. Adjutant General, Army of the Potomac, saying: "Please withhold appointments to fill vacancies occasioned by the discharge of Lieut. Colonel Mooney and Captains Harrington, Tobin and Lynch … until further advised."[38] Tobin and Lynch were reinstated with Mooney. Harrington was reinstated a few days later. There are a few hints as to what may have happened. The Company K muster roll dated February 28, 1862 lists Lynch as "waiting sentence of a court martial". The March 1862 muster rolls list Mooney and Tobin as "In arrest"[39]. As mentioned in the previous chapter Mooney had stated in a request for a leave in February

---

K, Thomas Ward, Co. D and Thomas Jones, Co. D died at various hospitals in the north. Patrick Hanlon, Co. G died at Falmouth, VA in December, just after Fredericksburg.

[36] Special Order No. 89, paragraph 5, A. G. O. April 23, 1862.

[37] Special Order No: 109, paragraph 3, A. G. O. May 16, 1862.

[38] New York State Archives, document 36.

[39] The record of Captain Harrington could not be located at the National Archives but it would not be surprising if he was also under arrest at the same time as the other officers.

that he had been "placed in arrest by General Stone on a trivial charge". That charged was related to the failure of Mooney and other regimental offices to appear before a board of examiners. It seems likely, although by no means certain, that all of these events can be traced back to the charges made by General Stone[40].

First Lieut. J. Garland, Regimental Quartermaster, USMHI

Captain Walter Tobin was no stranger to trivial controversy. In December 1861, while the senior officers were on leave, Captain Tobin was in temporary command of the regiment at Poolesville, MD when he authorized a horse to be used by the sutler servicing the regiment. The sutler's horse was ill and he had asked the regimental quartermaster, First Lieut. Garland, for use of a horse to make a trip to Washington. Garland in a letter to General Stone dated December 22, 1861 said that he had refused the sutler's request but that when the sutler made the same request to Tobin the captain "went in person without my knowledge to my principal teamster and ordered him to furnish a public horse for the above purpose". Tobin was informed of Garland's charge of "improper use

---

[40] Stone was arrested on February 8, 1862 and remained in prison without being charged until his release in August 1862.

of authority" and responded to General Stone that he was unaware that the original request made to the quartermaster had been refused and expressed his regrets for having authorized the use of the horse. Merry Christmas!

Also listed as "in arrest" on the muster roll of March-April 1862 is First. Lieut. James H. Conroy. Conroy's file does not provide a reason for his being under arrest but his letter of resignation to Colonel Charles written on May 24 says: " …It is now nearly four months since my case was before the courts martial. I have still been under arrest and nothing further satisfactorily seemingly to transpire … I feel justified in taking the steps I now do." Nearly four months would put the time of the courts martial around mid January. Is it a coincidence that Conroy ran into trouble in January? Perhaps, but it should be remembered that it was in January that Conroy, filed charges against Captain John Quinn, one of the original officers of the regiment, that resulted in Quinn's resignation. Exactly what happened at the courts martial is likely never to be known as an endorsement on Conroy's resignation request written by General Sedgwick dated May 24 reads: "It is well known that this officer was dismissed by the Courts Martial and Colonel Gantt informed me that the proceedings were in a chest that was lost on the march. I therefore approve of his discharge". Another endorsement by General Owen reads: "This officer is worthless in the service, has been in arrest four months and I respectfully urge the acceptance of his resignation."[41] On the same day, May 24, Conroy was discharged from the service by Special Order, No. 156, paragraph 3, Army of the Potomac.

The record of another officer, First Lieut. John Paine, adds to the complexity of the legal issues faced by the officer corps of the Tammany regiment. The same February 28, 1862, muster record that listed Captain Lynch as "Waiting sentence of court martial" lists Paine as "waiting trial of a court martial". Shortly thereafter Paine was transferred to Co. A. The record is silent on what if anything happened as a result of the courts martial. It is quite possible that Paine's case "disappeared" in the same way the actions against Lieut. Colonel Mooney and the other officers did.

---

[41]   NARA: record of James H. Conroy. The Colonel Gantt referred to in Sedgwick's endorsement was most likely Colonel Thomas T. Gantt, Judge Advocate, Army of the Potomac.

Paine, however, ran into trouble of a more serious nature while near Yorktown. Charges were brought against Paine by a group of officers from the First U. S. Cavalry. The three charges: conduct prejudicial to good order and military discipline, disobedience of orders and conduct unbecoming an officer and a gentleman were based on an incident that occurred on or about April 9, 1862 within the lines of sentinels of the 1st Regiment U. S. Cavalry near Yorktown. Paine was alleged to have, while intoxicated, unnecessarily fired his pistol, in violation of orders at a Negro boy, the servant of Captain Marcus A. Reno who had been sent to a house to buy potatoes.[42] The order that Paine was said to have disobeyed was General Order No. 113, Army of the Potomac, issued April 8, 1862. Paragraph VIII of that order specified that " ...men will ... preserve perfect silence ..." Additionally, orders were issued the same day to all commanders to prevent the unnecessary firing of weapons. A letter dated April 28 sent by Colonel Charles to a paymaster regarding a remark on the pay roll that stated that Lieut. Paine "was awaiting sentence of Court Martial" was a mistake. Charles said: "Paine was in arrest ... but had not been and has not been either sentenced or even tried by any Court Martial nor had any Court Martial been ordered in his case." On May 27, Paine submitted a letter of resignation that was forwarded with comment by Colonel Charles up the line to Generals Owen, Sedgwick and Sumner who all approved Paine's request. Charles' comments were very supportive of Paine stating: "On investigating the charges upon which Lieut. Paine was

---

[42] NARA: record of John Paine. The officer that filed the charges was Captain William T. Magruder, the brother of Confederate General Magruder. On May 31, 1862 Captain Magruder was proposed for promotion to the rank of Brigadier General by Edwin Stanton. "Journal of the Senate, Volume 37, Issue 2, page 323". The promotion was never approved. On October 1, 1862 Captain Magruder resigned his commission and thereafter joined the service of the Confederacy. He served as a captain on the staff of General Joseph R. Davis in A. P. Hills Corps. He was killed in action at Gettysburg. Marcus A. Reno graduated from West Point in 1857. With the rank of Major he was the senior surviving officer from the Battle of the Little Big Horn in 1876 commonly referred to as Custer's Last Stand. On April 1, 1880 Major Reno was dismissed from the service following his conviction on several charges one of which was "Conduct unbecoming an officer and a gentleman". "47th Congress, Senate Report No. 926, January 16, 1883. General Court Martial Order No. 20."

arrested it may be well to say that Lieut. Paine was at the time officer of the day, that he found the Negro in question, as he says he thought, marauding in the house alluded to, that he attempted to eject him forcibly, and that in the struggle his pistol, which he had drawn to intimidate the Negro, accidently exploded. I think the charge of intoxication is a mistake as I can say that I saw Lieut. Paine before and immediately after the transaction and did not myself perceive that he was under the effects of liquor." The story of Lieut. Paine does not end here.

Charles appeared to be quite frustrated by confusing correspondence with the office of the Adjutant General of New York in Albany related to the appointment of various officers to positions within the regiment. On May 10, Charles wrote to Albany outlining his need to obtain official commissions for appointments that had been made in February. After receiving a response, Charles again wrote Albany on May 20 stating: "I am in receipt of yours of the 16th in answer to mine of the 10th and have received the copy of the roster of officers of this regiment. I shall cease my endeavors to make the regimental record tally with it as it is simply impossible. The officers you name as belonging to the regiment in many cases I never saw or heard of having left long before I took command ... I now simply desire to secure the confirmation of those appointments I have made by your authority and who are and have been duly mustered and paid and long since doing duty ... I simply desire to obtain a commission ... for George W. Shaw who is now my adjutant ... and one for Septimus Cobb as Second Lieut."[43]

It is easy to see how miscommunication could occur between units in the field and administrative offices in Albany. In the field things were fluid with adjustments being made to deal with battlefield conditions and regimental needs. There was no time to wait for official documents to catch up with the reality of the field. Yet, regulations required detailed paperwork to provide the basis for payment of officers and in some cases determination of who was actually in command of a given situation. The amount of paper being handled by the adjutant general of New York had to be enormous considering the number of regiments in the field from the state. Two examples of correspondence related to the Tammany regiment

---

[43] New York State Archives: Documents 271 and 563.

may help to understand what days in Albany were like and what might be expected if you were waiting for Albany to act on a request you had made.

On May 20, 1862 S. M. Saunders wrote to Albany saying: "On the 15th I forwarded to your address the original certificate of Captain Call as to my having performed duty as First Lieut. Tammany regiment. My anxiety General, for a decision in my case ... I apologize for my frequent communication and fearing any accident might have happened in the transmission of the certificate I write this ..." Saunders' note has an endorsement showing that it was received and answered on May 21. Also on May 20, Saunders sent a letter to the Governor of New York requesting a certificate be issued to him to raise forty volunteers and be commissioned a First Lieut. Attached to that letter is a copy of a letter written to Saunders from the Adjutant General's Office in Washington, dated Oct. 12, 1861 showing that he was listed as the First Lieut. Co. H, of the Tammany regiment.[44] Several additional letters were sent by Saunders to Albany related to his obtaining appointments and requesting clarifications of details on dates of commissions. One of his letters written in June says: "I am most anxious to be in the service that so many of my countrymen (Irish) are now engaged and I feel every day a loss to me."[45]

During May 1862 a number of letters were received in Albany asking for certificates of enlistment for Tammany men that had enlisted in Boston. On May 3 the Relief Office at Boston City Hall sent a request to Albany asking for proof that Nicholas Quinn was a member of the regiment so that they could provide relief to his family. Similar requests were made in May on behalf of Uncle Pat, John Nugent, Michael Collins, John Hanlon, John Kelly and Patrick Conner. All the requests were related to a recently passed law in Massachusetts that provided for relief to families of men that had enlisted in regiments from other states. All of the requests were answered by the end of May.[46]

---

[44] New York State Archives: Documents 397 and 699. Saunders was indeed a Lieut. in the Tammany regiment. He was one of the officers that recruited men in Boston in 1861.

[45] New York State Archives: Documents 898 and 2722. Early in 1861, Saunders had been associated with the New York British Volunteers, a unit that was made part of the 36th New York Infantry. The roster of that unit does not include Saunders.

[46] New York State Archives: Documents: 39, 250, 341, 612, 674 and 1520.

The letters Colonel Charles sent to Albany in May also said: "We are so constantly on the move that I have but little time to communicate with your department ... We are on the eve of a great battle, at least we expect it." As the month of May came to an end the regiment camped near a place known as Fair Oaks or Seven Pines. Colonel Charles was right!

Chapter Seven

FAIR OAKS-SEVEN PINES

On May 21, 1862, the disposition of the Army of the Potomac was as follows. The advance guard under Brig. General George Stoneman was one mile from New Bridge on the Chickahominy River. V and VI Corps under Brig. Generals Fitz John Porter and William B. Franklin were three miles from New Bridge on the north side of the Chickahominy River and formed the right of the Army of the Potomac. II Corps under Brig. General Edwin V. Sumner was in the center near the York River Railroad line three miles north of the Chickahominy while III and IV Corps under Brig. Generals Samuel P. Heintzelman and Erasmus D. Keyes formed the Union left near Bottom's Bridge.[1] Retreating Confederate forces had burned the existing bridge but they did not defend the crossing. This allowed Brig. General Silas Casey's Second Division of the IV Corps to ford the river. After a personal reconnaissance of the situation at Bottom's Bridge by General McClellan, he ordered the rest of the IV and the III Corps to cross the Chickahominy and move toward Richmond on the southern side of the river.[2] It was this move by McClellan that set the stage for the upcoming battle. It put the Chickahominy River, notorious for its ability to flood and become a muddy nightmare, in between the III and IV Corps and the rest of the Union force. II Corps was kept on the northern side of the river; however it was the nearest body of troops that could be brought to the assistance of the two corps in the south, if aid was needed. It left the

---

[1]   Second Army Corps, page 19-20
[2]   Sears, Stephen W., To The Gates of Richmond, Ticknor and Fields, New York, 1992, page 110

smallest part of the Union force unprotected and in a position that made reinforcement difficult.

To understand this more clearly it is necessary to know the situation of the crossings of the Chickahominy in the area. There were a number of bridges including Bottom's Bridge and a nearby railroad bridge behind the Union left. There were others including Grapevine, Woodbury's, Duane's and Alexander's Bridges. All were unusable or had at some point been destroyed by the retreating Confederate forces. General Sumner had ordered two temporary bridges constructed with one at the site of the Grapevine Bridge and the other a bit further downriver. No bridges had been constructed for the crossing of the right column as yet although three were planned.[3] The river itself had been described as treacherous with it being hard to say where its banks would be at any given time[4].

On May 30, the Union forces had advanced with V Corps at Mechanicsville, VI and II Corps on the northern side of the river to Porter's left. II Corps was encamped near the Tyler House about a mile and a half from the river about half way between Bottom's Bridge and New Bridge[5]. III Corps was on the south bank with General Kearny's Division guarding Bottom's Bridge and General Hooker's Division on the southern flank facing White Oak Swamp.[6] On the night of May 30, there was a tremendous storm that turned the Chickahominy into a raging river with a strong current.[7]

What of the Confederate plans to deal with the defense of Richmond? General Joseph E. Johnson, commander of the Confederate Army of Northern Virginia became aware of the distribution of the Union forces on both sides of the Chickahominy and eventually finalized a plan to attack the southern two corps of Keyes and Heintzelman. This would hopefully destroy, or at least neutralize, 40% of the Union force before they could combine with the northern three corps and advance on Richmond. Johnston organized his forces into a Left Wing under Major General Gustavus W. Smith consisting of two divisions under Brig. General

[3] Second Army Corps, page 21
[4] Twentieth Massachusetts, page 91
[5] Ibid
[6] Gates of Richmond, supra, page 124
[7] Twentieth Massachusetts, page 91

W.H.C. Whiting and Major General A. P. Hill and a Right Wing under Major General James Longstreet with three divisions under Brig. General Richard H. Anderson and Major Generals D.H. Hill and Benjamin Huger. In reserve, under the overall command of Major General John B. Magruder, were two divisions commanded by Brig. Generals Lafayette McLaws and David R. Jones. Longstreet's divisions were to lead the attack with Whiting in support. A.P. Hill's troops were not part of the plan of attack having been assigned to protect against the northern approach of Union Generals Porter and Franklin.[8]

A lot has been written about the way the Confederate attack was executed. Issues related to the order of troop movements, clarity of command and efficiency of various leaders have been commented on and I need not go into those aspects of the battle to convey the impact that the Tammany regiment had on the events that unfolded on May 31. To do this, it is only necessary to follow the activity of the division under Whiting, containing five brigades, and the resulting battle with reinforced remnants of Brig. General John J. Abercrombie's brigade of IV Corps. Abercrombie was sixty-four years old and originally from Tennessee. His brigade consisted of the 65 and 67NY and the 23, 31 and 61PA infantry regiments. After the initial confederate attack on Couch's Division, Abercrombie's brigade became divided with several regiments separated from their commander. Several other regiments from different brigades within the same division also were isolated and had joined with Abercrombie. All together Abercrombie had under his direct command his own 31PA and 65NY as well as the 7MA from General Deven's brigade and the 62NY from General Peck's brigade who had picked up an officer and a small number of pickets from other commands[9]. He also had Battery H, First Pennsylvania Light Artillery under Captain James Brady with 4 Parrott cannon.

As Whiting was moving toward his assigned objective of supporting Longstreet he sent the brigade commanded by John B. Hood into the area between Seven Pines and Fair Oaks in an attempt to make contact with Longstreet's left flank. Generals Johnston and Whiting were riding with

---

[8]   Dowdy, Clifford, *The Seven Days Battles*, Fairfax Press, New York, 1964, page 90.

[9]   OR:S1, V11, 892: The pickets were members of the 100NY.

Whiting's brigade, currently commanded by Colonel E. M. Law, along the Nine Mile Road near Fair Oaks Station where the railroad crossed the road. This command group detected the presence of a small Union force across the railroad tracks and sent the 4AL regiment from Law's Brigade to deal with it.[10] This Union force was the reinforced half brigade led by Abercrombie that had been falling back toward the Chickahominy. The Union force, with its artillery separated into two sections, had taken up position, around 4 o'clock in the afternoon, on both sides of the small Adams House facing west. As the 4AL assaulted their position the combination of musket and cannon fire stopped the southerners in their tracks. Whiting continued the attack against Abercrombie by committing additional regiments from Law's Brigade. These units fared no better than the 4AL.[11]

Some three hours earlier, after the initial Confederate attack had commenced, activity was building on the north side of the Chickahominy. Sumner's II Corps had been ordered to prepare to assist the forces on the southern side of the river. Sumner had had his two divisions assemble and move to the bridgeheads waiting for the order to cross. Sedgwick's Division was at the Grapevine Bridge and Richardson's Division was at a nearby bridge just below Grapevine. Both bridges were recently constructed and were suffering from the effects of the heavy rains of the previous evening. By 2:30 PM Sumner had received his order to move and Sedgwick had started his lead brigade across the Grapevine Bridge. This brigade commanded by Gorman was made up of the 1MN, 34 and 82NY and the 15MA. The remaining troops of the division then crossed in the following order: Kirby's battery of Napoleans, the brigades of Burns and Dana and the rest of the division's artillery.[12] General Dana's brigade was short the 19MA which was then on picket duty down river between the Grapevine and Bottom Bridges. He also had been told to leave his "smallest" regiment behind to protect Grapevine Bridge and assist with the crossing of the artillery. This regiment was the 42NY.[13] The remaining three batteries of artillery were all from the First Rhode Island Light Artillery. In order of

10 The Seven Days Battles, supra, page 116
11 Ibid page 117
12 OR: S1, V11, 791-793
13 OR: S1, V11, 807-809

crossing the Chickahominy they were Battery A, under Captain John A. Tompkins, Battery B, under Captain Walter O. Bartlett and Battery C, under Captain Charles D. Owen. Overall commander of the Division's artillery was Colonel Charles A. Tompkins. In his report[14] he said: "The crossing to the swamp … was upon a narrow causeway … Kirby's battery was, by great exertion upon the part of himself, officers and men, got across, and arrived upon the field of battle in time to participate in the action … Notwithstanding the terrible condition of the causeway, rendered worse than at first by the crossing of Kirby's battery, Captain Tompkins, by great exertion of himself and command, got his battery through, and arrived on the field of action just at the close of the engagement. Captain Bartlett also succeeded in getting one piece of his battery across … arriving upon the field immediately after Captain Tompkins. A bridge which crossed a ditch in the causeway having broken through, and the continued rise of the water overflowing a portion of the causeway, it became necessary to unharness the horses and draw the remainder of Bartlett's and all of Owen's battery through by hand. In the performance of this arduous duty valuable assistance was rendered by Major Bowe, Forty Second New York Volunteers and 100 men of that regiment. By early dawn of the 1st instant all the remaining artillery, with the exception of two pieces of Owen's battery, was upon the field, and at 7 a.m. the remaining section of Owen's battery arrived."[15]

---

[14] OR: S1, V11, 793-795

[15] The number of Tammany men that actually assisted in the moving of artillery across the Chickahominy is a bit unclear. At least one company, Company I was on temporary duty unloading supplies at White Horse Landing until June 8. NARA: Record Group 94. Additional men were no doubt utilized as pickets protecting the bridge and surrounding area.

Grapevine Bridge over the Chickahominy River, Library of Congress

To get a better feel for how the men of the 42NY spent May 31 and June 1, 1862 it is necessary to look at the time line of those two days and what was accomplished. General Dana in his official report[16] said that his brigade was placed under arms shortly after 1:30 p.m. on the 31st. Dana's brigade was in the rear of the Division, followed only by most of the artillery, and the 42NY was at the end of the brigade. After crossing the river, Colonel Charles commanding the 42NY, was left to help with the artillery and secure the bridge. This took place around 4:30. Captain Tompkin's of Battery A, 1st RI Artillery reported that he left camp at Tyler's House at 2 p.m. and crossed the Chickahominy at 5 p.m. The remaining batteries reached the river and partially crossed between 6 and 7 p.m. The last piece was across the river by 5 a.m. Captain Tompkins does not mention the 42NY in his report but he did say: "Leaving the caissons to follow, I brought the guns to the front. ... At 4 a.m the battery was posted ... the caissons were placed under cover of the woods ... opposite Adam's House." It seems a reasonable assumption that the men of the 42NY must have assisted with the movement of Tompkin's caissons as well as the rest of the division's artillery and that the entire task took somewhere close to 12 hours, at night, between 5 p.m. on the 31st of May to 5 a.m. on the 1st of June. Captain Bartlett reported: " ...We crossed

---

16   OR: S1, V11, 807-809

the Chickahominy about 6 p.m. I proceeded with the right piece ... The second piece ... got struck by a horse tailing in a deep hole. This caused a long delay, as it was nearly 10 o'clock before the piece was got out. All the carriages after this one were unlimbered and pulled through by hand with the assistance of the 42nd Regiment. One caisson was so badly mired that it was necessary to take out the ammunition and pass it ashore." [17]

In another report the following graphic description of the crossing of the artillery appears: "After crossing the river we came to a stream of swift running water, formed by the overflow, which we found much difficulty in crossing. The cannoneers were in the water for an hour and a half, sometimes up to their waists. We finally reached what we thought to be solid ground, but such was not the case, as only a thin crust of earth covered the swampy land, which soon became spongy by constant travel, so that the guns and caissons would descend to the hubs in the mire. The horses would sink to their knees as they struggled with their heavy loads, so, in order to relieve them, they were unhitched from the guns and caissons, and led to one side, in order to obtain a firm footing. Then the prolonges were attached to the carriages, the horses hitched on, and the cannoneers with fence rails pried the wheels up out of the mud. Then the word would be given: "A strong pull, and a pull together," upon which the guns and caissons would be lifted out and go on a few yards further, when carriages, horses and men would again sink into the soft and spongy soil; at each occurrence the same maneuvers would be repeated. In this way, after six hours of toil and struggle, through mud and water, the battery finally reached firm ground and pushed forward." [18]

James Fennessy reported some detail on the events around the Grapevine Bridge. [19] Fennessy said: "The general's aide de camp came dashing at full speed to the colonel with the dispatch that his regiment must halt, stack arms, and get to work instantly in rescuing, from the now partially broken bridge ... all the divisional artillery ... and to attain this, if need be, the horses carriages, caissons, guns and all should have to be taken across on the men's shoulders. After several hours of fatiguing labor,

[17] OR: S1, V11, 796-798
[18] Rhodes, John H, The History of Battery B, First Regiment Rhode Island Light Artillery, Snow and Farnham, Providence, R. I. 1894, pages 88-89
[19] Irish American Newspaper, New York, June 7, 1862, page 2, column 3.

with the boys up to their necks in mud and water, the artillery was timely rescued from the swamps of the Chickahominy ... When the artillery had been righted the regiment was again ordered to guard the bridge." Fennessy went on to describe the scene following the battle: "Long trains of ambulances now arrived at the bridge but could not be conveyed across the stream, which ... had risen several feet carrying away a part of the bridge and overflowing almost all of the ground to the base of the hill beyond, thus causing all the wounded to be taken out of the ambulances, and rafted across ... an act most painful to the mangled and dying, and a sight most melancholy to those who assisted in their removal ... General Pettigrew, who was severely wounded when he fell into our hands, was allowed to stay in the ambulance, which the men managed to float over the swollen stream safely."

So it appears that the task in front of the Tammany regiment was a large one. To see how big we need to look at some numbers. Each battery was equipped with 6 guns. Battery A had 6-10 pound rifled Parrots, Battery B had 6-12 inch smooth bore Napoleons and Battery G had 6-3 inch rifles. While somewhat different all these pieces, with their associated limbers and ammunition (one chest of usually 32 rounds) weighed on average around 2300 pounds. Additionally, each gun had an assigned caisson carrying 3 extra ammunition chests for a total weight in the area of 1900 pounds.[20] Additional support wagons were also assigned to each battery but to be conservative, let's ignore them for this analysis. Again, being conservative, let's also assume that the 42nd New York did not assist in helping any of Kirby's Battery's caissons or Tompkins guns across the river. That would leave Tompkins six caissons, Bartlett's six guns and six extra caissons and Owen's six guns and six extra caissons. All together they assisted in the crossing of 12 guns and 18 additional caissons in the 12 hours between 5 p.m. and 5 a.m. A total weight of something like 61,800 pounds of ordinance, just fewer than 31 tons, and most of this work took place in darkness in a swamp! The Tammany regiment certainly did not do all the work alone. Each battery assisted in the movement of their guns. Assuming that each battery was at full strength, which was unlikely, there would have been 123 men in each, including officers. That breaks down

[20]   Johnson, Curt and Anderson, Richard C. Jr., Artillery Hell, Texas A and M University Press, College Station, Texas, 1995 pages 21-6.

to around 20 men per gun. To operate a gun properly in action required 10 men[21] meaning that half of the battery would likely have left for the action as soon as a gun was safely across the river leaving only around 60 men behind to help with the caissons. These men would also likely leave the area as their caissons reached firm ground. Therefore, it appears a safe assumption that the 100 men from the 42NY provided between 45-63% of the manpower required to move the equipment. There was also a complement of 146 horses assigned to each battery and while these animals surely made parts of the task much easier their care and handling would likely have needed the attention of trained personnel from the battery leaving a higher percentage of the grunt work to the infantry.

Additionally, General Richardson's division which was to cross the Chickahominy at a different bridge was rerouted to the Grapevine Bridge after their intended crossing had washed away after only General French's brigade had crossed. The remaining two brigades and all the batteries of the division reached and crossed the Grapevine Bridge by 3 a.m. on the morning of June 1 according to the report of Captain George Hazzard, Richardson's Chief of Artillery. While this statement appears somewhat in conflict with the times mentioned by other officers it is likely that Captain Hazzard was referring to the guns themselves and not the additional caissons. Captain Hazzard also stated, "the night proved extremely dark" adding the to the difficulty of the crossing.[22] Given the orders of the 42NY to protect the bridge and aid in the crossing of artillery it is also more likely than not that they assisted in the crossing of Richardson's four batteries of guns.

Once across the Chickahominy the troops and guns of Sedgwick's Division moved to the sound of battle some two miles away. The first unit to cross, the 1MN, arrived and was immediately sent to the right of the Union force headed by Abercrombie and Couch. Kirby arrived next with part of his battery of Napoleans and took position alongside two of the four guns in Brady's battery under the command of Lt. Fagan. Three of the regiments under Abercrombie, the 62NY, 82PA (formally called the 31PA) and the 65NY also formed to the right connecting with the 1MN. To the Union left, the arriving men of Gorman's Brigade took up

---

21   Ibid pages 27-28
22   OR: S1, V11, 767-768

positions with the 15MA supporting the artillery and the 82 and 34NY anchoring the left corner of the position. The two advancing regiments of Dana's Brigade, the 20MA and 7MI, arrived and were positioned on the extreme left connecting with the 34NY. At this point General Sumner assigned Sedgwick to command the right; Couch to command the center and Sumner took direct command of the left. Fighting was furious with regiment after regiment of rebel troops assaulting the Union line in piecemeal attacks. All met with tremendous volleys of musket and cannon fire. The four guns of Brady's battery and the five operational guns under Kirby were particularly deadly as they poured round after round of canister into the rebel troops. "When Captain Brady ran out of canister, he had his gunners fire shell and case shot without fuses so like canister they burst leaving the muzzles with the lethal effect of giant shotguns … Lt. Kirby recorded that his five guns fired 343 rounds at the enemy on May 31."[23]

In this author's opinion, Lt. Kirby, a graduate of the West Point class of 1861, deserves a tremendous amount of credit. This young officer's battery of five guns fired at a rate that must have been exhausting. All of the ammunition required to keep the guns firing was not at the battle site requiring caissons to be sent back towards the river to pick up additional ammunition. In his official report[24], Lt. Kirby stated that he fired 70 rounds of shell, 210 rounds of spherical case, 15 rounds of solid shot and 48 rounds of canister making up the total of the 343 rounds fired. He also reported that he arrived at the battlefield with 3 guns and one additional caisson at 4:45PM and was ordered into position by General Sumner. If we assume that the ammunition carried by these guns and caisson were normal loads there would have been 32 rounds in each chest carried by each gun and an additional 96 rounds with the caisson or a total of 192 rounds.[25] He immediately opened fire on advancing enemy infantry at about 1000 yards, using spherical case and shell ammunition. A short time later Lt. Woodruff arrived with two additional guns and went into action. The last gun of the battery arrived following the firing of a few rounds, under the command of Lt. French. Additional caissons did not accompany the last three guns. Therefore, the total ammunition available on the battlefield was 288 rounds,

---

23 The Gates of Richmond, supra, page 137
24 OR: S1, V11, 795-796
25 Artillery Hell, supra, page 27

mixed between the various types. One of the guns that arrived early broke down after having fired only four rounds making the battery a five-gun unit. After exhausting all of the spherical case and shell ammunition the wagons were sent back to get more from the equipment being dragged through the mud. This was not normal procedure for batteries were trained not to send wagons back to replenish ammunition without their guns. In the heat of battle the guns could be required to change position and the wagons sent back for ammunition would likely not know where the new positions were. Normal practice would have been for the entire battery to be pulled out of the action and sent back to replenish their supplies.[26] Until the new supply of the exhausted munitions arrived the battery fired solid shot at the enemy. When the replenished supply of spherical case and shell arrived it was fired until the enemy had closed to within 500 yards. At that range canister was fired. Later the enemy attacked again and was driven back by heavy canister fire from all five guns.

On average each of Kirby's guns fired 68 times during the battle, which, for them, lasted for about three hours and fifteen minutes from 4:45 to 8PM. That's around 21 times an hour or once every three minutes. A fully manned gun could be fired by a trained group of men once every 30 seconds.[27] However, that figure does not allow for repositioning guns as was required several times in the battle fought by Lt. Kirby. Quite an effort after having dragged the artillery pieces through the mud and rushed to the battlefield! And all accomplished under the command of a young man that had graduated from West Point less than a year before the battle. Unfortunately, the Union was to later lose the services of Lt. Kirby when he was killed at Chancellorsville.

In a letter by Lt. Col. Robert McAllister, who at the time was second in command of the 1NJ in Franklin's VI Corps on the north side of the Chickahominy, the battle was reported to have started at about 1PM and ended around 8PM.[28] In his letter McAllister stated: " ...The battle

[26] Ibid. page 30
[27] Nofi, Albert A., A Civil War Treasury, Combined Books, Inc. Conshohocken, PA, 1992, page 110
[28] "The Civil War Letters of General Robert McAllister", edited by James I. Robertson, Jr. Published for the New Jersey Civil War Centennial Commission, Rutgers University Press 1997. Lt. Col. McAllister later was the commanding

commenced about 1 P. M. and did not close till 8 this evening ... It continued long after dark, a very uncommon occurrence. I say it was terrible for the roaring of artillery and musketry was more terrific than I have yet seen or heard. It was rapid and constant. We think the battle will be resumed in the morning and that it will become general along the whole line ..."

The letter by McAllister sheds light on another aspect of what was happening on May 31. He mentions that the battle continued well after dark and that such an occurrence was quite unusual. From his position on the north side of the Chickahominy he thought that there was a real expectation that the battle would resume with intensity in the morning. If he felt that way from his position of safety, what were the men of the 42NY, charged with the moving of artillery and ammunition over the swollen Chickahominy thinking? I would think that there was a sense of urgency and fear that was overwhelming. The enemy was only a few miles away and little information was available. All the commanding generals were at the front and the sounds of the battle were deafening. It is not surprising that the men at the river worked all night in the dark and up to their waists in the swamp. There was no other choice. Tomorrow was coming and everything that could be brought to bear on the enemy was needed at the front. While it has been said that the 42NY was left behind at the bridge and did not take part in the Battle of Fair Oaks, it is this author's view that the Tammany regiment played an integral and important role in the events of May 31, 1862![29]

Colonel of the 11NJ in III Corps and eventually became a Brig. General commanding a brigade in the II Corps.

[29]   The record of William Schackleton, Pvt., Co. B, shows him as absent on the muster roll of May-June 1862 with the remark: "Wounded in New York hospital, rec'd his wound in the battle of Fair Oaks, May 31, 1862". He is listed on the rolls of U.S.A. General Hospital, Lexington Avenue and 51st Street, NY in September. While there is no record of where or when during the battle of Fair Oaks Schackleton was wounded, his record does show that following his return to the regiment he served mainly as a teamster on detached service with ammunition trains. Is it possible that he was so assigned at the time of his wounding? Schackleton was mustered out on July 17, 1864 in New York, as a wagoner. He arrived in New York on June 23 from Fortress Monroe. New York Times June 24, 1862.

Chapter Eight

SEVEN DAYS BATTLES

With the close of action at Fair Oaks/Seven Pines on June 1, the regiments of the Army of the Potomac settled into a period of several weeks of relatively quiet cleaning up the battlefield, fortifying positions and taking stock of and adjusting to what had happened within their ranks. The Tammany regiment was no exception.

Administratively, a number of promotions within both the enlisted and officer ranks took place. Most notably, First Sergeant Edwin Pierce was promoted to Second Lieut. and Second Lieut. William Hevey advanced to First Lieut.[1] Lieut. McLean, who had joined the regiment just before it left for the Peninsula was discharged for chronic diarrhea on June 20 at Fair Oaks.[2] Nineteen enlisted men that did not make the trip to the

---

[1] Hevey had been with the regiment from the beginning. He was promoted from First Sergeant to Second Lieut. September 17, 1861. He would continue to serve through most of 1862 and would resign his commission due to Chronic Rheumatism in early 1863. In his letter of resignation dated Jan. 26, 1863 he states "I have been suffering from Rheumatism for the last four months, and for the last month have been unable to perform duty". He was discharged by Special Order No. 32, paragraph 5, Second Army Corps, Feb. 15, 1863. NARA: record of William Hevey.

[2] McLean was discharged by S. O. No. 186, Army of the Potomac, June 20, 1862. He saw subsequent service with the Thirty Ninth New York Infantry, joining that regiment in December 1863 reaching the rank of Second Lieut. On July 7, 1864 McLean was dishonorably discharged for being absent without leave by Special Order No. 229, War Department, Adjutant General's Office. On July 26, 1892, twenty eight years later, the War Department revoked and set aside his dismissal. NARA: file of C. McLean.

Peninsula were discharged for disability at various locations in the first three weeks of June. Corporal Robert Deacon, Co. D and Private Phineas Norris, Co. H arrived at Fort Monroe on the steamship Vanderbilt on June 7 having gotten ill following their arrival on the Peninsula.[3] Michael Cafferty, Co. D arrived in New York on June 14 on the steamer Fulton carrying hundreds of sick and wounded from Ft. Monroe.[4] On June 25, the steamer Commodore arrived in New York carrying Corporal George W. O'Dell and John Donovan.[5]

Captain Edwin Pierce, USMHI, collection of Martin Schoenfeld

---

[3]   New York Times, June 8, 1862, page 1, column 5. The article in the Times lists the men arriving on the Vanderbilt as "wounded", however the NARA record of Phineas B. Norris lists him as sick. Norris, one of the Boston enlistees and a sailor by profession, had been a sergeant in Co. H but was reduced in rank to private in November 1861and assigned as a carpenter to the regimental Quartermaster. His record lists him as having deserted around September 1862. There is a record of a Phineas B. Norris having drowned in 1877 in Gloucester, MA at Pew's Dock. The dock was operated by John Pew and Son, the most famous of the Gloucester fishing companies, known more recently as Gorton's of Gloucester. The regimental listing for Robert Deacon, age 32, has him as having deserted in September or October 1862. It is quite possible that Norris and Deacon shared more than the ride on the steamship Vanderbilt.

[4]   New York Times, June 15, 1862. The article says that men from New York regiments were sent to Park Barracks and that the worst cases were kept on ship.

[5]   New York Times, June 26, 1862.

Scott Dean was recommended for appointment to Second Lieut. by Colonel Charles on June 7. However, Charles would again find that Albany moved as a snail's pace when it came to administration issues. On June 17, Daniel Delavan, a senior Tammany Hall politician, wrote to Governor Morgan asking that Dean's commission be sent to him directly. Another letter from Delavan was sent on June 24. In this letter Delavan said: "Not having heard anything in regard to the matter, I venture to write again, asking that the subject be favorably attended to at as early a day as possible. Not only am I anxious in regard to the appointments, but as the "Tammany Society" desires sending a suit of colors to the regiment, and no civilian being allowed within the lines, Mr. Dean, the new appointee, who will instantly join his regiment if commissioned by you, can, as an officer, take them down and present them."[6] Septimus Cobb was finally mustered in as Second Lieut. on June 17.

Lieut. Septimus Cobb, USMHI

---

[6]   Delavan would send yet another letter regarding Dean to Governor Morgan on August 28, 1862 in which he states: "He was directed to report for duty…there to receive his commission…He reported as directed and is now doing duty but his commission, by some miscarriage has not reached him and I respectfully ask your Excellency to direct that a new commission be issued. New York State Archives: Documents: 1629, 6574 and 1896. On December 19, 1862 Dean tendered his resignation giving his reason as "Chronic Rheumatism". An endorsement on the request written by Lt. Colonel Bomford reads: "Approved…as he has been unable to do more than twenty days duty since joining the regiment in July last." Dean was discharged January 8, 1863, S. O. No. 18, Right Grand Division. NARA: File of Scott Dean.

Eugene Sullivan described the activities of the regiment during June saying: "General Dana's brigade ... lay in our position at Fair Oaks Station, throwing up earthworks and performing such duties as were required of us until Sunday morning June 29, 1862 when we received orders to evacuate our trenches on the right of Fair Oaks Station and fall back to Grapevine Bridge."[7] What had happened to cause the retreat of Union forces? A lot!

Following the close of action at Fair Oaks McClellan continued to press Washington for the additional troops he believed he needed to press the attack on Richmond. On June 7, McClellan was advised that McCall's division of 9,500 men was being sent to the Peninsula by sea. McCall arrived at White Horse Landing on June 11 and was ordered to take positions north of the Chickahominy.[8] Additional requests for troops by McClellan were unproductive. Actually, McClellan should have been happy that he got McCall given that Washington was extremely nervous about weakening the forces protecting the capital following Stonewall Jackson's successful Shenandoah Valley Campaign in May and early June.

McClellan's plan called for moving the enormous firepower of his siege train to within range of Richmond. Once in place these huge weapons would subject the Confederate capital to continuous attack which, McClellan believed, would force evacuation of the city and the defeat of the South. On June 21 the movement of the siege train started from White House and by June 25 almost two dozen of the large guns had been advanced to positions north of the Chickahominy near Gaines Mills. A large percentage of the more than 100 pieces of heavy ordnance remained on ships in the Pamunkey and York Rivers.

While McClellan's army prepared the Confederacy was busy as well. The change of command that established Robert E. Lee as the commander of all troops in the region had occurred and a plan was being put together that would put pressure on all corners of the Union front and result in the group of battles referred to as "The Seven Days" and ultimately the full withdrawal of the Army of the Potomac from the Peninsula.

Lee was ready to take the offensive. He was convinced that attacking the Union army was the only way to save Richmond. He knew the general

---

[7] Eugene Sullivan, "Bringing Up the Rear", The National Tribune, Washington, DC, January 7, 1904, page 3.

[8] Dowdey, Clifford, The Seven Days, page 134.

disposition of the Union forces based on the recent battles but wanted more current information and specifics that would raise his confidence in finalizing his plan to move. He called on his leader of cavalry, General J. E. B. Stuart to execute a reconnaissance in strength, concentrating on establishing the strength and dispositions of the Union forces on the north side of the Chickahominy.

Stuart's force of about 1,200 cavalry included the First Virginia under Colonel Fitzhugh Lee, R. E. Lee's nephew, the Ninth Virginia under Colonel William Henry Fitzhugh (Rooney) Lee, the commanding general's son, as well as the Fourth Virginia, the Jeff Davis Legion and a two gun battery of horse artillery. Between June 12-16, this force moved north from Richmond to Hanover Court House, southeast to Tunstall's Station on the Richmond and York railroad connecting to White House Landing, further southeast crossing the Chickahominy at Forge bridge and finally to Charles City Court House and back to Richmond.

Throughout the entire circling of the Union positions messages were sent to Lee informing him of the dispositions of the Union troops. This allowed Lee to implement his plan to attack the force on the north side of the Chickahominy with the objective of destroying it and interdicting the supply line from White House Landing to the bulk of the Union troops on the south side of the river. If successful, the attack would force, at a minimum, the retreat of the forces threatening Richmond and could possibly result in McClellan having to leave the Peninsula entirely.

Along the way Stuart's men ran into numerous small groups of Union troops, mainly cavalry patrols and unescorted supply wagons. Two supply bases, Tunstall's Station and Garlick's Landing, two miles north of Tunstall's, were attacked and sacked. In total, Stuart destroyed two supply schooners, probably the Whitman Phillips and the Island City, some locomotives and rolling stock, approximately seventy-five supply wagons and sizable amounts of various types of stores. Stuart's force returned to Richmond with 150 Union prisoners and several hundred captured animals.[9]

---

[9]   OR: S1, V11, 1032 and Longacre, Edward G. "All The Way Around", Civil War Times, June 2002, page 59. The names of the two schooners come from: Mewborn, Horace, "A Wonderful Exploit, Jeb Stuart's Ride Around the Army of the Potomac, Blue and Gray Magazine, Summer 1998, page 19. The naming of

The attack on Tunstall's Station is of particular interest. Why? Four Tammany men: Captain James McGrath, Co. G, First Lieut. John Paine, Co. A, Corporal James P. Daly and Private Patrick Russell, both from Co. G, were captured and taken to Richmond.[10] Other men escaped and reported back what had happened. Why were these men at Tunstall's Station? Their regiment was encamped at Fair Oaks more than fifteen miles away. Had they been sent to procure supplies? Were they on some other mission? The most likely answer is that they were a detached Tammany force positioned along the railroad.

The Richmond and York Railroad was a key player in McClellan's plan. It stretched thirty eight miles from Richmond to West Point on the York River and had more than a dozen stations. The line was completed in 1859. It took a train just under two hours to make the trip from Richmond to West Point.[11] Tunstall's Station was just about in the middle of the line, eighteen miles from West Point and twenty miles from Richmond. An account of Stuart's raid said: " ...the railroad, over which are transported the supplies which keep in motion the vast Army of the Potomac ... has been left to be guarded ... from White House to the Chickahominy bridge by two companies of the Tammany Regiment of New York-a picket force which was in some places so scanty as really to invite the attacks of marauding bands ...".[12]

---

the Whitman Phillips is consistent with the entry for the same schooner in Army and Navy Series, Dictionary of Transports and Combatant Vessels Employed by the US Army, page 336.

[10] Ibid. The Blue and Gray article states that "at least nine enlisted men from the 42nd New York were captured at the depot". On June 21, the New York Times published an article that appeared in the Richmond Examiner on June 16. That article names McGrath and Paine (called Price) as the only two officers captured at Tunstall's and says that "there were about twenty regulars among the privates, the balance being members of the Forty-second New York Volunteers". The total number of privates reported captured was put at about 140 which would mean that 120 members of the Tammany regiment were captured, a number that is clearly incorrect.

[11] Richmond Dispatch, Monday, December 10, 1860.

[12] New York Times, June 20, 1862. "Affairs on the Right Wing". A similar reference is Longacre, Edward "All the Way Around", Civil War Times, June 2002, page 28. It reads: "Stuart closed up on Tunstall's, whose garrison, thought to consist of two companies of infantry..."

The likely scenario is therefore that Company G was positioned as a security force at Tunstall's Station when Stuart's men attacked. That would explain the capture of Captain McGrath and the two enlisted men. Whether another company of Tammany men was also positioned along the rail line is a question without an answer.

Why was Lieut. Paine at Tunstall's? Lieut. Paine had been under arrest since the incident near Yorktown when he fired his pistol at a servant of a cavalry officer. On May 27, Paine had submitted his resignation to Colonel Charles. The request was forwarded by Charles along with a statement presenting reasons why Charles thought that the charges against Paine were inaccurate. The recommendation was forwarded to General Sedgwick the same day but was not acted on until June 20 most likely due to the more pressing matters associated with the battle at Fair Oaks. There was also a second letter from Colonel Charles that read: "This officer has been in arrest on charges for some months, upon which he has never been tried. On several occasions he has been in the habit of leaving camp without leave. Latterly, he did so remaining absent the entire night and only saved himself from being placed under guard by faithfully promising to confine himself strictly to camp limits. He has despite this been absent from camp since Thursday last. On the afternoon of the attack of the enemy's cavalry at Tunstall's Station he was seen there in company with Captain McGrath of the regiment who was subsequently made prisoner. There is scarcely a doubt that he was made prisoner at the same time. A short time since he sent in his resignation which was duly forwarded with approval, together with a copy of the charges against him. My regiment is very short of officers and it is of the greatest importance that every commission should as far as possible be represented. I have good and brave men who deserve promotion and I earnestly request that the resignation of Lieut. Paine be accepted without delay".[13]

At the time of his capture McGrath was a popular officer within the ranks as well as with the command structure. This is clear from a letter written by General Sedgwick to Governor Morgan on August 8 from Harrison Landing. In his letter Sedgwick recommended that "Captain McGrath, now a prisoner at Richmond", be considered for promotion

---

[13]   NARA: Record of Lieut. Paine

to Lieut. Colonel of the Tammany regiment.[14] Actually, at the time of Sedgwick's letter, McGrath had been paroled at Aiken's Landing, his exchange taking place on August 12.[15] Whether this was known by Sedgwick is unclear. Paine was paroled along with McGrath and the two enlisted men and was told that he had been discharged while he was a prisoner by Special Order, No. 189, Army of the Potomac, dated June 23.

Adding to the saga of John Paine is the fact that more than a year after he had been discharged, he rejoined the Tammany regiment under circumstances that are far from clear. The regimental roster shows Paine as: "not commissioned First Lieut.; commissioned, but not mustered, Captain, October 21, 1863". On November 17, 1863, Paine, from Washington, D. C., wrote a letter to J. J. Johnson, Acting Assistant Adjutant General in Albany saying: "I joined my regiment on the fourth of this month and was with them until the 16th." Paine explained that he could not be mustered in because of confusion as to whose spot he would be taking. He signed the letter, John Paine, Captain, 42nd Regiment NY.[16] The documented record of John Paine ends with the November 17, 1863 letter.[17]

Once Robert E. Lee had the information provided by Stuart he implemented his attack plan aimed at the weaker part of McClellan's force north of the Chickahominy. He left about twenty percent of his strength south of the river under generals Magruder and Huger with the task of holding the attention of the Union forces in the area so that they would not shift quickly to the north. The rest of Lee's force on the Peninsula, as well as Jackson's troops coming down from the Shenandoah, would maneuver to engage the Union troops under Porter and McCall in the initial battles of the Seven Days.

---

[14] Letter, General Sedgwick to Gov. Morgan of New York, August 8, 1862, Harrison Landing, VA. Auction Catalog, Battles and Leaders, Collection of Civil War Letters, American Historical Auctions, Boston, MA. Februsry 24, 1996. Page 155, item 686.
[15] NARA: Record of Captain James McGrath
[16] New York State Archives: document 13589
[17] There is a record of a John Paine being mustered into the 11th NY Cavalry as Second Lieut. on March 12, 1864. Is he the same man? While the timing is consistent the man in the 11th Cavalry is listed as being 35 years old in 1864. If the age of the John Paine who served in the Tammany regiment was correctly entered when he joined the regiment he would have been only 29 in 1864.

Between Wednesday, June 25 and Saturday, June 28, battles were fought at Oak Grove, Mechanicsville/Beaver Dam Creek and Gaines Mills. These hard fought actions had Union generals Porter and McCall under continuous pressure from Confederate forces under D.H. Hill, A. P. Hill and Longstreet. Union troops held their ground in the early phases of the actions but were ordered to fall back as part of McClellan's newly formed plan of shifting his supply base from White House Landing to positions on the James River.

From the start of the Peninsula Campaign McClellan had planned to use White House Landing, on the Pamunkey River, with its rail connection to West Point and the York River as his main supply base. No attempt had been made to establish a James River base. To know that the shift to a James River base was not planned, all one has to do is read the official report of Lieut. Colonel Rufus Ingalls, Aide-de-camp to General Stewart Van Vliet, Senior Quartermaster of the Army of the Potomac, commanding White House, dated June 19, 1862. Ingall's report states: "With a depot stretching from Cumberland", a town only a few miles downriver from White House Landing, "to this point, with three hundred ships crowded into so small a river, containing all our supplies ..."[18] Surely, if there had been a plan to shift the base of the Union force to the James from the beginning of the campaign the top quartermaster officers would have known about it. The decision was apparently made after the attack at Mechanicsville and following McClellan's receipt of information on the movement of Jackson's troops. McClellan reacted quickly and in a way that was certainly uncharacteristic. He knew of the extent of Stuart's reconnaissance and the demonstrated vulnerability of the supply lines between White House and the troops on the south side of the Chickahominy. He had seen the strength of the attacks on Porter and McCall and knew that the Confederate force on the north side of the river could not be held for long. He had to act and he had to protect the two dozen pieces of heavy artillery of the siege train that had been unloaded and moved forward. It must be remembered that even the loss of a battery of light guns to the enemy was considered an embarrassing and demoralizing event. Imagine the effect on McClellan and the Army of the Potomac if a large number of heavy siege guns intended to force the Confederacy into submission had been captured

---

[18]   OR: S1, V11, 1032

and the main supply base of the Union destroyed. McClellan decided that the heavy guns could not be returned to White House Landing and reloaded onto ships for safe removal in a timely way so he ordered that they be moved overland to the James River. He ordered his infantry to delay the Confederate advance and to provide all the cover possible for the movement of the guns.

Sumner's Second Corps remained in place around Fair Oaks while the fighting at Mechanicsville occurred. As Porter's troops felt the full force of the Confederate attack at Gaines Mills, Sumner sent two brigades, under Meagher and French, to the support of Fifth Corps. The Second Corps men arrived late in the afternoon of June 27 and were able to help prevent a complete collapse of the Union front. By Saturday, June 28, the movement to the James had commenced in earnest and the roads were clogged with wagons carrying the guns of the siege train, supplies of all kinds and hundreds of sick and wounded troops.[19] By the evening of June 28, Sumner's remaining troops had received orders to pack up and prepare to move down the rail line toward Savage Station and protect the roads providing the intended line of march to the James River through White Oak Swamp. It was at this point that the men of the Tammany regiment joined the Seven Days battles as the rear guard of Second Corps.

Fortunately, we have several firsthand accounts of the activities of the Tammany regiment during this period. Unfortunately, each of the accounts concentrates on certain activities rather than the total picture so while many details are available it is for certain that gaps exist.

Eugene Sullivan, in his January 1907 article in the National Tribune went into deep detail on the activities around Grapevine Bridge and the subsequent movement of the regiment to Savage Station. He said: "The rear guard of an army on the march ... is never a pleasing detail. If the army be on the advance the stragglers must be kept up as well as possible with

---

[19] OR: S1, V11, 272-274. Report of Colonel Robert O. Tyler, First Connecticut Heavy Artillery, commanding siege train, July 15, 1862. In his report Colonel Tyler states that twenty-five of the twenty-six heavy guns of the siege train that had been unloaded from shipping were successfully moved to the James River overland. The only gun lost was a howitzer, left unserviceable at Savage Station. He also states that it was only on June 29th that the last heavy gun made it through White Oak Swamp joining those that had started earlier from their depot at Fair Oaks Station.

their commands, causing the rear guard to lose time which must be made up ... usually by double-quick ... If the army be on the retreat rearguard duty at once becomes both embarrassing and dangerous ... Knowing that the safety of the troops ahead depends in a measure on the conduct of the rearguard, that guard must always be on the alert ready to throw itself between the enemy and the retreating column." Sullivan's account describes how the Tammany regiment left Fair Oaks Station and crossed over Grapevine Bridge to the north side of the Chickahominy and that once on the north side was ordered to stop while the other regiments of the brigade continued on the march. At that time three companies, E, K and I, all under the command of Captain William O'Shea were detailed to destroy the bridge. The remaining seven companies, under the command of Colonel Charles were drawn up in line of battle on the high ground a short distance to the rear of the bridge.[20] According to Sullivan: "As our men were about to sever the last link one of McClellan's aides, at least we supposed him to be, came dashing to us on a spirited horse, which he forced into the river, asking in a loud and commanding voice: "Who is in command here?" Now Captain O'Shea enjoyed a decided impediment in his speech when excited. Eyeing the officer sharply, the Captain said: "I-I-I am in c-c-command". The officer said ... can I get a few pieces of artillery across here? O'Shea looked at him in amazement that he should ask such a question having seen for himself the condition of the bridge,

---

[20] Sullivan, supra. Sullivan is not specific as to the exact location taken by the seven companies not working on destroying Grapevine Bridge but it is reasonably clear that they must have been on the south side of the river. While William O'Shea did obtain the rank of Captain during the war, at the time of the action at Grapevine Bridge he was a Lieut. in company A. Since the account was written in 1904 it would be likely that Sullivan referred to O'Shea by his highest rank rather than the rank at the time of the action. The senior officers in the three companies mentioned by Sullivan were all either sick or otherwise away from their units so it is quite possible that O'Shea was selected by Colonel Charles to oversee the destruction of the bridge because of his prior service as Second Sergeant in Co. E. Command of a force containing three companies would normally fall to the Major or Lieut. Colonel of the regiment. Both Major Bowe and Lieut. Colonel Mooney were present so it is unclear why they did not command instead of O'Shea. Accounting for all ten companies also suggests that any men previously detached to provide security along the rail line had rejoined the regiment.

and the impossibility of getting artillery across, and it made the Captain rather angry, yet amused him too, and he stuttered: "I-I am in com-com-command here to s-s-see that this br-br-bridge is p-p-prop-prop-properly destroyed; b-b-but you c-c-can get artillery across if it be f-f-fly-fly-flying artillery, and ca-ca-can and travel on wings." Giving O'Shea a look of scorn the officer turned and rode back in the direction whence he came and in a little while afterwards Grapevine Bridge was a thing of the past."[21]

According to Sullivan, following the destruction of the bridge the Tammany men double-quick marched to catch up to the rest of the brigade ending up in position with the right of the regiment resting on the left of the railroad embankment about two miles west of Savage Station. About 1 o'clock in the afternoon the lead elements of the attacking Confederate army could be seen marching along the rail line with muskets thrown carelessly thrown over their shoulders. General Sumner ordered artillery to fire on the rail tracks and the right and left wings of the division were thrown forward, the right through the peach orchard and the left through the woods on the left of the railroad. Confederate troops left the tracks, formed on either side and returned fire but shortly fell back in disorder. It wasn't until four in the afternoon that the Tammany regiment was ordered to retreat to Savage Station, again following the bulk of Sedgwick's division.

Sullivan's account of the afternoon action at Savage Station leaves little to the imagination. He said: "Upon our arrival we found two of the brigades of our division in line of battle ... Two regiments of our brigade, the 7th Michigan and the 42nd New York were detached on our right flank parallel with and on the declining slope of the Richmond and York Railroad. The object was to protect our right ... We stood in line of battle with our backs almost squarely to the battlefield while the battle was raging within 25 paces of us, our backs to the foe as well as to our own men. We were not however, long in this position, until we had the enemy to our front as well as our rear. The enemy, with artillery on cars, came down the railroad and opened fire on us at short range, but the concentrated fire of the two regiments made short work of that attack. About dusk a general advance was ordered ... the two regiments were ordered to abut face, and taking position on the right of the brigade, again pushed forward on

---

[21]   Ibid

the enemy, who again gave way, disclosing another line of battle a short distance in their rear. Our men were ordered to lie down and seconds later a shower of bullets passed over our heads, when we were ordered to rise and go forward. Our brigade, which had reserved its fire, was ordered to fire and charge. With a solid volley and fixed bayonets, and with loud cheers, we dashed on the enemy's second line, which yielded and fell into disorder before us. Firing continued until ten P. M. The battle of Savage Station had been fought."[22]

How accurate is Sullivan's account written in 1904? Is it consistent with other accounts of the withdrawal to Savage Station? The only way to know is to look at what reports written closer to the events say happened.

A detailed account of the action between Savage Station and the arrival of the troops at the James River was written by a field reporter for the Irish American newspaper. It reads: " ...At daybreak, on Sunday morning, the works in front were evacuated, the troops falling back in line on the railroad, two miles back. The rear guard was formed by Gen. Sumner's Corps ... The march ... continued ... until the covering corps reached Savage Station. Here the troops were halted, both for the purpose of resting and to complete the destruction of the stores and railroad stock that had to be abandoned. Here, late in the afternoon, the enemy again appeared, with cavalry masking a battery of artillery, and with artillery on both flanks, and large masses of infantry in the rear ... presenting a triple line front of half a mile in extent ... Sedgwick's division formed the center, and maintained its ground well ... The station and all the property that could not be removed, were destroyed by the troops, and a train of cars standing on the track was set on fire and run into the river ... our troops remained in possession of the battlefield till eleven o'clock, when the protecting column resumed its line of march towards the James River. At one o'clock that night, it reached the White Oak Swamp Bridge and at three A.M. the 30th of June, our rear guard, consisting of a squadron of the 6th New York Cavalry, passed over. At five o'clock the bridge over the swamp was blown up." [23]

---

[22] Ibid. Sullivan's account ends with the night of June 29 at Savage Station. If he wrote additional articles they were not found.

[23] Irish American, New York City, July 12, 1862, page 2, columns 3-5.

According to accounts written in the History of the 20th Massachusetts, June 29th was an intensely hot day with a strong thunder shower, many men were sun struck on the march. Most blankets and knapsacks were thrown away. There was a house shaded by tall trees with about fifty tents holding sick and wounded men that had been left behind. Rail cars containing ammunition were on fire and exploding.[24] A New York Times reporter said: "Including the wounded of the battles of Mechanicsville and Gaines' Mill with those of Allen's Farm and Savage Station at least from three to five thousand wounded must have been left in the hands of the rebels."[25]

Savage Station Field Hospital, June 27, 1862, Library of Congress

Private Roland E. Bowen, Fifteenth Massachusetts wrote that the men had the ability to take whatever they could from the mass of supplies and that sugar and dried apples were high on the list. He talked about whiskey running down the hill like a river and tons of ammunition and clothing along with a quantity of old muskets and a long line of railroad cars being destroyed.[26]

In his report, General Dana stated: "At 11 o'clock of the 29th instant I received an order to hasten my command ... down the railroad to Savage Station. I ... detached the Forty-second New York Volunteers about

---

[24]   Twentieth Massachusetts, page 115-6.

[25]   New York Times, July 8, 1862, page 1, column 2.

[26]   Coco, Gregory A., From Ball's Bluff to Gettysburg...and Beyond. The Civil War Letters of Private Roland E. Bowen, page 106.

1,000 yards in the woods to the front, to observe the enemy and resist his approach. This regiment ... lost several men by the enemy's shells ... About the middle of the afternoon ... I was ordered to support the right by two of my regiments, the Seventh Michigan and the Twentieth Massachusetts ... The brigade marched about 10 p.m. across White Oak Swamp."[27]

The above relatively consistent accounts paint a picture of how the Tammany regiment spent Sunday, June 30, 1862. An article appeared in the New York Herald that is apparently based on an interview with Colonel Charles following his wounding at Glendale, capture, parole and return to New York on the steamer Vanderbilt from Fortress Monroe on July 22.[28] The article describes the events surrounding the movement from Fair Oaks Station to Savage Station and then goes into great detail on the retreat to Glendale where the Colonel was wounded in the groin. In part the article states: " ...The pickets of the Forty-second New York regiment were posted three hundred yards in front of the rifle pits ... orders were given to strike the shelter tents ... the secret order was deemed necessary ... as it would disclose to the watchful enemy in front that preparations were in execution for an evacuation of our line ... The troops ... commenced their retrograde movement at daylight, and by six o'clock A.M ... the Forty-second moved out of the fortification ... down the road seven miles to a point where were immense piles of commissary stores being prepared for destruction ... huge piles of goods were saturated with whiskey, to be ready for the final application of the torch ... the flames and smoke circling up in huge volumes to the skies ... The troops moved down to an open clearing called Beardsley's farm, Sumner's right resting on a large hill, while Sedgwick's division ... rested upon the railroad. The troops remained in position for some hours ... Several regiments were immediately deployed as skirmishers, and presently became engaged ... At twelve o'clock the Forty-second regiment was under the shade of a skirt of woods ... and were ordered to move by the left flank down the railroad to Savage Station with further orders to make the best time possible ... At five o'clock P.M., the rebels opened the attack in large force ... which lasted ... until almost dark ... a thunder storm set in ... the troops marched in retreat, for White Oak Swamp ... many of the troops falling by fatigue and hunger, by the

27 OR: S1, V11, 93-95. Report of General Dana, July 5, 1862
28 New York Herald, Interesting From Richmond, July 24, 1862.

roadside. Colonel Charles ... fell twice from his horse, by sheer fatigue, and to prevent a repetition of the act he dismounted and led his horse in order to keep himself awake ... our troops still marched on until they reached the bridge over which they were to pass the White Oak Swamp ... As soon as the last regiment had crossed the bridge was blown up ... The troops were then halted, and a few hours rest allowed ... Between three and four o'clock on Monday ... the march towards the James River was resumed ... At noon ... the pursuing enemy arrived at the point where the bridge was destroyed. Its passage was defended by Franklin's corps; but his force was deemed insufficient for the purpose, and Dana's brigade, which by this time had reached a point four miles beyond, was ordered to the rear over the ground that they had just traversed to assist Franklin ... Our brave soldiers ran four miles in double quick time ... The Forty-second was halted, formed in line of battle and then moved across an open space in the direction of a piece of woods ... The enemy now moved over the hill to meet the Forty-second; our men stood firm, with pieces loaded, ready for the conflict. For a time the enemy were checked, when an unfortunate shot struck the neck of Colonel Charles' horse, through the pommel of the saddle, firmly lodging in the Colonel's groin ... his horse became restive, whirling around with its rider, dashing through the woods and striking against a tree ... The wounded Colonel was supported on his horse and conveyed to Bracket's house and carried in there ... A strong dose of morphine was administered."

A letter was written by Lieut. Colonel Francis Palfrey to Colonel Charles's wife saying: "near the close of the Battle of Glendale your husband rode by me and inquired for a doctor, telling me that he was shot through the thigh and was dying. I did not see him again ... My man William, who knew the Colonel well told me ... he led him to a hospital where the Surgeon of his regiment examined the wound ... My impression is that the Surgeon must have remained with him as he's not rejoined his regiment".[29]

On Tuesday morning Colonel Charles surrendered his sword to Captain John Walter Fairfax, a member of General Longstreet's staff. He was paroled and told to make his way to Richmond as best he could. According to the article referred to above, Colonel Charles was placed in

---

[29] New York Leader, July 19, 1862, page 6, column 6. Letter dated Powhatan Mills, VA, July 8, 1862.

an ambulance on Wednesday, July 2. The wagon reached Richmond on Thursday and after attempts to find accommodations were unsuccessful, Colonel Charles found refuge at the State Prison Hospital, 20 Cary Street (Libby Prison).

The article says that "he was lifted from the wagon by one of the orderly sergeants of his own regiment, who had been made prisoner three weeks previous, by General Stuart in his raid on Tunstall's station." Earlier in this chapter four men were identified as having been captured at Tunstall's, two officers and two enlisted men neither of which was an orderly sergeant. Who could the orderly sergeant have been? There is no current answer to this question.[30]

---

[30]   Author's note: Statements like this one attributed to Colonel Charles can create a puzzle that is both challenging and frustrating. Significant time was spent reviewing documents and files trying to create a detailed roster timeline for all of the possible orderly sergeants that could have been the man referenced. At the time of Stuart's raid on Tunstall's Station there would have been a maximum of ten orderly sergeants (also called first sergeants) in the Tammany regiment. Each company would have had one. There might have been fewer than ten if the spot had not been filled after a casualty or promotion but there could not have been more than ten. Since the two enlisted men and the senior officer captured at the station were from Co. G, it seemed wise to look at Co. G first. John J. Ferguson was mustered in as First Sergeant of Co. G on June 23, 1861. He was promoted to Second Lieut. on August 28, 1862. James Culbert was the First Sergeant of Co. A from May 1, 1862 until his promotion to Sergeant Major on July 1, 1862. Edward Cauvet served as First Sergeant of Co. C from June 1861 until his promotion to Second Lieut. on October 17, 1862. Julian Ellendorff was the First Sergeant of Co. D throughout the Peninsula campaign and until his promotion to Second Lieut. on April 4, 1863. James McConvill held the rank in Co. E from Oct. 21, 1861throughout the war. John Kurnan served as First Sergeant, Co. F from the beginning of the war until he was promoted to Second Lieut. on July 1, 1862. Maurice Fitzharris was First Sergeant of Co. H from Feb.19, 1862 until his promotion to Sergeant Major on August 15, 1862. James J. Monaghan held the position in Co. K during the Peninsula campaign. He became ill and died in the hospital at Frederick, MD on September 29, 1862. Edwin R. Pierce was the First Sergeant of Co. B until his promotion to Second Lieut. on June 1, 1862. On July 1, 1862 John Sharkley was promoted from Second to First Sergeant. Although there is a gap of one month that includes the raid on Tunstall's Station it seems highly unlikely that there would have been an interim promotion. More likely that the position was simply unfilled officially for the month of June, but

Numerous accounts of what had happened during the retreat of the Army of the Potomac to Savage Station, Glendale[31], Malvern Hill and finally to Harrison's Landing were published in New York newspapers. Most were fairly accurate but there were some that provided information on casualties that were incorrect and no doubt caused much agony to family members anxiously seeking information on loved ones in the battle zone. Lieut. Colonel Mooney was incorrectly reported as having been killed.[32] Colonel Charles also was reported as having died following his wounding and capture.[33] Colonel Charles was actually in a Richmond hospital on July 10 and arrived at Fortress Monroe on July 19. He was officially exchanged for Colonel E. C. Cook, thirty-second Tennessee by General Order No. 118 on August 27, 1862.[34]

Looking at the Seven Days battles as a whole the Tammany regiment suffered their largest losses since Ball's Bluff. Five Tammany men were among the casualties at Savage Station. Captured were: Corporal Nickolas Quinn (also wounded) and Richard McAuliffe, Co. H (both Boston men), Bernard Lavery, Jr. Co. A, and Edward Kelly Co. D. Henry Roach, Co. E was wounded. Edward Kelly is sometimes confused with another Edward Kelly, a Boston man in Co. H who served most of the war as a baker and pioneer; however the record of the Co. D man shows he was

---

that Sharkley filled the role in the field. None of the records for these men show that they were captured during any part of the Peninsula campaign. Research has not identified any man holding the rank of orderly sergeant in Co. I in June of 1862. William Hevey held the rank until his promotion in September 1861. Rudolph Knapp was promoted to the rank in January 1863 from his position as Third Sergeant. Joseph Schneider was promoted from Third Sergeant to Second Sergeant in April 1862 and served as a regimental color bearer. Francis Reynolds, who would reach the rank of Captain commanding Company I, was Fifth Sergeant in April 1862. George W. Crandell and Robert Moore served as sergeants in Co. I from the start of the war through 1862 but did not reach the rank of orderly sergeant. None of these men were listed as captured during the Peninsula Campaign. George W. Crandall died in October 1899. New York Times, Oct. 19, 1899.

31   The action at Glendale is also referred to as Nelson's Farm and Frazier's Farm.
32   Irish American, July 12, 1862, page 2, column 3-5.
33   New York Times, July 13, 1862.
34   New York Times, July 19, 1862 and New York Times July 23, 1862, page 3, column 2.

captured at Savage Station. The four captured men were paroled within three months.[35]

Another thirty-nine men were killed, wounded or captured at Glendale. The seven killed were: Co. A: Thomas Dugan, Co. C: John B. Walsh, Co. D: John Diamond and James Roach, Co. G: Jacob N. Bedell, Co. H: James Monahan, (a Boston man) and Co. K: Patrick Riley.

Thirteen were taken prisoner (nine of those captured were also wounded). Wounded and captured: Colonel Edmund Charles, Co. D: William Wilson and John Maher, Co. H: Augustus Bauer and Sgt. Thomas Delaney (a Boston man), Co. I: Corporal William Charlier, Daniel Lane, William McCaully and Andrew Wolf. Captured but not wounded: Surgeon John Q. Osborne, Asstistant Surgeon George Fossard, Co. H: John Smithwick (a Boston man) and Co. I: Daniel McPeek. All were paroled within three months except W. Wilson who died while a prisoner in Richmond.[36]

Nineteen were wounded and avoided capture.[37] Eleven returned to the regiment, five were discharged for disability within six months and two were listed as having deserted from hospitals.[38]

---

[35]   N. Quinn spent many months in hospitals and was transferred to the Invalid Corps in December 1863. McAuliffe, Kelly and Roach returned to the regiment. Lavery's record is unclear but does list him as having deserted following his parole.

[36]   Sgt. Delaney's record is unclear after he spent many months in hospitals. Smithwick and Charlier returned to the regiment. No further record was found for McPeek. The other enlisted men were discharged for disability within six months. Also captured was Mike Walters, servant to Colonel Charles. New York Times, July 24, 1862, page 2, column 2-4. Richmond Dispatch, July 12, 1862, page 3, column 2.

[37]   Wounded: Second Lieut. George H. Smith (slight thigh), Michael Madden (medal of honor winner for action at Mason's Island), John Noonan, John Shoby, Dennis Leary, John Allendorfer, Samuel Ferguson, Barney Flannagan, John Hazlett (severe), Timothy Keenan, John Kelly, Hiram Lippencot, Patrick Murphy (finger), Jackson Ray (slight wound to hand), Conrad Ringold, Patrick Sheehans, Peter Brentzer, Dennis Callahan and John Kemp. New York Times July 12, 1862, page 2, column 3 and individual records.

[38]   On their return to the regiment Jackson Ray served as the officer's cook and H. Lippencott served with the brigade commissary. Timothy Keenan and John

Second Lieut. George H. Smith served from the start of the war. His wound was slight and he remained with the regiment being promoted to First Lieut. on July 1, 1862 and then to Captain on October 24, 1862. His health worsened and on January 1, 1863 he resigned giving chronic rheumatism as the reason.

Surgeon John Q. Osborne was mustered into the regiment on July 17, 1861. On several occasions, early in the war, he made trips to New York carrying money to families following regimental pay days. Following his parole on July 22, 1862 he served in the hospital at Harper's Ferry and in Washington until early 1863. He was discharged for disability by Special Order 194, Adjutant General's Office on April 29, 1863 suffering from Chronic Scorbutic Diarrhea.[39] George H. Fossard served as Assistant Surgeon from June 1861. Following his parole in July he returned to the regiment serving until he was dismissed from the service for incompetency by Special Order No. 37, Adjutant General's Office dated January 23, 1863.[40]

Kelly are listed as having deserted while in hospital. No further records were found on C. Ringold.

[39] Dr. Osborne died in January 1868 at his home at 680 Broadway, New York City. He was a bachelor. The settlement of his estate created some complex legal issues ending up in court. New York Times May 6, 1870 and Nov. 18, 1871.

[40] Dr. Fossard served with the 146th New York as Assistant Surgeon from September 22, 1863 through October 17, 1864 when he was discharged to take the position of Surgeon of the 56th New York Infantry. Fossard died in May 1907. At the time of his death he lived at 1013 Putnam Avenue, Brooklyn, New York and was Inspector of Customs at the Barge Office in Manhattan. He was married and had one daughter. Brooklyn Standard Union, May 4, 1907.

Asst. Surgeon George H. Fossard, USMHI

During the war three additional men served as surgeons in the Tammany regiment. William Burr was mustered in as Surgeon on May 22, 1863 filling the opening created by Osborne's discharge. He had served previously as the Assistant Surgeon of the fifty-ninth New York. George B. Parker joined the regiment on September 3, 1862 as Assistant Surgeon. He served just about a year resigning on August 12, 1863 to accept an appointment in the U. S. Volunteers. Parker was nominated for a promotion to Lieut. Colonel by brevet on January 15, 1866.[41] Platt R. H. Sawyer joined the regiment as Assistant Surgeon on March 1, 1863. He served on special duty with the Nineteenth Massachusetts during December 1863 and with divisional hospitals in February and March of 1864[42]. In addition to the Surgeons and Assistant Surgeons there was

---

[41]   Parker's file shows that he was Surgeon in charge at Hospital No. 2, Annapolis Maryland from August 1863 to May 1864. Brevet promotion: Journal of the executive proceedings of the Senate of the United States, January 15, 1866.

[42]   Special Order 205, Headquarters 2d Division, 2d Corps, November 24, 1863. Special Order 28, 2d Corps, Feb. 10, 1864. Reported as wounded in DC hospital: New York Military Museum document page 12. In 1881 Dr. Sawyer was living in Bedford, New York. New York Times October 29, 1881.

a regimental Hospital Steward. The position was held by Hugh Dinnin throughout the war.[43]

The retreat from Fair Oaks was accomplished. The men of the Tammany regiment along with the rest of the Army of the Potomac continued the move to Harrison's Landing and the James River passing through Malvern Hill.

---

[43] Born in Ireland he was by occupation a plumber. Dinnin was a very active member of the regimental veteran's association after the war. He died on July 23, 1895. His obituary says: "at the close of the war he returned to this city, married, and again conducted a plumbing business...Almost as fast as he made money it slipped through his hands...He died in poverty...On the left upper corner of the door was a foot-square, black tin sign..." High Positions are Like the Summit of Steep Rocks-Eagles and Reptiles Alone can Reach Them"." New York Times, July 24, 1895.

Chapter Nine

HARRISON'S LANDING WITHDRAWAL FROM THE PENINSULA

As the Army of the Potomac poured into the area southeast of Malvern Hill on July 2, General McClellan had already finalized the new location to be occupied by his army as a region of land bordering on the James River surrounding Berkeley Plantation. The original mansion at Berkeley had been built in 1726. One of the early owners of the plantation was Benjamin Harrison, a signer of the Declaration of Independence and father of William Henry "Tippecanoe" Harrison, who in 1841 became the ninth President of the United States. Benjamin was also the great grandfather of Benjamin Harrison, the twenty-third President.

McClellan's Headquarters was at the mansion. On July 4, in a letter to President Lincoln, McClellan described the position: "We now occupy a line of heights about two miles from the James, a plain extending from there to the river. Our front is about three miles long. These heights command our whole position, and must be maintained. The gunboats can render valuable support upon both flanks. If the enemy attack us in front we must hold our ground as we best may, and at whatever cost. Our positions can be carried only by overwhelming numbers".[1]

The details behind the establishment of the perimeter of the defensive position had been worked out just the day before and were recorded by Brig. General John G. Barnard in his official report. He said: "On the 3rd

---

[1]   OR: S1, V11, 72

of July the army commenced moving out to more eligible positions ... The left stretched for upwards of a mile along the left bank of Kimage's Creek, which excavated a deep ravine in the table-land through which it flowed, and the lower half of the stream was so deep and marshy as to make an impassable obstacle. In front were cleared fields exposed to the fire of our gunboats, while on our own side were woods, which covered our movements and concealed our positions. From near the head of the creek the line turned at right angles and stretched three-quarters of a mile to the eastward, on the mill pond, the line was resumed, ran easterly through the woods about half a mile, and then southeasterly a mile and a quarter through the cultivated fields of Westover, and then southerly a half mile to a point on Herring Creek, near Westover Church. It will be seen that of this line, 4 miles long, that portion on Kimage's Creek was naturally very strong, and with the aid of the flanking fire of the gunboats might throughout be considered (with proper defensive arrangements) unassailable, and that portion of the line parallel to James River the mill pond covered nearly a mile of front, so that it could not be assailed, and that the half mile of line constituting our right flank and the approaches thereto by the Charles City Road were flanked by the fire of our gunboats".[2]

The James River's northern bank, heading south from just below Turkey Creek near Malvern Hill, passed Haxall's Landing and Shirley Plantation, the home of Robert E. Lee's mother, before it curved to the east at Eppe's Island. From that point it ran mainly east; pass Harrison's Point, Berkeley Landing and Westover Landing. Kimage's Creek was located west of Harrison's Point and ran north to a point about due west of Shirley Plantation. Herring Creek was located to the east of Westover Landing not far from a place called Wilcox's Wharf and ran northwest to where it had been dammed at Rowland's Mill, creating Rowland's Mill Pond.

As Union troops arrived on July 2, confusion was common and the Tammany regiment was no exception. James Jackson, Co. B fell behind and was captured.[3] William Curran, Jacob Beer, Philip Coyle and James

---

2   OR: S1, V11, 122

3   James Jackson was born in Scotland and was a shoemaker by trade. Following his parole in September 1862 he spent many months in various hospitals. His records contain numerous references to his being considered a deserter, however all charges were dropped against him in 1864.

Scott, all from Co. B, also struggled on the march and became separated from the rest of the regiment.[4] Thomas Dempsey, Co. A, had been left sick at Savage Station but had avoided capture and made his way to the landing.[5]

Captain Joseph W. Tobin, commander of Co. F was captured at Bottom's Bridge, near where the railroad crossed the Chickahominy, on July 1. The circumstances surrounding his capture are not clear but it is reasonable to assume that he was somehow separated from the rest of the regiment in their retreat toward Harrison's Landing. Tobin was paroled on August 12 along with the officers that had been captured at Tunstall's Station.

Eventually order was established and commands were assigned to positions within the defensive perimeter. The bulk of the heavy artillery was camped around the landing at Berkeley. V Corps was assigned positions on the eastern side of the line behind Herring Creek; VI, III and IV Corps were assigned to areas on the northern edge of the perimeter with IV Corps the most westerly of the group. II Corps was along Kimage's Creek, connecting with IV Corps with Sedgwick closest to the creek and Richardson between Sedgwick and Berkeley Plantation.[6]

Part of Jeb Stuart's cavalry command was in pursuit of the retreating Union army. On July 2, Lieut. Colonel W. T. Martin, commanding the Jefferson Davis Mississippi Legion and the Fourth Virginia Cavalry had reached Shirley Plantation and started heading east when he ran into and engaged the Tammany Regiment. In his report he said: " ...I was enabled to open fire unexpectedly upon this regiment, which proved to be the Forty-second New York (or Tammany) Regiment, one of the best, it is said, in the service of the enemy. This force was soon driven in confusion and rapidly toward Berkeley. Our skirmishers had captured three prisoners of

---

[4] Beer was transferred to the Invalid Corps in Oct. 1863. Coyle never returned to the regiment following treatment in various hospitals. Curran and Scott returned to duty. In 1864 Curran, born in Ireland, was captured at Weldon Railroad and died in Andersonville Nov. 15, 1864.

[5] Dempsey was evacuated to Alexandria, VA. His records show him as having deserted at Alexandria on August 17, 1862.

[6] Official Military Atlas of the Civil War, Plate XIII, No. 3, Sketch of the Army of the Potomac at Harrison's Landing, 1862, accompanying report Of General McClellan.

this regiment and killed three. Pursuit was made rapidly as the skirmishers could proceed through the woods. The Tammany Regiment, however, was too fleet for us, and reached the main body of McClellan's army, at Berkeley, before we could overtake it …"[7] The three men taken prisoner might have been: Oramel R. Burdick and William Davis, both from Co. B, and Frederick Kinegar, Co. I.[8] Who the three men mentioned as having been killed were is not clear. One might have been Timothy Hanly, Co. E. He had been shot through the body by the James River (exact date unknown) and was eventually evacuated on the Spaulding, arriving in Philadelphia on August 9.[9]

While the Confederacy would continue to harass the Union force at Harrison's Landing they would not attempt to attack the position. On July 6, Robert E. Lee wrote to President Davis stating: " …These considerations include the opinion that it may be better to leave a small, light force with the cavalry here and retire the army near Richmond, where it can be better refreshed and strengthened, and be prepared for a renewal of the contest, which must take place at some quarter soon. I beg that you will take every practicable means to reinforce our ranks … and which will require to be strengthened to their full extent to be able to compete with the invigorated force of the enemy." [10]

On July 4, McClellan addressed the troops saying: "Soldiers of the Army of the Potomac- Your achievements of the last ten days have illustrated the valor and endurance of the American soldier attacked by superior forces: and without hope of reinforcements you have succeeded in changing your base of operations in a flank movement, always regarded as the most hazardous of military expedients. You have saved all your material, all your trains, and all your guns, except a few lost in battle, taking in return guns and colors from the enemy. Upon your march you have been assailed day after day with desperate fury by men of the same

---

[7]   OR:S1, V11, 531

[8]   Individual men's records and New York Times, August 14, 1862, page 2, column 4-5. All three men were paroled on July 25 and admitted to Chesapeake Hospital at Fortress Monroe on July 26. They were evacuated to area hospitals around DC and never returned to the regiment.

[9]   New York Times, August 14, 1862, page 2, column 1-4.

[10] OR: S1, V11, 635

race and nation, skillfully massed and led. Under every disadvantage of number, and necessarily of position also, you have in every conflict beaten back your foes with enormous slaughter. Your conduct ranks you among the celebrated armies of history. No one will now question that each of you may always with pride say: "I belong to the Army of the Potomac". You have reached the new base complete in organization, and unimpaired in spirit. The enemy may at any time attack you. We are prepared to meet them. I have personally established your lines. Let them come, and we will convert their repulse into a final defeat. Your government is strengthening you with the resources of a great people. On this, our nation's birthday, we declare to our foes, who are rebels against the best interests of mankind, that this army shall enter the capital of the so called confederacy; that our national Constitution shall prevail, and that the Union, which can alone insure internal peace and external security to each State, "must and shall be preserved," cost what it may in time, treasure and blood.[11]

On July 8, President Lincoln arrived at Harrison's Landing to look over the situation. He had to decide whether to withdraw the army entirely from the Peninsula, or, as suggested by McClellan, to remount a drive on Richmond from the new base on the James. Lincoln returned to Washington and conferred with General Halleck, General Chief of the Armies. Ultimately, on August 3, the decision was made to withdraw McClellan's army and unite it with General Pope's command.[12]

The men of the army spent the month between arriving at Harrison's Landing and the decision to leave the Peninsula doing what soldiers always do. Parades were frequent and sometimes elaborate. Unfortunately, large numbers of men were sick with a variety of diseases that would kill many of them either before they left the Peninsula or soon thereafter. Conditions in the camp were terrible. Surgeon Jonathan Letterman, Medical Director of the Army of the Potomac described the situation in his official report by saying: " ...The army when it reached Harrison's Landing was greatly exhausted. The malaria from the borders of the Chickahominy and from the swamps throughout the Peninsula to which it had been so freely exposed now began to manifest its baneful effects on the health of the men ... The labors of the troops had been excessive ... They were called

---

[11]   New York Irish American, July 12, 1862, page 2, column 6.
[12]   OR: S1, V11, 80

upon to subsist on a scanty supply of food … They had little time for sleep, and even when the chance presented itself it was to lie in the rain or mud … Scurvy had made its appearance … It was impossible to obtain proper reports of the number of the sick in the army when it reached Harrison's Landing … After about 6,000 had been sent away on the transports 12,795 remained."[13]

The Tammany Regiment lost four men to disease while at Harrison's Landing. James McKibbin, Co. I, and Thomas Woods, Co. E, died on July 14. Woods is buried at Glendale National Cemetery, Grave C-20. Patrick Smith, Co. D, died on July 21 from Typhoid Fever and on August 5, Edward Cleary, Co. A, passed away. Cleary had been paroled in February after being imprisoned for four months following Ball's Bluff. Hugh Gilchrist, Co. C, another Ball's Bluff prisoner, also died from disease but at the Annapolis, MD hospital on July 20. Disease took Edward Connolly, Co. D, in New York City on July 14 and Michael Trainor, Co. B, on June 28 near Brandy Station, Virginia.

Many other Tammany men were sick or wounded and some had to be transported to various hospitals by ship. Captain William A. Lynch, Co. K, was taken to Washington D. C. on July 1 aboard the 365-ton steamer Commodore, General McClellan's flagship before it was converted to hospital duty, and was admitted to Judicial Square Hospital on July 10 with Typhoid.[14] John Donovan, Co. B was also on the Commodore. First Lieut. Henry L. Twiggs, Co. E, (sick) and Josiah Stout, Co. G, (kidney disease), left on the steamer John Brooks to Annapolis, July 2.[15] On July 4, the steamers Vanderbuilt and Louistana arrived in Washington, D. C. On board were Barney Flannegan, Co. C and John Kelly, Co. K, both of who had been wounded at Glendale.[16] John Hazlet, Co. G, also wounded at Glendale, arrived in Philadelphia on August 9 on the St. Marks. The same day the Elm City arrived in Philadelphia carrying five sick Tammany

---

13 OR: S1, V11, 211
14 New York Times, July 10, 1862, page 2, column 1
15 New York Times, July 7, 1862, page 2, column 1 and New York Times, July 11, 1862, page 1, column 5. Twiggs submitted his resignation, based on health reasons, on July 5. His resignation was accepted by SO 30, Middle Department, July 11, 1862.
16 New York Times, July 6, 1862, page 8, column 4.

The Tammany Regiment

men: Thomas Murray, Co. K, Corporal James L. Reedy, Co. D, Corporal Daniel Sullivan, Co. G, and John Anderson (a Boston man) and Dennis Burns, Co. H. Also arriving in Philadelphia sick, on the Spaulding, was Sergeant William Lynch, Co. A. On July 6, the Knickerbocker, an 858 ton side-wheel steamer equipped as a hospital ship, arrived at Old Point near Fortress Monroe carrying band musician Stephen Corbin, Michael Karretts, Co. G, and Henry Roach, Co. E. When the steamer Atlantic reached New York in mid-August it carried a sick Thomas Curley who was sent to a hospital in Newark, New Jersey. Jacob Hecker, Co. C, John H. Mann, Co. B, John Gillan, Co. F and James McCabe, Co. K, were sent to the U.S. General Hospital in Annapolis, MD on September 6, 1862.[17] Of these twenty-one men only five: Captain Lynch and Privates Murray, Roach, Curley and Mann would ever return to action with the regiment.[18]

Six men are listed as having deserted at Harrison's Landing. Company A: Sgt. Edward Cunningham, James Farrell, Peter Snedden and Patrick Ferry. Company D: James Kenneth. Company H: John Hoyne.

Occasionally, rebel activity would flare up and cause concern for the troops. On July 3, General Kimball, leading a brigade of recently arriving men that joined II Corps the previous day, probed the area east of Herring Creek on the extreme right of the Union positions running into a force of enemy supported by four pieces of artillery.[19]

More significant, but still only minor aggravations were attempts by artillery to interfere with and destroy the shipping along the James. On

---

[17] New York Times, August 14, 1862, page 2, column 1-4 and New York Times, July 6, 1862, page 2, column 3. All three men listed as sick. Also, New York Times September 9, 1862, page 2, column 4 and New York Times August 21, 1862, page 3, column 1-2.

[18] John Donovan would recover from his illness sufficiently to serve from September 1, 1862 to December 22, 1863 with the 11th NY Cavalry in positions around Washington. He would eventually be hospitalized with a large ulcer and discharged for disability on February 18, 1864. By March 1863, the other fifteen and Timothy Hanly, were discharged for disability from various hospitals. Discharged for disability in Washington during July were: John Welch and Thomas McDermott, Co. A, Clement Reed and Peter Grew, Co. B, and at Camp Parole, MD Anton Schlessinger, Co. K.

[19] OR: S1, V11, 922

165

July 5, Captain C. W. Squires, First Company, Washington Artillery was ordered to take his four gun battery to a position 100 yards from the river near Wilcox's Wharf just east of Herring Creek where they fired on a Union ship heading towards Harrison's Landing. The next day the force was increased to seven guns and moved about nine miles further east along the riverbank. On the morning of July 8, the guns opened fire on the 263-ton steamer Juniata, causing several casualties and some minor damage to the ship. Later the same day a tugboat towing two transports was taken under fire resulting in the tug cutting free the transports, one of which was sunk and the other damaged by the artillery fire.[20]

The most ambitious attempt to attack the shipping lanes occurred around mid-night on July 31. Lee had ordered a large force of 43 pieces of artillery to move to Coggin's Point on the south bank of the James River across from and midway between Harrison's and Westover Landings. The guns fired about 1,000 rounds into the Union camps and at the nearby shipping. The attack killed 10 and wounded 15 men and several ships were damaged. Fire from Union gunboats forced the artillery to depart. As a result of the action General McClellan ordered a force to cross the river and occupy the point to prevent another incident.[21]

Of great significance was the signing on July 22, of the Dix-Hill Cartel. This agreement between Union General John A. Dix and Confederate General D. H. Hill formalized the parole and exchange of prisoners. It provided an equitable, man for man, exchange based on rank with provisions for substitutions of privates for men of senior ranks. For example, a colonel or navy captain could be exchanged for a man of equal rank or fifteen privates or common seamen. Other key provisions provided for: equal footing for privateers, the process of parole followed by documented exchange, handling of captured civilians such as sutlers, a time of parole to be within ten days of capture, descriptions of tasks not allowed to be performed by paroled but not exchanged men and the selection of Aiken's Landing, VA and Vicksburg, MS as the main places for sending paroled prisoners.[22] For weeks after the signing of the agreement Union shipping was almost entirely dedicated to handling sick and wounded prisoners

---

[20]   OR: S1, V11, 924
[21]   Wise, J. C. "The Long Arm of Lee", 1991, pages 234-5
[22]   OR: S2, V4, 266-8

released from Richmond and Confederate men that were exchanged. According to the Medical Director of the Army of the Potomac, Surgeon Letterman, some 3,845 sick and wounded Union released prisoners were sent north to hospitals in Baltimore, New York and Philadelphia.[23]

In late July Lieut. Colonel Mooney and Major Bowe once again renewed their campaign against the Governor of New York and his policy of appointing men to the officer ranks that, in their opinion, were not the equal of others. On July 31 both Mooney and Bowe wrote letters of resignation. Bowe's was sent to Mooney and Mooney's was sent to General Sedgwick. Mooney's letter, which was essentially the same as Bowe's said: "I regret extremely the necessity of tendering my resignation … but in defense of my reputation and the claims of meritorious non-commissioned officers under my command for consideration and promotion compels me to insist that my resignation be accepted … to take effect immediately. Governor E. D. Morgan … has appointed to this command without recommendation from these Headquarters several Lieutenants from civil life, many of whom, though they had opportunity in our recent contests, have through want of experience, and incapacity shamefully abandoned their proper positions in the presence of the enemy. Recently appointments have been made by the same authority, the appointees arriving lately to take position over brave, and gallant Sergeants, who were distinguished in all the battles in which our regiment has participated … Can a commanding officer fail to see the dispiriting effect it produces upon the whole command; even now the original officers are preparing their resignations, disappointed and aggrieved in consequence of this great injustice to men who under their direct observation have acted nobly and are entitled to the reward suggested. As there is not in my opinion any opportunity to correct this injustice of the Governor of the State of New York, I again, most respectfully, urge the acceptance of this my resignation, in order to be relieved from circumstances so unpleasant and prejudicial to the best interests of our service." Mooney and Bowe had gone too far. General Sedgwick recommended the acceptance of the resignations of Mooney and

---

[23] OR: S1, V11, 211. By the third week of August more than a dozen Tammany men were paroled, including Captain Timothy O'Meara, who had been captured at Ball's Bluff and held hostage until his release on Aug. 17.

Bowe with strong endorsements that were forwarded to General Sumner. On Mooney's request Sedgwick said: "Lieut. Col. Mooney is not in my opinion fit to command a regiment ... and is not ... worthy of being an officer. He has led the young officers into a confederation to resist the authority of the governor." On Bowe's request Sedgwick said: "There is a confederation in the regiment to resist the governor. The Lieut. Colonel and Major have indecently drawn into it most of the company officers, who have sent in their resignations. For this act alone I think he is unworthy of holding a commission of field officer." Both requests were approved by General Sumner and Lieut. Colonel Mooney and Major Bowe were discharged on August 2, 1862 by Army of the Potomac Special Order 223, paragraph 2.[24] The news of Mooney's and Bowe's resignations spread quickly to New York City. A newspaper account of what had happened said: " ...Lieut. Colonel Mooney and Major Bowe tendered their resignations, which were accepted. They have consequently set out for the Empire City. The remainder of the commissioned officers forwarded their resignations but these were not accepted. The General said that the officers had erred in interfering with the "rights" of Gov. Morgan; and that their next offence in that line would be more severely dealt with. So it seems Gov. Morgan is empowered with the "right" to appoint ignorant and pusillanimous striplings over brave and patriotic soldiers, who will doubtless fall a sacrifice on the field, where experience, good judgment and courage would be a means of preserving valuable lives. But Major General Morgan is invested with certain "rights" conflicting with justice, and he will exercise that "right" notwithstanding the feelings of "mere Irishmen."[25]

The resignations of Mooney and Bowe left a gaping hole in the top ranks of the Tammany regiment. Colonel Charles was in New York

---

[24] Records of Lieut. Col. Mooney and Major Bowe. Mooney, the grandson of the original Grand Sachem of the Tammany Society, died in 1897 at the age of 70, leaving no family. He was active in New York City politics for many years after the war holding the position of Assemblyman in 1872 and Alderman in 1885. New York Times, November 16, 1897. Bowe died in 1903 at the age of 71, leaving a wife but no children. New York Times, March 3, 1903.

[25] Irish American, New York, August 23, 1862, page 4, column 4. "The Tammany Regiment" Harrison's Landing, August 9, 1862. It is unclear exactly who wrote this article. It is signed "Erin". Most articles written for the Irish American were done by James Fennessy.

recovering from his wounds and the Lieut. Colonel and Major positions were unfilled. Two immediate appointments were made on August 2. George N. Bomford was promoted from Captain Co. B to Lieut. Colonel and James E. Mallon was named Major by Governor Morgan.

George N. Bomford had been with the regiment from the start and had been promoted to Captain in February 1862. He came from a distinguished military family. His father James Voty Bomford had graduated from West Point in 1832 and served in the Blackhawk, Seminole and Mexican Wars. When the Civil War broke out he was Lieut. Colonel of the Eight U. S. Infantry.[26] George Bomford, his grandfather was one of the first graduates of West Point in 1805.[27]

James E. Mallon was born in Brooklyn, New York September 12, 1836. His older sister Theresa married Edward John Riley who in 1861 was appointed Adjutant of the 40th NY Infantry. By June 1861 the command structure of the 40th NY had changed and Riley was its Colonel. Mallon had served as a Lieut. in the 40th NY, the Mozart regiment, since August 1861.[28] He was wounded at Fair Oaks while serving as an aide to General Kearny with the third division of III Corps. The exact date that Mallon joined the Tammany regiment is unclear. As late as August 20 he was serving as Acting Assistant Adjutant General on General Kearny's staff.[29]

---

[26] James V. Bomford was brevetted Brigadier General, US Regular Army on March 13, 1865. He died January 6, 1892 in New Jersey at the age of 80.

[27] George Bomford is credited with the invention of the Columbiad coastal defense gun. He served as the Chief of Ordnance of the United States Army in 1832. He died in Boston in 1848.

[28] Colonel Riley was injured while serving on the Peninsula and was discharged shortly thereafter. He died in February 1918 at the age of 87. New York Times February 22, 1918. At the start of the Civil War Mallon had been a member of 7th Regiment, New York State National Guard and served with that unit as a private. The Mozart regiment was formed by Fernando Wood, Mayor of New York who in his second term as Mayor in 1861 suggested that New York City secede and declare itself a free city so that it could continue to trade with the south. Wood had been a leading member of Tammany Hall and served as Mayor of New York from 1854 until he was ousted in 1857 after displeasing members of the political machine. He formed Mozart Hall, a rival organization and was re-elected in 1859.

[29] OR: S1, V11, 842. Mallon was aboard the steamer Express on Aug. 20 when he signed General Order No. 44, First Division, III Corps. OR: S1, V51, 748.

A number of other changes took place in early August. Thomas Mallon, the younger brother of James, joined the regiment as Second Lieut. Co. B. Thomas Wright was promoted from Second Sergeant to Second Lieut. Co. G. Captain Samuel Giberson was ordered by General Sumner to take charge of the Corps Ambulance Train and report to the Medical Director, Army of the Potomac.[30] First Lieut. Frederick Skeete was appointed regimental Quartermaster filling the spot previously held by First Lieut. John M. Garland who had been transferred to be Chief of Ambulances on General Sumner's staff.[31] Maurice Fitzharris, one of the Irish Fenians, was promoted to regimental Sergeant Major replacing James Culbert who had held the rank for only six weeks.[32]

Ambulance Train, 1st Division, II Corps, Library of Congress

Kearny was killed at the battle of Ox Hill on September 1, 1862.
[30] SO No. 73, Headquarters, 2nd Corps, August 8, 1862, Camp near James River. Two months later Giberson would be discharged for disability.
[31] SO No. 147, Headquarters, Army of the Potomac, Aug. 2, 1862, Camp near Harrison's Landing, established the regulations for the organization of the ambulance corps and the management of the ambulance trains. OR: S1, V11, 218.
[32] Culbert was reduced to the ranks for drunkenness on August 15, 1862. His promotion to Sergeant Major on July 1 followed the promotion of Patrick Condon, the previous Sergeant Major, who had held the position since March 1862, to Second Lieut.

McClellan would eventually obey Halleck's order to leave the Peninsula, but first he decided to make a reconnaissance back to Malvern Hill to see if the situation had changed and perhaps opportunities existed to advance. On August 5, a force of some 17,000 men under General Hooker was sent to occupy Malvern Hill. The force, which included men from II Corps, reached Malvern Hill, occupied it for a short time, engaged a small force of enemy infantry taking sixty prisoners after strong resistance, remained on picket duty and then returned to Harrison's Landing on August 7.[33] Along the way, two Tammany men were captured on August 8, Louis Schaefle, Co. B and William H. Davis, Co. D.[34]

The evacuation of Harrison's Landing had been going on continually since the Army of the Potomac had arrived. In the early stages priority was given to moving sick and wounded troops to safety. McClellan had been told to make the withdrawal without calling much attention to what was happening. Even his own troops were not to know what the orders were. Halleck's order had read: " ...withdraw your army ... covering the movement the best you can. Its real object and withdrawal should be concealed even from your own officers. Your material and transportation should be removed first ..."[35] The troops were to depart to Aquia Creek to join Pope's army near Washington. McClellan had a problem in that at some point there would be too few troops at the landing. There was a big risk that the Confederates could then over run the base. While there were large numbers of vessels available to McClellan, many of the larger ones were unable to move down the James to the landing and therefore, another plan needed to be implemented if large numbers of troops were to be evacuated quickly. The plan developed by McClellan called for moving infantry by foot away from the landing to points down river that would allow the large ships to pick them up. Sedgwick's Division left the

[33] Lash, Gary G., "History of Edward Baker's California Regiment", Army of the Potomac Series, Butternut and Blue, 2001, page 247.
[34] Richmond Dispatch, August 8, 1862 reported the capture of William H. Davis. William H. is not to be confused with William Davis of Co. B also referred to in this chapter. William H. was paroled on September 13, 1862. He returned to the regiment and served as a teamster with the Quartermaster. Schaefle was paroled the same day and was discharged for disability in early 1863.
[35] OR: S1, V11, 81

landing on August 16, marching roughly six miles from their positions near Kimage's Creek to Charles City Court House on the River Road. On Sunday, August 17, they marched fifteen hours covering sixteen miles to the mouth of the Chickahominy River. The next morning they crossed the river at Barrett's Ferry and marched another five miles before camping for the night. On August 18, they marched through Williamsburg and on August 20, they reached Yorktown. Their march ended in Newport News on Aug. 22 where they waited their turn to board steamers to take them north. On Aug. 25, the Tammany Regiment and the rest of their brigade boarded the steamer Atlantic and headed north.[36]

McClellan's attempt to take Richmond and bring the war to a close was over, ending in defeat. Despite his loss, McClellan had successfully extracted his army when he had come very close to losing it all. Robert E. Lee had risen to the eminent position that he would maintain throughout the rest of the war even though he had not inflicted the degree of damage to the Army of the Potomac that he had wished to. He had chased the enemy away from the gates of Richmond and the Confederacy could breathe a bit easier and plan what would happen next.

---

[36] Twentieth Massachusetts, 140-143. Some of the teamsters, including Frank Kennedy, Co. G, who served as the cook for the teamsters of the regiment temporarily remained behind with the teams. Along the march eight men were reported to have deserted: Co. B: Thomas Carroll; Co. C: James Moore, John Hanlon, Francis J. Campbell and Wagoner Patrick Daly; Co. F: William Matthews and Patrick Devine; Co. K: Daniel Sheehan. Michael Quigley, Co. A, who had been in the hospital at Fortress Monroe was discharged for disability on Aug. 20. Other Tammany men in various hospitals on the Peninsula and countless more were ill but not sufficiently to warrant hospitalization. Left at Newport News Hospital: Thomas Coleman, Co. B, serving as a nurse, Thomas Coffee, Co. I, and Patrick Kehoe, Co. G. Left at Yorktown Hospital: James Lynch, Co. A, and James Fallon, Co. H. Eugene Mazzochi, Co. G musician remained behind at an unknown hospital. Many records are incomplete as most of the regiment's books were abandoned for want of transportation during the move to Harrison's Landing. Record Group 94, National Archives, Roll 119.

Chapter Ten

PRELUDE TO ANTIETAM

In Early August, General Jackson crossed the Rapidan River and headed toward Culpepper, VA. He had left the Peninsula in July and moved to Gordonsville. Other Confederate forces joined him and it was Union General Pope, in command of the newly strengthened Army of Virginia that stood between the Confederate advance and Washington. Pope's original command, formed in late June, consisted of the disjointed forces operating under Generals McDowell, Banks and Fremont which became I, II and III Corps of the Army of Virginia. Upon the merger of the Army of Virginia into the Army of the Potomac they became XI, XII and I Corps of McClellan's former command, now under Pope. Additional forces under Burnside had been pulled out of the Carolinas and became the new commands IX Corps. On August 9, Banks engaged Jackson at Cedar Mountain. By August 20, the bulk of Lee's army was across the Rapidan and in the minds of the Union high command, their biggest nightmare; an attack on Washington was looking like a real possibility.[1]

Early August was also when President Lincoln ordered the raising of 300,000 recruits to fill the ranks that had been depleted by the Peninsula Campaign. General Orders No. 99 dated August 9, laid out the details whereby the states would be required to meet quotas set by the War Department for enlistments. If the quotas were not met by voluntary enlistments by August 15, a draft would be conducted to make up any

---

[1]   Swinton, William, Campaigns of the Army of the Potomac, pages 168-78, Blue and Grey Press, 1988

deficiencies. New York's quota was set at 59,705.[2] The short time frame set for responding to General Order 99 caused a flurry of activity but it became clear that insufficient time had been allocated. On August 14, Governor Morgan wrote to Secretary Stanton saying that 30,000 volunteers had been enrolled, in part due to the fear of a draft, and that an equal number could be raised in another three weeks.[3] Additional efforts were ongoing to fill the ranks of old regiments like the 42nd NY. Federal bounty programs that had been paid to all new recruits had recently expired but there was a desire to continue paying bounties to men that volunteered to fill the ranks of existing regiments. Washington asked that the states establish programs that would supplement federal efforts.[4] On August 30, Governor Morgan issued a proclamation that directly responded to Washington's request. It read: " ...I ... offer on behalf of the State a ... bounty of $50 ... to be paid to private soldiers who may enlist to serve three years or the war, to fill up the regiments ... which were in the field before the 2d day of July 1862 and to those only".[5]

From August 21-30 military action was continuous with movements of large numbers of troops by both sides that culminated in the battle known as Second Manassas. Pope was finally outmaneuvered by Jackson and hit hard by Longstreet resulting in a large-scale retreat toward Washington. The Tammany regiment was not engaged at Second Manassas, they were part of the defenses of Washington.[6]

On August 25, as the steamer Atlantic carrying the Tammany Regiment headed north to the Potomac River and Aquia Creek most of the Army of the Potomac had already departed Harrison's Landing and had followed orders to join General Pope. Sumner's II Corps originally had similar orders but on their arrival at Aquia Creek on August 26, instead of unloading and heading toward the Rappahannock, they were ordered to continue by ship to Alexandria.

---

[2] OR: S3, V2, 291-2, OR: S3, V2, 333-5, 342.

[3] OR: S3, V2, 385

[4] OR: S3, V2, 452

[5] New York Times, September 1, 1862, page 8, column 4.

[6] Dennis Downing, the regiment's first Sergeant Major, and brother of Patrick Downing, was captured on August 30 while serving as First Lieut. and Adjutant of the 97th NY. He was paroled at Aiken's Landing on September 24.

At 1:15 in the afternoon on August 27, General McClellan, in Alexandria, sent a message to General Halleck saying: " ...will it not be well to push Sumner's corps here by water as rapidly as possible, to make immediate arrangements for placing the works in front of Washington in an efficient condition of defense! I have no means of knowing the enemy's force between Pope and ourselves ... Should not Burnside take steps at once to evacuate Falmouth and Aquia, at the same time covering the retreat of any of Pope's troop who may fall back in that direction? ... Are we safe in the valley?"[7]

The sense of panic in McClellan's message was shared by most of the high command around Washington. Communications had broken down, command was in a state of disarray and the exact location of the enemy was unknown. In response to McClellan, Halleck ordered II Corps to be positioned at Chain Bridge, near Washington and upriver in the direction of Leesburg.[8] Further communications between Halleck and McClellan refined the II Corps positioning.

On August 29, McClellan suggested: "I had better send a brigade or two of Sumner's to near Tannallytown (north of Georgetown), where ... they can watch both Chain Bridge and Tannallytown ... Would it meet your views to post the rest of Sumner's corps between Arlington and Fort Corcoron?" On August 30, McClellan wrote: "Have ordered Sumner to leave one brigade in vicinity of Chain Bridge, and to move the rest via Columbia Pike on Annandale and Fairfax Court House ... I will also send my only remaining squadron of cavalry with General Sumner. I can do no more. You now have every man in the Army of the Potomac who is within my reach".[9]

The Tammany Regiment and the rest of their brigade were in this last group. In the early morning hours of August 31, they marched into and through Georgetown, crossed the Potomac using the Aqueduct Bridge and reached Fairfax Court House at midnight.[10]

The cavalry mentioned by McClellan was a squadron of the Second U. S. Cavalry commanded by Captain Thomas Hight. It had been sent

---

[7] OR: S1, V12, 689
[8] Second Army Corps, page 89
[9] OR: S1, V11, 101
[10] Twentieth Massachusetts, page 144

ahead of the infantry column by Sumner to scout the area and report on enemy positions. At 11:30 p.m. on August 31, McClellan sent the following message to Halleck: "The squadron of Second Regular Cavalry that I sent with General Sumner was captured ... some three miles from Fairfax Court House ... by Fitzhugh Lee, with 3,000 cavalry and three light batteries ... Pope has no troops on that road ... I fear the total destruction of the army ... The question is the salvation of the country".[11]

Halleck apparently reacted quickly. At 3 p.m. on September 1, General Pope sent a message to Sumner stating: "The reconnoitering party of cavalry which you sent out early yesterday morning under Captain Hight, has ... been captured by the enemy's cavalry. It is essential that your right be carefully watched. I desire you at daylight to push a reconnaissance of not less than one brigade ... to the Little River turnpike and beyond ...". Two hours later Pope sent a second message to Sumner adding: "The reconnaissance is only designed to ascertain whether there is any considerable movement of the enemy's infantry toward our right and rear ... I do not wish any engagement brought on at present on that ground ..."[12]

The nearest troops other than Sumner's were the First Brigade, First Division, VI Corps under Colonel Alfred T. A. Torbert comprising about 1,600 men of the First, Second, Third and Fourth New Jersey regiments. In Torbert's report he comments on the capture of Captain Hight[13] and the brigade of II Corps sent to his location saying: "General Pope ... ordered a brigade, five regiments (Dana's) under command of Colonel Hinks ... to report to me ... None of them arrived until ... September 1, about 8 a.m. when I put two regiments on picket, the others in position, with the right resting on Germantown".[14]

Pope sent two additional messages around noon on September 1. One went to Colonel Torbert ordering his brigade to join the brigade under Hinks at Germantown and the other to Hooker ordering him to Germantown

---

[11]   OR: S1, V11, 103

[12]   OR: S1, V12, 82

[13]   Captain Thomas Hight, Second U. S. Cavalry was exchanged on September 21 for Captain W. W. Roberts, CSA.

[14]   OR: S1, V12, 538

to take command of all the troops in the area.[15] September 1, was also the day of the Battle of Chantilly (Ox Hill) where Union generals Philip Kearny and Isaac Ingalls Stephens were killed.[16] Following the battle the Union forces in the area fell back to the defenses around Washington with Hinks' brigade serving as the rear guard around Germantown.

The brigade saw little action but the Tammany Regiment suffered one casualty. First Lieut. Morgan Doheny, Company I, the son of the regiment's first Lieut. Colonel Michael Doheny, was captured near Chantilly on September 1. He was paroled at Aiken's Landing on either September 24 or October 6 and reported to Camp Parole on Oct. 9.

Interestingly, no other member of the regiment is listed as having been killed, wounded or captured on September 1. What was Doheny doing when he was captured? The answer is not clear. One possible answer is that he might have heard of the death or capture of General Kearny and ventured off to see what actually happened. To be sure Kearny was a familiar and significant figure in New York at the time the Tammany regiment was formed. It is most likely that Kearny had been a close acquaintance of the senior Doheny, who himself was a major figure within the Irish community of New York. While serving during the later battles on the Peninsula, Kearny's command included the 40th NY or Mozart Regiment, a unit formed by former members of Tammany Hall and the unit in which James E. Mallon, appointed on Aug. 2 by the Governor of New York to be the Tammany Major had served before becoming a member of Kearny's staff. At Williamsburg, Kearny had just been promoted to division command from his previous position as commander of First Brigade, First Division, I Corps. His brigade consisted of four New Jersey regiments, the same troops that were under Colonel Torbert when the

---

[15]   OR: S1, V12, 84-5

[16]   Major General Philip Kearney had a long military career including service with the French in Algeria and with Napoleon in Italy and the Crimea. He served in the war with Mexico, losing his left arm at Churubusco. During the Battle of Chantilly he mistakenly rode into a group of the enemy and was shot while trying to escape. His body was returned to Union lines. Major General Isaac I. Stephens was in command of the First Division of IX Corps when he was killed at Chantilly. Born in 1818 in Andover, Massachusetts he had graduated first in his class at West Point in 1839 and had been assigned to the engineers. He served in the Mexican War and was the first Governor of the Washington Territory.

Tammany regiment reached Germantown on September 1. The interest of these men in the fate of their former commander would naturally have been quite high and it is not unreasonable to consider the likelihood that it, combined with the interest as to the fate of James Mallon could have influenced the actions of Lieut. Doheny.[17]

As the tail end of the retreating Union army moved to Washington the Tammany regiment, along with the rest of their brigade, returned to Chain Bridge early on September 3 just after General McClellan had been restored to command of the Army of the Potomac. On the fourth the brigade moved to Tanallytown, north of Washington and bivouacked just about the time Robert E. Lee's troops crossed the Potomac into Maryland. On September 5, the brigade moved to Rockville where they remained until moving to Middlebrook, on the road to Frederick City, September 10. The next day they moved through Clarksburg to Hyattstown and on September 12 they reached Urbana. On September 13, they crossed the Monocacy River and entered Frederick City. In the evening of September 13, McClellan obtained a copy of Robert E. Lee's Special Orders, No. 191 containing all the details on the movement anticipated for the Confederate army. Union plans were adjusted sending the Tammany regiment's brigade toward Boonsborough on September 15, turning off to Centerville into the area around Sharpsburg.

In these three weeks the 42nd NY had lost but a single man to enemy action, Lieut. Doheny, but they had lost quite a few men to other causes. Records show that 19 men left the regiment without authorization between the time they unloaded in Alexandria and when they reached Centerville. Other events thinned the ranks as well. Discharged for disability were: Patrick Malone, Co. D, at Philadelphia and John Murphy, Co. E, at New York City. William Russell, Co. D, William Murray, Co. B, and James Downey, Co. E, died from disease.

---

[17] James E. Mallon was still serving on the staff of General Kearney as they headed back from the Peninsula. On August 20, 1862, more than two weeks after he had been appointed to the position of Major in the Tammany Regiment by the Governor of New York, he issued, in his capacity as Acting Assistant Adjutant General for Kearny, General Order No. 44, Headquarters First Division, III Corps from the steamer Express. OR: S1, V51, 748.

The men were tired. They had marched almost continuously since they left Harrison's Landing and were hardly ready for what was about to unfold on September 17 as they headed into the West Woods after crossing Antietam Creek. Ball's Bluff had been terrible. Glendale had taken its toll. Disease had done a job that Confederate minnie balls could not do. No one could have known what was about to happen at Antietam or how those events would shape the future of the Tammany regiment.

Chapter Eleven

ANTIETAM

As evening fell on September 16, 1862 General McClellan's Army of the Potomac was assembled for a major confrontation with Robert E. Lee. What happened on September 17, around the town of Sharpsburg, MD and along a stream with the name of Antietam Creek has become one of the most written about battles of the Civil War. It is not my intent to cover all aspects of the battle, but rather, to concentrate on those actions that involved the Tammany regiment or had a meaningful effect on their situation. To say that their role was significant is to understate what occurred. Their losses were enormous and the effect of the battle on the regiment was far reaching.

To be able to follow what happened during the battle it is critical to have clarity on the organization of General Sumner's II Corps. The corps had three divisions. The first commanded by Richardson, the second under Sedgwick and the third under French. All together II Corps numbered approximately 19,000 men.

Focusing in on Sedgwick's division there were three brigades, Gorman's first (15MA, 1MN, 34NY, 82NY, 2 companies of MA Sharpshooters), Howard's second (69PA, 71PA, 72PA, 106PA) and Dana's third (19MA, 20MA, 7MI, 42NY, 59NY). The division had two batteries of artillery assigned to it, Woodruff's Battery I, 1st US and Tompkin's Battery A, 1st RI. Both batteries contained six guns.

II Corps had encamped around the town of Keedysville, a little over three miles to the northeast of Sharpsburg. On the evening of September 16, McClellan ordered General Mansfield's XII Corps across Antietam

Creek to support the positions of Hooker's I Corps, already in contact with Confederate units.[1] The same order had Sumner ready II Corps for movement just before daylight on the 19th. Together I, II and XII Corps were to form the northern branch of McClellan's multi-directional attack.

Sumner received the order to move westward across Antietam Creek, toward the positions of I and XII Corps, at 7:20 AM on the 19th. According to his report he moved Sedgwick immediately in three columns, followed by French. Richardson was ordered to wait about an hour until relieved by Morell's division of V Corps.[2]

The delay of Richardson's division was the first of a number of events that had pronounced effect on what was to occur that morning. Sumner was not one to wait for everything to be perfect before he acted. He was also a general that believed his place was in front with the troops doing the fighting. These traits were made quite clear by his aggressive actions at Grapevine Bridge and at the front lines during the battle of Fair Oaks four months earlier, a time when II Corps comprised only two divisions instead of its current three.

Why was Richardson delayed? The answer is in the location of Keedysville in the center of the Union force, with its connections to the supply lines McClellan depended on. Morell had reached Keedysville at five o'clock in the afternoon on September 16 and had relieved Richardson from the position he had held at that time. The Twenty-second Massachusetts, part of Morell's division, was ordered to "fall in" at 8 AM and moved about a mile to relieve Richardson around 8:30 at his location: "on the east side of Antietam Creek on the main road leading to Sharpsburg, and directly opposite the center of the enemy's line, thus filling the interval between the right wing and General Burnside's command, and guarding the main approach from the enemy's position to our train of supplies ... It was necessary to watch this part of our line with the utmost vigilance, lest the enemy should take advantage of the first exhibition of faltering to push upon us a vigorous assault, for the purpose of piercing our center and turning our rear, as well as to capture or destroy our supply trains. Once having penetrated this line, the enemy's passage to our rear could have

---

[1]   OR: S1, V19, 275-6
[2]   Ibid.

been met with but feeble resistance, as there were no reserves to re-enforce or close the gap".[3]

A number of heavy artillery batteries (20-pound Parrott) had been positioned around the area. General Meagher's Irish brigade of Richardson's division (29MA, 63NY, 69NY, 88NY) was positioned directly in front of these heavy batteries on the east side of Antietam Creek just east of the middle bridge on the Keedysville-Sharpsburg Pike.[4] McClellan would always look after his artillery; he would not risk the loss of these heavy batteries. Just look at the extent he went to in saving the siege train on the Peninsula.

So the reasons for requiring Richardson to be relieved before moving are quite clear. What is not clear is why Morell's division was not alerted earlier, or if they had been why they did not reach Richardson before 8:30? McClellan certainly knew the situation. His headquarters were located at the Pry House, just about a mile to the southwest of Keedysville, quite close to where Richardson was. Signal stations were located all over the area and communications were excellent. Regardless of the reason, the delay of Richardson separated Sumner from one-third of his strength; forces that could well have been used later in the morning.

As Sedgwick moved out, Dana reported that his brigade made up the center column and that the first and second brigades were on his right and left respectively. The formation crossed Antietam Creek at Pry Mill's Ford and headed west. After moving about a mile to the west the formation was shifted to face the direction of the Hagerstown Pike and what has become the famous East Woods, in three lines: first brigade in the front line, third brigade in the middle and second brigade in the rear. A distance of about 50-75 yards separated the lines. What the exact distance was between the lines is hard to pinpoint but it is clear that it was not very much and the formation was extremely tight. Sedgwick took his position between the first and second line along with Sumner who, as would be expected, chose to be with the lead division in the attack.[5]

---

3   Parker, History of the Twenty-second Massachusetts, pages 189-191.
4   OR: S1, V19, 53-65 and 205-207. The batteries were those of Taft, Langner, Von Kleiser and Wever. Each had 4 20-pound Parrot rifles. Also, Priest, Antietam, page 8.
5   OR: S1, V19, 319-21

One report by General Francis Walker, Assistant Adjutant General of II Corps, lists the regiments in the three lines as follows from left to right: Gorman's brigade: 34NY, 15MA, 82NY, 1MN; Dana's brigade: 20MA, 59NY, 7MI, 42NY, 19MA; Howard's brigade: 72PA, 69PA, 106PA, 71PA.[6]

A major question that needs an answer is whether the order of the units, especially in Dana's brigade, listed by Walker is accurate? Dana's report listed the regiments from right to left as: 19MA, 20MA, 59NY, 42NY, 7MI.[7] The two listings agree only on the position of the 19MA on the extreme right. It is the opinion of this author that Dana's report is the correct one. As will be seen shortly, Dana includes in his report details of the battle that fixes the position of the 7MI and 42NY. Dana was with them as the battle unfolded. Should additional evidence be needed one has only to look at the report of Colonel J. Suiter of the 34NY. There is full agreement that the 34NY was on the extreme left of the first rank or Gorman's brigade. In his report he states: "Arriving near the battlefield, we were moved by the right flank through a piece of timber land ... At this point we were considerably crowded, the Seventh Regiment Michigan Volunteers being crowded in my ranks, causing considerable confusion".[8] For the 34NY to have been so close to the 7MI is consistent with the location of the regiments in Dana's report and would be inconsistent with Walker's listings, which would put the 20MA on the left with the 7MI in the center of Dana's brigade.

By the time Sedgwick was approaching the East Woods the battle had been going on for several hours. The troops under Hooker and Mansfield had been heavily engaged and suffered severe casualties in and all around the East and West Woods, the nearby cornfield and the open spaces between the wooded areas. Both Hooker and Mansfield had been wounded, Mansfield mortally. The three lines of Sedgwick's troops advanced through the East Woods, crossed the corn field and the Hagerstown Pike north of Dunker Church and entered the West Woods, all the time under the fire of Confederate artillery from the heights to the west and northwest. Upon clearing the West Woods additional musket fire greeted the tightly grouped

[6]   Second Army Corps, page 101. This listing was written in 1887.
[7]   OR: S1, V19, 319-21
[8]   OR: S1, V19, 315-6

formation. Because of the limited space between ranks many men could not fire without fear of hitting their comrades. Some friendly fire did occur resulting in additional casualties. The left side of the Union formation was turned resulting in chaos, with the 7MI and Tammany regiments bearing the brunt of the force within Dana's brigade. General Dana was wounded and turned command over to Colonel Hall of the 7MI as he was carried from the field. Generals Sedgwick and Sumner personally tried to restore order to the left side of the formation. Sedgwick was wounded and had to turn command of the division over to Howard. Eventually, the division retired to the northeast and rallied sufficiently, with the support of their two batteries of artillery, to stabilize the line and deny further advances to the enemy.

Sumner's choice of where he would be and his actions during the battle directly affected the ability of II Corps to act as a unit. When he left Keedysville, Richardson's division was already separated. By taking a position between the first and second lines of Sedgwick's division, Sumner in effect, was acting as either a brigade or division commander. No one was actually in command of II Corps, that is, with the ability to coordinate the movements of the three divisions. Sumner should have allowed his experienced division commander, Sedgwick, to do his job while he paid attention to getting the maximum effort out his combined divisions. Had Sumner taken a proper position to the rear of Sedgwick and between Sedgwick and French he would have been able to direct the movements of all three divisions in a more effective manner. Instead, French veered off to the left, exposing the left flank of Sedgwick and Richardson followed French's move to the left.

General Sumner's Staff, Nov. 1862, Library of Congress
Left to right: Capt. W. G. Jones, Aide, Major Lawrence Kip,
Aide, Lt. Col. Joseph Taylor, Chief of Staff, General Sumner,
Capt. John M. Garland, Tammany Regiment, Chief of
Ambulances, Capt. Samuel Sumner, Aide (bent right leg), Lieut.
Alonso Cushing, Topographical Engineer, Lt. Col. William
Teall, Chief Commissary (son in law of Gen. Sumner)

To his credit, General Sumner did dispatch his son and aide, Captain S.S. Sumner to General French. According to French's report: "Captain Sumner communicated to me, from the general commanding the corps, that his right divisions were being severely handled, and directed me to press the enemy with all my force".[9] French attacked, but not in a direction that would have aided Sedgwick. Sedgwick and his brigade commanders could have taken actions that would have prevented the surprise that developed on the left. Where were the skirmishers or pickets that normally were posted to establish connections with supporting elements? None were posted. The division advanced totally exposed.

Unfortunately, there are no official reports by members of the Tammany regiment. We do however have a report sent to the Irish American Newspaper by Fennessy covering the battle. He wrote: "Ere the boom of the first gun was heard on the memorable 17th September, the

---

9   OR: S1, V19, 323-4

"Tammany" was under arms, and fully prepared for the conflict, each man being previously served with eighty rounds of ammunition. Between us … and the enemy's chosen position in the woods and heights beyond, runs a deep, narrow stream, known as Antietam Creek, from which the battle takes its name, and which the regiment, with all the others of the division, forded. Scarcely had the last battalion of the division crossed the stream than line of brigade was formed … In rear of these two lines of glimmering steel was another no less formidable, namely-Burn's brigade … Here, then, advancing in three lines, could be observed the flower of the Army of the Peninsula- one of the most, if not the most, distinguished division of McClellan's army, commanded by a gallant General. When the command, "Fix bayonets, forward, double quick" was given, cheer after cheer, from both officers and men; rent the air that almost drowned the sound of the artillery. In vain did the enemy essay to check our advance by shelling us, the deadly missiles falling thick and fast between the brigade lines, sub soiled the field, and slivered fence rails to atoms, but doing no other injury. As the advance was executed in double quick across the Creek, through lots, woodland, and over fences, about thirty of which we had to clear before we came face to face with the rebel masses, it is to be wondered at that the men were exhausted when they arrived at the position where their physical strength was again to undergo a severe test? … But it is for us to obey and for him to command; and while some may condemn what they consider rashness in a General, all must admire the pluck and bravery of a gallant commander. In front of these woods is a cornfield, through which we advanced over the dead and dying there laying in thousands on the field … The contest here was of a desperate character, as the rebels occupied the best position, and were numerically superior in force, besides being well generaled. Each moment saw our ranks decimated with our brave and noble comrades dead and bleeding at our feet. As each battalion of the steadfast enemy was mowed down, its place was filled by another. It was the reverse of this with us. Sedgwick's division had no support. His entire command was engaged at the same time. The regiment on our extreme left, the 34th New York, was forced to fall back, then the enemy gained a position from which they could deliver a cross fire on us, which they did, doing fearful execution to our ranks. The division was then ordered to fall back; and the artillery opened, mowing the rebels down in columns. The last regiment, or rather remnant of a regiment to retire from the woods was the "Tammany", for which Gen. Dana offered, and joined in giving, three hearty cheers for the gallant "Tammany", which was considered a compliment, and was duly received and responded to as Irish soldiers know how. The regiment has passed through many an ordeal, from the slaughter of Ball's Bluff, where some of its best blood bedewed the soil, on the 21ˢᵗ of October 1861, to the recent tremendous battle of Antietam, where 172 of its members were killed and wounded. There were 32 buried in the battlefield, but many have since died of wounds received, and were interred near "Sedgwick's Division Hospital," between Keedysville and Sharpsburg."[10]

A few clarifications need to be made to Fennessy's report. The dead and dying men referred to were mainly from the earlier battles fought by Hooker and Mansfield over the same ground and included both Union and Confederate men. The mention of the position of the 34NY is again consistent with other reports. The statement that the Tammany regiment was the last to leave the field is not accurate. The details relating to casualties suffered by the regiment will be discussed a bit later in this chapter.

Throughout the literature there are numerous references to what happened to the Tammany regiment during the Battle of Antietam. Presented here are selections of comments that either directly mention the Tammany regiment or describe details that provide insight into what happened during those few hours in the morning of September 17.

There is a report of two Tammany men being killed by artillery fire on the evening of September 16. If true, it is most likely that two of the fatalities listed for the main battle are these men.[11]

General Howard's Official Report states that he took command of the division after Sedgwick was wounded, around 11 A.M. He also singled out Major Mallon, Forty-second New York "for his gallantry in rescuing in person his fallen flag under a sharp fire".[12]

General Dana's report discussed earlier contains many additional details. He states: "The division was ordered to advance and I received directions to keep my line about 75 yards in rear of the first line. After

[10] Irish American, New York, October 25, 1862, page 1, column 8.
[11] Lamb, The History of Edward Baker's California Regiment, page 261
[12] OR: S1, V19, 305-8

advancing through fields ... the division entered a piece of woods, on emerging from which another dense woods appeared in front, separated from us by a narrow clear space; and a line of troops lying on the ground, which I took to be the first line, was immediately in my front, and I accordingly halted and ordered my men to lie down, but they were hardly on the ground when I received an order to move forward at the double quick and enter the woods in front ... The first line was hotly engaged in front, and hardly had my left regiment entered the woods when a tremendous musketry fire opened on my left and front, apparently perpendicular to my line of march and flanking the first line. Almost immediately a regiment of infantry came running in great disorder from the woods on my left, and the Seventh Michigan regiment commenced to deliver an oblique fire to the left. There was no time to wait for orders; the flanking force, whatever it was, was advancing its fire too rapidly on my left. I permitted the three right regiments to move on, but broke off the Forty-second New York Volunteers, with orders to change front to the left and meet the attack which had apparently broken through the first line on my left and front and was now precipitated with fury on my left flank. The Forty-second moved nobly to its work, but before it was formed in its new position, and while it was in disorder, the enemy was close up on it, and the fire which was poured upon it and the Seventh Michigan was the most terrific I ever witnessed. I remained with these two regiments, and although the shattered remnants of them were forced by overwhelming numbers and a crossfire to retreat in disorder, I bear them witness that it was after nearly half the officers and men were placed hors de combat ... I desire to express my admiration of the gallant and meritorious conduct of Major Mallon, of the Forty-second New York Volunteers, who was distinguished for coolness and bravery and for his active endeavors to rally and reform the regiment under fire."[13]

Colonel Norman Hall, Commanding the Seventh Michigan, reported on events following the start of the collapse of the left: "While falling back ... I saw General Dana riding slowly to the rear ahead of me ... General Dana was wounded ... he directed that I should take command of the brigade, as I understood. I afterward learned that the general said "This wing of the Brigade." At this time the Seventh Michigan was the

---

[13]   OR: S1, V19, 319-21

only regiment in my sight. The Forty-second New York, after having made quite a successful attempt to rally a few rods in rear of its first position in battle, was broken completely, and its colors carried to the rear by Lieutenant-Colonel Bomford, commanding the regiment. I observed the most efficient and fearless service on the part of Major Mallon, Forty-second New York Volunteers, in keeping the men in ranks under fire, and in gallantly recovering the fallen color from the advancing enemy ... I found Captain Leach, assistant adjutant-general ... to General Dana. Captain Leach ... went in search of the Forty-second and the Fifty-ninth New York Volunteers. A portion of the former was on the road a considerable distance farther to the rear, where it had been ordered to stop fugitives from the battle ... They were ordered to rejoin the brigade ... The Forty-second New York joined me some hours later ... Lieutenant-Colonel Bomford, who had received much injury from a fall, I believe, was taken to hospital ...".[14]

General French, in his report states that he crossed Antietam Creek and when he: "had cleared the ford a mile, the division faced to the left, forming three lines of battle adjacent to and contiguous with Sedgwick".[15] This is confirmed in the report of General N. Kimball who commanded French's First brigade that occupied the third line of the division. Kimball's report reads: "My brigade ... formed line of battle on the left of General Sedgwick's division, and in the third line, Generals Weber and Morris forming the first and second lines".[16] These descriptions place the two divisions together about half way between Antietam Creek and the Hagerstown road. As Sedgwick attacked in a westward direction, French diverged more to the south creating a gap. The exact reason for French's move is not clear. However, if Sumner had been present he should have been able to correct the movement of French.

As the 15MA advanced in the center of Sedgwick's first line it suffered from friendly fire. Lieut. Colonel J. Kimball's report reads: " ...a portion of the 59NY ... had closed upon and commenced firing through my left wing on the enemy. Many of my men were by this maneuver killed by our own forces, and my most strenuous exertions were of no avail either

---

[14]   OR: S1, V19, 321-3
[15]   OR: S1, V19, 323-4
[16]   OR: S1, V19, 326-8

in stopping this murderous fire or in causing the second line to advance to the front. At this juncture General Sumner came up, and his attention was immediately called by myself to this terrible mistake. He immediately rode to the right of the Fifty-ninth regiment, ordered the firing to cease and the line to retire, which order was executed in considerable confusion".[17] While this action by Sumner can be credited with stopping a terrible and unfortunate situation where friends were firing on each other, it also shows that Sumner was so occupied with the details of the action that the big picture was nowhere to be seen. As he rode from hot spot to hot spot no one was in command of II Corps. Clearly, some men were saved by Sumner's actions but many others were to lose their lives and the entire northern prong of the battle would fail.

General Gorman's official report confirms the positioning of his regiments as right to left: 1MN, 82NY, 15MA and 34NY and states the distance between Sedgwick's brigades as about 50 yards. As the lead brigade they passed through the East Woods, across the open fields to the West woods, all the time under artillery fire, and emerged in the clear to encounter the Confederate infantry. Gorman mentions that he encountered a Union force in the woods to his left that was from Crawford's brigade of Mansfield's XII Corps (10ME, 28NY, 46PA, 124PA, 125PA, 128PA). The presence of Union troops on the left of Sedgwick could provide an answer to why French may have thought he was still in contact with Sedgwick as he headed to the left. Gorman's report goes on to say: " …I gave an order, reached no one but Colonel Sully, to move quietly by the right flank so as to unmask the second and third lines, to enable them to direct their fire to check the rapid advance of the enemy on my rear, and to enable them to fire without endangering my left regiment". The 34NY, on the left of Gorman's line had actually drifted to the southwest and become somewhat separated so it is not quite clear if Gorman's reference to "my left regiment" is talking about the 34NY or the 15MA that was next in line on the left and actually did suffer the effects of friendly fire.[18] Colonel Sully, upon hearing the order from General Gorman retired to the right and was joined by the 82NY, and the 19MA from Dana's brigade. These three regiments, forming the northwest corner of Sedgwick's position, fought as a unit for

---

[17] OR: S1, V19, 312-4
[18] OR: S1, V19, 310-2

the rest of the battle.[19] Their movement, coupled with the separation of the 34NY, left the 15MA alone in the front rank of the division.

Both the East and West Woods, "were not like the Peninsula swamp forest, filled with underbrush and creeping vines, black stagnant marsh and stifled air, but open and clear, with large trees and firm ground underneath and spreading branches overhead".[20]

The History of the Twentieth Massachusetts reads: "As our first line stopped when the firing commenced, the lines crowded very closely together. No one in the second or third line could fire a shot. The men of the Twentieth stood leaning on their muskets, and some of the officers commenced smoking. We had remained in this position some minutes, the most advanced one reached, watching the line in front firing and falling, when suddenly the cry was raised, "The enemy is behind us!" There they were, not twenty rods from us, coming in on the left flank, and the regiments there were breaking. Howard's brigade went first and very quickly, while other regiments held their ground or ran away according to their courage and discipline. The Twentieth faced about, but was so crowded in the center of the division that only a few could fire without killing men on our own side ... When the regiments on the left gave way, the enemy poured it upon our rear, and for a time the loss of life was fearful".[21] The references: "crowded in the center of the division" and "when the regiments on our left gave way" add further to the conclusion that the 20MA could not have been on the extreme left of the brigade as suggested by Walker.

The roles played by the two batteries assigned directly to Sedgwick's division provide details that help define what happened. Lieut. Woodruff, commanding Battery I, First US Artillery, reported that he positioned his guns in a clear field about three hundred yards from a woods occupied by the enemy and that at that time the Union infantry had broken and was retreating rapidly. Although he does not identify the infantry regiments it is certain that the units were from the group comprising the 42NY, 7MI, 34NY and the remnants of XII Corps in the area, especially the 125PA. The position he was in was just near the southwest corner of the

---

[19] OR: S1. V19, 314-5
[20] Waitt, History of the Nineteenth Massachusetts, page 136.
[21] Twentieth Massachusetts, page 169-171

East Woods. Woodruff reported that he fired 168 rounds of canister, 75 spherical shot and 27 solid shot for a total of 270 rounds or an average of 45 per gun.[22] Captain John A. Tomkins, commanding Battery A, First Rhode Island Light Artillery reported that he had crossed Antietam Creek on September 16 under orders to support Hooker. The next morning he was put into position near some burning ruins, most likely the Mumma Farm. Around 9AM he performed counter-battery fire and at 9:30 engaged enemy infantry to his right front. He mentions the presence of General French's troops to his left and indicates that he fired in support of their attack. In total Tomkins' Battery fired 1,050 rounds including 83 canister, 67 solid shot, 427 shell and 454 of case shot. On average his guns fired 175 times each during the 2½ hours they were engaged, roughly every fifty seconds.[23]

French's division, in its divergent movement to the south, separated from Sedgwick by more than half a mile as they both met the enemy. Richardson crossed Antietam Creek around 9:30. By the time he had reached the battle area and moved to the left of French, most of Sedgwick's battle had already taken place.[24] II Corps had been committed piecemeal and had suffered the consequences.

Antietam is another battle where Barksdale's Mississippi brigade and the 42NY were in action either directly against each other or in extremely close proximity. What had started at Ball's Bluff almost a year before Antietam would repeat itself again and again throughout the war. There is a report of six of Barksdale's men in pursuit of a flag of a regiment on Sedgwick's left. Just before the Mississippians reached the flag it was picked up by a Yankee and carried across the Hagerstown Pike to safety. Canister from Woodruff's Battery knocked down three of the rebels.[25] Could this be the event surrounding the action of Major Mallon described in the reports of General Dana and Colonel Hall? The timing and unit locations seem right.

By early afternoon the action in the northern part of the battlefield had ended. Soldiers of I, II and XII Corps that had survived the battle

---

[22]   OR: S1, V19, 309-10
[23]   OR: S1, V19, 308-9
[24]   Twentieth Massachusetts, page 169
[25]   Priest, Antietam, The Soldiers Battle, page 150

and their Confederate adversaries regrouped and licked their wounds. Hospitals were full and the bodies of the fallen waiting to be buried were many. Action would continue to the south for the rest of the day and many more would fall on both sides, but for the men of the Tammany regiment the day was over.

Coming up with an exact accounting of the number of Tammany men that were present at Antietam or the number of total casualties is not easy but a close approximation can be made. A good place to start is with the figures presented in Fox's Regimental Losses, Chapter X, as used in the Official Record. In the listing of the 42NY it has a total of 345 men engaged with 35 killed, 127 wounded and 19 missing for a total of 181 casualties (52.5%).

Through examination of a portion of the personal records of members of the regiment and various newspaper and other accounts of the battle, I have identified by name a total of 145 casualties. Included are 43 killed[26], 11 mortally wounded who died shortly after the battle[27], 86 wounded[28]

---

[26] The 43 Tammany men killed at Antietam: Co. A: J. Duffy, J. Eagan, T. McAvoy, J. Norton, Co. B: H. Hull, W. Allen, O. Healy, P. McClafferty, W. Robbins, B. Sharkley, Co. C: Captain C. McPherson, P. Darey, T. Hill, S. Nixon, H. Pardy, C. Parron, C. Sparrows, Co. D: G. Hawksby, M. Gallager, P. Hayes, W. McCue, J. Wilson, Co. E: D. O'Neill, J. Cassidy, T. Dubbins, M, Ringwald, Co. F: First Lieut. S. Dexter, W. Brahaney, T. Connor, Co. G: R. Standiford, M. Burk, J. Carr, M. McConnell, F. Murray, T. O'Keefe, Co. H: First Sergeant J. O'Brien, Co. I: P. Asman, F. Assman, S. Stahek, H. Wiltacher, Co. K: M. Cusack, R. Heany, W. Lee.

[27] The 11 men mortally wounded were: Co. B: J. Roe (died Oct. 30), Co. C. P. Trainor (died Nov. 5), Co. E: C. Donohoe (died September 23, Hoffman House Hospital), R. Crow (died September 19, Hoffman House Hospital), P. Reilly (died Oct. 10, US Hospital Frederick, MD), L. Souvey (died September 22, Franklin's Hospital), Co. F: F. Grawe (died Oct. 10), P. Sullivan (died in December), J. Welsh (died Oct. 7), Co. I: P. Downs (died Oct. 17), A. Winter (died Oct. 4, Frederick, MD).

[28] Wounded were: Staff: Lieut. Colonel Bomford, Co. A: J. Canady, J. Casey, B. Docherty, M. Henratty, J. Kennedy, D. Leary, J. McCarty, W. Rutledge, H. Vickerage, Co. B: J. Kellit, J. Quinn, J. White, S. Wolfer, Co: C: Lieut. S. Cobb, S. Barnett, J. Elsom, J. Craig, J. Gallagher, J. Meyers, J. Shoby, Co. D: First Lieut. P. Cooper, C. Blackburn, J. Brien, R. Cook, T. Dolan, W. Sharkey, Co. E: Captain T. Abbott, First Lieut. Van Voast, First Sergeant J. McConvill,

and 5 who were taken prisoner. I expect that a more thorough examination of the records would identify additional men who were wounded.

Going into action the Tammany regiment was under the command of Lieut. Colonel Bomford[29] as Colonel Edmund Charles was in New York recovering from his wounding and capture on the Peninsula. Second in command was Major Mallon, recently transferred from the 40NY and the staff of General Kearny. The company commanders were: Second Lieut. O'Shea (A), Captain McGrath (B), Captain McPherson (C), First Lieut. Cooper[30] (D), Captain Abbott (E), Captain Tobin (F), First Lieut. R. Wright (G), Second Lieut. Lennon (Uncle Pat H), Captain Downing (I) and Captain Lynch (K). Included in the casualties were: Lieut. Colonel Bomford (w), Captains McPherson (k), Abbott (w), Downing (w) and Lynch (w). Additionally, First Lieutenants Cobb, Co. C, Cooper Co. D, Van Voost, Co. E and T. Wright, Co. K were wounded and First Lieut. Dexter, Co. F was killed. Two First Sergeants, eleven other Sergeants and fifteen Corporals were also included in the casualties. Nineteen of the casualties were former Ball's Bluff prisoners. The five men captured at Antietam were paroled within three weeks.[31]

Only 26 (18%) of the 145 casualties I have specifics on returned to see duty with the regiment again. The majority of the others were discharged

---

J. Joyce, J. Kerns, L. Lynch, J. Malloy, M. McDonogh, M. Reddy, E. Tief, D. Tivenan, Co. F: A. Johnson, P. Lahy, A. Whyte, Co. G: A. Charters, W. Curran, E. Gilbert, M. Maher, A. McKnight, J. McLaughlin, P. Prior, G. Russell, J. Sugar, W. West, Co. H: J. Byron, W. Byrne, J. Conley, B. Dolan, T. Manahan, B. McGovern, A. Mullen, J. Nugent, J. Smithwick (all from Co. H except Conley were Boston men), Co. I: Captain P. Downing, First Lieut F. Reynolds, E. Ahrend, J. Braws, J. Carr, W. Charlier, B. Deary, J. Fitzgerald, M. Gerrin, W. Helffenstein, J. McSweeney, R. Moore, P. Ryan, T. Ryan, J. Vilbert, J. Wollman, R. Woodrich, H. Zuirnau, Co. K: Captain W. Lynch, First Lieut. T. Wright, D. Callaghan, D. Daly, J. Fitzgerald, M. Madden, D. Mahoney, J. Noonan.

29   Bomford's injury was the result of his horse falling on him after being shot. New York Times, October 19, 1862.

30   Cooper's injury was slight-a slight grazing of the skin of the instep of his foot. New York Times, October 19, 1862.

31   Captured were: Corporal James P. Daley, Co. G, (also wounded, previously captured at Tunstall's Station), Edward Flood, Co. A, (also wounded), William McHaney and William Smith, Co. C and Bernard Reynolds (a Boston man), Co. H (also wounded).

for disability at various locations. A few were transferred to the Veteran's Reserves or Invalid Corps and some remained in hospitals until they were mustered out of the service or were transferred to the 82NY when the Tammany regiment was mustered out. Several are listed as having deserted from the hospitals they were recovering in.

To say that Antietam had a tremendous effect on the Tammany regiment is to state the obvious. Roughly every other man became a casualty. The vast majority of these veterans were never to rejoin their comrades. The Tammany regiment had left New York in June 1861 with a full complement of over 1000 soldiers and was now, just 15 months later, a skeleton of itself with only a few more than 200 men.

Chapter Twelve

MOVEMENT TO FREDERICKSBURG

Following the battle at Antietam the surviving troops of II Corps licked their wounds, took care of their dead and wounded and tried to recover from the terrible ordeal in any way they could. Probes by Union forces soon discovered that Lee's army had crossed the river back to Virginia. General Sumner moved his men to Bolivar Heights near Harper's Ferry. On October 9, with General Sumner on leave, command of II Corps was transferred to Major General Darius N. Couch[1]

On October 16, a reconnaissance in force was conducted under General Hancock toward Charlestown, West Virginia. In addition to his own division Hancock was given a strengthened brigade under the command of Colonel William E. Lee, 20th Massachusetts, a former Ball's Bluff prisoner and Schooner Savannah hostage. Lee's command included the 20MA, 7MI, 42NY, 59NY, 1MN, 71PA and 72PA. The 1MN was detached as skirmishers and the 20MA was detached to another brigade leaving Lee with five regiments.

As Lee moved beyond Halltown he was forced to move forward in line of battle and provide support to artillery firing on the enemy. Lee formed in two lines with the 42NY, 7MI and 71PA in front and the two remaining regiments in the rear on the right and left flanks of the line. Movement continued along the road to the suburbs of Charlestown where the 42NY was placed as pickets on the right flank of the town where they remained, without taking any casualties, until withdrawn the next day.

---

[1] Second Army Corps, 127-8. Also SO 274, HQ, Army of the Potomac, Oct. 7, 1862. OR: S1, V19, 400.

The reconnaissance made little contact with the enemy and returned to camp at Bolivar Heights.[2]

On October 30, II Corps left Bolivar Heights and headed south along the eastern side of the Blue Ridge Mountains taking positions at strategic towns protecting various gaps. On November 3, 1862 they were at Snickersville, the next day they camped at Uppersville and on the 6th they moved to Rectortown. On that day General Sumner rejoined the Army of the Potomac but not as commander of II Corps.

General Burnside replaced General McClellan on November 7, just before II Corps reached Warrenton. One of Burnside's first actions was to reorganize the Army into three large units called "Grand Divisions", each comprising two corps. The Right Grand Division under the command of Sumner had II and IX Corps. The Center Grand Division under Hooker was made up of III and IV Corps and the Left Grand Division under Franklin contained I and VI Corps. On the day Burnside took command the Army of the Potomac totaled almost 128,000.[3]

McClellan's departure was impressive. Almost 100,000 men were drawn up in line as he rode past. As he approached each regiment's colors were dipped and the troops presented arms. Artillery fired salvos from the nearby hilltops. Although McClellan had never brought victory to the Army of the Potomac the men he commanded held him in very high regard and had affection for him that would last well beyond his departure.[4]

Burnside decided to move ahead on a plan that required the taking of Fredericksburg and a subsequent strong attack on Richmond. II Corps left Warrenton on November 15, and reached Falmouth, directly across the Rappahannock River from Fredericksburg, in the early afternoon of November 17.

[2]   OR: S1, V19, 95-6
[3]   Second Army Corps, 132-9
[4]   Waitt, Nineteenth Regiment, Massachusetts Volunteers, 158

Captain Ed Cauvet, USMHI, collection of Martin Schoenfeld

Many changes took place within the Tammany Regiment during the time between Antietam and the start of the action at Fredericksburg in mid-December. Replacements for lost company commanders at Antietam were assigned with Ed Cauvet being promoted to Captain, Company C on September 18, replacing Captain McPherson who had been killed in action. On the same day First Lieut. William Hevey was transferred from Company A to take command of Company I and First Lieut. George W. Shaw took over command of Company K filling the gaps created by the wounding of Captains Downing and Lynch. On Oct. 24, George H. Smith was promoted to Captain and took over Company A. In early December First Lieut. Pierce was transferred from Company B to take command of Company E, filling in for the wounded Captain Abbott and First Lieut. Van Voast[5]. Although Lieut. Colonel Bomford had been injured when his horse had been shot out from under him during the action at Antietam he remained with and in functional command of the regiment.

---

[5]   Captain Abbott's wound was a compound fracture of his left thigh bone that resulted in a shortening of his leg by three inches. Letter, January 24, 1863 from A. B. Mott, Surgeon accompanying request for discharge. Abbott was discharged for disability by paragraph 23, SO 402, AGO, September 8, 1863, after being absent from the regiment for over six months. First Lieut. Van Voast was discharged by SO 36, Army of the Potomac, Feb. 19, 1863.

On November 11 and December 10, Lieut. Colonel Bomford made a number of recommendations to the Governor of New York for further promotions to fill openings in the officer ranks of the regiment. Recommended for promotion were: William O'Shea, Patrick H. Lennon (Uncle Pat), Henry Van Voast (who was at the time recovering from his wounds), Maurice Fitzharris, James McConvill, John McGuire, Jullian Ellendorf, John Ferguson and Francis Reynolds.[6]

What prompted this flurry of activity? Each of Bomford's letters starts out with the phrase: "In accordance with instructions received from Headquarters, Army of the Potomac dated Oct. 7, 1862". On that date McClellan received a communication from Washington in which General Halleck said: " ...The Governor of New York wishes a list of officers, non-commissioned officers, and privates, to fill vacancies. He will also call in a few days for officers to take charge of drafted men, to fill old regiments. Have lists made of those who can be spared for that purpose ...".[7]

On October 13, Second Lieut. Patrick Condon was arrested for insolence and drunkenness. On October 19, he wrote a letter to Albany asking for a copy of his commission.[8] He was reduced in rank by Lieut. Colonel Bomford to Sergeant Major on Oct. 31, but refused to accept the demotion. He was further reduced to private on Feb. 7, 1863 and transferred to the ambulance corps as a driver. Condon did not take what happened to him easily. It is quite clear that it bothered him for a long time. Some ten months later, on September 5, 1863, after Bomford had left the regiment, Condon wrote a detailed letter to Major General Meade, Commander of the Army of the Potomac, asking to be reinstated to his rank of Second Lieut. It never happened.

First Lieut. Morgan Doheny requested a discharge on Nov. 20, while he was a paroled prisoner of war, having been captured at Chantilly

---

6 New York State Archives, Series B04-62-84, boxes 33-41, documents 4256, 2596, 3624, 4241 and 15499.

7 OR: S1, V19, 393

8 New York State Archives, Series BO4 document 10940. Condon, a native of County Cork, Ireland, a former soldier in Europe and a stonecutter by trade, had been the First Sergeant of Company K at Ball's Bluff. He had been promoted by Regimental Order 81, dated July 6, 1862 to Second Lieut., with a date of rank of July 1, for his gallant behavior in that battle. At the time of his promotion he was serving as the Sergeant Major of the regiment.

on September 1, 1862 and paroled on September 24. His request was submitted to Lieut. Colonel Sangster, Commander of Paroled Prisoners at Camp Parole, Annapolis, MD. The letter said: "Colonel, I beg leave to tender my resignation as 1st Lieut. in the 42nd Regiment New York State Volunteers. Cause: The recent death of my father has left his family affairs in much confusion and my presence is urgently required that everything may be righted. I have been an officer in the service for more than eighteen months during which time I was not absent one day from my Regiment until I became a paroled prisoner of war and I have not any desire to leave the service now only that a case of absolute necessity requires my doing so. Hoping that it will meet with your approval I am sir, very respectively, your obedient servant, Morgan Doheny, 1st Lieut. 42nd Regiment NY Vol. Paroled prisoner of war." The request was forwarded to Headquarters, 8th Army Corps and on November 21, it was accepted.[9] Looking at the November 20 request in isolation presents a picture that makes sense as far as it goes. However, like so many events in the Civil War there is a lot more to the story.

A quick review of several facts is important to help understand this somewhat complex event. Morgan Doheny was the son of Michael Doheny, the first Lieut. Colonel of the Tammany regiment and a very famous and respected Irish nationalist. He had been used in 1861 as a recruiting officer with the understanding that he would not go to war with the regiment. He died suddenly on April 1, 1862. When Morgan was captured at Chantilly, he was the only member of the regiment to become a casualty of any kind and the circumstances behind his capture are unclear. James Mallon, formally from the Mozart regiment (40NY), a unit formed by dissident members of the Tammany Society, had just been appointed as Major of the 42NY. At the time of Morgan's resignation request, Mallon was still serving in that position and under Lieut. Colonel Bomford. These two men were now in positions previously held by two of the original Irish officers, Lieut. Colonel Mooney and Major Bowe.

There are a number of other facts that will bring what really happened better into focus. On October 17, President Lincoln sent the following note to Secretary of War, Edwin M. Stanton: "Executive Mansion, Washington:

---

[9] Doheny's request was accepted by Major General John Wool and Special Order 162, HQ 8th Army Corps. Baltimore, MD was issued on November 21, 1862.

Today Gen. Corcoron, calls and asks that Morgan Doheny, now a Lieut. in the 42nd New York Vol., may be a Lieutenant in the regular Army. There are special reasons for this, and perhaps the rule might be departed from in so low a place as a 2nd Lieut. I wish to oblige Gen. Corcoron; the Sec. Of War will oblige me if he will find a way to do it. Yours truly, A. Lincoln".[10] On November 10, 1862 Doheny wrote the following letter to President Lincoln. "Washington DC, To his Excellency, Abraham Lincoln, President of the United States, Sir, being unable to get an audience with you and my leave of absence having expired I enclose a letter of introduction from General Corcoron. I understand from the General that you (at his request) had sent my name to the War Department for a Lieutenancy in the Regular Service. If it is not asking too much, I would wish to know what has been done in regards to this matter. Hoping that I have not in any way transgressed by writing to you. I am very respectively your obedient servant. Morgan Doheny, Lt. 42 Reg. NYS vol. Paroled Prisoner of War, Annapolis, MD". Attached to the letter in the presidential files is the note: "Respectfully returned. The application referred to by Lt. Doheny has not been received in this office. James B. Fry, Asst. Adj. General, Nov. 27, 1862".

Less than a week later, on December 3, Morgan sent the following letter to General Corcoron: "Brooklyn, My dear General, I enclose you all the papers in relation to the position you had obtained for me in the Regular Army. Your letter of introduction I sent to him enclosed in another letter written by myself, both of which were this day returned to me from the Adj. General's office in Washington. The papers will explain exactly how the case stands and I submit the same for your consideration. I am now without any position whatever having (as I stated to you in a previous letter) resigned my commission in the 42nd NY Vol. and as it will not do for me to be idle you will confer a great favor by letting me know what course I may pursue. I am General very respectfully, Your obedient servant, Morgan Doheny. Direct to the care of Mr. O'Mahoney, 6 Centre Street."[11]

---

[10]   Letter, A. Lincoln to E. M. Stanton, October 17, 1862. Collected Works of Abraham Lincoln, Volume 5.

[11]   Letter to General Corcoran from Morgan Doheny, December 3, 1862 (sends papers), The Abraham Lincoln Papers at the Library of Congress, Series 1, General Correspondence, 1833-1916. The reference to Mr. O'Mahoney is to John O'Mahoney, the extremely active, Irish nationalist (Fenian) leader.

On February 11, 1863, Governor Seymour of New York wrote a letter to Colonel Charles expressing an interest in reinstating Morgan Doheny in the Tammany Regiment. On March 2, Colonel Charles, from his home in New York City wrote the governor recommending Doheny's restoration of rank.[12] He was reappointed on March 30 and mustered back into the 42NY on April 2, 1863.

It seems likely, from the timing of events, that Doheny was unhappy with his prospects in the 42NY following his parole and sought to find a better position in the regular army, enlisting the help of General Corcoron, an old friend of his father. When the possibility of such a position disappeared further attempts by Corcoron to have the governor of New York reappoint Doheny to his former position were successful. The big question is why was Doheny motivated to leave in the first place? Was it a loss of power of the Irish in the regiment? Unlikely, as Mallon was an Irishman whose parents had come from Ireland. More likely, Doheny felt that the old line, which had a strong allegiance to his father, was being replaced and therefore he may have feared that his future would be uncertain.

On Monday evening, December 15, 1862 Morgan Doheny joined Captains Tobin, McGrath and Downing in New York City to present the original, tattered colors of the regiment to the Tammany Society. An article in the Irish American newspaper described the meeting. " ...A committee of three was appointed. It consisted of the Hon. Elijah Purdy, J. M. Marsh and Sheriff Lynch. These gentlemen were the conductors and introducers of Captain Downing ... addresses of welcome were delivered by the Grand Sachem, the Hon. Nelson J. Waterbury, on behalf of the Society". Captain Downing replied: "I have the honor of being the bearer

---

[12] New York Archives, BO4 document 3280. "Governor: A copy of a letter dated Feb. 11, last has been placed in my hands by Lt. Morgan Doheny, the original of which he states had been forwarded to Headquarters of my Regiment in which you express an interest in his behalf and your willingness to reinstate him in his former position as a 1st Lieut. in my command. Lt. Doheny left the regiment from no fault that I am aware of- I was wounded and a prisoner in Richmond at the time- he has always performed his duties faithfully and I respectfully beg leave to recommend him for restoration, with rank from the date of issue of his commission. I am sir, Edmond Charles, Col. 42nd NY Infantry."

from the officers and men of the Tammany regiment of that which to soldiers is the most cherished and deeply venerated object, next to god and country, the national colors borne by our regiment. It carries with it recollections of the privations and hardships we have undergone since the commencement of the rebellion. It has been present on every field of battle during the Peninsula Campaign and at Ball's Bluff, always, I am proud to relate, with honor to our corps, which our diminished numbers sadly attest. When our regiment first left this city with the devoted and talented Colonel Kennedy, the first who gave his life to the cause, we were eleven hundred; now we are long short of two hundred fighting men. It is this remnant, on behalf of their dead comrades, who now seek a resting place for the emblem which they strove to uphold, in the hearts and custody of the donors, our patrons. It of itself is a proof of the patriotism and devotion of those who have gone, for the bearing of the name of this honorable and patriotic society. They hope that you will receive it for this reason as well that it is the pride of those of us who survive and have preformed our duty and because the memory of our departed comrades hallows every hole and rent of its glorious shreds".[13]

The rolls of the regiment continued to shrink. Nine men died from disease and forty-two were discharged for disability between September 18 and December 13.[14]

Correspondent Private James Fennessy described the arrival of the 42NY in front of Fredericksburg in an article written on December 4 and published on Dec. 20.[15] He said: "There is nothing of moment

---

[13] Irish American, New York, December 13, 1862, page 4, column 8. Also document from the Byron S. Miller Collection, MSA SC 227, Maryland State Archives, Location 00/10/02/34 (numbers 1-7), remarks on presentation of colors of the Tmmany regiment to the Tammany Society.

[14] Men that died from disease were: First Sergeant J. Monaghan, Co. K (Sept. 29) at Frederick, MD, Sergeant W. Smith, Co. C at Newport News on Sept. 25, Henry Ruben, Co. I (Oct. 6) at Fairfax Seminary Hospital, VA, Seventh Corporal Joseph Hartley, Co. C (Oct. 22) at Douglas Hospital, Washington (buried at Soldier's Home Cemetery), George Devoe, Co. F, at Fairfax Hospital (Nov. 6), Corporal George O'Dell, Co. C, in Warrenton, VA (Nov. 11), Benjamin Dowe, Co. C, at Bolivar Heights (Nov. 17), Thomas Ward, Co. D, in Baltimore (Nov. 17) and Thomas Jones, Co. D, in Philadelphia (Dec. 1).

[15] Irish American, New York, Dec. 20, 1862, page 4, column 1-2.

transpiring here, save that the enemy can be seen fortifying his position and going through the general routine of camp duty, in drilling, guarding and picketing. We too, have been observed by him passing through the same maneuvers". Fennessy describes the way the two sides were camped just across the river from each other and how they would try to exchange words. He also described the way the local forests had all been chopped down to provide shelter and called the area a "wild waste of land". The quiet was about to end!

Chapter Thirteen

FREDERICKSBURG

Fredericksburg can be a very complex battle to write about. Much has been written about Lincoln's decision to appoint General Burnside as McClellan's replacement and the President's desire to speed up the Union offensive. With good reason the Union disaster in assaulting Marye's Heights and the terrible losses incurred in that attack have received justified top billing in works that cover the battle. The men of the Tammany regiment were not part of the main assault on Marye's Heights but instead were assigned, along with the rest of their brigade, a different mission which could well have been just as devastating to their ranks.

To fully understand the role of the Tammany regiment in the attack on Fredericksburg it is important to look closely at the timeline of events leading to the attack. Burnside assumed command of the Army of the Potomac on November 7, 1862 and re-organized the Army into three Grand Divisions, one of which, the Right Grand Division, was commanded by Sumner. Second Corps, under Couch and part of Sumner's command, left Warrenton, VA on November 15 reaching Falmouth, directly opposite Fredericksburg across the Rappahannock River, midday on the 17th.[1] Couch's Second Division commanded by O. O. Howard included three brigades, the third of which was led by Colonel Norman J. Hall. It was with Hall's brigade that the Tammany men awaited their orders to attack.

The march to Falmouth covered some 40 miles. Half way through the weather got cold and snowy making the trek more difficult for the men, many of whom had no winter clothing and shoes that were unable

---

[1]   Second Army Corps: 140.

to protect against the wet and cold. It was reported that Sumner wanted to cross the 400 foot wide river immediately, as it was low and looked easily fordable, but he was ordered to encamp and await the arrival of the engineers with their bridging equipment.[2]

To be sure the ordering of the engineers to advance and deploy the necessary bridges has been one of the most controversial aspects of the attack on Fredericksburg. Did Burnside issue the order in a timely way? Was there confusion in Washington regarding the orders for the engineers? Was there a suitable sense of urgency attached to the movement of the engineers? Whatever the answers are to these questions the reality is that the engineers and the necessary equipment did not arrive in Falmouth until November 25, eight days after Sumner.[3]

Fredericksburg, Crossing the Rappahannock, Library of Congress

---

[2] Nineteenth Regiment Massachusetts Volunteers, compiled by E. L. Waitt, Salem Press, Salem Mass. 1906, 159-60. Hereinafter cited as "Nineteenth Mass".

[3] Bridge Building in Wartime, Colonel Wesley Brainerd's Memoir of the Fiftieth New York Engineers, edited by Ed Miles, University of Tennessee Press, Knoxville, 1997, page 97. It is reported here that the order for the movement of the engineers was written on the same day that McClellan was replaced but was somehow not conveyed to the engineering command for about a week. It wasn't until November 16, that the 50th NY Engineers were in full preparation to depart. On November 19, the engineers left Washington.

Streets of Fredericksburg, Library of Congress

More importantly, the actual crossing of the river did not take place until December 11, more than two weeks after the bridging equipment had arrived. What took Burnside so long? Perhaps it was the inability to finalize the locations for the bridges.[4] Bridges were to be built in a number of locations to facilitate the attack. The men of the Tammany regiment were only concerned with the upper spans, those being constructed directly into the city. Attempts by the engineers to construct the spans were thwarted by enemy fire from the city streets. After some hours a plan to cross the river using the pontoon boats to carry infantry was put into motion. The men of the 7th Michigan crossed the Rappahannock first, closely followed by the 20th Massachusetts. Upon reaching the opposite bank these two regiments secured the shoreline allowing the engineers to complete the construction of the bridges. Colonel Hall described the events in his report saying: " ... The moment the bridge was ready the Forty-second and Fifty-ninth New York Volunteers and the One-hundred and twenty-seventh Pennsylvania Volunteers moved across and the Twentieth Massachusetts was formed in column in the street ... Upon attempting to cross the second street, it became evident that the enemy was in considerable force, and could only be dislodged by desperate fighting. It was fast growing dark ... Platoon

---

[4]   Ibid, 98-105

after platoon was swept away, but the head of the column did not falter. Ninety-seven officers and men were killed or wounded in the space of 50 yards ... The Forty-second New York was ordered to advance by a street to the left, but for fear of firing upon our own men, the order was countermanded ... The positions occupied when the firing was ordered to cease were held till late in the night, when it was found that the enemy had retired from the buildings throughout the town. The brigade was relieved at light."[5] The men of Colonel Hall's brigade had fought through the streets of Fredericksburg against Confederate General Barksdale commanding many of the same men that had been at Ball's Bluff.

It wasn't until midday on December 13 that the Tammany regiment and the rest of Hall's brigade once again saw action in the final stages of the attack on Marye's Heights. Hall's report described the afternoon as follows: " ...I was directed to form a second line of battle behind Colonel Owen's brigade, to support General French's attack on the enemy ... I met generals Couch and Hancock. The latter ordered me to charge the rifle pits of the enemy, in column up the road. I formed as broad a column as the street would admit of, and advanced the command, then less than 800 men, to execute the order. But happily, General Couch changed the order after I had gone a short distance, and a line of battle was formed on the right of the road, with directions to charge upon the rifle pits and wall in front of the enemy from that position ... A portion of the Seventh Michigan, Forty-second and Fifty-ninth New York fell back, as did the Nineteenth Massachusetts a moment later. The Twentieth Massachusetts stood firm and returned the fire of the enemy, till I had ... reformed the line and commenced a second advance ... The advance was renewed ... but gave way from the left ... Further attempts to advance were hopeless. I reported that I could hold my position, and was ordered to do so. The remainder of the day, till late at night, was spent under a fire of shell from our own guns as well as those of the enemy ... After mid-night the brigade was relieved ... and withdrew to the city. The Forty-second New York was detailed for picket duty the next day."[6]

Sumner's official report described the events of December 15, saying: " ...there was continuous picket firing, and the enemy was more active

5   OR: S1, V21, 282-4
6   Ibid

than on the previous day with his artillery. On the night of this day orders were received to withdraw the command to the left bank of the Rappahannock. The order was executed quietly and promptly, without loss or confusion ..."[7]

Reviewing the command structure of the Tammany regiment during the action at Fredericksburg helps to paint a picture of what the men who crossed the bridge and fought in the streets must have experienced. Colonel Edmund Charles was in New York recovering from severe wounds. Lieut. Colonel Bomford was with the regiment despite having been slightly injured at Antietam when his horse was shot out from under him. Major Mallon started with the regiment when they left for Falmouth on November 15. On December 9, just two days before the attack, Special Order No. 40, Right Grand Division transferred Mallon to duty as Provost Marshal on General Sumner's staff, leaving Lieut. Colonel Bomford the only senior officer in the field.[8] The company officer ranks were also depleted with only a single company having a Captain in the field that had been in the position more than two months.[9] Despite the appearance of a lack of senior officers it has to be remembered that the regiment had been reduced to an effective strength of less than 200 so the rank and file would have had more than adequate leadership going into battle.

Casualties in the Tammany regiment were quite low compared to many of the other regiments engaged at Fredericksburg. One officer, First Lieut. Thomas Wright, Co. G, and eight men were wounded. Lieut. Wright had been named regimental adjutant in January 1863. Third Sergeant Rudolph Knapp, Co. I, was wounded in the face, through both cheeks. While recovering at Carver General Hospital in Washington he was promoted to First Sergeant in January, 1863. On October 3, 1863 he was discharged

---

7 OR: S1, V21, 218-20

8 NARA: Record of James Mallon. As Provost Marshal, Mallon was responsible for administering activities of sutlers and other civilians and all things related to police and discipline. Craighill, William P. The 1862 Army Officer's Pocket Companion. D. Van Nostrand, 192 Broadway, New York, 1862, 29-31.

9 Captain William Lynch, Co. K had just returned on Oct. 15 after recovering from being wounded at Antietam. Captains George Smith, Co. A, Ed Cauvet, Co. C and Robert C. Wright, Co. G had been promoted on October 24, September 18 and Nov. 1, 1862 respectively. The other six companies were commanded in the field by junior officers.

to accept an appointment as a Hospital Steward in the US Service. Dennis Collins, Co. D, received a GSW to the arm. John Allendorfer, Co. F, was wounded in the leg. He had been wounded previously at Glendale. He and Patrick Walsh, Co. C, spent the rest of the war in various hospitals. Third Sergeant Charles Malloy, Co. C, spent three months in Union Hospital, Georgetown before returning to the regiment. Three Boston men of Co. H were wounded. Phillip Cratton, James Boyce and James Byron all recovered and returned to the regiment.[10] The records of two men: Felix Angus, Co. I and Herbert (aka Albert) Stout, Co. F, show that they were captured at Fredericksburg and paroled shortly thereafter.[11] Most likely they were captured while the regiment was on picket duty as mentioned earlier.

General Sumner's official report speaks highly of a number of members of his staff, as was the usual custom, including "Captain J. M. Garland, the master of ambulances and Major J. E. Mallon, provost marshal".[12] Mallon would be promoted to Colonel of the Tammany regiment in March.

Garland has been mentioned in a number of other chapters but a detailed account of his time with the Tammany regiment best fits here. What follows is quite complex, and certainly open to interpretation. To be sure Garland's story is unique.

---

[10]   NARA: Files of individual men. Also, Irish American, Dec. 20, 1862, page 2.

[11]   Both men were captured on Dec. 19 and paroled on Dec. 20, 1862. Upon their parole they were sent to Camp Parole, Annapolis, MD and carried on the roll of Co. C, 2nd Battalion Paroled Prisoners as authorized by G. O. No: 72, War Dept. June 28, 1862, until their release. F. Angus, age 30, enrolled in May 1861and for awhile held the rank of Corporal. A note in his record says he was sent back to the Army of the Potomac on May 15, 1863. He is listed on the muster roll of U. S.A. Hospital, 65th and Vine Streets, Philadelphia, PA for May-June 1864. Herbert Stout, age 27, enrolled June 8, 1861. He was born in Germany and was a Tarnisher by trade. He is shown as present on the regimental rolls starting in May 1863. He would be captured again in 1864.

[12]   OR: S1, V21, 220

Staff of Gen. George Stoneman, Library of Congress
Captain John M. Garland, Tammany Regiment,
Chief of Ambulances, far left.

John M. Garland had been on the rolls of the Tammany regiment since July 28, 1861, when he enrolled and was mustered in as First Lieut. and Quartermaster, replacing 41 year old William C. Rhodes, in Washington. New York State documents list Garland as 32 years old when enrolled.[13] What else do we know about Garland? We know that on October 23, 1861, he was a member of the party that crossed the Potomac into Virginia under a flag of truce following the action at Ball's Bluff to recover the body of Captain Alden.[14] We know that on Dec. 22, 1861, he wrote a letter to General Stone informing him that Captain Tobin, who was acting in command of the regiment, had improperly provided a sutler use of a government horse despite Garland's refusal of the sutler's request for assistance.[15] We know that Garland was in charge of the Ambulances of II Corps at Antietam and was transferred on November 27, 1862 to take charge of the Ambulance Corps of the Right Grand Division, under

---

13 Documents of the Assembly of the State of New York, 1901, Vol. VI, No: 30, Part 3, Albany, page 963.

14 New York Times, November 13, 1861. (see chapter 3)

15 NARA: File of Joseph Tobin. (see chapter 6)

General Sumner.[16] We know that a request that Garland be assigned to the Ambulance Corps of the Cavalry Corps was made on Feb. 17, 1863, by Medical Director, G. L. Pancoast, in which he says: " ...We need a good intelligent officer in that position and I believe Captain Garland to be such ..." On Feb. 18, Jonathan Letterman, Medical Director of the Army of the Potomac, added his favorable endorsement. Garland was transferred on Feb. 18, 1863 to be commander of the Ambulance Corps of the Cavalry Corps of the Army of the Potomac.[17] It is clear that Letterman thought highly of Garland. In his report detailing the activities of the Medical Department of the Army of the Potomac covering operations between July and November 1862, written on March 1, 1863, Garland is specifically singled out as performing excellent service.[18]

We know that Garland was the son of a Dr. Garland, a slave owner. How do we know that? The official report of Lieut. D. Wonderly, Acting Signal Officer, written December 18, 1862, has the following message being transmitted by telegraph: "Headquarters Second Corps, A Negro, just in from the enemy's lines, states that those in front fell back last night, and that there are but a few men left; that Jackson went to Port Royal. This Negro belongs to Dr. Garland, father of Captain Garland, ambulance corps. The doctor is here, and believes what he says is true. General Kimball gave the alarm. D. N. Couch, Major General."[19] This message provides

---

[16] Special Order No: 24, HQ, II Corps, Falmouth, VA. By order of General Couch. NARA file of J. M. Garland

[17] Special Order No: 49, HQ, Army of the Potomac, Camp near Falmouth, VA. By order of General Hooker. NARA file of J. M. Garland.

[18] OR: S1, V19, 110. In his report on Antietam Letterman says: "The Second Corps was more fully equipped, and did most excellent service under the charge of Capt. J. M. Garland, who labored diligently and with great care until all his wounded were removed." The Ambulance Corps was defined in SO 147, Army of the Potomac, August 2, 1862. OR: S1, V11, 218. The Ambulance Corps of Second Corps would have had a Captain, 2 First Lieut., 7 Second Lieut., 30 Sergeants, and 381 men assigned to ambulance duty with 30 transport carts, 261 two horse ambulances and 90 four horse ambulances. Armstrong, Marion V., Unfurl Those Colors, McClellan, Sumner and the Second Army Corps in the Antietam Campaign, University of Alabama Press, 2008, Chapter 3, page 30.

[19] OR: S1, V21, 165-7.

lots of information but it also raises a number of questions to which answers are not easily provided.

Looking first at the last sentence of the message helps to set the timing of the arrival of the information. General Nathan Kimball was commander of the first brigade, third division, II Corps and on December 12, he crossed the pontoon bridge and formed his brigade in the streets of Fredericksburg. At around noon on December 13, he moved his brigade through the town to engage the enemy in the area of Marye's Heights. During this action Kimball was severely wounded in the thigh and carried from the field.[20] That means that for Kimball to have given the alarm as mentioned in the message the information had to have been provided to him roughly in the twenty-four hour period between midday on the 12th and the 13th. This timing would only be consistent with the phrase: "that those in front fell back last night and that there are but a few men left" if the reference was to Confederates that were in the town, namely those under the command of Barksdale who did "fall back" after dusk on the 12th. Does all this mean that the Negro that "belonged" to Dr. Garland was in Fredericksburg on December 12, gave his information to General Kimball and then crossed the bridge to Second Corps HQ where Dr. Garland was? It does seem likely. What about the phrase: "Jackson went to Port Royal"? One of Jackson's divisions, under D. H. Hill was at Port Royal until December 12 and the rest of Jackson's men had been positioned to support D. H. Hill as late as December 5.[21] Port Royal is about 20 miles from Fredericksburg, in Caroline County, VA. Moss Neck, where Stonewall Jackson spent the winter following the Battle of Fredericksburg, is also in Caroline County. Is it possible that Dr. Garland was from Fredericksburg or the area between Fredericksburg and Port Royal?

Perhaps the biggest question raised by the message is, why was Dr. Garland, a southern slave owner, at the Headquarters of General Couch discussing movements of the Confederate army? The answer seems clear. Like his son, Dr. Garland must have been in sympathy with the North. One doesn't have to look too far to find another relevant example.

Brevet General John Spottswood Garland was born in 1792-3 in Albemarle County, Virginia (not close to Caroline County). He joined

---

[20]   OR: S1, V21, 289-91
[21]   OR: S1, V21, 550-556, Report of Robert E. Lee.

the army and served in the War of 1812. His daughter married James Longstreet in 1848 but that connection did not alter J. S. Garland's dedication to his country.[22] He stayed in the U. S. army until his death. What makes General Garland part of this discussion on J. M. Garland? Perhaps more than is immediately obvious!

Let's first ask another question? How could John M. Garland, a thirty-two year old son of a Virginia slave owner obtain the position of Quartermaster in the Tammany Regiment? Does it seem likely that he just walked into a recruiting office and offered his services in June, 1861? Was there more at work here? If we look deeper into the record of General Garland we find that he had spent a significant amount of time as a Quartermaster. In 1829, Garland was the Quartermaster at Fort Crawford, Wisconsin serving under Major Stephen W. Kearny, the future general, Military Governor of New Mexico and uncle of Major General Philip Kearny, a close associate of many New York politicians. Between 1830 -1845, General Garland's assignments were closely aligned with General E. V. Sumner. He was also close with Major General Thomas Jesup, the twelfth Quartermaster General of the United States. When Jesup, considered the father of the modern Quartermaster Corps, died in 1860, Garland was one of his pall bearers.[23]

Perhaps the most relevant part of General Garland's career was his command of the Eighth U. S. Infantry. At the time of his death in June 1861 he was the commanding officer of the Eighth Infantry stationed in New York City. Two men closely associated with the Tammany regiment are also tied to the Eighth Infantry.

Most importantly, Colonel Milton Cogswell the commander of the Tammany regiment when John M. Garland was appointed Quartermaster had spent significant time in the Eighth.[24] George M. Bomford was First

---

[22] There was another Civil War General named Garland. Samuel Garland served in the Confederacy and was killed at South Mountain in 1862. Samuel Garland was born in Lynchburg, VA. (Not close to Caroline county.). It should be pointed out that the Garland family is one of the oldest in America. There are two main branches called the northern (Massachusetts and New Hampshire) and southern branches (Virginia, North Carolina and Arkansas).

[23] The Evening Star, June 11 and June 14, 1860.

[24] Cogswell was appointed Second Lieut. 8th Inf. Aug. 4, 1849, First Lieut. Aug. 15, 1855 and Captain May 13, 1861.

Lieut. and Adjutant of the Tammany regiment at the time of John M. Garland's appointment as Quartermaster. His father James V. Bomford was the Lieut. Colonel of the Eighth Infantry stationed in Texas when Ft. Sumter was fired on and a prisoner at the time General Garland died.[25]

Is there a definitive connection between the appointment of John M. Garland and General John Garland? No. Is there reason to believe that John M. Garland could have been looked at as a favorable candidate because of some unknown connection to a general with a strong background as a Quartermaster who happened to have been a recent commanding officer of the colonel of the Tammany regiment and was until his recent death the current commanding officer of the father of the adjutant of the Tammany regiment? Yes. Perhaps future research will provide the real answer.

So at this point, you, as a reader, must be about at the end of your attention span in dealing with the complex details of the story of Quartermaster Garland. Please accept my apologies. However, the Garland story is far from over. From what has been presented so far you probably view John M. Garland as a loyal Unionist that performed his duties diligently and was well respected by his superiors. On April 5, 1863, Garland was officially recommended for promotion to Captain, although he had been accepted as holding that rank for quite some time.[26] His career was on the upswing. Right? Wrong!

25   In May 1864, James V. Bomford was named Colonel, 8th U. S. Inf.
26   Letter from Col. Mallon to Brig. Gen. Sprague, Adjutant General, New York. From HQ 42NY near Falmouth, VA. NY State Archives, document 5026.

Post Office, Army of Potomac, Library of Congress

On April 6, 1863, the day after his recommendation for promotion, General Orders, No. 89, War Department, Adjutant General's Office, Washington was issued. That order read:

> "The case of 1st Lieutenant J. M. Garland, 42d New York Volunteers, having been submitted to the Judge Advocate General, the following facts appear from his report, viz: On the 27th of February last a letter was addressed to the Reverend Elliott H. Thompson, Shanghai, China, and deposited in the post office of this city. The stamps upon it, however, amounted to but thirty-six of the ninety cents required to be prepaid, and it was, in consequence, returned to the General Post Office, to be there examined under the regulations, with a view to its restoration to the writer. On opening it, it was found to be from Lieutenant J. M. Garland, of United States Volunteers, and to disclose on his part a state of feeling towards the Administration, and towards the rebels making war upon the Government, which seems to be in complete conflict with the duties imposed upon him by the sword he wears.

After some discussion of political topics, and comments upon current events, Lieutenant Garland says that "the Administration have at last shown their hands, and that their principles and their hearts are blacker than the "n----r" they are fighting for;" and he pronounces the President's proclamation "as unconstitutional as it is unjust". He explains to his friend that, while entertaining these sentiments, he does not resign, though anxious to do so, because "to tender his resignation now would be to ask his disgrace," and for the further reason that recently, at his own request, he had been transferred from the Quartermaster Department to the Ambulance Corps, which he alleges will prevent him "from coming into actual contact with the South" and will enable him, during an action, "to render the same assistance to the other side as well as his own men". He adds: "At Antietam I had the pleasure of bringing from the field a large number of Confederates, among them some of our old friends, all of whom I saw well cared for, and some of whom I have heard from since their return". He further states that when he saw Fredericksburg bombarded "tears ran down his cheeks and he cried like a child." He appears to have found only sorrow in the service, except where enjoying the pleasure of ministering to the comfort of those who had been wounded while stabbing at the life of the country whose commission he held.

It is difficult to conceive of a position of deeper dishonor than that in which this officer has placed himself by the treacherous concealment of his sentiments from the government whose confidence he was enjoying, and upon whose treasury he was living. Although not seeming to realize this self-inflicted degradation himself, he appears to be conscious that it would be realized by others, were his real opinions and feelings become known. Hence he says: "Were it known that these were my sentiments, I would not only be summarily dismissed the service, but probably boarded, at the expense of Uncle Sam, in Fort Lafayette, or some other sea-side prison, for the benefit of my health, until the war is over".

It is entirely certain that no public interest can be safe in the hands of an officer so hostile to the Administration charged with the conduct of the war, and so profoundly sympathizing with the rebels, as Lieutenant Garland has confessed himself to be.

Although up to this time, so far as known, his sympathy has manifested itself only in weeping when one of the enemy's strongholds was bombarded, and in rejoicing when ministering to the wants of wounded rebels, no guaranty exists that at some critical conjuncture in our military movements, this sympathy would not take a more active and manly, and for the government, a far more fatal form of development.

1ˢᵗ Lieutenant J. M. Garland, of the 42d New York Volunteers, is therefore, by direction of the President, dishonorably dismissed the service of the United States. By Order of the Secretary of War: E. D. Townsend, Assistant Adjutant General"

What a shock General Order No. 89 must have been. It appears from the timing of events that the commanding officer of the Tammany regiment had no idea that actions were being contemplated against one of his officers. Would he have recommended Garland for promotion the day before the order was going to be released if he had the slightest knowledge of what was happening?

Looking closely at the details contained in the dismissal order, the letter addressed to Rev. Elliott H. Thompson was written on Feb. 27, nine days after Garland had been appointed to the Cavalry Ambulance Corps. Who was Elliott H. Thompson? As a member of the Protestant Episcopal Church, Thompson served as a missionary to China for more than fifty years. In 1851 he was a "Candidate for Holy Orders" at the 56ᵗʰ Annual Convention of the Episcopal Church held in Staunton, VA.[27] In 1859 he was listed as a Deacon and "Missionary to China" in the Journal of the General Convention of the Church.[28] He is mentioned in numerous additional Church documents, from 1865-1882, referencing his activities at Our Savior Church in Shanghai.[29]

---

[27] Convention held at Trinity Church, May 21-24, 1851. Journal of the 56ᵗʰ Annual Convention of the Protestant Episcopal Church in Virginia, John T. Towers, Vol. 56-63, Washington, 1851, page 29.

[28] Journal of the Proceedings of the Bishops, the Clergy and the Laity of the Protestant Episcopal Church of the United States of America. General Convention, 1859. St. Pauls Church, Richmond, VA, Oct. 5-22, 1859. Philadelphia, King and Baird printers, 607 Sanson Street. 1860. Page 439.

[29] American Quarterly Church Review, Ecclesiastical Register, Vol. XVII, 1865-6, page 672. N. S. Richardson, 37 Bible House, Astor Place, New York, 1866. Also, Journal of the 53ʳᵈ Annual Convention of the Episcopal Church in Ohio, Trinity Church, Columbus, June 6-10, 1870, page 10. Also, Farrington, William G. The Protestant Episcopal Tract Society Church Almanac, Cooper Union, New York,

The dismissal order refers to Thompson as "his friend" and quotes Garland as saying that after Antietam he assisted "Confederates, among them some of our old friends". Since Thompson was clearly a "man of the cloth" it would be helpful to know whether Garland was writing to him merely as a friend or as something more. We don't know when or where Thompson was born but we do know that he was married in 1896 and that he died in 1921.[30] Doing the math tells us that there were about sixty one years from his recorded arrival in Shanghai to his death and eight years before that he had been accepted as a "Candidate for Holy Orders" meaning that he had already been recommended by a Bishop and accepted by the Standing Committee of the Episcopalian Church.[31] The current age requirement for becoming a member of the Holy Orders is 24. Assuming that requirement was in place in the 1850s, Thompson would have been twenty to twenty three years old when he was a Candidate for Holy Orders. That places his birth around 1830. We know that Garland was 32 when he was mustered into the Tammany regiment in mid 1861 so he would have been born about 1829. While the exact dates are unknown it is clear that Garland and Thompson were most likely childhood friends or possibly cousins. The reference to seeing "some of our old friends" is certainly reasonable considering that there were more than forty Virginia regiments at Antietam.

Information provided in the order also suggests that Garland was not a frequent writer to Thompson. In the letter he talks about events that took place as far back as August 1862 when he was transferred to the Ambulance Corps following the Peninsula campaign. So it appears that it had been at least six months since Garland had written his friend in Shanghai.

1873. Also, 98th Convention of the Episcopal Church in Pennsylvania, May 4, 1882. Also, The Churchman, Vol. 99, Jan. 2, 1909, New York. Rev. Dr. Elliott H. Thompson honored for completion of fifty years of continuous service in China.

[30] Religion, Religious Ethics and Nursing edited by Marsh Diane Mary Fowler, Springer Publishing Co. 2012. New York. Chapter 7, Missionary Nursing 139-143. Elizabeth McKechnie, first graduate nurse in China, graduated from Philadelphia Woman's Hospital Dec. 19, 1883, arrived in Shanghai in1884 and twelve years later married Archdeacon E. H. Thompson. She remained in Shanghai until her husband's death in 1921.

[31] Episcopal Church, glossary of terminology.

There is also the issue of the postage. The letter "was deposited in the post office of this city", Washington, and had "thirty-six of the ninety cents required to be prepaid". In 1863 the postage required to send a letter from Washington to Shanghai depended on both the weight of the letter and the chosen route selected to be followed. It was customary for a sender to write the desired route on the envelope so that a postal clerk could be certain that the correct postage was affixed. Without being able to examine and weigh the envelope and letter in question it is only possible to say that both thirty-six and ninety cents were possibilities. If the letter was to be sent by British mail, thirty-six cents would not have been enough regardless of the weight, a minimum of forty-five cents being required. However, if the letter was to be sent using French mail, thirty-six cents would have been sufficient provided the weight were ¼ ounce or less. A ninety cent rate would have been needed if the letter went by French mail and weighed ¾ ounce.[32] It is hard to believe that Garland, an experienced Quartermaster and a man known for his organizational skills would not have known the rules for mailing a letter to Shanghai and taken the time to write the desired route on the envelope and affix the appropriate postage. If the letter had been handed to a postal clerk it would have most likely had any additional required postage added immediately. Was Garland at the post office when the letter was deposited? Had he sent many letters to Shanghai? The answer to both of these questions is likely no.

Details contained in the order tell us a lot about the state of mind of Garland. The Emancipation Proclamation had been issued on January 1, 1863 freeing the slaves in most of Virginia, including the area most likely the home of Garland's family. Could that have really come as a surprise to Garland? He had chosen to be in the Union army. Perhaps he was

---

[32] Authors Note: As a long time member of the American Philatelic Society, I inquired about the postal rates in place in 1863 to China. There was no official rate. The most likely to have been used for this letter were (1) British mail via Southampton that cost 45 cents for the first ¼ oz. and added an additional varying charge for each additional ¼ oz. (2) British mail via Marseille that cost 51 cents for the first ¼ oz. A ½ oz. letter would have cost 57 cents and additional weight added a variable additional cost. (3) French mail cost 30 cents for ¼ oz, 60 cents for ½ oz. with additional cost per ¼ oz. There were also rates that would have routed the mail through Bremen or Hamburg. Those rates were very similar to British mail. E-mail Dr. Charles J. Di Como to F. Wexler, March 3, 2009.

motivated by the preservation of the Union rather than the abolishment of slavery, but surely, he had to have known that slavery was going to be abolished if the North prevailed. He appears to be in a state of depression as he describes the actions at Antietam and Fredericksburg as the war hits home. It seems that he had hit a really low point and was lost as to what to do next. As it turned out a mere fifty-four cents made that decision moot!

So what happened to John M. Garland after he was dismissed from the service? We do know that copies of his dismissal, being a General Order, were distributed far and wide.[33] Interestingly, Major General David Hunter, known for issuing his own Emancipation Proclamation in May 1862, referenced Garland's dismissal in a letter he wrote to President Lincoln on April 25,1863 saying: " ...thank you for ... the order ... dismissing dishonorably Lieut. J. M. Garland ... from the service, which he stood ready to betray whenever opportunity offered ...". The phrase "which he stood ready to betray whenever opportunity offered" is a far cry from what actually is said in the order. It appears that General Hunter had a vivid imagination in fabricating his communications as well as his own authority to issue orders reserved for the President of the United States.[34]

Garland's file contains a letter written on Jan. 27, 1867 from Little Rock Arkansas. It is addressed to Major General E. O. C. Ord, commanding, Department of Arkansas. The letter reads: "General, I have the honor

---

[33] Garland's file has records of the order being received at Ft. Trumbull, CT on April 13, at Fort Halleck, Nebraska Territory on May 23 and at Camp Boise, Idaho Territory on June 11, 1863. New York Times, April 10, 1863 simply listed Lieut. J. M. Garland, Forty-second New York as having been dismissed from the service by order of the President.

[34] OR: S1, V14, 447. On May 9, 1862, General David Hunter issued General Order No. 11, Department of the South. It read: "The three States of Georgia, Florida and South Carolina, comprising the military department of the south, having deliberately declared themselves no longer under the protection of the United States of America, and having taken up arms against the said United States, it becomes a military necessity to declare them under martial law. This was accordingly done on the 25th day of April, 1862. Slavery and martial law in a free country are altogether incompatible; the persons in these three States — Georgia, Florida, and South Carolina— heretofore held as slaves, are therefore declared forever free." General Oder No. 11 was immediately rescinded by President Lincoln. Hunter was a graduate of West Point class of 1822. He had strong anti-slavery views and advocated the enlistment of black soldiers.

to respectfully call your attention to General Orders 89 from War Department, Adjutant General's Office, dated Washington, D. C., April 6, 1863 dismissing John M. Garland as an officer from the United States Service for the utterance of disloyal sentiment against the government he was then serving.

Since that time said Garland was ordered out of the Department of Western Virginia under guard, while an employee of the Quartermaster Department (a fact well known to some of the officers and many of the employees of the QM department here) by order of the Quartermaster General.

The said Garland-contrary to precedent and Orders now disgraces the Service as an employee in the Capacity of Superintendent of Transportation under Lt. Col. A. Montgomery, Chief Quartermaster for this department as the undersigned is most credibly informed.

Believing that the honor of the Service requires an investigation of the circumstances of this case, I remain, Very Respectfully, Your Obt. Servant, John Smith, Late U. S. Army"

The letter has an endorsement saying it was received on January 17, 1867 and "Gen. will anything be done in this matter? The com. is anonymous." It also has an endorsement that reads: "No notice need be taken of this paper. E. O. C. O."

So what does the letter, if we assume that the facts are accurate, tell us about what happened to John M. Garland after his dismissal? The letter fixes Garland as having been working in the Department of Western Virginia prior to being with the Department of Arkansas. The only known date is the date of the letter, January 25, 1867. Therefore, between the dismissal date of April 6, 1863 and January 25, 1867, Garland left Washington, landed a position with the Quartermaster Department most likely in either Cumberland, Maryland, the HQ of the Department of West Virginia or Wheeling, W. Virginia, the major supply base of the department.[35] He was ordered out of the Department of West Virginia, under guard, and eventually made his way to Arkansas.

---

[35]   Captain John G. Farnsworth commanded the Quartermaster Department at Wheeling, WVA, the principal supply base of the department, from Feb. 1864-Nov. 1864. He was Chief Quartermaster of the Department of WVA, based in Cumberland, MD from Nov. 1864 to Sep. 1865. Farnsworth was born in 1832

Since Garland was ordered out under guard it might be a reasonable assumption that the event happened before the war ended. That would put the event between April 1863 and April 1865. What do we know about the Department of West Virginia during that two year period? West Virginia was admitted as a state on June 20, 1863 and the Department of West Virginia was created in March 1864 under the command of General Franz Sigel. On May 21, 1864 Sigel was replaced by, believe it or not, General David Hunter, the same man that had referenced Garland's dismissal in a letter to President Lincoln two years earlier. Hunter remained in command only two months. He was replaced by General George Crook on July 25, 1864. Did Hunter have anything to do with Garland being escorted out of the department under guard? Probably not, but it wouldn't have been out of character.

The timing of Garland's arrival in Arkansas is unknown. The anonymous letter mentions Lt. Col. A. Montgomery, Chief Quartermaster. Alexander Montgomery was appointed Chief Quartermaster of the Department of Arkansas on Oct. 3, 1866.[36] Although the endorsement on the anonymous letter suggests that no action was going to be taken, it is interesting that Lt. Col. Alexander was transferred out of Arkansas on Feb. 26, 1867, just about one month after the letter was received by General E. O. C. Ord's office.[37]

---

in Elmira, NY, the son of a Presbyterian minister. He was appointed Adjutant General of the State of New York on Jan. 1, 1883 by Grover Cleveland, Governor of New York and future President of the United States. Farnsworth died on Aug. 10, 1895. Wheeling Daily Intelligencer, Dec. 5, 1864 and New York Times, April 11, 1895. No connection has been found between Farnsworth and Garland.

[36] Montgomery was a West Point graduate of the class of 1834. Between 1834 and 1861 he served as quartermaster in various western and southern commands. He died Oct. 13, 1893 in Coburg, Canada at the age of 82.

[37] General Order No: 4, Department of Arkansas, Feb. 26, 1867 reads: "Upon being relieved by Lt. Col. Peirce, Lt. Col. Alexander Montgomery, Deputy Quartermaster General, will proceed in accordance with orders of the War Department, to Buffalo, N. Y. and report for duty. In relieving Colonel Montgomery, the General Commanding takes pleasure in testifying to the zeal, economy and sagacity with which he has administered to the affairs of his department."

Lastly, notice has to be taken of Augustus Hill Garland, born 1832 in Tennessee. His family can be traced to the Virginian Garlands. They moved to Arkansas in 1833 and Augustus grew up to become a famous Arkansas lawyer and politician living in Little Rock from 1856. He was opposed to succession but eventually gave his support to the Confederacy. He served in the Confederate House of Representatives. After the war he was pardoned by President Johnson on July 15, 1865. A. H. Garland was clearly an important individual in Arkansas politics at the time that J. M. Garland would have been working for Colonel Alexander. Augustus Garland was Governor of Arkansas from November 1874- January 1877. Is there a connection? Probably not- but there just could be more to the story. Unfortunately, no more is known about what happened to John M. Garland, First Lieut. and Quartermaster of the Tammany regiment.

Chapter Fourteen

WINTER 1863

As might be expected the Union defeat at Fredericksburg left the Army of the Potomac in a sad state. According to one author "the morale ... was seriously impaired ... it would be impossible to imagine a graver or gloomier, a more somber or unmusical body of men".[1] General Burnside was not yet done making life for his men difficult. He formulated a plan that became known as the "Mud March" that would have the army cross the Rappahannock during the third week of January. Almost constant rains turned the landscape into a muddy quagmire forcing Burnside to abort the operation. The men of the Tammany regiment, along with the rest of Second Corps, had orders to remain in their positions across from Fredericksburg and were spared the ordeal of the Mud March. On January 26, 1863, President Lincoln replaced Burnside with Joseph Hooker.[2]

Between Fredericksburg and April 27, 1863, the start of the Battle of Chancellorsville, numerous changes took place within the Tammany regiment. Several junior officers resigned their commissions.[3] The rank

---

[1] Swinton, William: Campaigns of the Army of the Potomac, Blue and grey Press, Secaucus, NJ, 1988, page 256.

[2] General Orders No. 9, Headquarters Army of the Potomac, Jan. 26, 1863. "By direction of the President of the United States, the Commanding General this day transfers the command of the army to Maj. Gen. Joseph Hooker." New York Times, Jan. 27, 1863.

[3] First Lieut. William George Shaw enrolled in Feb. 62, served in Co. K and as regimental adjutant. He was discharged for disability (Rheumatism) on Dec. 2. An endorsement on his request for dismissal by Lieut. Col. Bomford reads: "Approved and respectively forwarded. The within named officer has been a

and file was reduced by 103 men that were discharged for disability from various locations.[4] On January 17, Sergeant James O'Brien, Co. F died of disease while in hospital at Frederick, MD.

The positions of Quartermaster and Commissary Sergeants were held by very few men during the war, but even these posts were affected during the winter of 1863.

Daniel Cummings, 30 was mustered into the regiment as Corporal Co. D. He was promoted to Commissary Sergeant around August 1, 1861, holding that position until Feb. 12, 1862. He was discharged for disability on Feb. 28, 1862.

James H. Welch was the regiment's first Commissary Sergeant having assumed that position on June 23, 1861. On August 1, 1861 he was appointed Quartermaster Sergeant but returned to the position of Commissary Sergeant when it was vacated by Cummings. Welch held the position until January 6, 1863 when he was reduced to the ranks. He spent the rest of the war as an ambulance driver.

Joseph Callender, age 19, was born in Manchester, England and mustered in as a Sergeant on June 28, 1861. Almost immediately he was detailed as a Quartermaster clerk. He was promoted to Commissary Sergeant Jan. 6, 1863 replacing Welch. He re-enlisted as a veteran on Feb. 22, 1864, receiving a furlough for 35 days to New York. His record states that he failed to return from the furlough and was listed as a deserter on April 12. However, his record must be incomplete as he is listed as having been transferred to the 82nd NY. He is also found on the rolls of the

---

useless encumbrance to the regiment for the past three months". First Lieut. Septimus Cobb, Co. C was discharged for disability on Dec. 6. He had served previously in the 83NY. Cobb enrolled in the regiment in Feb. 62 and had been wounded at Antietam by a musket ball that entered at the interior extremity of his left seventh rib and came out the opposite side of his body. Subsequent to his discharge he served as Second Lieut., 3rd Regiment, Veteran Reserve Corps, resigning that position November 21, 1863. First Lieut. William Hevey, Captain George Smith, First Lieut. Henry Van Voast and Second Lieut. Scott Dean were discharged for disability on Feb. 2, Jan. 12, Feb. 19 and Jan. 8 respectively.

[4]   Some companies were hit harder by discharges than others: A:16, B:10, C:12, D:7, E:9, F:13, G:12, H:5, I:12 and K:7. Three of the men discharged from Co. H were from the original Boston enlistees: Pat Flattery, James Kennedy and John Lynch. Another Boston man, John Driscoll deserted on April 13.

59th NY as Joseph Challender, Commissary Sergeant with promotions to Second Lieut. on January 4, 1865 and to First Lieut. on January 19, 1865.

George B. Ruddy, 37 years old and born in Ireland was mustered in as Private, Co. G on July 7, 1861. He was promoted to Quartermaster Sergeant Feb. 14, 1862 when James Welch was transferred to be Commissary Sergeant. Ruddy re-enlisted as a veteran on Feb. 22, 1864, according to the provisions of War Department General Order 191, and was promoted to Second Lieut. Co. C on April 24, 1864. On May 12, 1864 he was slightly wounded at the Battle of Spotsylvania Court House. Nineteen days later, on May 31, he was killed while on picket duty.

Felix Fagan joined the regiment in September 1861 and was captured at Ball's Bluff. Upon his parole he served at the Provost Marshal's Office, Annapolis, MD until the early part of 1864. Fagan was promoted to Sergeant, Co. C, March 1, 1864 and to Quartermaster Sergeant on April 17, 1864, holding that position for the rest of the war.

Colonel James E. Mallon
Kreis, Philip. "Col. James E. Mallon," Under two flags, the
adventures of Philip Kreis; story of the Tammany Regiment
of New York ... John Shaw Pierson Civil War Collection
(W), Rare Book Division, Department of Rare Books and
Special Collections, Princeton University Library.

The most significant change was at the top, with the colonelcy of the regiment. On March 17, Edmund Charles, who had been colonel from early 1862, was discharged for disability resulting from his wound received at Glendale and his subsequent imprisonment in Richmond. Colonel Charles died on April 25, 1863 in New York City.[5] Charles was replaced on Saint Patrick's Day, March 17, by James E. Mallon who at the time was Major of the regiment on staff duty as the Provost Marshal of Second Corps. The order appointing Mallon to the position of Provost Marshal of Second Corps is General Orders No: 12, dated March 13, 1863, meaning that officially Mallon held that position for only four days.[6]

On March 16, Mallon tried a case involving a member of the Tammany regiment. The facts were reported in the New York Leader as follows: " ... sutler while in Washington purchased a heavy stock of goods consisting of, besides the legal articles, a large amount of contraband property, bargained with the Quartermaster that the illegal goods be brought to Aquia Creek, under pretense that they were Quartermaster stores ... The Quartermaster immediately ordered the arrest of the sutler ... The property confiscated consisted of 720 bottles of whiskey ... which when retailed to the men would be equivalent to $2000." The Quartermaster was First. Lieut. Frederick Skeete who at the time was detailed as Brigade QM. The finding was against the sutler. What happened to the whiskey? Was it destroyed or was it treated according to General Orders No. 18 with one fourth going to Skeete and the rest to the Tammany regiment hospital fund?[7] Whether Skeete was actually at the trial is unclear as he had requested and

---

[5]   New York Times, April 27, 1863 and Apr. 30, 1863. The body of Col. Charles was taken to the Governor's Room at City Hall where it laid in state in a flag draped coffin guarded by a company of men. On top of the coffin were the colonel's sword, belt and cap and a cluster of white flowers in the shape of a cross. A procession of military detachments escorted the coffin down Broadway to South Ferry.

[6]   Mallon had been Provost Marshal of the Right Grand Division prior to being appointed to the same position with Second Corps.

[7]   OR: S1, V25, 119-122. General Orders No: 18, Army of the Potomac, March 3, 1863. Paragraph XVI reads: "All sutlers will confine their traffic to the regiment they are appointed...goods and property of those violating this order will be confiscated...one fourth to the benefit of the informer and the remainder to the benefit of the hospital fund of the regiment of the officer or soldier who gives the information..."

was granted a ten day leave of absence on March 14 to visit Washington and Philadelphia on business.[8]

Mallon's promotion to Colonel was not without controversy.[9] According to the New York Times, Mallon had been given the position of Colonel " …on the direct and earnest recommendations of Gen. Hooker … and also of his immediate corps, division and brigade commanders … Mallon was raised to the Colonelcy of the regiment, by Gov. Seymour, against decidedly strong political pressure in favor of another officer."[10] Who might the other officer have been? The most likely candidate would have been Lieut. Colonel Bomford. He was, after all, the ranking officer in the regiment, the son of a well known regular army officer and the grandson of a famous general (chapter 9). Why then wasn't the command given to Bomford?

---

[8]   New York Leader, April 4, 1863, page 7, column 1. Frederick Skeete was 37 years old when he enrolled in the Tammany regiment in May 1861as First Lieut. Co. H. He was the officer in charge of recruiting in Boston in June 1861. He assumed the position of Regimental Quartermaster on Aug. 15, 1862, after John Garland was transferred to the ambulance service. Regimental Order No. 88. He was assigned as Acting Assistant Brigade Quartermaster in Jan. 1863. On May 13, 1863 Skeete requested and was granted a medical leave of 20 days based on a surgeon's certificate stating he was suffering from acute nephritis. Although he never returned to the regiment and was carried on the roster as absent without leave after June 9, 1863, he was one of a number of Tammany men that contributed to the presentation of a sword to Major General Sedgwick by members of Second Corps after the Battle of Gettysburg. Correspondence of John Sedgwick, Vol. 2, page 146-8. On Feb. 5, 1864 Skeete was dismissed from the service by paragraph 34, SO No: 57, War Department for being absent without leave.

[9]   Mallon's appointment might, in part, stem from his former position with the Mozart or 40NY regiment that was associated with Fernando Wood. Wood had on January 6, 1861 recommended that New York City secede from the Union to be able to continue its business dealings with the south and continued making speeches that did not sit well with supporters of the Union. The men of the 40NY rejected any association with Wood through a resolution issued on April 6, 1863 saying: "…we indignantly repudiate any claim of Fernando Wood's to our sympathy, our obligations or our respect…that we have no sympathy with his principles, no respect for his character, and hope that the day is not far distant when such traitors will be shunned as lepers…"

[10] New York Times, Oct. 21, 1863. Obituary for Col. Mallon.

General Orders: No. 18, referenced above, was an extensive order issued on March 3, by General Hooker with a goal of improving discipline and efficiency. Paragraph V of that order lists the Forty-second New York as one of a number of regiments considered to have been at less than a desired state of readiness and for whom all leaves were cancelled.[11] Just eleven days later, March 14, Hooker issued General Orders No: 27 removing the restriction on leaves from the Tammany regiment.[12]

On Feb. 25, a week before the restriction on leaves was imposed, Bomford applied for a leave to visit his father who was on recruiting duty in Indianapolis, Indiana. His request was approved and forwarded with an endorsement by brigade commander Gen. Joshua Owen that read: " ...this is considered an exceptional case, one of the field officers (Col. Charles) being absent wounded and another field officer Major Mallon being detailed on detached duty."[13] Was Bomford simply seeking to see his father, who he said he had not seen for five years, or was he going to consult with a politically connected father on his future? Was he aware that his regiment had not been judged ready by the inspections conducted under Hooker's orders? Was he aware that Colonel Charles was about to resign? Was he aware that Hooker was about to recommend that he be discharged from the service? The answer to all of these questions is probably yes.

On March 9, Hooker sent a letter to Major Thomas M. Vincent, Assistant Adjutant General, War Department recommending that a number of officers be honorably discharged, one of whom was Bomford. Vincent responded on March 17, saying "at the expiration of his leave of absence,

---

[11] OR: S1, V25, 120. Paragraph V reads: "The inspection reports...giving evidence of the necessity of strong exertions on the part of every officer...to bring them up to a proper state of discipline and efficiency, no further leaves of absence or furloughs will be granted to these commands and all officers absent there from must be recalled, and their leaves revoked..." The Tammany regiment was one of over twenty five regiments and batteries specified in the order.

[12] OR: S1, V25, 137-138. Paragraph VIII of GO No. 27 reads: "As the inspection reports of the following named regiments and batteries show that they have greatly improved...they are relieved from the disability as to leaves of absence... Forty-second New York..."

[13] Leave was granted for 10 days. S. O. 42, Feb. 25, 1863.

Lieut. Col. Bomford should be brought before an examining board".[14] It seems certain that Bomford actually appeared before an examining board before Vincent's letter was received in Hooker's headquarters. On March 13, Bomford wrote to General Sprague, Adjutant General of the State of New York, recommending the promotion of First Lieut. Thomas Wright to be Captain. Attached to that recommendation was a list of the current officers carried on the rolls of the regiment regardless of whether they were actually with the regiment at the time, including seven Captains (Abbott, Cauvet, Cooper, Downing, Halstead, R. Wright and Lynch), five First Lieut. (Skeete, Towne, Ellis, T. Wright and Lennon) and six Second Lieut. (O'Shea, T. Mallon, Fitzharris, Ferguson, Ellendorf and Reynolds)[15] The next day, March 14, Lieut. Colonel Bomford submitted his resignation, addressed to Brig. General Sully, President Examining Board saying: "I have the honor herewith to resign my commission … Being an only son and all the male portion of my family (my father and two uncles) being in the service of the United States, I consider it my duty to resign". The request was forwarded with a recommendation of acceptance by Sully. General Couch, commanding Second Corps forwarded the request with the following endorsement: "Lt. Col. Bomford not having sufficient experience to hold the position, to which his commission entitles him, will be discharged from the service".[16]

---

[14] Vincent was responsible for the organization, mustering and payrolls of the volunteer armies of the United States. An 1853 graduate of West Point he had held the position of Asst. Adjutant General since July 17, 1862.

[15] New York State Archives, document G3975.

[16] NARA: File of George N. Bomford. Discharged by SO No: 61, paragraph 5, Second Corps, March 14, 1863. Following his discharge Bomford enlisted as a private in the U. S. Infantry in August 1864. By October he had been promoted to First Lieut. He remained in the army after the war. George N. Bomford died at his home at 214 West 14th Street, New York City at the age of fifty-six on September 5, 1897, from a kidney infection. New York Times, September 6, 1897. His wife, Sallie R. Bomford died from heart failure Nov. 23, 1896 at the same address. She was forty-five. They were married at Fort Shaw, Montana in 1873. New York Times, Nov. 25, 1896. Their son George N. Bomford, Jr. was born in 1874. While a Lieut. with the Fifth Infantry in Santiago, Cuba he married Katherine Muellock on Nov. 9, 1898. New York Times, Nov. 10, 1898. There is a record of a Lieut. George N. Bomford, Jr., Fifth U.S. Infantry having

Bomford's departure was reported in the New York Leader of April 4, saying: " ...It is only a few days ago that Lt. Col. Bomford took up his line of march for the north, having his "final papers" in his pocket. He raised from Lt. to Lt. Col. and reigned since July 1862. The next senior officer of the regiment, Major James E. Mallon, having returned from acting as Provost Marshal, has assumed command. Heretofore in the absence of Lt. Col. Bomford, the command devolved on the senior Captain, William A. Lynch of Co. K. It is said there are several aspirants to the vacancy. The question is, then, who shall be the lucky one, that is, if the advancement should prove to be such, since it often brings down on the person so raised the reverse of luck ..."[17] If the vacancy mentioned is that of the Colonelcy, could William A. Lynch have been one of the aspirants? Probably not, considering that he had already been passed over when Mallon was promoted to Major. Lynch had other plans.

Of the officers listed by Bomford several were on special assignments away from the regiment. Captain Abbott and First Lieut. Lennon (Uncle Pat) were on medical leave. Lieut. Towne and Lieut. Ellis were with the Signal Corps and Lieut. Skeete was assigned to Brigade QM. Fitzharris, Ferguson and Ellendorf had recently been recommended for promotion by Bomford and had previously been senior sergeants.

---

died in the Philippines on August 5, 1902. He is buried at San Francisco National Cemetery, California, Plot PP/NE98.

[17] New York Leader, April 4, 1863, page 6 col. 7. From Our Tammany Correspondents: In Camp at Falmouth, VA, March 29, 1863. The statement on the potential for bad luck for the person getting promoted was quite accurate as Colonel Mallon would be killed in battle six months after taking command.

Lieut. Maurice Fitzharris, New York Public Library

Maurice Fitzharris, an Ireland born member of the Fenian Brotherhood, joined the Tammany regiment in May 1861 as a 22 year old private. Following Ball's Bluff he moved quickly through the enlisted ranks in Company H, with promotion to Corporal on November 1, 1861, to Fifth Sergeant on January 1, 1862 and to First Sergeant on Feb. 19, 1862. On August 15, 1862 he was promoted to Regimental Sergeant Major. He was recommended for promotion to Second Lieut. in November 1862 and assumed that position in March 1863.[18]

John J. Ferguson, age 21, joined the regiment as Teamster, Co. G on May 5, and was appointed First Sergeant Co. G on June 23, 1861. On August 28, 1862 he was mustered in as Second Lieut. on Dec. 8, 1862. His service record has a muster sheet showing him at the U. S. General Hospital, Harpers Ferry for an unknown period between September and October 1862. On Feb. 26, 1863 Ferguson requested ten days leave to visit his family in New York and to purchase equipment. He did not return from his leave and was listed as absent without leave from March 14-April 13, 1863. Ferguson was dismissed from the service by sentence of

---

[18] Fitzharris was wounded at Gettysburg (gunshot wound to the thigh), promoted to First Lieut. in October 1863, wounded at Spotsylvania Court House, was hospitalized at Carver Hospital and mustered out while on medical leave on July 17, 1864.

a General Courts Martial on May 20, 1863.[19] Apparently, his dismissal did not bother the veterans of the Tammany regiment as he was one of five Tammany men that carried the battle flags of the regiment in the Decoration Day parade on Fifth Avenue in New York on May 31, 1895.[20] Ferguson died in Hoboken, New Jersey on May 15, 1906.[21]

Julius M. Ellendorf (AKA Julian), age 21, joined the regiment on June 6, 1861, was mustered in as Fifth Sergeant, Co. D on June 22, the next day as Third Sergeant and to First Sergeant a year later in July 1862. Ellendorf was promoted to Second Lieut., Co. H on April 4, 1863. He was mustered in as First Lieut. and Adjutant of the regiment on November 18, 1863 officially filling the role he had performed since April 1863. He was wounded at Cold Harbor June 3, 1864 (right foot) and was promoted to Captain on June 23, 1864 but never mustered in at that rank. Ellendorf was mustered out on July 13, 1864 while recovering from his wounds.[22]

Ed Cauvet was mustered in as First Sergeant, Co. C on June 22, 1861, promoted to Second Lieut. October 17, to First Lieut. Feb. 18, 1862 and to Captain on September 18, 1862. He served continuously except for a seven day leave of absence in October 1861 to visit his dying mother, a

---

[19] General Order No. 54, Army of the Potomac, May 20, 1863.

[20] New York Tribune, May 31, 1895, page 2. The other 4 men were Stephen Wolfer, Henry Bird, John McCloughlin and Philip Kreis.

[21] Pension records for John J. Ferguson show that his wife Selina filed for a widow's pension on June 27, 1913, Application Number 1010323. Another application was filed for an invalid pension on Oct. 26, 1892, Application Number 1135638. No Certificate Numbers appears on the record indicating that the pensions were not granted.

[22] New York Times, June 8, 1864 lists Lieut. J. M. Ellendorf in article "Wounded Officers at Washington". An invalid pension file exists for Julius M. Ellendorf, filed July 25, 1888, Application number 637101 and Certificate Number 640057. There are records for a Julius Marea Ellendorf, who was born in Berlin June 24, 1840 and died in Norwalk, CT July 23, 1893. He married Clara Whitehead, born in Milburn, NJ. The 1870 census lists the family living in New Jersey and the 1880 census has them in Norwalk, CT. Records also exist showing Julius M. Ellendorf as Adjutant, 93rd New York National Guard (100 day, 1864). This unit was mustered in on July 20, 1864. Julius M. Ellendorf is also listed as First Lieut. of the 1st Regiment, US Veteran Volunteer Infantry with a date of rank of January 14, 1865 and as Adjutant, Brevet Captain with date of rank of March 13, 1865. It is most probable that all of these men are the same person.

medical leave of 30 days because of an ulcerated left leg in February 1863 and a 10 day leave in December 1863. For the first three months of 1864 Cauvet was assigned as a battalion commander of the 7th Michigan and was appointed Commander of the Provost Guard of Second Corps by General Hancock on March 30, 1864.[23]

Captain Richard Halstead, collection of Martin Schoenfeld

General Sedgwick's Staff, Library of Congress
Captain Halstead, Tammany Regiment, Aide, 3rd
from right, left hand at waist of grey pants

23 Special Order 221, Second Division, Second Corps, Dec. 29, 1863. General Orders 12, Headquarters Second Army Corps, March 30, 1864. OR: S1, V33, 772. Cauvet went into the plumbing business after the war moving to Minneapolis in 1874 where he died February, 26, 1896. New York Sun, Feb. 28, 1896, page 7.

Captain Richard Halstead requires some explanation. He never actually spent time with the Tammany regiment. At the beginning of the war he was mustered in as Major of the 40NY. In May 1862, Halstead was brought up on charges of "Disobedience of Orders" and dismissed from the service.[24] Generals Kearney and Sedgwick requested that the case be taken under reconsideration. On July 11, Sedgwick wrote a recommendation that Halstead, who was serving as a "volunteer aide" on his staff, be appointed to a colonelcy.[25] Politics were certainly in play on this issue as the NY Leader, the newspaper of Tammany Hall, wrote on July 12: "Fortieth Regiment ... Major Halstead for acts unbecoming soldiers ... the disgraceful end ... is characteristic of men who overstep the bounds of justice and honor".[26] On July 21, Halstead wrote to Albany requesting that he be appointed as a First Lieut. saying " ...in some regiment in the Army of the Potomac in order to enable me to return there at once upon staff duty while awaiting a decision in the matter of appointment to a colonelcy as recommended by General McClellan ..."[27] On December 24, 1862 Halstead was mustered into the Tammany regiment as Captain of Co. F and immediately transferred to the staff of General Sedgwick where he served until Sedgwick was killed in 1864.[28]

The promotion of James Mallon was not the only controversy. On April 5, Mallon wrote to Albany saying: "A few days since Captain Wright of this regiment left camp on ten days leave. I have learned since his departure that he intends visiting Albany to secure for himself the vacant Majority of this regiment. Before making such appointment I respectfully

---

24 Special Order 160, May 26, 1862, Army of the Potomac.
25 New York State Archives, document 3053. OR: S1, V11, 82 references Halstead serving as volunteer aide to Sedgwick during the Peninsula Campaign.
26 New York Leader, July 12, 1862, page 6, col. 7.
27 New York State Archives, document 3569
28 Halstead was a frequent author of letters, on behalf of General Sedgwick, to the general's sister Emily who it seems Halstead had romantic feelings for. Emily married Dr. William Welch of Norfolk, CT. She died May 5, 1902. Correspondence of John Sedgwick, Army of the Potomac Series, Butternut and Blue, 1999, Volume 2, 136. Upon Sedgwick's death Halstead accompanied his body back to Connecticut. Halstead continued to serve in staff positions throughout the war. He died in Sing Sing, NY May 24, 1881.

request that you will give deliberate consideration to what I have to say … He makes a good Captain but is not fitted by either education or military knowledge to properly discharge the duties of Major. Capt. P. J. Downing who ranks next to Captain Wright is much the superior in anything that makes the soldier. If you consider it important that the position in the Field of this regiment, now vacant, be filled, I ask for the good of this command, in which there is so much of interest that is personal to myself in character and reputation, to commission P. J. Downing Major."[29]

Captain Robert C. Wright had requested a leave of 10 days on April 1, 1863 the purpose of which was stated as "visiting my family in New York". Several days earlier, on March 28, Wright wrote a letter to Mr. T. McCann, New York City saying: "In addressing these lines to you I do so to a man whose greatest pleasure it always was to serve his friends whenever an opportunity offered itself. I wish to secure your reliable assistance and … in a case that concerns my promotion, a promotion I feel justly entitled. Permit me to state the case. By resignation of our late Colonel and the recommendation of his successor to his place, a vacancy for the rank of Major exists in our regiment which has to be filled. I have received information that certain parties … are secretly working to secure that place setting aside entirely my superior claims as senior Captain of the regiment. It needs no comment to show how injurious to the Service as unjust it would be to allow them to succeed. The favor therefore I would ask of you … is to write at once to the Honorable Thomas Fields, Assemblyman, and beg of him in my name, to use all of the influence he can command in my favor stated before, my past service as well as my position as Captain of the regiment justly entitle me to the Majority."[30] The letter made its way to Albany, being received there on April 8 with a notation reading "Applying for the Majority of his regiment".[31]

---

[29] New York State Archives. Document 5026.

[30] Exactly who T. McCann was is not clear. There was a boxer and gang member in New York named Tom McCann. Thomas C. Fields was a member of the New York State Assembly from the 17th District in 1863. He was a member of the notorious "Tweed Ring". In 1872 he fled New York and died a fugitive from justice in Quebec, Canada in 1885.

[31] New York Archives. Document 4945.

Robert C. Wright was one of the original officers of the regiment being mustered in as First Lieut. Co. G in May 1861 at age 22. He was officially promoted to Captain after Antietam. His younger brother Thomas Wright enrolled at age 20 as a private and was immediately appointed 2nd Sergeant, Co. G, serving with his brother. Thomas was captured at Ball's Bluff. Following his exchange he was wounded at Antietam and advanced to the rank of First Lieut. when his brother was made Captain. Thomas was again wounded at Fredericksburg.[32]

The outcome of the controversy related to who should be appointed Major of the regiment is clear although following the paperwork is almost impossible. Not surprisingly, Albany followed the recommendation of the new colonel and the position went to Captain Patrick J. Downing. However, a record in Downing's service file states that he was not mustered in as Major until April 17, 1864. Another record dated War Department: Dec. 10, 1890, related to a pension application, establishes that Downing was officially considered Major of the Tammany regiment since March 17, 1863, the same day that James Mallon relinquished the position to take the Colonelcy.[33] Downing should best be remembered as the senior Fenian nationalist in the regiment having fought unsuccessfully against the British for Irish independence before coming to the United States. On April 21, 1863, 162 members of the Tammany regiment donated $493.50 to Irish Relief. A letter sent with the donation read: " …We hope it may contribute, if only to a small degree, to stop the stream of Irish immigration, and to keep our friends from starvation, so that, this war in which we are engaged being ended, there may, be some of our race left at home who we can aid in placing beyond the fear of recurrence both the miseries of famine and the horrors of landlordism." Donations were made by eight officers: Colonel

[32] Thomas Wright would be mustered out of the regiment on February 26, 1864 to accept appointment as Captain, 31st, U.S. Colored Troops. He would be promoted to Major, 31st USCT and was again wounded (gunshot flesh wound right side of thorax) on July 30, 1864, at the Crater, after assuming command of his regiment. He was recommended for promotion to Lieut. Colonel by Brevet by President Johnson on July 9, 1866. Thomas Wright died September 26, 1918 in St. Louis. Pension record card, Certificate: 84551.

[33] Interestingly, Captain Robert Wright would be appointed to the position of Lt. Col. of the regiment later in 1863 following the death of Mallon, but was never mustered in at that position.

Mallon, Lt. Col. Lynch, Captains Downing (not listed as Major), O'Shea, R. Wright, T. Wright and Lieut. Fitzharris and Reynolds.[34]

If, as a reader, you are not confused right now consider yourself special. To get a better understanding of all the changes to the command structure we need to look just a bit deeper at one of the men mentioned above, William A. Lynch. In the above paragraphs Lynch is mentioned several times both as the senior Captain and as Lieut. Colonel. His service with the regiment started in May 1861 with an appointment as First Lieut., Co. K. He was promoted to Captain on Dec. 1, 1861 filling the spot created by the death of the previous captain at Ball's Bluff. He came down with Typhoid Fever while on the Peninsula, was wounded at Antietam and was in command of the regiment when the more senior officers were absent, which was quite frequent.[35] On March 17, the same day Mallon was appointed Colonel, a letter was written from the regiment's camp in Falmouth to the Governor of New York, recommending that Lynch be appointed Lieut. Colonel of the regiment. It was signed by six officers: Robert Wright, Thomas Wright, Julius Ellendorf, Maurice Fitzharris, Francis Reynolds and William O'Shea. The letter reads: "We the undersigned, Officers of the 42d (Tammany) Reg. respectfully recommend the name of Captain William A. Lynch, to fill the vacancy occasioned by the resignation of Lieut. Colonel Bomford. In offering this recommendation to your Excellency, we only consult and give expression to the wishes of every member of the regiment. The distinguished services, Captain Lynch so faithfully rendered to his country and its cause, as well as the many sterling qualities of his character as an officer and a gentleman have endeared him to us all and won our heartfelt admiration and friendship. We feel, that, in offering his name for

---

[34] Irish American, May 9, 1863, Page 2, Column 4. Officers of the Tammany regiment were often publically named as supporters of the Fenian movement. Upon the death on April 1, 1862 of Michael Doheny, the first Lt. Col. of the regiment and a revered member of the Fenians, an article appeared in the New York Leader, April 5, 1862, page 4, Column 4-6 listing numerous Union officers that were in support of John O'Mahoney, leader of the Fenians in New York. On that list were: Captain James McGrath, Lieut. Patrick Downing, Lieut. William O'Shea, Lieut. Morgan Doheny and Lieut. Patrick. H. Lennon (Uncle Pat) of the Tammany regiment.

[35] NARA, John J. Ferguson file. Document dated March 19, 1863, signed Wm. A. Lynch, Captain, Commanding Regiment.

the above position, we do justice to a gallant and deserving officer, to the cause we all unitedly strive to advance, and to the Society whose name we bear, and whose honor is ever dear to our hearts. It is needless to state, that, by attending to this petition, your Excellency will serve both the interests of our country, in rewarding merit of the highest order, and the wishes and desires of a regiment whose greatest ambition it ever was and ever will be, to maintain untarnished the honor of that Order, whose proud banners have floated over us on many a hard fought field." The letter was hand carried by Lynch to Albany along with two further recommendations signed by Tammany officials Daniel Delevan and Elijah Purdy on March 25. From the text of the letter from Purdy it is absolutely clear that the position being lobbied for is that of Lieut. Colonel not Colonel.[36]

There are numerous dates in Lynch's file that speaks to when he was actually mustered in as Lieut. Colonel. It appears that the actual date is April 4, 1863. After Gettysburg, Lieut. Col. Lynch would suffer the return of symptoms of Typhoid Fever. On November 20, 1863, General A. S. Webb, commanding Second Division, requested that Lynch be brought before an examining board saying "I deem him inefficient and incompetent". Lynch also spent significant time in New York City on recruiting duty. He returned to the regiment in late May.[37] On June 4, 1864, at the Battle of Cold Harbor, Lynch was wounded by a gunshot wound to his right leg and was mustered out on July 13, 1864 while in the Officers U. S. A. Hospital, Annapolis, MD.[38]

It is certainly possible that deep down Lynch hoped he would get the Colonel's position. There was no Colonel and Major Mallon had been on

---

[36]   New York Archives, document 4557

[37]   Special Orders No. 375, War Department, paragraph 1, August 22, 1863 granted Lynch 30 days leave of absence on a Surgeon's Certificate of Disability. On the endorsement of General Webb's request there is a note saying: "See SO 264". That order could not be located. Special Orders No. 41, Second Division, Second Corps, Feb. 10, 1864 and Special Orders No. 26, Adjutant's General, March 24, 1864 ordered Lynch to New York on recruiting duty between February and April 1864. Lynch is listed on the rolls of the "Rendezvous of Distribution" near Alexandria, VA, May 19, 1864.

[38]   After the war Lynch was the Treasurer of the United Service Society of New York, an organization of Union veterans headed by Major General G. K. Warren. New York Times, June 24, 1865

various assignments in staff positions. However, once a decision was made appointing Mallon the picture was quite clear and "for the good of the service" everyone had to move on.[39]

James Fennessy, writing for the Irish American, said: "The Paymaster has just paid us a flying visit. It must be said however, our anticipations were not realized, as he paid us only four months pay, which was little more than half our dues; still we feel that half a loaf is better than no bread ... Up to this writing there is prevailing here a remarkable tranquility, which the wise ones believe forebodes an approaching storm".[40]

The Tammany regiment was reorganized with its command structure overhauled and it was ready for the next phase of the war, Chancellorsville.

[39] Lynch received an appointment to Colonel of the Tammany regiment on November 21, 1863 but was never mustered in at that rank possibly because of General Orders, War Department, Adjutant's General Office, No. 182, June 20, 1863. This order reduced the number of officers a regiment could have dependent on the number of active men it had. If a regiment was below half strength the position of Colonel was not to be filled. OR, S3, V3, 389. William A. Lynch died in New York City on Tuesday August 4, 1874. Brooklyn Eagle, August 6, 1874, page 2. His pension file shows both an Invalid (107905) and Widows pension (428027).

[40] Irish American, Feb. 14, 1863, page 2, column 8.

Chapter Fifteen

CHANCELLORSVILLE
SECOND FREDERICKSBURG

By April 1863 Hooker had completed his plan for bringing the war to the enemy and had re-configured his Army of the Potomac, now containing seven Corps, in a way that he believed would be up to the job. On Monday, April 27 the troops started to prepare and initial movements of artillery and regiments began. No one on either side had any idea of what was going to happen in the next week and a half but the Union troops knew that it would be significant. Spring had arrived.

For the men of the 42nd NY, under the command of Colonel James E. Mallon, April 27th started like many other days. From their camp near Falmouth they were detailed to relieve the 61st NY (Colonel N. A. Miles) and the 64th NY (Colonel Daniel G. Bingham). These units had been providing protection for two batteries of artillery. Both regiments were from Hancock's First Division and were to move from their position near the Lacy House in preparation for crossing the Rappahannock. The 42nd NY, along with the rest of Gibbon's Second Division, would remain behind attached to Sedgwick's command while the bulk of II Corps moved up river.[1]

Chancellorsville ranks right up there with the most important battles of the Civil War. It was the victory that gave Robert E. Lee the confidence to move north into Pennsylvania and set the stage for the historic days at

---

[1]   OR: S1, V25, 323, 339-346. The Tammany regiment occupied the camp vacated by the 64NY.

Gettysburg. It was where General Stonewall Jackson was mortally wounded by fire from his own troops. It was where the Union, once again, found out that mere advantage in numbers would not lead to success. Because of the magnitude of the action at Chancellorsville, the role played by the men of the Tammany Regiment can in no way be considered major. But they did have a role and they did their part. Many Union regiments fought gallantly at Chancellorsville and many others did not. Many Union commanders were brilliant but most left a lot to be desired. The Tammany men and their leaders were in none of these categories. They had a specific job to do and they did it.

General Gibbon had been attached to General Sedgwick's command for a number of reasons beyond the obvious one of providing additional strength. Sedgwick had commanded Gibbon's division before he had been promoted to the command of VI Corps. In the plan that was to unfold Gibbon was to provide cover for Sedgwick's right flank in and around the town of Fredericksburg, a place Gibbon's men knew well from last December.

The 42nd NY was part of Third Brigade, Second Division under Colonel Norman J. Hall, the former commander of the 7th MI. There were currently six regiments in the brigade although most of them were mere remnants of their original strength due to large losses at Ball's Bluff, The Peninsula, Antietam and disease. Many of the veterans of these regiments had crossed in boats or on the pontoon bridges spanning the Rappahannock in December when Burnside attacked Fredericksburg. The 7th MI, 19th and 20th MA and the 42nd NY had fought through the streets of Fredericksburg and could be depended on to know the area better than others. They knew Sedgwick and he knew them and they had fought together in many battles. This was an advantage that other Union corps commanders did not have with units they would have to depend on during the upcoming action.

It is not my intent to cover the battle at Chancellorsville in all its detail. There are many excellent works available to the reader if such an in depth treatment is desired. In order to understand the role of the Tammany regiment in the battle it is important to follow the activities of General Sedgwick's command. By doing so the reader will see how, like at Fair Oaks, while the regiment was not in the hottest part of the battle, their role was important and contributed to the positive aspects of the Union attack.

As the overall attack plan was put together Sedgwick was placed in command of the left wing of the Union forces, about 50,000 men, located around Fredericksburg and down river from the town. In addition to VI Corps, Sedgwick had command of I Corps under Reynolds, III Corps under Sickles and Gibbon's Division of Couch's II Corps.[2]

More support was available as well. General Hooker's Chief of Artillery, Brig. General Henry J. Hunt had placed a number of batteries from the artillery reserve in initial positions determined to be important to Sedgwick's objectives. These included the two heaviest batteries in the Army, Batteries B and M of the 1st CT Heavy Artillery, each battery having four, four and a half inch siege rifles. Battery B was placed at Bank's Ford along with the four 20-pound Parrotts of the 29th NY Artillery. These batteries were placed to be able to bring enfilading fire on the enemy's rifle pits and the fortified positions on the heights overlooking the city as well as providing cover for the troops that would be placing bridges at Fredericksburg.

Battery M was placed at Franklin's Crossing, named for the place of General Franklin's crossing in December 1862, slightly down river from town. With Battery M were six 20-pound Parrotts of the 30th NY Artillery, five light batteries of VI Corps and K Battery, 4th U. S. Artillery belonging to III Corps. This large formation, under the command of Colonel C. H. Tomkins, Chief of Artillery, VI Corps, was charged with covering the pontoon bridges that were to be placed at this part of the Rappahannock.

Still further down river near Pollock's Mill were forty guns of I Corps, under Colonel C. S. Wainwright, Chief of Artillery, charged with covering the crossing at that location. A mile further down river near Traveler's Rest, were the 5th NY Artillery (4-20 pound Parrotts) and the combined 12, 3-inch guns of the 15th and 32nd NY Artillery, all from the general artillery reserve. This group, under Lt. Col. E. R. Warner, Inspector of Artillery, controlled the left of the entire army front as well as the bridge across the Massaponax River. If enemy troops were to come from the direction of Port Royal they would come under fire from this position.

---

2   Letter by Captain Halstead to Sedgwick's sister, May 13, 1863. Correspondence of John Sedgwick, page 110-128, Volume 2, Army of the Potomac Series, Butternut and Blue. 1999.

The rest of the artillery reserve was parked near Falmouth slightly upriver from Fredericksburg.[3]

Some changes in the positions of the above batteries, especially those near Falmouth, took place during the next few days and batteries generally moved with their corps, but the bulk of the reserve batteries positioned in Sedgwick's area of operations remained in place. There can be no question that the need for supporting Sedgwick in what he was going to be asked to accomplish was paramount to Hooker.

What were Sedgwick's orders? To say that they were clear would be an over simplification, but orders at that level were rarely clear. On the other hand they were clear enough for Sedgwick to know what he was expected to do. They were not clear at all on when or how far he was to move.

Captain Halstead, Aide-de-camp to Sedgwick, described the orders as: "These three corps, under the General, should make a strong demonstration just below Fredericksburg, at and below the place where Franklin made his crossing under Burnside, while Hooker was to make the main attack, if possible, on their rear and left flank. Our movements depended entirely on the movements of the enemy. He might force us to convert our feigned attack into a real one, and for this reason a strong force was left there".[4]

On the rainy night of April 28, the men of the Light Division (a strong brigade), VI Corps under Colonel Hiram Burnham brought the boats to the river from the pontoon train some two miles away. In the early hours of Wednesday, April 29 the boats reached the river and the men of General Brook's division, VI Corps, crossed the Rappahannock under light enemy fire, and secured the riverbank for the placement of three bridges. Further down river, I Corps also succeeded in crossing and establishing a bridgehead. For the rest of the day, sparring between artillery and infantry units took place but no significant changes in position occurred. Sedgwick had complied with the initial orders he had received. The enemy, seeing numerous bridges being placed across the river at locations of significant crossings just a few months earlier, would reasonably believe that a major attack was likely to come in this sector.[5]

---

[3]   OR: S1, V25, 246-50. Report of Gen. Henry Hunt.
[4]   Correspondence of John Sedgwick, supra, page 111
[5]   OR: S1, V25, 557-562. Report of Gen. Sedgwick

On Thursday, April 30, III Corps was withdrawn from Sedgwick's command and ordered upriver to United States Ford and several bridges were taken up and sent to Bank's Ford.[6]

Sedgwick received an order from Hooker at 5PM on Friday, May 1 ordering a "demonstration in force at 1 o'clock, May 1". The order said: "to let it be as severe as possible without being an attack; to assume a threatening attitude, and maintain it until further orders". As the time for the "demonstration" had already passed by several hours, Sedgwick ordered his men to act. A division of VI Corps was ordered to protect the bridges of I Corps and the Light Division was sent across the river to support General Brooks. Upon executing these movements Sedgwick received another order, countermanding the order to make the demonstration.[7]

On Saturday, May 2, I Corps was withdrawn from Sedgwick and ordered to head upriver. A division of VI Corps was sent to take up the bridge at the I Corps crossing. At 6:30 P.M. the order was issued to pursue the enemy along the Bowling Green road toward Fredericksburg. Another order was received by Sedgwick telling him to "cross the Rappahannock at Fredericksburg and move in the direction of Chancellorsville until connected with the major-general commanding; to attack and destroy any force on the road, and be in the vicinity by daylight". When Sedgwick received the order he was already on the south side of the river. Rather than cross over and then re-cross at Fredericksburg, he advanced down the Bowling Green road and entered the city, his troops fighting all the way. Confederate troops were in strong positions along the stone wall and on Marye's Heights, positions well known to all Union troops as the scene of the disaster of December '62.[8]

On Sunday, May 3 the bridges across the Rappahannock at Fredericksburg were completed and the troops of Gibbon's division of II Corps crossed and moved to support Sedgwick's right until checked by the location of a canal. Artillery pounded the positions on Marye's Heights but Sedgwick was unable to take the Confederate works. He decided to make a direct assault. The men of VI Corps charged the enemy works and took Marye's Heights capturing many prisoners and artillery pieces.

---

[6]   Ibid
[7]   Ibid
[8]   Ibid

Once the heights were taken, VI Corps continued in pursuit of the enemy establishing a line near Salem Church. What Sedgwick did not know was that large Confederate forces were moving to envelop him and hit him from the rear.

Early in the morning of Monday, May 4, Sedgwick was told that a force of 15,000 enemy troops had re-occupied Marye's Heights, in his rear, cutting off his communications with Fredericksburg. He also received a dispatch from Hooker stating that: "he had contracted his lines, that I must look to the safety of my corps". Sedgwick moved VI Corps to Bank's Ford and re-crossed the Rappahannock early in the morning of Tuesday, May 5, taking up the bridges behind him. In total Sedgwick had almost 5,000 casualties, had taken 1400 prisoners and captured and removed 9 artillery pieces.[9]

Looking more closely at the actions of Gibbon's troops on May 3-5 provides interesting insights. The division was made up of three brigades supported by two batteries of artillery. First Brigade, under Colonel Laflin had the 19th ME, 34th and 82nd NY, 15th MA and 1st MN. Second Brigade, under General Owen comprised the 69th, 71st, 72nd and 106th PA. Third Brigade, under Colonel Hall, had the 19th and 20th MA, 7th MI, 42nd and 59th NY and the 127th PA. The two assigned batteries, each with six guns, were Battery A and B, 1st RI Light Artillery, however Battery G, 1st RI, had replaced Battery A, which had been sent along with the rest of II Corps to United States Ford. A company of Massachusetts's sharpshooters was also assigned to Gibbons.

The entire Second Brigade had been ordered to Bank's Ford and actually never participated in any of the actions of the division during the engagement at Fredericksburg, although they played an important part in setting up the path for Sedgwick's eventual movement to safety.[10] The 19th ME was left on the north side of the river to protect telegraph lines, leaving four regiments in the first brigade.[11]

In Third Brigade, the 7th MI had 222 effective men on May 3. Of these, 87 were left on picket or guard duty in Falmouth, leaving only 135

[9] Ibid
[10] OR: S1, V25, 350-1. Report of General Gibbon
[11] OR: S1, V25, 352-3. Report of Colonel Laflin.

to make the attack.[12] The 19th MA reported on March 16, a strength of only 217 enlisted men ready for duty.[13] Records of the Tammany regiment indicate that their strength was similar to the 19th Massachusetts. According to Major Henry Abbott of the 20th MA, the entire brigade numbered less than 1200 men.[14] This figure seems reasonable as it is consistent with that made by Brig. Gen. Warren, Chief Topographical Engineer of the Army, in his report that placed the strength of Gibbon's attacking division at 2500.[15]

As Gibbon moved out in the early morning of May 3, he crossed the Rappahannock on recently placed pontoon bridges and met with Sedgwick who had just arrived in Fredericksburg. The terrain to be covered during the attack was well known to both generals who were joined in town by engineering General Warren. It is fortunate that an eyewitness account by James Fennessy is available to cover what happened. In his May 6 and 11 articles for the Irish American, he said: "Having been an eye witness to the scene enacted in the immediate vicinity of Fredericksburg, from the opening to the closing of the sanguinary action, the writer of this is, therefore, enabled to describe what may be appropriately called the "Second Battle of Fredericksburg", the movements for the opening of which were progressing for several days before it became known where and by what corps the passage of the Rappahannock should first be forced. Gen. Sedgwick's corps crossed without much resistance about three miles on the left flank of the city, while the forces under the personal command of Gen. Hooker crossed the stream at two points up the river, at Bank's and United States fords. The operation of these forces on the right will be chronicled by the correspondents that witnessed them. It is the terrific fighting of the left wing of the army that will be treated of here. On Sunday, the 3rd of May, ere the sun had fully displayed his brilliance above the Eastern horizon, a long roll of musketry, accompanied with loud cheering, tells the advance of Sedgwick's column. His artillery following

---

[12]   Report of Lt. Col. Steele, 7th MI, Michigan State Archives, Townsend, David, The Seventh Michigan Volunteer Infantry, Southeast Publications, Ft. Lauderdale, FL, 1993, page 104.

[13]   Nineteenth Massachusetts, page 199.

[14]   Scott, Robert Garth, Fallen Leaves, page 175

[15]   OR: S1, V25, 193-206. Report of Gen. Warren.

the infantry closely opens a brisk fire on the retreating enemy, who falls back on the third line of defenses, being covered by a tremendous fire from their works on the heights. While this artillery duel is going on, the third brigade of the second division, second corps, without resistance, throws a pontoon over the stream opposite the town in the very same place one was laid which met with such stubborn resistance on the 13th of last December. This brigade was also the first to enter the city at that period. It is composed of the 42nd New York (Tammany Regiment), the 19th and 20th Mass., 59th New York and a nine-month's regiment, 127th Pennsylvania. (The author omitted the 7th Michigan, which was a long-standing member of the brigade.) In the campaigns of McClellan it was commanded by Gen. Dana, and since the battle of Antietam by Col. Hall. Having safely crossed the bridge, the brigade advances toward the "flats" or table land on the right of the city, under the muzzles of the enemy's guns, posted on the heights, at a distance of three or four hundred yards only. Not a single shot does the enemy fire at the brigade at this time. Having formed column by battalion right in front and thrown out a requisite number of skirmishers, the brigade moves toward the fortified heights. Here is a great spectacle. The men advance in splendid order. The question arises; will the batteries in the redoubts surrender or resist this advancing column? It is no longer a doubt. A volume of smoke is seen curling over the embrasures of one of the forts and instantly a plunging fire of shot and shell is hurled against the brigade. The enemy's skirmishers are deployed and coming into contact with ours; they are forced to make "about face" and seek shelter in their trenches. Our artillery, which crossed the bridge, cannot reply effectively, owing to the low position on which the pieces are posted. The enemy concentrates a tremendous fire on our advancing column. For a moment this human tide seen under the thundering storm that seems to sweep in its deadly course all before it surges on the billows of battle, now steadily rolling upwards toward the fortified hills again slowly receding before the deadly hail of metal. Sixty of the men fall in their gore, three of them being instantly killed, the rest wounded. It is a miracle the brigade escapes so fortunately, considering the amount of powder expended essaying to annihilate it. If however, the stone wall in their front, can be gained, it may afford a partial shelter. Another move is therefore ordered, and through a plunging fire of grapeshot, the wall is gained. Skirmishers again are thrown out, and a feint is made to move on the heights. The enemy concentrates his forces to meet this apparent intended attack. Now is the moment for Sedgwick to make a vigorous attack, while the enemy has weakened his forces to reinforce the troops threatening the third brigade. The attack is made and the heights carried at the point of the bayonet. I confess a more magnificent scene I never before witnessed. Truly grand it was to see a line of men charging up the green slope in the face of a terrific fire mounting the parapet of the redoubt and planting thereon their colors. The first battery is carried and the column advances by the right flank along the summit of the range of hills, capturing many prisoners and six or seven pieces of artillery. This is a complete success. It is to be regretted that subsequent events allow the enemy to advance heavy masses and reoccupy them, which they accomplished on the following day, Monday the 4th, to the chagrin of the late victors. The forces of Sedgwick having carried the heights move direct to the right to form a junction with those that crossed at Bank's ford. The only troops left in and around the city are those of the third brigade already alluded to here; and those guard a circuit calculated to measure five miles. Against our line the enemy comes in mass, sweeping everything standing in its way; and flushed with success their peculiar cheer can be heard far and wide. Nor do they remain satisfied with their re-occupying the works, their skirmishers are instantly deployed, but we met them, with some companies of the 42nd New York posted in the graveyard in the rear of the city. This position is an admirable one, being a square lot, surrounded by a brick wall four feet high and about one foot in thickness. The wall is musket proof, lucky for its living inhabitants, but it showed the strongest evidence that it could not resist a 12-pounder. Picket firing at this juncture seems the order of the day. Over the dust of the dead the cracking of musketry never ceases till the troops re-cross the river at early dawn, on Tuesday the 5th of May. Thus ends the second great battle of Fredericksburg."[16]

Fennessy continued saying: "May I crave space for a special from the Tammany Regiment? On the morning of the third of May, about one o'clock, the regiment marched to the Lacy House, from whence it passed over the pontoon into the city of Fredericksburg, with the command to

16 Irish American, May 23, 1863, page 1, column 5-6. Sedgwick's Attack, by James Fennessy. Falmouth, May 6, 1863.

which it belongs. The head of the column marched by the right, on the immediate right of the city, where the regiments form line of battle on the open plain, three hundred fifty yards distant from the Heights, from whose summit a lava of the most destructive fire was emitting. About noon, the regiment marched to the left, and soon after moved briskly up the slopes of the fortified hills, which they took possession of, and held until withdrawn to the city that evening by the commanding officer of the Brigade, and posted at intervals around its suburbs as a picket guard. The regiment re-crossed the river on the Tuesday following, together with the whole command of Col. Hall, who is commanding officer of the 2d Brigade … James O'Brien, from the city of Cork, served through the whole engagement as a volunteer in Captain Patrick J. Downing's Company. If I were to particularize the individual bravery displayed by the enlisted men, it would extend this communication to a greater length than intended. As for the commissioned officers, I will take liberty to chronicle that Captain Patrick J. Downing is as dashing a field officer as ever wielded a blade, his pluck and marked coolness under fire or artillery charge are themes amongst the men when the battle is ended. There is also Captain Wm. O'Shea, who has plucked a laurel wreath from the battlefield; his bearing at this late battle adds another chaplet to that wreath so glowingly gained on the field of action. There are others who are well deserving of notice".[17] One has to remember that the Irish American newspaper always glorified the performance of members of the Fenian Brotherhood.

From the above it is clear that Gibbon was sent to the right of the town to support the main attack of Sedgwick. Other reports throughout the Official Records agree with J.F.'s account. With the two batteries placing supporting fire on the heights, protected by the 11th RI Infantry from Sedgwick's Corps, Gibbon's two attacking brigades spread out between the right edge of Fredericksburg and the Rappahannock across from Falmouth along a line parallel to the canal and the River Road with First Brigade closest to the river and Third Brigade near the town. After Sedgwick had secured the heights and the crossing of the canal was prevented by the lack of an intact bridge, the right was abandoned with all troops moving back into town and onto Marye's Heights.

---

[17]   Ibid, page 1, column 4. Tammany Regiment, Falmouth, May 11, 1863.

Sedgwick continued with his advance toward Chancellorsville as ordered and Gibbon's troops were left on the heights with orders to protect the city and the bridges. Colonel Laflin was ordered to move his brigade back across the river and deploy to protect the bridges and support the artillery positions near the Lacy House.[18] This left the Third Brigade as the only troops on the southern bank of the river. Colonel Hall reported that following the support of the attack by Sedgwick, during which his brigade captured over one hundred prisoners, he was ordered back to the town and spent the rest of the night of May 3, collecting wounded, burying dead and securing property. It is reasonable to assume that this last duty could well have been on the minds of all commanders based on the massive destruction of private property that had occurred in December. Hall posted pickets, established a bridge guard and set up outposts around the city.[19]

So who, if anyone, was charged with occupying the heights? Surely, such a formidable position, the scene of such loss to the Union in December 1862 and the strong point of the defense met so far by Sedgwick, was to be defended. Apparently not! Sedgwick was following his orders to link up with Hooker. Gibbon believed that he was ordered to protect the city and the bridges and routes across the Rappahannock as a security force between the rebel forces and the supply and artillery positions of the Army of the Potomac reaching as far as Aquia Creek. As far as the Union was concerned possession of Marye's Heights was not a priority.

Could Gibbon have held the heights? An interesting question, the answer is likely not. His under strength brigades supported by only two light batteries would have had no chance to repel an enemy advance on the heights. The enemy force that had just been dislodged was superior to what Gibbon could have brought to bear if he had dedicated his entire strength to the defense of the heights. Who then would have protected the town; the bridges and the Union supply routes? There was nobody else! All the other troops were upriver with Hooker. If the I or III Corps had been left under Sedgwick, things would likely have been different. But that was not the case. Gibbon and his small force were separated from all other Union

---

18   OR: S1, V25, 352-3. Report of Col. Laflin.
19   OR: S1, V25, 258-60. Report of Colonel Hall.

troops and had but one escape, the bridges across the Rappahannock at Fredericksburg.

As the Confederate troops released by Robert E. Lee from Chancellorsville to attack Sedgwick approached Fredericksburg and Salem Church, Colonel Hall distributed his brigade and made plans to defend the town and withdraw to safety. From the report of J. Fennessy and that of Major Abbott, 20th MA, the Tammany regiment was posted as pickets around the outskirts of the town with several companies located in the graveyard in the rear of the town. As the enemy approached the town these pickets put up resistance for several hours until driven back into town.[20] The brigade supported by the First Company of Massachusetts Sharpshooters, and some 225 men from the VI Corps continued the fight and started to withdraw. In the evening of May 4, the wounded and ambulances of VI Corps as well as many other wagons, prisoners and seven pieces of captured artillery were moved across the river. Additionally, the main roads were ditched and rear guards were posted to cover the withdrawal. That night two companies of the 127th Pennsylvania, a six-month regiment whose term was about to end, created a false alarm and fired into the Tammany Regiment. Colonel Hall commented that Colonel Mallon took prompt and judicious action and mentioned the good conduct of the Tammany Regiment in preventing unfortunate results from the incident. On the morning of Tuesday, May 5, the bridgeheads were destroyed and the bridges picked up with the last remaining troops re-crossing in boats.[21]

The Tammany regiment suffered 10 casualties during the battle. Sergeant John Maher (hand), Sergeant Andrew Clines (thigh), Co. K, Privates John Hess, Co. C, Owen McDermott, Co. D, mortally wounded thigh, died on 5/14, Michael McDonough, Co. E, Matthew McNally (hand), James Kilduff, Thomas Ryan, Co. I, Thomas Murray (leg), Co. K and Horace Adams, Co. H.

I have always believed that there has been confusion in the way the Battle of Chancellorsville has been referred to in various regimental histories and other works that I have read. In some records unit historians have said that their units did not take part in the battle when from this author's perspective they clearly did. I see it this way. The Battle of Chancellorsville

---

[20]   Ibid and Fallen Leaves, supra, page 175
[21]   Ibid and OR: S1, V25, 361. Report of Captain William Plumer.

encompasses all the activities put into motion by Hooker's plan of attack and the reactions to it by the Confederate forces under Lee. This includes the sweeping river crossing movements on the Union right, the bridge building and artillery placements on the Union left and everything in between. The confusion comes, in my opinion, in discussions of various actions that were components of the Battle of Chancellorsville. A perfect example is Salem Church. Was Salem Church a part of the Battle of Chancellorsville? Of course it was. To say that it was not is to say that the role of Sedgwick was not part of the plan. Few historians would take this position. Of course referring to Salem Church does pinpoint a specific segment of the Battle of Chancellorsville and therefore helps focus a reader's mind in the same way referring to Pickett's Charge focuses a reader to a specific part of the battle of Gettysburg. Likewise, the actions of Gibbon's Division, as part of the force under Sedgwick, are clearly part of the Battle of Chancellorsville. References to Second Fredericksburg also help take a reader to a part of the battle but readers, and authors, should not lose sight of the overall plan when considering the order of battle involved in Chancellorsville.

Chapter Sixteen

GETTYSBURG

The Tammany regiment spent the six weeks following Chancellorsville in camp near Falmouth. Administratively, events altered the regiment's roster although not anywhere as drastically as the command changes that had recently occurred. Nine additional men were discharged for disability from various locations. Joseph Benoit, Co. D, was assigned as a commissary guard at brigade, Philip Catton, Co. H, a Boston man, was assigned to Battery A, 1st RI Artillery, John Hudson, Co. E, was attached to 2nd Division Provost Guard, Ed Kelly, Co. D, was detached as a pioneer with Brigade Commissary, Joseph Murphy, Co. G, was detached as Brigade Farrier (blacksmith) and John Wilson, Co. C was serving as the regimental tailor.

Changes to the officer ranks saw Captain Tobin returning to the regiment and taking command of Co. F. Captain P. Cooper returned from a month's medical leave for chronic diarrhea and was assigned as Acting Assistant Inspector General, at brigade HQ. Morgan Doheny was appointed Acting Quartermaster.

Second Lieut. John Kurman and Captain James McGrath were dismissed for desertion.[1] Kurman enrolled in Co. F in May 1861 and served as First Sergeant until his promotion to Second Lieut. on July 1, 1862. He spent significant time in hospitals and on recruiting duty in New York prior to being listed as absent without leave on November 18, 1862. James McGrath had been captured on the Peninsula during Stuart's ride

---

[1]   Special Orders No. 217, War Department, paragraph 18, May 15, 1863.

around McClellan.[2] His record shows him carried as absent without leave since Nov. 28, 1862.

On May 15, Colonel Mallon recommended a series of promotions in a letter to General Sprague in Albany. T. Mallon, M. Fitzharris, F. Reynolds and J. Ellendorf were recommended for advancement to First Lieut. First Sergeant Stuart A. Standiford was recommended for promotion to Second Lieut. with the comment "Sgt. Standiford behaved with great gallantry in the late battle at Fredericksburg".[3]

In early June 1863 General Lee initiated a plan that would result in a confrontation in Pennsylvania that, for many, would be the "high water mark" of the Civil War. Certainly, the action at Gettysburg, on July 1-3, would remain entrenched in the minds of all who lived at the time just as it remains in the forefront of all modern Civil War discussions. Lee's army moved from their winter positions near Chancellorsville to the northwest, through the Blue Ridge Mountains, crossing the Potomac River and advanced into Pennsylvania headed in the general direction of Harrisburg.

In reaction to Lee's movements the Army of the Potomac broke camp around Falmouth and took up the chase. Second Corps left Falmouth on June 15 and after a nine-mile march camped near Aquia. The next day a march of eighteen miles brought the corps via Dumfries to the banks of the Occoquan River at Wolf Run Shoals. At nightfall on June 17, Second Corps settled into camp at Sangster's Station on the Orange and Alexandria Rail Road. The corps left Sangster's Station on June 20 moving to Centerville, then west to Gainesville and reached Thoroughfare Gap on June 21 covering a total of eighteen miles. June 25 took II Corps back to Gainesville and then north across Bull Run to Gum Springs a march of sixteen miles. On June 26, II Corps, now under Hancock, crossed the Potomac at Edwards Ferry after a march of ten miles, bringing back vivid memories to the men of the Tammany regiment and others that had taken it on the chin more than a year earlier at Ball's Bluff. Two days later, after walking another 35 miles, they reached Monocacy Junction near Frederick, MD and were told of the leadership change in the Army of the Potomac that relieved Hooker and put General Meade in command. June

---

[2]   McGrath was exchanged for Lt. A. M. De Bree, CS Navy, GO. WD, No. 118, August 27, 1862.

[3]   New York State Archives. Document 6158. All five men received their promotions.

29 saw an additional march of over twenty miles (some reports say as much as 33 miles) from Monocacy Junction through Liberty and Johnsonville to Uniontown. On July 1 after a total march of over one hundred and ten miles in just over two weeks time, Hancock's command reached Taneytown just south of the Pennsylvania border and about twelve miles southeast of Gettysburg.[4]

Along the march, Private Patrick Killan, straggled and was captured near Dumfries, VA on June 17. Killan's record is quite interesting and is presented here in its entirety as an example of how complex service in the regiment could be for those in the rank and file. Killan, age 25, born in Ireland, joined the regiment on June 11, 1861 as a Private in Co. C. He had black hair, stood five feet, five inches high and was a silverplater by profession. He was engaged at Ball's Bluff where he escaped being captured, fought throughout the Peninsula campaign, at Antietam, Fredericksburg and Chancellorsville.[5] Muster sheets in Killan's record show him listed as "Deserted" June 17 near Dumfries, VA taking with him "one Springfield Rifle and a full set of accoutrements". On Oct. 10 he is listed as "returned from prisoner of war, was dropped from roll in error as deserter". On November 12, 1863 he was under arrest with the Division Provost Guard and sentenced "to hard labor for the rest of his term of service" on Dec. 11, 1863.[6] His sentence came as a result of a conviction on December 8, 1863 by a General Court Martial on three charges: conduct prejudicial to good order and discipline, disrespect towards his superior officer and mutinous conduct.[7] While there is no way of knowing what prompted Killan's behavior a good guess is that he lost it when he returned and found out he

---

4   Second Army Corps, 261-2 and OR: S1, V27, 140: Itinerary of the Army of the Potomac.

5   NARA record, Volunteer Descriptive List, Dec. 10, 1863, signed by Capt. Ed Cauvet, Commanding Co. C showing that he owed the government $45.48 for clothing. Clearly this document was completed in connection with the sentencing of Killan to hard labor.

6   Ibid, Letter from Lieut. William Harmon, Provost Marshal saying: I send you Private Patrick Killen, 42NY...and copy of order promulgating his sentence. Dec. 11, 1863.

7   Ibid. General Orders No. 195, HQ 2nd Division, Second Corps, Dec. 8, 1863. The sentence was approved by General Webb. A muster sheet has him being transferred by order of Court Martial to Rip Raps, VA.

had been considered a deserter. On April 20, 1864, Killan was admitted to Armory Square General Hospital in Washington. On June 16, a Surgeon at Armory Hospital requested instructions on what should be done with Killan as he was ready to be returned to duty but that an endorsement on his admission record said he was "under sentence of Court Martial". Killan was kept in the Central Guard House, Washington until August 17. On October 27, 1864, Killan was captured near Petersburg, VA and confined in Richmond on Oct. 29. He was transferred to Salisbury, N. C. Nov. 14, 1864, paroled at Aiken's Landing on Feb. 17, 1865 and admitted to Hospital, Division 1, Annapolis, MD on Feb. 23. The date of his capture is after the Tammany regiment was mustered out. Killan is not carried on the published rolls of the 82NY and 59NY so what actually happened in August, near Petersburg is somewhat of a mystery.

As the forces deployed in and around Gettysburg confrontation was inevitable. On July 1, Union cavalry took up and defended positions awaiting the arrival of the Union I and XI Corps under generals Reynolds and Howard. In the ensuing fight Reynolds was killed. Upon hearing of the fight and the loss of Reynolds, Meade ordered Hancock to turn over II Corps to Gibbon and proceed to the scene of the fight and take command of Union forces in the area. Hancock's temporary assignment lasted but a few hours after which he rejoined II Corps and as the end of July 1 gave birth to July 2 his troops settled into position just to the south of the town of Gettysburg along the Taneytown Road on some slightly high ground called Cemetery Ridge just north of the hills known as the Round Tops.[8]

The early hours of July 2 found the men of the 42NY to the left of the clump of trees on the ridge near several artillery batteries. While there were some artillery and picket actions nearby and the sounds of significant fights could be heard in the distance, little of consequence was occurring directly in their area. One of the picket details was made up of Tammany men, Companies F and D, Captain Tobin and Second Lieutenant Maguire commanding respectively. In total this picket force amounted to only 36 enlisted men.[9]

Early in the afternoon, General Sickles moved III Corps into a position somewhat forward of the main line established along Cemetery Ridge down

---

[8] Ibid, 264-8, Order, HQ, Army of the Potomac, July 1, 1863, 1:10PM.
[9] OR: S1, V27, 451-2. Report of Colonel Mallon

to the Round Tops. As the Confederate attacks against Little Round Top, the Peach Orchard and the Wheat Field unfolded during the afternoon Sickle's position came under attack and faltered. Between 5 and 6 P. M. an order was given to the 42NY and 19MA, under the combined command of Colonel Devereux commander of the 19MA, to move to the assistance of General Humphreys and his Second Division of Sickle's III Corps.

Colonel Mallon described the action in his report stating: "The staff officer who conducted us led the commands, they marching by the right flank until they were well brought under musketry fire. At this time all the troops to the front were precipitately retiring in great disorder. To avoid the enfilading effect of the fire, which was now rapidly thinning the ranks; to infuse confidence in the hearts of those who among those retreating might have some manhood left; to present a disciplined, unwavering front toward the rapidly approaching and confident enemy, the two regiments formed a line. From the moment of the commencement of this movement, I saw nothing of the staff officer who conducted us. When the rebels had arrived within 50 yards of the line, Colonel Devereux and I consulted as to the best course to be pursued. Already we were receiving fire from both flanks. We concluded that the best thing to be done was to retire. After having poured into the rebels several volleys, the regiments, the 19MA covering, moved to the rear. When we had retired 200 yards, we were ordered by Captain Leach of the brigade staff to rejoin the brigade. During this engagement the regiment lost 3 killed and 12 wounded".[10]

Fortunately we have additional descriptions of the action described by Colonel Mallon. Colonel Devereux, commanding the combined force of the19th MA and 42nd NY in his official report written July 7, 1863 states that he was ordered, around 5PM, to follow a staff officer and provide support for units of Humphreys' Division of III Corps. Both regiments combined amounted to only 290 men. The two regiments took prone positions behind the crest of a small knoll and waited until numbers of retreating Union soldiers passed, then delivered front and rear rank volleys slowing the enemy advance. To avoid being overrun the men of the combined force under Devereux retreated in good order firing several additional volleys and taking several prisoners. Additional Union reinforcements arrived and by dark all was quiet with the two regiments returning to positions

---

[10] Ibid

on Cemetery Ridge in support of a battery with the rest of the brigade in front by the stone wall.[11]

An account presented in the History of the Nineteenth Massachusetts says: " ...the two regiments, in all about 400 men are on the march at the double quick ... The two regiments move forward, but the terrible flank fire forces them to quickly halt. The men are ordered to lie down ... Col. Devereux says to Colonel Mallon: Order your men to stand up, fire a volley by the rear and front rank and you will clean out those in front of you and stop them. Then face about, go back to the old line on the double quick, face about again and wait for the Nineteenth ... As the regiments fall back ... a line of men from the Fifth Corps is met ... the two regiments fall back ... plug away at the foe coolly as if they had not already lost a quarter of their men ... It was now quite dark ... the regiments returned to the old position of the Second Corps, where they arrived at 2 AM".[12]

As the men of the Tammany regiment settled into their positions on Cemetery Ridge they had no idea that the action that they had just been through would pale in comparison to what was going to happen in just a few hours. As the sun came up on July 3 Confederate troops and artillery were massing on Seminary Ridge about a mile away from the Union lines. According to Colonel Mallon, the artillery barrage started about 1PM and lasted about four hours. Following the barrage enemy infantry attacked and came directly toward the position of the regiment about 100 yards behind the front line. Mallon's described "Pickett's Charge": "When those of the enemy who approached our brigade front had been successfully disposed of, and when those who had with great energy and persistence penetrated that portion of our line to our right, near the corps batteries, I caused the regiment to be formed in line facing the decisive point. The line was but fairly established and but just started in the direction of the contested point, when Colonel Hall, with words of encouragement, cheered us forward ... the regiment vigorously advanced, and in that charge which rescued our batteries from the hand of our foe, which saved our army from disaster and defeat, which gave to us glorious, triumphant success, this regiment was foremost and its flag in the advance. The color bearer, Sergeant Michael Cuddy ... displayed the most heroic bravery, when he

---

[11] OR: S1, V27, 442-4. Report of Col. Arthur Devereux, 19MA.
[12] Nineteenth Mass. 230-232

fell, mortally wounded, he rose by a convulsive effort, and triumphantly waved in the face of the rebels, not 10 yards distant, the flag he loved so dearly, of which he was so proud, and for which his valuable life, without a murmur, was freely given up".[13]

Colonel Mallon's description is of the final few minutes of the attack on July 3. The decisive point mentioned was the "Copse of Trees" on Cemetery Ridge that has been written about by every author that has discussed Gettysburg. It is today surrounded by a protective fence on the National Battlefield and it is impossible to stand near it and not be overwhelmed with emotion thinking about what happened at that spot. Mallon is describing the part of the battle when Confederate forces breached the defenses of the stone wall and overran Cushing's Battery; the part of the battle in the movie Gettysburg when general Armistead, with his sword holding up his hat, led his Virginians across the wall and into the trees.

For those who want to know the details of the entire action on July 3, there are numerous accounts available. It is, however, worth mentioning what several others have said about the final moments of the battle. Colonel Devereux said: "At around 1PM ... a most terrific cannonade ... lasted two hours. The battery which we lay behind was disabled in the first hour's cannonading ... about 3 O'clock the enemies cannonade slackened and columns of attack appeared emerging from the woods across the field in our front. They advanced gallantly upon our position ... General Hancock appeared on the left of my regiment. I ran to him, and asked permission to advance ... I marched my regiment with all speed and reached the desired point directly behind Mallon's regiment, which being on my right when we started, had reached there first. There was considerable confusion here, from the men running to the rear from the first line, and the two mentioned regiments coming up on a short space closely following each other ... For an instant it seemed to hang in the balance whether we should drive the enemy out of our works, which they had entered, or they succeed in carrying the position; but I firmly believe that the extraordinary exertions of a few officers, among whom were conspicuous the brigade commander and staff, Lieut. Haskell, of the division staff, Colonel Mallon, and some officers of my own regiment whom I saw, the line was carried back to the

---

13   Official Report of Colonel Mallon: OR: S1, V27, 451-2, July 16, 1863.

rifle pits, driving the enemy out. Just at this moment the enemy ... threw down their arms in a body, burst into our lines by hundreds, delivering themselves up as prisoners, and the battle was won".[14]

In July 1889, Colonel Devereux wrote another account of the battle saying: "Hancock came furiously riding up. I halted him, pointing to the enemy's colors crossing the stone wall and asked permission to put my men in there. His prompt direction was "To get in G-D quick". I went in on the run. Mallon with the 42NY taking up the same movement, as he stood by my side when this interview occurred between me and Hancock; and he had been substantially under my command since the middle of the afternoon of the previous day".[15]

Perhaps the most descriptive account of the hand to hand fighting that took place at the Copse of Trees was written by Lieut. Colonel Rice of the 19th MA in 1887. He said: " ...This is one of those periods in action, which are measurable in seconds. The men near seem to fire so slowly, those in the rear, although coming up at a run seem to drag their feet ... The crush toward the enemy in the copse becomes greater. The men in gray are doing all that is possible to keep off the mixed bodies of men who are moving upon them swiftly and without hesitation, keeping up as close and continuous a fire that it effects at last, become terrible. I can feel the touch of the men on my right and left as we near the edge of the Copse. It is fairly jammed with Pickett's men in all positions lying and kneeling. Back from the edge many are standing and firing over those in front. By the side of several who are firing while lying down are those with their hands up in token of surrender. I notice two men in particular not a musket length away. One is aiming so that I can look into his musket barrel; the other lying on his back is coolly ramming home a cartridge, and a little further on is one on his knees waving something white in both hands. Every foot of ground is occupied by men engaged in mortal combat who are in every possible position which can be taken while under arms, or lying wounded or dead ... Seconds are ages ... This close musketry fight could not last long ... I feel a sharp blow as a shot strikes me. Then another, I whirl

14 OR: S1, V27, 442-44. Report of Colonel A. F. Devereux, 19th MA, July 7. 1863.
15 Ladd, David L. and Audrey J. The Bachelder Papers, Morningside Press, Dayton Ohio, 1994. 1609-1610.

around, my sword is torn from my hand by a bullet or shell splinter, as I go down my men rush past me".[16]

Colonel Norman Hall, commanding Third Brigade, Second Division, Second Corps reported that the flag of the 22 North Carolina was Private Michael McDonough of the Tammany regiment. General William Harrow, commanding Second Division praised Captain Poinsett Cooper of the Tammany regiment who was acting as Assistant Inspector General of First Brigade.[17]

The battle was won but the price paid was extremely high. Looking to the numbers provided by Colonel Mallon we can see that the three day battle dramatically thinned out the ranks of the already far under strength Tammany regiment. If we take the strength of the two companies sent out as skirmishers, 36 enlisted men, as typical the regiment would have totaled around 200 men. The actual number is probably a bit lower since the combined total of the 42nd NY and 19th MA was put at between 290-400 men in descriptions written by Devereux. Using the 200 number and the final casualty figure in Mallon's report of 15 killed, 55 wounded and 4 missing for a total of 74, it comes to 37%, a bit more than every third man.

Accounting for the casualties by day is not completely possible but some facts are known. Again, looking to the numbers provided by Mallon, casualties on July 2 were 3 killed and 12 wounded meaning that on July 3 additional casualties, excluding the missing, were 12 killed, 43 wounded. What follows is an analysis based on data from the regimental roster, individual soldier's records and listings in "These Honored Dead, The Union Casualties at Gettysburg".[18]

---

[16] Account of Pickett's Charge by Lieut. Col. Rice, 19th MA, April 19, 1887, written at Ft. Totten, Dakota Territory. Vol. 1, Gettysburg Volume, Abner Doubleday Papers, NY Historical Society, NYC, Gettysburg National Military Park Library, Box B:46. Ft. Totten was established in 1867 on the south side of Lake Minnewaukan (Devils Lake). It closed in 1890. The account was written at the request of Gen. Doubleday for inclusion in a book he was writing.

[17] OR: S1, V27, 441. Report of Col. Hall. There is some question as to whether the flag was actually captured by McDonough. OR: S1, V27, 419-22. Report of Gen. Harrow.

[18] Busey, John W., These Honored Dead, Union Casualties at Gettysburg, Longstreet House, Hightstown, NJ, 1996 pages 133-5. Listed are 26 men, including those who were mortally wounded. Service records of men usually

Sixteen men (probably including one of the men listed by Mallon as missing) are recorded as being killed in action: Thomas James, Neil McAlean, Thomas Curley, Derby Constant, Thomas Barren, John Smith, Michael Brennan, Peter Fent, Patrick McMorrow, James Cullen, Michael Riley, Hugh Murphy, Sergeant Christopher Stone, Color Sergeant Michael Cuddy, Corporal Peter Brentzer and Frederick Tibell. Only Michael Riley is known to have been killed on July 2.

Ten men were mortally wounded: Corporal Henry Wooley, Corporal Frederick Schultz, Daniel Barrett, Sergeant Charles Moore, Daniel O'Shea, Ambrose Paine, Felix McGraw, First Sgt. William Flynn (Boston man)[19], Peter West and Corporal William Byrne.[20] McGraw and Byrne are recorded as wounded on July 2.

Forty six others are known as having been wounded, seven have some mention in their records of their being wounded on July 2.[21] In Patrick

---

contain individual muster sheets listing the date of causality as well as a Casualty Sheet completed in August 1878 that reads "Date of Casualty: July 2 & 3, 1863".

[19] Obituary for First Sgt. Flynn, Roxbury City Gazette, July 30, 1863, page 2, column 4. The obituary reads: "...At Gettysburg he was, during most of the third days' fight, in command of his company, Lt. Lennon, the only commissioned officer, having been wounded...and fell mortally wounded towards the close of the battle."

[20] Ibid. These Honored Dead list the ten mortally wounded as: F. McGraw, shot in the right leg, died August 14, W. Byrne, right ankle fractured by a gunshot, amputated, died July 24, H. Wooley, shot through the head, died July 6, F. Schultz, shot in the right lung, died July 25, D. Barrett, shot in the shoulder, died July 29, C. Moore, shot in both ankles, died September 5, D. O'Shea, shot in the right leg, died July 24 or 25, A. Paine, shot in both legs, died July 23, W. Flynn, wounded in the spine and left lung, died July 12, P. West, shot in the right leg, amputated, died July 23 or 24.

[21] Seven soldiers have a record of being wounded on July 2 or conflicting records of when they were wounded: P. Bishop, J. Burke, J. Coffee, J. Kennedy, R. McAuliffe, T. Ramsdell and P. Russell. Review of the service records of the following men contain confirmation of the date of their wounds as July 3: P. Cain, J. Casey, A. Cronier, J. Dougherty, J. Elsom, S. Ferguson, Lieut. M. Fitzharris, P. Flaherty, P. Flynn, J. Hudson, Lieut. P. Lennon (uncle Pat), M. Lynch, Lieut. T. Mallon, M. Marrowe, W. McHaney, J. Noonan, Capt. W. O'Shea, M. Queenan (Boston man), Sgt. John S. Ritter, W. Rutledge, J. Smithwick, Lieut. S. Staniford, J. Vilbert and Captain R. Wright. The records of R. Allen, J. Ash, C. Bach, J. Falton, P. Fitzgerald, J. Gilbert, W. Jamieson, T. King, J. Malloy, J. McCarthy,

H. Lennon's (Uncle Pat) file is a document written on July 9, 1863 saying: " ...he is recovering from a gunshot wound of right arm received in action at Gettysburg, PA July 3, 1863." Twenty-three men recovered from their wounds sufficiently to return to the regiment. One man, Patrick Genatty, is recorded as being wounded and captured on July 3. He died of disease on December 14, 1863 at Confederate States Armory Hospital, Richmond. Almost certainly he was one of the "missing" listed by Mallon. Another man James Pepper has a record that is unclear. He is listed as being sent to General Hospital on July 4 with no further record[22].

The above accounts for the 74 casualties Mallon listed. However, only one of the fatalities and seven of the wounded of July 2, have been documented. Given that the regiment did not return to Cemetery Ridge until well after midnight on July 2, it is not surprising that the records do not agree.

Patrick Downing wrote a letter to John O'Mahony, head of the Fenian Brotherhood in New York saying: "I am sitting by Denis' bedside. He has had his leg amputated above the ankle otherwise he is in excellent health. For myself, I am all right, which all things considered, I think rather strange. Of the 42d, O'Shea and Fitzharris are seriously hurt ..." Downing was speaking of his brother who was the original Sergeant Major of the Tammany regiment and fought at Gettysburg with the 97NY as a Captain.[23]

D. McCrystal, R. Murray, J. Owens, B. Quinn and N. Rogers have not been reviewed so, as of this writing, no confirmation was found on their casualty date.

[22] These Honored Dead, supra, list him as "apparently died of wounds in an unidentified hospital".

[23] Irish American, July 18, 1863, page 2, column 5. Denis Downing left the Tammany regiment before Ball's Bluff. In his letter he restricted his comments mentioning only the fate of prominent members of the Fenian Brotherhood.

Tammany Regiment Monument at Gettysburg
Kreis, Philip. "Tammany Monument at Gettysburg," Under
two flags, the adventures of Philip Kreis, story of the Tammany
Regiment of New York, John Shaw Pierson Civil War Collection
(W), Rare Book Division, Department of Rare Books and
Special Collections, Princeton University Library.

Tammany Regiment veterans at dedication of Tammany monument
at Gettysburg, September 24, 1891. Courtesy of Sheila Vaughn,
great granddaughter of James Elson, front row fourth from left.

On September 24, 1891 the twenty seven foot, bronze and granite monument to the Tammany regiment that currently stands on Hancock Avenue near the Copse of Trees at Gettysburg National Battlefield, was dedicated. To say the least it is impressive with its design of a tepee and artwork depicting the Native American culture upon which the organization of Tammany Hall was based. Many visitors mistakenly think that Native Americans served in the Tammany regiment. Research by this author did not identify a single member of the regiment that was a Native American.

The dedication ceremony was an elaborate affair attended by 72 of the surviving members of the regiment. Captain Eugene Sullivan of the veteran organization opened the ceremony and the statue was unveiled by the son of Colonel James E. Mallon. General Daniel Sickles delivered an oration and presented the monument to the Gettysburg battlefield memorial association.[24] Sickles said: "There is a day and an hour in the annuals of every nation when its life hangs on the issue of a battle; when it stands or falls by the sword. Such a battle was Gettysburg. You are now standing on the field where the destiny of this republic was decided. Right here, are some of the brave soldiers, veterans of the Forty-second, who helped to win the decisive victory for the Union. You stand, right here, on a spot that was a vortex of battle; man to man, steel against steel, rifle and cannon and sword, shot and shell, the hoarse voices of desperate combatants, the smoke and flame and the clash of arms; right hear near this clump of trees."[25]

It should be pointed out that there was a tremendous amount of controversy over where monuments should be placed at Gettysburg. A rule adopted on May 5, 1887 resolved: "that hereafter regiments erecting monuments on the ground of the Association would be required to locate and place them in the position held by the regiment in the line of battle,

---

[24] Brooklyn Eagle, September 24, 1891, page 6. Exactly where Eugene Sullivan obtained the rank of Captain is unclear. Could he and Philip Kreis, who is also listed as a Captain, have been awarded that rank though their positions in the veteran's organization?

[25] Proceedings of the Dedication of the Monument to the Tammany Regiment, Tammany Society, New York 1892. Page 20.

but that they would not be prohibited from erecting such markers on the field, to indicate secondary or advanced positions, as the Association might determine." The only regiment that placed their monument in a more forward position was the 72nd PA. The placement of that monument, at the stone wall instead of a position in line with that of the Tammany regiment, was challenged in the Supreme Court of Pennsylvania by the Gettysburg Battlefield Association. The court refused to change the placement decision saying "the Commonwealth … has the right to designate the position where any of her regiments specially distinguished themselves". The left side of the monument reads: "The regiment reached this Angle at 1 a.m., took position in rear of this monument supported Cushing's Battery A, 4th US Artillery. At 6 p.m. assisted in repulsing an attack of the enemy and in making a counter charge driving them beyond the Emmitsburg road, capturing 250 prisoners."[26]

In 1893 the survivors of the Tammany regiment planned a return visit to the battlefield. At that time of the more than one thousand original members only seventy four remained.[27]

---

[26] Supreme Court of Pennsylvania, May Term 1891. #20 30. Middle District. Appeal of the Gettysburg Battlefield Memorial Association from the decree of the Court of Common Pleas of Adams County.

[27] New York Times, May 15, 1893.

Chapter Seventeen

BRISTOE STATION
MINE RUN

Gettysburg had reduced the Tammany regiment to just over one hundred men, about the strength of a single company. Most of Second Corps shared the same fate and the loss of experienced men was being felt everywhere. Within a year many of the regiments recruited at the beginning of the war would be mustered out of service and there was no apparent way to replace them. Actions along the Mississippi River, including Vicksburg, coupled with the losses at Chancellorsville and Gettysburg impacted thinking in Washington resulting in the implementation of a plan to add new fighting men to the ranks that would have far reaching impact on the Tammany regiment and the entire Union army. The stage had been set on March 3, 1863 when the Federal Enrollment (Draft) Act was passed.[1] This law provided the structure for registering all men between the ages of twenty and forty five so that if they were needed they could be called into service by order of the President. The various sections of the law defined certain exemptions from service and created a process whereby men, if they were selected, could pay a substitute $300 to perform their service.

Another part of the plan was put into motion on June 25, 1863 by General Order No. 191 which created a process whereby experienced soldiers could re-enlist and receive sizable bounties for their continued service. General Order 376, Nov. 21, 1863, modified the benefits of

---

[1]   An Act for enrolling and calling out the national Forces, and for other purposes, Congressional Record. 37th Cong. 3d Session. Ch. 74, 75. 1863. March 3, 1863.

re-enlisting to include the granting of a furlough of at least thirty days with transportation costs being paid by the Quartermaster Department. It was this provision, a chance to go home for a visit with family that did the trick for many soldiers. More than fifty Tammany men re-enlisted between December 10, 1863 and March 30, 1864.[2]

On June 15, in response to Confederate military movements, President Lincoln issued Proclamation 102 calling into federal service for six months one hundred thousand militia from the states of Maryland, Pennsylvania, Ohio and West Virginia. On July 2, a call was made for three hundred thousand men under the provisions of the Enrollment Act.[3]

The first lottery drawing in New York was made on July 11, the second on July 13. Rioting broke out in the streets over the following days resulting in the destruction of numerous city buildings and the murder of over one hundred residents. More than ten members of the black community of New York were killed and others were forced to leave the city in fear of their lives. Order was eventually restored with the assistance of Union troops including some from mid-west regiments within the Army of the Potomac. While the New York Draft Riot is the most well known, civil unrest broke out in many other cities.[4]

---

[2] OR: S3, V3, 414-16. General Orders No. 191, War Department, June 25, 1863. Veterans had to have served not less than nine months and had to pass certain mustering regulations to be accepted and called "Veteran Volunteers". Each man would receive one month's pay and a bounty of $402 to be paid in installments over the following three years or at the conclusion of their service. Men could remain in their current regiments but if their regiment was to be mustered out before the full term of their enlistment they would be transferred to new units. For men of the Tammany regiment transfer would initially be to the 82nd NY and then the 59th NY. OR: S3, V3, 1084. General Orders No. 376, War Department, November 21, 1863. OR: S1, V33, 347. On January 5, 1864, General Meade informed Gen. Halleck that through January 2, 1864, 16,189 men had re-enlisted as Veteran Volunteers, each receiving an average furlough of thirty five days.

[3] New York Times, July 9, 1863. Another call for 300,000 men was made by Presidential Proclamation 107, Oct. 17, 1863.

[4] On July 14, 1863, rioting of a much smaller degree broke out in Boston. Other cities where disturbances broke out included Philadelphia, Chicago, St. Louis and Detroit.

To fully appreciate the impact the draft had consider that between October 1, 1861 and July 11, 1863 only 69 men were enrolled in the Tammany regiment. Between July 11 and September 30, 1863, 250 new men were enrolled. The experience level of the regiment as a whole was dramatically reduced. Two out of every three men in the regiment had been in the army less than three months. To handle the influx of new men orders were issued sending senior officers and enlisted men to New York to serve at Riker's Island handling new recruits. Periodically, groups of new men were sent to Virginia escorted by a veteran of the regiment.[5]

In rare cases special arrangements were made for individual soldiers to be sent on recruiting duty. Private James Ostrander, joined the regiment on September 2, 1863 as a substitute. On Feb. 1, 1864 a letter from the Executive Department of the State of New York to the Secretary of War, signed by William Kidd, Military Secretary, requested that a ten day furlough be granted to Ostrander to go to Albany to visit his sick father. The request was forwarded, after being received on Feb. 5, to HQ Army of the Potomac on Feb. 8 and then to Second Corps HQ. On Feb. 10, Ostrander was assigned to recruiting duty in New York and left Virginia the next day.[6]

Men were assigned to the Tammany regiment periodically throughout the period between July 11 and September 30 but the largest number, 53, were enrolled on August 26. Between August 24 and August 31, 115 men

---

[5] Men detailed on recruiting duty included: Col. J. Mallon, Lt. Col. W. Lynch, Captain P. Downing, Lieut. J. Maguire, Sergeants A. Cline, S. Ferguson, P. Gaffney, E. Sullivan, J. Daley, M. Thomas, C. Malloy, A. Brandt and Private W. Carey. Men served on recruiting duty for various time periods between July 63 and Feb. 64 and several remained in New York through most of the rest of the war. In December 1863, a recruiting office was set up at 6 Centre Street in Manhattan. SO No: 171, HQ, Second Army Corps, July 26, 1863. Captain W. O'Shea was ordered to Elmira, New York in March of 1864 to assist in recruiting activities. Special Orders No.189, State of New York, Headquarters of the Acting Assistant Provost Marshal General, Northern Division. March 7, 1864.

[6] NARA: record of J. Ostrander. Following his return to the regiment he was captured on June 22, 1864 at Weldon RR. He was paroled on Dec. 10, 1864.

joined the ranks and were assigned to companies as needed.[7] New men tended to be somewhat older with almost 30% being over age 30.

Desertions among the new men were significant. Between September 21 and October 13, fifteen newly enrolled Tammany men are recorded as having deserted.[8] The exact circumstances associated with most of these desertions are likely lost to history, however some details are known.

John Beltz, John Beleler and Jacob Stuher had all enrolled and been assigned to Co. G on August 26. The three men deserted from the regimental camp on the Rapidan River on September 25-26. Beltz was captured and sent to Andersonville.[9] What happened to the other two men is unknown.

Peter Smith, born in Vermont, had joined Co. K as a substitute on July 11. He was 22 years old, stood five feet four and had blue eyes and brown hair. According to his record on October 2, 1863 while acting as a vidette (scout) he deserted to the enemy taking with him his Springfield rifle and the rest of his equipment.

Desertion could lead to execution or other severe consequences. Such was the case of Adam Wigand, born in Germany, who had joined the regiment as a substitute on September 2, 1863 in Brooklyn, NY. He was 25 years old, stood five foot two and had blue eyes and brown hair. He deserted from camp near Sommerville, VA on September 24 and was apprehended almost immediately carrying $195.50. Wigand was tried by a General Court Martial in March 1864 and sentenced to serve the rest of the war at Fort Jefferson Prison, Dry Tortugas, Florida.[10]

---

7   The 247 new men that joined between July 11 and September 30, whose company assignments are known, were distributed as follows: A: 31, B: 24, C: 21, D: 25, E: 18, F: 28, G: 31, H: 17, I: 23, K: 29.

8   Men listed as having deserted are: Daniel Morton, John Rall, Herman Konig, Adam Wigand, William Wolf, John Beltz, John Beleler, Jacob Stuher, Arculus Simons, Charles Hug, John McDermott, William Bottez, Charles Rock, Peter Smith and William Degmeier.

9   Beltz was transferred to Camp Lawton, Millen, GA on November 11, 1864. No further records were found.

10   Fort Jefferson, Dry Tortugas, was considered one of the worse federal prisons and was not used to house Confederate prisoners. Mainly used as a prison for Union criminals and trouble makers the combination of hard labor, terrible heat, insects

Private Philip Kreis
Kreis, Philip. "Philip Kreis," Under two flags, the adventures of Philip
Kreis; story of the Tammany Regiment of New York. John Shaw
Pierson Civil War Collection (W), Rare Book Division, Department
of Rare Books and Special Collections. Princeton University Library.

The August 26 group and more specifically the men of that group assigned to Company B deserve to be looked at closer for a special reason. Philip Kreis, the author of "Under Two Flags, A History of the Tammany Regiment" says in his book that he joined the Tammany regiment on August 26, 1863 and was assigned to Company B.[11] There is absolutely no doubt in the mind of this author that Philip Kreis did join and serve in the Tammany regiment, however he is not listed anywhere in the records. Why is that? It is this author's opinion that Philip Kreis served under an assumed name, that of John Vaze. Is there absolute proof of that? No. Is there enough evidence to support that conclusion? Absolutely!

---

and disease resulted in a high mortality rate of inmates. The fate of Wigand is unknown.

[11] Kreis, Philip: Under Two Flags, the adventures of Philip Kreis; story of the Tammany Regiment of New York. John Shaw Pierson Civil War Collection (W), Rare Book Division, Department of Rare Books and Special Collections, Princeton University Library. Hereinafter cited as "Under Two Flags".

In Under Two Flags (UTF) Philip Kreis (PK) describes in detail his service in the Confederacy. He goes into great detail about his service in the Tammany regiment during the Battle of Bristoe Station but provides almost no detail of the anything past Bristoe. PK does say that he was seriously ill but there is no mention of his being discharged for disability.[12]

Seven men are recorded as having joined Company B on August 26. They are: Frederick Diterick, Peter McGourty, Daniel McGuire, John Otto, Isaac Propper, James Sheridan and John Vaze. Otto was captured at Bristoe Station and died in prison. Propper was wounded in the Wilderness and Sheridan and Diterick were discharged for disability. McGourty and Sheridan were over 35 years old and McGuire was 28. PK would have been almost 20 in August 1863. John Vaze is listed as a 21 year old former Confederate soldier. It is hard to imagine that PK would have joined the Tammany regiment the same day as another former Confederate, served with him at Bristoe Station and yet did not mention that fact in his story.

Attempts to find the service records of PK at the National Archives failed. A service record for John Vaze was obtained but was very limited in detail about his service other than mentioning his service in the Confederacy. PK is not listed on the rolls of the 82nd or 59th NY regiments, where he would have been reassigned after the Tammany regiment was mustered out. John Vaze is recorded on the rosters of both regiments and is listed as absent sick in Carver Hospital.

A search for pension records of both PK and John Vaze provided additional reasons to suspect that the two men were in fact the same man.[13] Although copies of a pension application exist for PK there is no record of any pension being granted. Record cards do show that confirmation of his service was requested by the Pension Department but apparently none were found sufficient to allow the granting of a pension. His pension application, filed after his death, says that he served under his own name, however it is quite possible that his wife did not know that he

---

[12] Ibid

[13] Over the years I was able to contact Fred Kreiss, the great-grandson of Philip Kreis. He was able to provide me with copies of pension documents that were filed in an attempt to obtain a pension by Philip Kreis's wife after his death. I am deeply indebted to Fred for his assistance.

served under an alias as such service was considered shameful.[14] It should also be remembered that if PK was captured and found to have been a former Confederate he faced execution, a fact that PK mentions several times in UTF.[15]

There is also a record card for a request of service for John Vaze in connection with a pension application. The National Archives could not locate a pension file for Vaze and there is no record of him that could be found prior to the war or after the war in census data.

The pension record cards of both PK and John Vaze have on them the names of Congressmen James R. Howe and F. H. Wilson respectively. Both men were Congressmen from Brooklyn, New York serving together representing neighboring wards. Both men were members of the same social club, the Union League Club of Brooklyn. PK's pension application was filed by the law firm of Butts and Phillips, experienced lawyers known for their connections to the Grand Army of the Republic and the Pension Department, yet they could not establish the service record of PK. Perhaps someday in the future clear evidence will surface to either prove or disprove whether John Vaze and Philip Kreis are the same person.

The battle at Bristoe Station on October 14, 1863 does not rank among the major engagements of the Civil War. The numbers of troops engaged, the casualties suffered, the ground taken or lost and the impact of the outcome of the battle on the rest of the war pales in comparison to what happened just a few months before at Gettysburg. Nevertheless, Bristoe Station is an important event in the history of the Tammany regiment for reasons that will become apparent as this chapter continues.

For the Army of the Potomac Bristoe Station was the first significant fight following the infusion of conscripts described above. Many of the regiments no longer reflected the character they had started the war with. The Tammany regiment now had as many men of German descent as there were Irishmen. Gone were so many of the battle tried and proven officers

---

[14] Miller, Richard F. Harvard's Civil War, University Press of New England, 2005, page 285. Reference to James Degan who had served as a substitute under an assumed name and felt that "giving the alias was an act I felt ashamed of at the time and one that I regretted since."

[15] Supra, "Under Two Flags"

and enlisted men and valid questions were being asked as to whether or not the new men would measure up and perform adequately under fire.

Bristoe Station was a stop on the Orange and Alexandria Railroad that ran between Culpeper and Manassas in Virginia. A small village had once existed where the station was but only a single house remained. The station was located just to the west of Broad Run, a significant stream that ran roughly perpendicular to the rail line, a road connecting the small towns of Brentsville and Milford passed directly by the station.

Following Gettysburg the Army of the Potomac had returned to Virginia and seemed content to spend time refurbishing itself. To a large degree the Confederate forces did the same. One major exception was that General Longstreet was sent to reinforce General Bragg in Tennessee. Washington responded to that move by detaching the Eleventh and Twelfth Corps from the Army of the Potomac and sending them to reinforce the Army of the Cumberland. Fearful that additional Union troops would be sent west Robert E. Lee decided that an offensive action had to be undertaken in Virginia to freeze the federal troops. It was this decision that resulted in the fight at Bristoe Station.

During the first ten days of October rebel activity was being reported by cavalry pickets and a number of small engagements of cavalry troops occurred to the north of the railroad on both sides of the Rappahannock River. As the frequency of these encounters increased General Meade became convinced that a major rebel attack was in the making that would threaten his supply base and ordered the Army of the Potomac to be prepared to move.

Second Corps, under the command of Major General Gouverneur K. Warren since August 12, 1863, received its orders from General Meade and Warren readied his force consisting of 587 officers and 8,243 enlisted men with 32 pieces of artillery manned by an additional 16 officers and 537 enlisted men.[16] On October 11, II Corps moved from Culpeper across the Rappahannock using the railroad bridge and settled in near Bealton traveling about eighteen miles. The next day orders sent the troops back across the river to prepare for an expected attack toward Culpeper that never materialized. Early in the morning of October 13, following new orders, II Corps crossed the river again and headed east. A final decision

---

[16] OR: S1, V29, 235-44, Report of General Warren.

had been made to have the Army of the Potomac retreat eastward and II Corps was to be the rearguard of the army. As II Corps moved eastward it occupied positions initially near Fayetteville, moving to Three Mile Station on the Warrenton Branch rail line after the rest of the army had safely left the area. The corps ammunition trains and ambulances, a column of 225 wagons extending for two miles on the road, were left behind at Three Mile Station under the protection of Colonel Carroll's brigade of the Third Division. The rest of II Corps continued east, crossing Turkey Run setting up camp just east of Cedar Run near the small village of Auburn. At 2 A.M. orders were received for II Corps to head south to Catlett's Station and then to move east along the railroad. It was this movement that would bring II Corps and the Tammany regiment, to Bristoe Station.[17]

Four days before the battle, Colonel Mallon wrote to General Sprague, Adjutant General of New York saying: "Some time since I recommended 2d Lieut. Thos. B. Riley to be promoted to 1st Lieut. He cannot be mustered in as 2d Lieut., the regiment not having the number of men required by the War Department. This will be handed to you by Lt. Riley himself for whose fitness and capacity I can safely vouch. His services as an officer are now sadly needed-the conscripts recently sent to the Regiment suffering from want of good drill master. Please issue the commission as 1st Lieut. as soon as possible, the good of the service requires that no time be lost." Mallon's reference to the low training level of recently arrived men was shared throughout the Army of the Potomac's command structure.[18]

---

[17]   Ibid

[18]   New York Archives, document 11901. Thomas B. Riley, born 1833, was very well known to Colonel Mallon. He was the brother of Colonel Edward John Riley, the husband of Mallon's sister Theresa. He had served with Mallon in the 40th New York, under Colonel Riley as a Captain. He was mustered into the Tammany regiment on October 10, 1863 at Culpeper, VA. Following the death of Colonel Mallon, Riley was detached to Brigade Headquarters as A.A.D.C. (Acting Assistant Aide-de Camp) to Colonel Morehead on Dec. 7, 1863 by Special Order 195, II Corps. He was discharged on January 25, 1864 by Special Order 37, paragraph 3, War Department for physical disability. Following the war he lived in Brooklyn and ran for a seat in the New York Assembly in 1892 but lost to George A. Stevens. Riley died on Sunday, Feb. 6, 1898 at his home at 289 Livingston Street, Brooklyn, New York.

The exact date Mallon arrived back in Virginia, from his service at Riker's Island, New York is unclear, but it was after September 25. On that date, from Riker's Island, Mallon wrote a letter to Albany requesting that his brother Thomas be commissioned as the regimental Quartermaster of the Tammany regiment saying: "Lt. Mallon was severely wounded in the thigh at Gettysburg in consequence of which, I am informed, he will always be unfit for foot service."[19]

While details of the movements of II Corps enroute to Bristoe are somewhat confusing what happened to the Tammany regiment during the battle on October 14, is fairly clear. A good place to start is the official report of Captain Robert C. Wright, who at the time of the battle commanded the regiment.[20] He said, " …on the 14th day of October, near Bristoe Station, Va., while marching by the right flank, the enemy appeared advancing on us in line of battle. I was immediately directed by Colonel Mallon to take up position behind the bank of the railroad, which was directly in our front. We there awaited the advance of the enemy … Our fire was reserved until they came close to us. Then we opened with terrible effect, and succeeded in repulsing them with severe loss and capturing many prisoners. I then sent out two companies to follow up the retreating foe, and act as skirmishers in our front. They advanced about a quarter of a mile to a wood, and there found the enemy in force and advancing. They then fell back according to orders and joined the regiment. Colonel Mallon, of the regiment (in command of the brigade), while gallantly leading his command, was killed … The men of this regiment surpassed all anticipation in coolness and bravery, most of them being substitutes or conscripts, having joined but a few days previous to the engagement …"[21]

Philip Kreis's account of the battle adds some important details. He said: " …As soon as we came within gunshot, they began firing … The regiments formed in battle lines. It happened that my company came on

---

[19] New York Archives, document 11138.

[20] Following Gettysburg and during the period when many senior officers were in New York on recruiting duty the Tammany regiment was often commanded by a Captain. On August 31, 1863 the regiment was under the command of Captain Edward C. Cauvet. OR: S1, V29, 121.

[21] OR: S1, V29, 287, Report of Captain Robert C. Wright, Company G, Commanding the regiment.

top of the railroad track. We were ordered to lie down and cover ourselves behind the rails. The other companies came behind the embankments. We lost a good many men, being in an exposed position. The command was given to retreat a little from the railroad behind a little hill. There I saw Colonel Mallon killed ... We took quite a number of prisoners. I was detailed to guard them."[22]

PK's account places Company B of the Tammany regiment at the intersection of the Orange and Alexandria Railroad and the Brentsville Road. It was only at this spot that men were denied the cover of the embankment.[23] It also seems likely that Company B was not one of the two companies sent forward by Captain Wright.

In the report filed by James Fennessy with the Irish American newspaper he said: " ...Our brigade, having been posted along the side of the railroad ... our pickets were driven in by the enemy's skirmishers ... our men preserved their fire until this line was quite close, when volley after volley was poured into them. Their advance was checked; their line was broken into pieces and hundreds of them slain ... The Tammany has lost, I regret to say, it's gallant Colonel. He had command of the brigade at the time, having been senior Colonel of the brigade since last August ... Mallon was equaled by few-surpassed by none. The bullet that pierced him, struck down forever one of the brightest stars in our Irish military horizon- one to whom we, Irish soldiers, used to point with proud feelings, for his dashing bravery on the field of battle. In camp and bivouac he was a strict disciplinarian-strict perhaps to a fault in the opinion of some; but whatever may be or have been the opinions of a few on this point, none will deny that in Colonel Mallon were combined the qualities of a true soldier. He was an accomplished scholar, and that combined with military genius, caused his society to be courted by those within his sphere. In his death the army has sustained an irreparable loss, and old Ireland a true

---

[22] Supra, "Under Two Flags", page 9

[23] Author's Note: On October 12-14, 2013 at the 150th Anniversary of the Battle of Bristoe Station, I was fortunate to be part of the commemoration program and had the opportunity to walk the ground fought over by the Tammany regiment. It is clear to any observer that men that were positioned at the intersection of the rail line and the Brentsville Road were exposed in a way no others experienced. The width of the road is no more than 25 feet.

friend and enthusiastic lover. I will not attempt to describe what must have been the feelings of another of Ireland's valiant and faithful sons, Captain William O'Shea, as he took the dying Colonel from where he had fallen and had him placed in the rear … Over the grave of the heroic Mallon may there be an Irish Shamrock planted, and let it be strewn with the choicest flowers that will bloom each springtime in token of the Irish ashes that under them smolders."[24]

Mallon's death was mentioned in many official reports. General Warren said: "Colonel Mallon, commanding Third Brigade, Second Division was killed. A portion of his command was placed where the railroad changes from cut to embankment and afforded no shelter. Here this brave man took his stand to encourage his troops and fell."[25] General Webb, Commander of the Second Division said: "Colonel Mallon, commanding Third Brigade, was mortally wounded, rallying a few men of one of his regiments who were driven back from the most exposed position on his line. I lost in him an able commander and a brave, intelligent gentleman."[26]

Lieut. Colonel Ansel Wass, 19th Massachusetts said: "The enemy's line advanced … it broke and retired in confusion … A party of about 20 took position in a ruined building within 100 feet of our line, and continued firing until they were surrounded and the entire party captured by men of the Forty-second New York … During the advance of the enemy, and while the fire was the hottest a part of the line of the Forty-second New York, composed principally of conscripts, and much exposed where the road crossed the track, gave way. In attempting to rally them Colonel Mallon, commanding the brigade, was shot through the body and died in an hour afterward. Through the exertions of the officers and non-commissioned officers of the Forty-second the break was filled …"[27]

A somewhat more detailed account of Mallon's last moments was described by Major Henry Livermore Abbott and Doctor John Perry, both with the 20th Massachusetts. Abbott said: " …just after rallying a company of his regiment which broke, that Col. Mallon was killed. Ever since the battle of Gettysburg and particularly since he commanded the brigade,

[24] Irish American, New York, October 31, 1863, page 2, column 5.
[25] OR: S1, V29, 245
[26] OR: S1, V29, 277-8
[27] OR: S1, V29, 283-4

we have been on the most intimate terms. I loved him almost as a brother, and while his eyes were glazing and he could no longer see me, he told me of his friendship. He was going towards me to speak to me when he was hit." Perry said: "I begged him not to, saying that he would surely be shot, but he answered "No, I cannot stand the suspense, and it will take but a moment", whereupon he rose, and was instantly shot through the abdomen. I dragged him down to a little muddy stream, the only place of safety, where the poor fellow lay with the water almost running down his throat. He lived until the fight was almost over and finally expired in my arms."[28]

Colonel Mallon's Obituary said: " ...Acting Brig. General Mallon was of Irish American parentage, and born in the City of Brooklyn, Sept. 12, 1836. Having received a good commercial education, he was employed first ... in the house of Wright, Gillett and Rawson and subsequently in the firm of Holcomb and Harvey, both in the wholesale commission business in the City. He commenced the same line of business on his own account, and speedily secured for himself an honorable position on the floor of the Corn Exchange and of the new Produce Exchange ... Having been a member of the Fourth Company (Capt. Riblet) Seventh Regiment, NYSNG for many years ... he went with his regiment as a private ... in April 1861, to Washington ... General Mallon was five feet seven inches high, and of remarkably sinewy frame ... In religion, Gen. Mallon, like all his family was a Catholic; in political conviction he was a Conservative Republican; but he never had anything to do with, had no taste for, practical politics. His remains reached the residence of his family

---

[28]   Scott, Robert Garth, Fallen Leaves, The Civil War Letters of Major Henry Livermore Abbott, Kent State University Press, Kent Ohio 1991, page 224 referencing Perry, Letters from a Surgeon of the Civil War, 112-3. Major Abbott would be killed in action in the Wilderness. In his 1863 letter Dr. Perry said of Mallon "He was just married". Actually, Mallon married Anna E. McCormick four years earlier on August 31, 1859, at the Church of the Assumption of the Blessed Virgin Mary, 64 Middagh Street, Brooklyn, New York. Ancestry. com Message Boards, UN64B0, April 25, 2007. They had 2 children, James Edward born Aug. 16, 1860 and Anna born Jan. 4, 1862. Anna E. McCormick Mallon was the daughter of Patrick and Sarah McCormick from Perth Amboy, New Jersey. Anna never remarried. She received a widow's pension (Application 37963, Certificate 25436). Anna died Jan. 14, 1913.

in Little Water Street, Brooklyn on Monday, under care of his brother, Lieut. Thomas Mallon ... His funeral will be strictly private in obedience to the frequently expressed wishes of the fallen hero."[29]

In fact Mallon's funeral was anything but private. Newspaper articles described it in detail saying: "The remains of General J. E. Mallon ... were conveyed to their last resting place in Flatbush cemetery by the largest and most impressive funeral cortege that our city has ever witnessed. The high social reputation and the military fame of the deceased patriot and soldier drew together an assemblage of eminent civilians and soldiers, honorable to our city and a justly paid tribute to the memory of a faithful citizen, a tender husband, an affectionate father, and a brave and gallant soldier. The funeral services were celebrated at the Roman Catholic Cathedral in Jay Street ... The coffin, covered with a handsome American flag, was placed in the middle aisle and the seats immediately surrounding it were filled by the relatives and friends of the deceased and the military officers that had come to pay the last tribute of respect to their fallen companion". Following the service and an emotional eulogy delivered by Father Keegan, of the Church of the Assumption where Mallon was married, the funeral procession formed and escorted the flag draped coffin from the church up Jay Street to Flatbush Avenue and then to Flatbush Cemetery. Captain Patrick Downing of the Tammany regiment was one of the pall bearers.[30]

Other casualties sustained by the Tammany regiment at Bristoe, were two men killed- Privates Alexander Breadner, Co. A and Adam Walter, Co. I. Both men joined the regiment on August 24, 1863. Another Tammany man, Philip Cratton, a Boston enlistee, died while serving with Battery A, First Rhode Island Artillery.[31] Nine men have been identified as having

---

29   New York Times, October 21, 1863. James Mallon's father was Hugh Mallon, born 1799 in County Armagh, Ireland. He died July 8, 1845 in Brooklyn, NY. Brooklyn Eagle, July 9, 1845, page 2. Mallon's mother was Ann McFarland Mallon, born in Ireland in 1805. She died July 1, 1888 at 728 Lafayette, Street, Brooklyn, NY. The family arrived in the U. S. in 1822.

30   Irish American, October 24, 1863, page 2, column 5 and October 31, 1863, page 2, column 5. Brooklyn Eagle, October 21, 1863, page 3.

31   Record of P. Cratton and OR: S1, V29, 308-9, Report of Captain Arnold. Cratton had been wounded at Fredericksburg in Dec. 1862 and assigned to the RI Artillery since May 1863.

been wounded and thirteen were taken prisoner.[32] Of the twenty-two wounded and captured men eighteen had been with the regiment less than two months. Company E sustained the most casualties, seven, suggesting that they might have been one of the two companies sent forward by Captain Wright.

Edward W. Bates a private in Co. K and one of those captured at Bristoe Station served as the Court Clerk in the trial of the "Raiders" at Andersonville. He was a member of a prisoner petition committee sent to Washington in August 1864 to discuss prisoner exchanges and was a witness at the trial of Henry Wirz, commandant of Andersonville following the end of the war.[33]

Another Tammany man was slightly injured (left thigh) at Bristoe.[34] Captain Poinsett Cooper was serving as AAIG (Acting Assistant Inspector General) of the Third Brigade, Second Division, II Corps on Colonel Mallon's staff. Cooper has been mentioned periodically in previous chapters. His story is quite interesting.

---

[32] Wounded were: G. Stein, Co. A, J. Murray, Co. D, Corp. J. Pigot, J. Malloy, E. Robbins and J. Hudson, Co. E, L. O'Sullivan, Co. F and A. Caleb and G. McGinnis, Co. H. Taken prisoner were: S. Boyle, J. Otto and W. Rapp, Co. B, M. Dougherty, Co. C, R. Smith, Co. D, A. McGiveney, W. Foley and W. Broom, Co. E, G. Cline, Co. F, C. Strewing, Co. H, H. Stockfish and J. Fink, Co. I and Edward Bates, Co. K. Cline, Stockfish, Otto and Fink died while in Richmond. Boyle and Smith died at Andersonville. W. Broom was released April 1, 1865 and mustered out in New York City on July 8, 1865.

[33] The Andersonville Raiders were a group of rouge prisoners that terrorized fellow prisoners. On July 11, 1864 the six leaders of the Raiders were hanged. Bates arrived from Hilton Head, South Carolina around August 19, 1864 on the steamer Arago. Irish American, New York, September 3, 1864, page 2, column 7-8. The petition can be found in its entirety at OR: S2, V7, 615-18. Bates was discharged for disability in New York City on November 15, 1864. On January 20, 1864 a letter was sent to General Benjamin Butler at Ft. Monroe asking about the state of health of Edward W. Boate (aka Bates). His wife Henrietta had made inquiries stating that she believed that her husband was in a dying state. OR: S2, V6, 858.

[34] New York Times, October 16, 1863. Listed as Capt. B. Cooper.

Captain Poinsett Cooper, collection of Martin Schoenfeld

Cooper was born in 1836 in Connecticut to Commodore Benjamin and Elizabeth Hicks Cooper. His father Benjamin, born in New Jersey in 1793, served in the US Navy during the War of 1812.[35] Benjamin died in 1850 when Poinsett Cooper was just 13. Poinsett's grandfather, Commander James Britton Cooper, born in New Jersey in 1761, served in the Revolutionary War.[36] James attained the rank of Commander in 1841 and commanded the Africa Squadron from 1848-9.[37] Commander Cooper died in New Jersey in 1854.

Poinsett's first cousin Rebecca Morgan Cooper married Loudon Campbell, born in Virginia. At the start of the Civil War he was a Second Assistant Engineer in the US Navy. He resigned and joined the Confederate Navy serving as a First Assistant Engineer on a number of

---

[35] Commodore Benjamin Cooper served in the War of 1812 on the USS Hornet, a sloop of war, under the command of James Lawrence of "Don't Give Up the Ship" fame.

[36] James Britton Cooper was the last living survivor of "Lee's Legion" commanded by Light Horse Harry Lee, father of Robert E. Lee.

[37] The Africa Squadron was a group of US warships sent to patrol the coast of Africa and suppress the slave trade. Between 1844 and 1862 more than 30 vessels were seized by the squadron but it was generally considered ineffective.

vessels including the Merrimac. Loudon Campbell is buried in Arlington National Cemetery.[38] There is little doubt in the mind of this author that Poinsett Cooper was also related to the famous writer James Fenimore Cooper and noted industrialist Peter Cooper the uncle of Tammany Lieut. George Hewitt Wallis discussed in detail in Chapter 2.[39]

Poinsett Cooper joined the Tammany regiment as First Lieut. Co. D, March 18, 1862, having previously served as a Private in Co. F, 7th New York State National Guard and as a Second Lieut. in the 82nd New York. At Antietam he received a slight wound to the foot and was promoted to Captain on November 12, 1862.[40] Between February and May of 1863 Cooper was on medical leave in New York. On June 14, 1863 he was appointed Acting Assistant Inspector General of the 1st Brigade, 2nd Division, II Corps by SO 146 and then to the same position with Mallon's 3rd Brigade by SO 175, July 30, 1863.

In May 1864 at the Battle of the Wilderness, Cooper, on the staff of General Alexander Webb, 1st Brigade, 2nd Division, II Corps was again wounded by a GSW to the right leg.[41] On his way to the hospital he was for the fourth time wounded by a bullet to the chest. He was admitted to First Division General Hospital, Alexandria, VA on May 12, 1864 being listed as single with his nearest relative being his mother Mrs. Benjamin Cooper. He spent the rest of the war recovering from his wounds.

Poinsett married Louise W. Cooper (AKA Lillie) who was 10 years his junior. They lived in Brooklyn, New York and had a daughter Alice, born in 1865.[42] Poinsett Cooper died February 8, 1895 and is buried in Greenwood Cemetery, Brooklyn, NY, Lot 3962, Section 122.[43]

---

[38] Pittsburg Gazette Times, November 18, 1912. Loudon Campbell to be re-buried in Arlington Cemetery.

[39] James Fenimore Cooper sent a letter to Commodore Benjamin Cooper while he was on duty with the Africa Squadron, August 20, 1849 discussion family matters.

[40] New York Times, October 19, 1862. Colonel Charles reports that Lieut. Cooper "received a slight wound in the foot, the ball passing over the instep, but fortunately doing but little injury beyond breaking the skin."

[41] OR: S1, V36, 437. Report of General Webb.

[42] United States Census, 1880.

[43] United States General Index to Pension Files, 1861-1934. Pension applications were filed in 1871 and 1895.

Following the Battle at Bristoe Station Robert E. Lee sent a report to Jefferson Davis saying: "During the night of the 14th the enemy continued his retreat and is now reported to be fortifying at Centerville. I do not deem it advisable to attack him in his entrenchments, or to force him father back by turning his present position … I can see no benefit to be derived from remaining where we are, and shall consequently return to the line of the Rappahannock".[44] It seems clear that Lee was fine with settling into winter quarters in order to prepare for what was going to be a difficult 1864. Washington and General Meade had different ideas and put into motion a plan that became known as The Mine Run Campaign.

In the overall scheme of things the Mine Run Campaign is vastly overshadowed by other battles fought by the Army of the Potomac in 1863-64. Most books spend little time going over the details of Meade's last attempt to make up for his lack of pursuit of Lee after Gettysburg. Perhaps the best way to cover the Mine Run Campaign is to let the New York Times do it. An extensive article had the following headline: "The Army of the Potomac: A Comprehensive Review of General Meade's Late Campaign. The Manner and the Causes of Its Failure. The Object, the Plan, the Advance and the Retreat."[45]

The Times article details the movements of the Union's roughly 80,000 men and the 50,000 Confederates who between November 27 and December 2, 1863 jockeyed for position and fought along the Rapidan River, the various fords in Orange County, Virginia and along a small waterway called Mine Run. It was at this spot that General Lee adopted defensive positions that could well have resulted in massive Union causalities were it not for the keen eye of Union General G. K. Warren, who upon seeing the potential disaster decided not to make an attack against Lee.

Although Meade's plan had merit it depended on coordinated movements and attacks by several Corps. While bad weather had its effect, it was the command of Third Corps by General William H. French that has received most of the blame for the failure of the campaign.[46]

---

44   OR: S1, V29, 407-8. Report of Robert E. Lee, October 17, 1863.

45   New York Times, December 12, 1863

46   Third Corps was re-organized out of the Army a few months later and General French was mustered out of volunteer service on May 6, 1864 but served for the

The movements of the Tammany regiment during the Mine Run Campaign are well documented in the report of Colonel Turner G. Morehead who commanded Third Brigade of General Webb's Second Division of II Corps. They crossed the Rapidan on November 28, at Germanna Ford around 4 P.M. and spent the night about three miles from the ford. The next day they moved to Robertson's Farm. For the next few days the regiment occupied various positions in the line of battle and on December 2nd at 10 A. M. the division re-crossed the Rapidan at Culpeper Ford. The Tammany regiment served as the divisional picket line for six hours after the rest of the division had withdrawn.[47]

Two Tammany men are known to have been captured during the Mine Run Campaign. Christian Sands, Co. K was captured on Dec. 2, most likely while serving as a picket.[48] Much more is known about Heinrich (Herman) Carl Platte who was captured on November 28. Heinrich was born in Germany in 1839, was a turner by trade and signed on with the Tammany regiment on September 12, 1863 as a substitute for Theodore D. Holmes who had been drafted in the Fifth District of New York. Heinrich is said to have been 5 feet, 10 inches tall with blue eyes. Following his capture he was confined in Richmond on December 3, 1863 and transferred to Andersonville on March 8, 1864. He was transferred

---

remainder of the Civil War on various boards in Washington, reaching the rank of Colonel in the regular army.

[47]   OR: S1, V29, 729-30

[48]   Sands enrolled on August 24, 1863 in the Fourth District of NY at age 34. His military record is silent on what happened after his capture. He is listed as transferred to the 82nd and 59th NY regiments as a POW in the records of the State of NY. On the roster of the 59th NY, Sands is said to have been paroled on an unknown date and is listed as absent at Camp Parole since June 22, 1864 and at the muster out of his company. Interestingly, there is a record of a Christian Santz arriving in New York from Bremen, Germany on August 17, 1863. That man is listed as having been born in 1827 in Prussia. His destination is listed as Minnesota. There also is a record of a Christian Sand, age 44, as having been a member of the Grand Army of the Republic in Faribault, Minnesota in 1869. Is it possible that all of these men are the same individual and that the Christian Sands that served with the Tammany regiment joined just a week after having arrived in the United States instead of continuing on to Minnesota and at the end of the war followed through on his original intentions? The dates while not a perfect fit are close enough for this to be a real possibility.

to work in the Engineering Workshop at Savannah, Georgia and was paroled by General McLaws on October 25, 1864. Platte was one of 79 men, considered to have been escaped prisoners that were sent north from Hilton Head, S. C. by the Provost Marshal General, Department of the South on January 1, 1865 escorted by Lieut. A. Jansen, 21st USCT. The men were to be delivered to the Provost Marshal General in New York City. Platte had been carried as a deserter on the regimental muster rolls since his disappearance on November 28, 1863. On November 7, 1865, Platte was relieved of the charges of desertion by Special Orders, No. 257, paragraph 4, signed by Major General Hooker, based on "satisfactory evidence having been given that he was a prisoner of war from November 1863 until January 1865 and that since that time, prior to October 16, 1865, under medical treatment and not able to travel". [49]

The Army of the Potomac settled into winter quarters to await the arrival of General Grant and what would be the last seven months of the existence of the Tammany regiment.

---

[49] Records with the Pension Department show both invalid (application #1164346, certificate #910018) and widow pensions (application 741973) were applied for. Herman C. Platte died November 23, 1900.

Chapter Eighteen

WINTER 1864

Although no direct account of where the Tammany regiment spent the winter of 1863-64 has been found there is a very detailed description of how the 20th Massachusetts, brigaded with the Tammany regiment, prepared for and filled the time between December 7, 1863 and May 3, 1864. "The men at once commenced to build huts ... constructed of logs, roofed with canvas, with wooded chimneys plastered over with Virginia mud ... There were plenty of pine forests from which to draw the requisite material ... The army was encamped in a half circle around Culpeper Court House, facing the Rapidan, with headquarters at Brandy Station. Extensive picket lines were established and supported by reserves. Beyond the infantry and nearer the enemy was a line of cavalry videttes ... During a period of five months thousands of men, drawn in detachments from each regiment, were to walk their beats over the same line of twenty miles ... it was their duty to report any movement seen, or any suspicious sounds heard, to always be alert, and ever ready to offer resistance to any hostile demonstration ... the peace ... remained practically undisturbed."[1]

Two Tammany men are known to have become casualties during the months at Culpeper. On Feb. 6, near Morton's Ford, Corporal Luke Keenan, Co. D, received a gunshot wound fracturing the last phalanx of the third finger on one of his hands.[2] The action at Morton's Ford can best be characterized as a demonstration conducted by Second Corps in support

---

[1] Twentieth Massachusetts, 324-5
[2] Keenan joined the regiment at age 30 on July 6, 1861. He was not to rejoin the regiment and was mustered out while recovering from his wound.

of a plan that had General Butler advancing on Richmond from the south with the Army of the James. It was hoped that when Lee saw Union troops advancing across the Rapidan he would not be quick to withdraw troops to counter Butler's attack. The Tammany regiment's role in the action at Morton's ford was minor as their division crossed the Rapidan late in the afternoon and was withdrawn later that same evening.[3] Corporal Edward Williams was not so fortunate. He was captured near Kelly's Ford on March 23 and died in Andersonville August 2, 1864.[4]

Winter quarters served as a time for adjutants to catch up on paperwork, commanders to fill vacancies and medical officers to evaluate the men. All of these activities were designed to prepare for the military actions that were sure to start with the arrival of spring.

High on the priority list was the recruitment of new men to fill the ranks. The practice of sending officers and senior enlisted men, discussed in previous chapters, to New York for this purpose was continued.[5] To assist in the process General Hancock, who had recovered from his wound received at Gettysburg and again assumed command of the Second Corps, commenced a recruitment campaign on February 7 in New York City designed to add 10,000 men to the ranks of the nineteen regiments from New York State that served in Second Corps. According to newspaper accounts Hancock's efforts focused on taking advantage of the likelihood of the expiration of national bounties and an unspoken promise that

---

[3] Second Army Corps, 394-5 and Twentieth Massachusetts 338. General Butler's advance on Richmond failed.

[4] Williams was born in Canada, stood 5 feet, 9 inches tall, had hazel eyes and had been a fireman. He enlisted at Buffalo, NY and was assigned to Co. D on August 10, 1863 and was promoted to Corporal in Jan. 1864. A note in his service record dated March 5, 1888 states that he was taken to Castle Thunder in Richmond on March 28, transferred to another prison in Richmond on April 15, 1864 and sent to Andersonville on May 31. There he was admitted to a hospital on August 2 with acute dysentery and died the same day. He is buried in grave 4522.

[5] New York Leader, January 30, 1864, page 4, column 2-3. "Tammany Regiment: The veteran regiment commanded by Colonel W. A. Lynch is now stationed at Culpepper, VA in the advance guard of the Army of the Potomac. Only 190 of the original volunteers are now in the regiment...The regiment is now in need of volunteers to fill up its ranks...and Captain J. W. Tobin has been detailed to recruit men in this city..."

service in Second Corps would allow men to be in on the attacks that would finally take Richmond. One article said: " ...there is the nature of the service to which Gen. Hancock's command will be assigned. By the terms of the order under which he is filling up his corps it is to be assigned to "special service". What this service is does not appear ... we think public anticipation does not greatly outrun probability when it fixes Richmond as the objective which will be aimed at by Hancock's column ... We do not take it upon ourselves ... and say that this, is the mission for which the Second Corps is designed, yet we make bold to prophesy that those who act on this suspicion will not be greatly mistaken."[6] Hancock's efforts continued well into March. On March 7 a meeting was held at Tammany Hall that was reported in newspapers with the headline: "Tammany and the Army: Grand War Meeting at Tammany Hall in Behalf of the Second Army Corps, Great Enthusiasm Manifested Speeches by Major General Hancock."[7]

How successful was Hancock? It is unclear exactly how many men responded directly to the efforts exerted by Hancock but some numbers can be looked at to get a sense of what happened. Between February 8 and March 31, 1864, 70 new men joined the ranks of the Tammany regiment and were distributed throughout the ten companies. If it is assumed that all of the new men had responded to Hancock's efforts and that the results within the other eighteen New York regiments were similar to that of the Tammany regiment only 1330 new men would have joined Second Corps, far short of the 10,000 sought.

Ten men enlisted in April but their presence was more than offset by the twenty men that were discharged for disability between April 24 and April 28 in Stevensburg, VA. One of the new recruits, Isaac C. Hadden wrote a series of letters to his wife and brother that provides a firsthand account of the movements and activities of the Tammany regiment that would otherwise not have been available.[8]

---

6   New York Times, February 8, 1864.
7   New York Times, March 8, 1864.
8   Letters relating to Hadden, Isaac from camps during the Civil War and death as a prisoner of war. New York Historical Society Manuscripts Collection. Hadden enrolled on April 4, 1864. He wrote to his wife on April 6 from Hart Island, New York City and again on April 18 from the regiment's camp at Brandy Station, VA

One event that was probably not anticipated was the enactment of an act by Congress on February 24, 1864 that read in part: "Any person now in the military service of the United States who shall furnish satisfactory proof that he is a mariner by vocation, or an able seaman, or ordinary seaman, may enlist into the Navy, under such rules and regulations as may be prescribed by the President ... it shall be the duty of every officer commanding a company ... to forward all the applications made to him ... together with proof that the applicants are mariners ..."[9] The act was incorporated into General Order No. 91 from the War Department on March 4 and into General Orders No. 12, Headquarters Army of the Potomac, March 29, 1864. Signed by General Meade the order required that "corps and other independent commanders will at once appoint a board of three officers, whose duty it shall be to examine into all applications for transfer to the Navy ... and who will make ... a daily report to these headquarters of all cases that meet the foregoing requirements. Such report will give ... all the facts necessary to authorize a transfer." Within two weeks twenty-three Tammany men were transferred to the Navy. All of the transferred men had joined the Tammany regiment after Gettysburg either as enlistees, draftees or substitutes.[10]

The service records of two of the men, John Price and John Benson, provide some interesting details. John Price, age 36, was mustered in on Aug. 27, 1863 and almost immediately was assigned to Battery A, First Rhode Island artillery where he remained until being transferred to the Navy on April 12. He had previously served in the Confederate army. John

---

stating that he had arrived on April 17 and was in need of various supplies that he couldn't get locally as the sutlers had left the area. In a letter dated April 27, Hadden said that a division sutler was in camp and that he could obtain butter for sixty cents a pound, cheese for thirty cents, condensed milk 50 cents a can and "all other things in proportion."

9   OR: S3, V4, 151. New York Times, March 19, 1864
10 OR: S1, V33, 760. Men transferred to the Navy were: Co. A: Samuel Armour, Henry Lamkie, Sgt. Francis Mahoney, George S. Walsh, Peter Daniels, Co. B: Peter Brown, Daniel Forester, Michael Marooney, Robert Travers, Co. C: Robert Burns, Donald McKay, Co. E: William Johnson, John Sweeney, Co. F: Thomas Mooney, James Reney, William H. Steadman, Co. G: George Taylor, Co. I: John Price, Joseph Smith, Charles Statewell, Co. K: Arthur Blackburn, John Benson and Joseph Crowley.

Benson was mustered in on July 11, 1863 from the Ninth Congressional District of New York receiving a bounty of $25. Company muster roll sheets for Nov. 63- Feb. 64 show him as being charged for the loss of a shelter half by neglect. One entry has the charge being $1.62 and the other entry is for $1.89. His service record contains a letter dated April 11, 1864 sent to Captain Charles H. Baines, AAG, 1st Brigade, 2nd Division, 2nd Corps, signed by Julius Ellendorf, Adjutant of the Tammany regiment that contains an approval endorsement from Captain Robert Wright. The letter makes application for the transfer of Benson to the Navy under the provisions of General Orders No. 12 and specifies that Benson had previously served four years in the British Navy, three years as an American merchant seaman and one year in the U. S. Navy for a total of eight years of service at sea. According to the report of the Adjutant General of New York, Benson was 22 years old when he was mustered in. If that age and the service time are accurate, Benson would have been serving in the British Navy when he was a young boy.

The number of Tammany men available for potential combat was also reduced by those that were detailed to special jobs or temporary duty assignments. John Boyd, James Merrick, Charles Mulholland, James McNailis and Amasa Soper were assigned as pioneers or to perform other wood cutting duties.[11]

John Ellicott, Co. G, enrolled in June 1861 and held the rank of Corporal until sometime around the start of 1863. Between August and October 1863, Ellicott was detailed to take care of Colonel Mallon's horse. Following Mallon's death at Bristoe Station, Ellicott served as an orderly at regimental headquarters until he was assigned to a regimental wood detail in January 1864.

Dennis Mooney, age 34, Co. D, joined the regiment in July 1863 and was detached to serve as a brigade blacksmith in January 1864. Around

---

[11] John Boyd, Co. B, Charles Mulholland, Co. G and James McNailis, Co. K, joined the regiment in 1861and were assigned as pioneers (wood cutters/road builders) between November 1863 and January 1864. James Merrick, Co. H, a Boston man, had spent some time in the hospital sick during early 1862 and was assigned as a regimental wood cutter in March 1864. Amasa Soper, Co. I, was mustered in on August 24, 1863 and was assigned to the Second Corps saw mill sometime around January 1864.

the end of June, Mooney, suffering from Chronic Diarrhea, arrived at De Camp Hospital on David's Island in New York Harbor and was carried on the hospital's muster roll until the end of the war.[12]

Thomas Coffee, Co. I was assigned as a guard at Brigade Headquarters in February 1864 and became a Brigade cook in March. Coffee had enrolled in 1861 at age 28.[13] Following the Peninsula Campaign Coffee is listed as "absent sick at Newport News" during July and August, 1862. The company muster sheet for September shows Coffee as "dropped from the pay roll as deserter according to General Orders, absent sick." No specific order is mentioned but it was likely General Orders, No. 92, War Department, July 31, 1862, issued under the signature of Secretary of War Stanton. The provisions of General Order 92 are extremely interesting and no doubt had far reaching impact on large numbers of soldiers. General Order 92 cancelled, on August 11, 1862, all leaves of absence and furloughs not issued by the War Department and required all units to have a muster call on August 18 with those not officially excused from being present being declared as deserters. It also contained provisions that punished officers that did not comply and established networks of special provost marshals throughout the nation to arrest soldiers.[14]

---

[12] Casualty sheet in the record of Dennis Mooney references Book 4, page 426 of the Hospital Register of the New England Soldier's Relief Association. In 1862 the association occupied 194 Broadway in New York City, having a dormitory for housing 86 men as well as a "Sick Ward" for convalescents and cases of serious illness. How much time, if any, Mooney spent at 194 Broadway or another facility of the association is not known. For a description of the workings of the association see New York Times, December 21, 1862: New England Soldiers Relief Association: Report of Operations. The association closed on September 1, 1865.

[13] Coffee was born in Galway, Ireland, stood 5 feet, six inches tall and was a bricklayer by trade. His record indicates that he was placed under arrest by order of General Stone on December 16, 1861 and was carried on the muster sheets as "absent-in arrest" for 11 days ending December 31, 1861.

[14] General Orders No. 92, War Department, Adjt. General's Office, Washington, July 31, 1862 reads: "The absence of officers and privates from their duty under various pretexts, while receiving pay, at great expense and burden to the Government, makes it necessary that efficient measures be taken to enforce their return to duty, or that their places be supplied by those who will not take pay while rendering no service. This evil, moreover, tends greatly to discourage

It may require several readings of the full text of General Orders No. 92 before the full impact of the content becomes clear. Try to imagine

---

the patriotic impulses of those who would contribute to support the families of faithful soldiers. It is therefore ordered by the President that on Monday, the 11th of August, all leaves of absence and furloughs by whomsoever given, unless by the War Department, are revoked and absolutely annulled, and all officers capable of service are required forthwith to join their respective commands, and all privates capable of service to join their regiments, under penalty of dismissal from the service, or such penalty as a court-martial may award, unless the absence be occasioned by lawful cause. The only excuses allowed for the absence of officers or privates after the 11th day of August are: the order or leave of the War Department, disability from wounds received in service or disability from disease that renders the party unfit for military duty. But any officer or private whose health permits him to visit watering places or places of amusement, or to make social visits, or walk about the town, city or neighborhood in which he may be, will be considered fit for military duty, and as evading duty by absence from his command or ranks.

On Monday, the 18th of August, at 10 o'clock a. m., each regiment and corps will be mustered. The absentees will be marked, three lists of the same made out, and within forty-eight hours after the muster one copy shall be sent to the Adjutant General of the Army, one to the commander of the corps, the third to be retained; and all officers and privates fit for duty absent at that time will be regarded as absent without cause, their pay will be stopped, and they dismissed from the service or treated as deserters, unless restored; and no officer shall be restored to his rank unless by the judgment of a court of inquiry, to be approved by the President, he shall establish that his absence was with good cause.

Commanders of corps, divisions, brigades, regiments and detached posts are strictly enjoined to enforce the muster and return aforesaid. Any officer failing in his duty herein will be deemed guilty of gross neglect of duty and be dismissed from the service. A commissioner shall be appointed by the Secretary of War to superintend the execution of this order in the respective States.

The United States marshals in the respective districts, the mayor and chief of police of any town or city, the sheriff of the respective counties in each State, all postmasters and justices of the peace, are authorized to act as special provost-marshals to arrest any officer or private soldier fit for duty who may be found absent from his command without just cause and convey him to the nearest military post or depot. The transportation, reasonable expenses of this duty, and five dollars will be paid for each officer or private so arrested and delivered. By order of the President: E.M. Stanton, Secretary of War"

OR: S3, V2, 286-7 and New York Times, August 1, 1862.

the amount of paperwork generated and the potential for error in the handling of individual soldier's circumstances. Consider the likelihood that protecting one's own reputation and position would result in decisions made on less than adequate facts and the temptation for monetary gain that could result in large numbers of soldiers being arrested.

Thomas Coffee returned to duty in November and was reinstated into the ranks of the regiment. On June 19, 1863 he was admitted to Fairfax Seminary Hospital in Virginia suffering from "General Debility" complaining of general weakness and lack of appetite. On July 10 he was considered well and placed on duty in the hospital. He received a furlough from the hospital from October 30 to November 14, 1863 and rejoined the Tammany regiment in January 1864. It seems quite possible that his history of illness prompted his assignment as a guard and cook.

Another Tammany man caught up in General Orders No. 92 was Jacob Martin, Co. B. Martin was mustered in on June 22, 1861 and between March and August 1862 was carried as sick in hospitals in Poolesville, MD and Washington, D.C. The company muster sheet for September and October 1862 reads: "Deserted, sent to hospital and not heard from since and dropped in accordance with General Order No. 92. Charged with one rifle and complete set of accoutrements." Martin is listed as having returned from desertion on January 13, 1864 in Philadelphia where he was detailed to the Provost Guard of that city by order of the War Department, serving in that capacity for the rest of the war.

Some men spent months and even years in various hospitals following their recovery from illness or wounds before returning to their regiments. John H. Mann, Co. B is one example. Mann enrolled in June 1861 and on August 9 he was admitted as sick to the General Hospital in Annapolis, MD. Between September 1, 1861 and January 1864, Mann was carried on regimental muster sheets as on detached service in General Hospital as an attendant, waiter or nurse. On February 1, 1864, Mann was detailed as a nurse in the Second Division Hospital.

A more complex example is the record of Dennis Collins, Co. B. Collins was mustered in at age 24, on June 22, 1861. In April 1862, during the Peninsula Campaign, he was admitted to the hospital at Hampton,

VA and arrived in New York by transport ship on May 22.[15] His record has him listed as "absent sick in hospital" from June through August and as "deserted" on the September 1862 muster sheet, most likely as a result of General Order 92. Collins rejoined the Tammany regiment on November 20 and was wounded at Fredericksburg in December. He was admitted to Hammond General Hospital, Point Lookout, MD on December 16, suffering from a flesh wound caused by a Minnie ball in his left forearm about 2 inches below the elbow. The wound is said to have healed about March 1, 1863 and that Collins remained at the hospital serving as a nurse until November 29, 1863. On February 8, 1864 Collins was assigned to Judiciary Square General Hospital in Washington, D. C. and on March 25, re-enlisted as a veteran before Captain Robert Wright while at Stevensburg, VA.[16] What Collins did during the rest of the war is a bit unclear. His record shows him listed as "present" on the Muster Roll for January-February 1865 of the Second Battalion, Paroled Prisoners, Camp Parole, Annapolis, MD.[17] No details related to his capture appear in his record. The records of the Adjutant General of New York have him transferred to the 82NY and 59NY regiments in 1864 while a prisoner of war and as mustered out at Munson's Hill, VA on June 20, 1865.

[15] New York Times, May 25, 1862, page 8. Arrived on steamer Kennebec listed as sick or wounded.
[16] Collins is listed on his re-enlistment papers as having been born in Clare, County, Ireland and as a blacksmith by trade. He had brown eyes and hair and stood five foot four inches tall.
[17] A note on the muster sheets says: "This organization was formed from paroled prisoners of war for duty compatible with their parole by G. O. No. 72, June 28, 1862..."

Fairfax Seminary Hospital, Alexandria, VA, Library of Congress

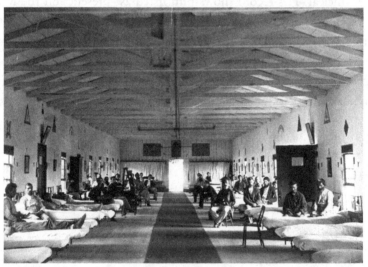

Ward K, Armory Square Hospital, Washington, Library of Congress

Serving as an ambulance driver was another detail that reduced the number of available fighting men within the ranks. There is good reason to believe that being assigned to drive an ambulance was not a job that was sought after. In fact, in some cases it was a detail given either as a punishment or simply as a method of removing a soldier that had lost favor with the regimental command. Edward Mullin, Co. B had been with the regiment since the beginning of the war and had risen through the ranks to First Sergeant. On January 9, 1864 Mullin was reduced to the rank of Private and detailed to service in the Ambulance Corps. James H. Welch, Co. C has a record similar to that of Mullin. Welch had held the rank of Commissary Sergeant until he was reduced to the rank of Private on January 6, 1863. He is listed as having spent March and April 1863 sick in the hospital and on a wood cutting detail and in May he was placed on detached service with the Ambulance Corps, where he remained for the rest of the war.[18]

John Brown, Co. F joined the regiment on June 22, 1861. Records show Brown as sick and on the Muster Roll of Stanton General Hospital, Washington, D. C. from March through August 1863. He returned to the regiment and was detached to the Ambulance Corps in January 1864. Sometime after March he rejoined the regiment and was captured near Petersburg on June 22.[19]

The clearest story of a man that was to spend time with the Ambulance Corps is that of Patrick Condon. Condon's story has been presented in part in several previous chapters but it is well worth repeating in its entirety here.[20] Condon was born in County Cork, Ireland in 1825, stood five foot, eight inches tall, had blue eyes and was a stone cutter by trade. Prior to coming to the United States he had served as a British soldier in Europe.

---

[18] Mullin was promoted to 8th Corporal June 1, 1862 and to 4th Sgt. On September 18, 1862. Neither Mullin's nor Welch's records show a reason for their demotion.

[19] A special thank you is given to Justyna Carlson, Secretary of the North Adams Massachusetts Historical Society for her assistance in providing some details on the life of John Brown. Through her I was able to contact Nelson Noel the great-grandson of John Brown. I also was provided with an obituary for John Brown that provided the following: "John Brown died...in the 77th year of his age. Mr. Brown was a native of Ireland, but went to England with his parents when a child and came from England to this country when a young boy. He settled in New York and later learned the tailor's trade. He worked in that city till the breaking out of the Civil War, when he enlisted in the 42d New York Volunteers...He was taken prisoner and held at Andersonville for six months..." Brown is buried in St, Joseph's Cemetery, North Adams, Massachusetts. North Adams Transcript, Monday, February 13, 1911, page 5.

[20] See Chapters 5 and 12. Patrick Condon should not be confused with another man Patrick J. Condon, Captain 63rd New York, a well known Fenian Brotherhood leader.

In June 1861, Condon, age 36, was appointed Orderly Sergeant, Co. K.[21] He was wounded at Ball's Bluff[22] in October 1861 and was recommended for promotion to General Stone by the members of Company K.[23] No promotion was immediately forthcoming. Why? While there is no clear answer to this question, there are certainly a number of reasons why General Stone would not have received the recommendation favorably. The most likely reason is that General Stone had much more important things on his mind. He was being blamed for the disaster at Ball's Bluff that resulted in the death of Colonel (Senator) Baker, a close friend of President Lincoln. The recommendation, while glowing in its appraisal of Condon, had not come through normal channels and was not signed by the commanding officer or any individual officer of the regiment. What the letter does tell us is that Condon was extremely well thought of by the men he served with and that the men in the ranks considered him to be a superior soldier with leadership qualities that would be needed as the war continued.

After recovering from his wound, Condon was assigned, still with the rank of Orderly Sergeant, to recruiting duty in New York City, where he

---

[21] Condon was originally mustered in as Orderly Sergeant of Company I but transferred almost immediately to Co. K where he was listed as a musician. The Orderly Sergeant of Co. K, Jacob Amene, had been reduced to the ranks and transferred to Co. I. Amene deserted several weeks later. Condon replaced Amene as Orderly Sergeant of Co. K. Record of Officers and Privates of regiments organized in New York, Adjutants General's Office, Vol. II, Albany, Comstock and Cassidy, N. Y. 1864, pages 104-6.

[22] In his letter to General Meade in 1863, Condon states that he was wounded twice. The details on the second wound are unknown.

[23] On October 28, 1861 a letter was sent to Brig. General Stone, HQ Corps of Observation, Poolesville, MD saying: "It is the unanimous voice of Company K, Tammany Regiment, to elevate our brave Orderly Sergeant, Patrick Condon to a Lieutenancy in this company. His long experience as a soldier on the Continent of Europe; his unflinching bravery and devotion to us on the battlefield of the 21st instant gives us entire confidence in his ability as an able commander, and further, we can bear the highest testimony to his reputation as a gentleman as well as to the highly and efficient manner in which he has, both theoretically and practically discharged his duties as a true and faithful soldier since the organization of the company. Written at the request of the members of Company K, Tammany Regiment, Camp Lyon" NARA, file of Patrick Condon.

remained until early 1862. On April 1, 1862 Condon was promoted to Regimental Sergeant Major and on July 1 to Second Lieut. by order of Lieut. Colonel Mooney.[24] It was at this point that Condon had reached the peak of his career with the Tammany regiment; it would be a steep downward spiral going forward.

In August, 1862, Lieut. Colonel Mooney left the regiment while Colonel Charles was recovering in New York from his wounds and time in a Richmond prison. Lieut. Colonel Bomford assumed field command of the regiment. Exactly what happened shortly after the Battle of Antietam is unclear. What is known is that on October 9, Condon wrote a letter to New York Adjutant General Hillhouse in Albany requesting a copy of his commission.[25] On October 13, 1862, before the letter to Albany was received, Condon was placed under arrest by Lieut. Colonel Bomford for "Insolence toward Lieut. Col. Bomford while serving as Officer of the Day and being under the influence of liquor". Condon denied both charges. On October 31, at Snicker's Gap, VA, Condon was told that he was to be released from arrest and required to serve as Regimental Sergeant Major instead as Second Lieut. Condon refused and was detailed to the Ambulance Corps where he served for the rest of the war. What a shock these events must have been for the rank and file of Co. K, mostly Irishmen, that just a year before had recommended Condon for promotion.[26]

---

[24] Regimental Special Order Number 2. Regimental Special Order No. 81, July 6, 1862, stated that Condon's promotion to Second Lieut. was to be with a date of rank of July 1 and that he was filling the position vacated by the promotion of George H. Smith.

[25] The letter written by Condon from Bolivar Heights, VA to Albany dated Oct. 9, 1862 reads: "Having been appointed Second Lieut. in this regiment by Lieut. Col. James J. Mooney, on the 1st day of July 1862, from which period I have been performing duty in that capacity; and being desirous of obtaining my Commission, which I have been assured have been applied for, but not forthcoming, I do hereby, most respectfully solicit your attention to it." New York State Archives document 10940. The document contains an endorsement that states the letter was received in Albany on October 22 and answered on Oct. 23 but no details on what the response was is noted.

[26] Condon re-enlisted as a veteran in January 1864. A Pension record document states that Condon was granted an Invalid pension in October 1890, Cert. Number 669736 and that he died in 1902.

Condon would not forget what had happened to him and it is clear that his pride was deeply hurt. He had been a professional soldier and had obtained the respect of his men through battle. He made one last attempt to regain his rank, most likely prompted by the resignation of Lt. Col. Bomford on March 14, just before the Battle of Chancellorsville. On September 5, 1863, Condon wrote a lengthy letter to Major General George Meade, stating that he had had previous discussions with General McClellan about his case and was requesting a review of his status and his return to the rank of Second Lieut. The request was referred to General Warren, Commander of Second Corps who endorsed the request saying: "The claim of Patrick Condon to be regarded as a commissioned officer was fully considered by all intermediate commanders and decided adversely by Major General Sumner, Commander of the Right Grand Division, who ordered that Condon be returned to duty as Sergeant Major. There seems to be no reason for reopening the question. The original papers are stored in Washington".[27]

---

[27] The letter to General Meade dated September 5, 1863 reads: "Since your advent as Commanding Officer of this Army, there is one quality developed in your administration of Military Affairs which has gained you the affection and confidence of your men more than all others and that is your being the soldier's friend. It is in the hope of enlisting your attention and favorable consideration that I lay before you the following remarks and I most respectfully trust that the issue will be that which General McClellan himself verbally gave me to hope for, but unfortunately for my interests that gentleman was removed from his command a day or two after. I will put the fact of my case in as few words as possible consistent with intelligibility. June 17, 1861-I was appointed 1st Sergeant, Co. K, 42nd NY Infantry. March 24, 1862 Promoted to Regimental Sergeant Major. July 1, 1862 Promoted to 2nd Lieut. by Regimental Order No. 81 (Copy attached). July 24. In charge of company, Captain and 1st Lieut. absent, to Oct. 13, 1862. 31 Aug. 1862, Mustered at Fairfax, VA as 2nd Lieut. and entered on Pay Roll as such. October 13, 1862-Placed under arrest by Lt. Col. Bomford. Requested copy of charges but was refused. Learnt that they were "Insolence toward Lt. Col. Bomford whilst officer of the day and being under the influence of liquor", both of which charges I most earnestly and unhesitatingly deny. Lt. Col. Bomford struck out and did not call my name at Snicker's Gap, VA while the regiment was being mustered, and the same day the adjutant informed me that Lt. Col. Bomford released me from arrest and required me to do duty as Regimental Sergeant Major, which I respectfully declined. Thus sir, as is shown

Condon's time with the ambulance corps was certainly a form of punishment. It seems extremely sad that such a superior soldier would have not been utilized to the best of his ability. On the other hand, spending time in the ambulance corps when the rest of the Tammany regiment was facing some of the deadliest battles of the war, probably saved his life.

A number of men were disciplined for a variety of reasons while the regiment was in winter quarters. Mathew Hillman, Co. F was convicted and sentenced by General Orders, No. 44, Second Division, Second Corps on April 20 for "Conduct prejudicial to good order and Military Discipline". He was to forfeit eight dollars a month for six months and was to be drummed through each regiment camp of the Division with a placard marked "Rumseller" on his breast.[28]

Lycurgus O'Sullivan had been wounded at Bristoe Station. He deserted at Jersey City, NJ while being transferred to a New York Hospital sometime

---

above after four months duty as 2nd Lieut. and being obliged to incur considerable expense for outfit and equipments, I was placed on the roll as an enlisted man and deprived of the pay and position I honorably gained having been present at every engagement with my regiment and wounded twice. Your own sound military discretion, Sir, will at once perceive that the above is not only subservice of military discipline but is calculated to destroy that which prevails among good soldiers to distinguish themselves and over to honorably gain by hard service what money or interest could not procure, viz. promotion. General, in concluding this, permit me to say, I am an old British soldier and while such I never witnessed the case of a man applying to his General for redress of a wrong, who did not, if he deserved it, get full and ample justice done him and I have but to refer you to Lieut. Colonel Lynch and the other officers of this regiment who can testify to my deportment and conduct during the time comprised in the above statement of facts and thereby I feel convinced I shall obtain that due and favorable consideration of my case, which although delayed will be all the more welcome when it arrives. I most respectfully leave the matter in your hands and pray you will see fit to restore me to the position I gained and held for four months until deprived of the same by the partial treatment of a man who has since been obliged to leave the service under circumstances which deny him from the Society of brave men." NARA record of Patrick Condon.

28 Hillman has been mustered in on September 12, 1863. He would be wounded in the Wilderness (gunshot wound to the right hand) and would spend time at Stanton General Hospital, Washington, DC between June-July 1864.

about Nov. 1, 1863. He was arrested in New York City on Dec. 21 and dishonorably discharged on January, 29, 1864.[29]

Patrick Killan was tried, convicted and sentenced by General Orders No. 195, HQ Second Division, Second Corps on December 8, 1863 for "Conduct prejudicial to good order and military discipline, Disrespect towards his superior officers and Mutinous Conduct". He was sentenced to forfeit all pay and allowances currently due him and ten dollars per month for the remainder of his term of enlistment and to be confined at hard labor on public works for the same period. Details of the charges against Killan are not in his file but there are muster sheets showing that he had previously been dropped as a deserter June 17, 1863 near Fair Fax Station and returned Oct. 10 with a reference to his having been a prisoner of war and listed as a deserted in error. What actually happened to Killan following his conviction is a bit unclear. On April 19, 1864 he was admitted to Armory General Hospital, Washington, DC and stayed there through June 16. On September 24 he was at Second Division, US General Hospital and said to be: " ...this day returned to duty, he claims to belong to Co. C, 42d Reg't NY Vol. and that his term of service has expired but it is now questionable whether he has not been discharged from that regiment and enlisted in another". His record shows that he was captured near Petersburg, VA on October 27, 1864 and was confined in Richmond and Salisbury, N. C. between October 29 and November 4, 1864. He was paroled at Aiken's Landing on Feb. 17, 1865 and admitted to Hospital Division 1, Annapolis, MD on Feb. 23, 1865.[30]

James Fallon, Co. H, a Boston man, was arrested in Roxbury, MA as a deserter on September 12, 1863. He was sent from Fort Independence

---

[29] O'Sullivan had been with the Tammany regiment from the beginning of the war. He stood five feet five inches high, had hazel eyes and brown hair and was a printer by trade. At the time of his discharge he was 25 years old.

[30] Killan was a native of Ireland and had lived in Newark, New Jersey before enrolling in the Tammany regiment in June 1861. He was five foot five, had black hair and was a silver plater by trade. Oct. 27, 1864 is the date of the Battle of Burgess Mill near Petersburg in which II Corps was engaged. If Killan was captured there it would have been after the men of the Tammany regiment had been transferred to the 59th NY. Killan did not re-enlist as a veteran but it is possible that his enlistment would have been extended to take into account time that he had spent in confinement following his conviction.

to Washington, DC and there confined in the Forrest Hill Guard House. He escaped on October 23, 1863 and was re-arrested in Roxbury on November 16.[31]

Several Tammany company level officers were promoted or otherwise significantly impacted by events during the winter of 1863-4. While these men have been mentioned previously in various chapters their careers are presented here in their entirety.

Stuart A. Standiford was promoted to First Lieut. Co. G on December 22, 1863. He was 24 years old when he joined the regiment in June 1861 as a private. By the time of Antietam Standiford had risen to the rank of Orderly Sergeant, Co. G. Wounded at Gettysburg, he recovered and was promoted to Second Lieut. on Aug. 14, 1863. In February 1864 Standiford suffered from Diarrhea and was on medical leave for two weeks. Promoted to Captain[32] on April 24, 1864, Standiford was captured on June 22 at Weldon Railroad and spent time in Richmond, Charleston, Camp Asylum Columbia S. C. and Macon, GA prisons[33]. He was paroled at NE Ferry, N. C. on March 1, 1865 and mustered out of the service on March 12, 1865.[34]

Edwin R. Pierce had joined the regiment in June 1861 as a private and was promoted to Sergeant, Co. B in November 1861, to Second Lieut. Co. I in June 1862, to First Lieut. Co. B on August 28, 1862 and to Captain, Co. B on November 23, 1863. He was on sick leave with chronic Diarrhea

---

[31] Fallon stood five feet three inches, had blue eyes and dark hair. He was 21 years old when he enlisted in Boston. There is a note in his file stating that he deserted a third time after May 3, 1864 and returned from desertion on May 27. He also is said to have served a year in the Navy.

[32] Standiford's promotion to Captain was not officially documented until December 30, 1908 by a notation in his service record.

[33] On September 23, 1864 Standiford's father wrote a letter from Trenton, New Jersey to Lieut. Col. Woodford, a member of the staff of General Q. A. Gilmore, Commanding the Department of the South, stating that he had a son that was a prisoner in Charleston and that he was wishing to send him a parcel of articles that he thought his son would need. The letter was received on Oct. 1 and the box was sent to Col. Woodford but there is no record of whether the box was ever delivered. NARA records.

[34] Mustered out by Paragraph 18, Special Order No. 121, War Department, Washington D. C. March 12, 1865. Standiford's widow was granted a pension filed on Jan. 17, 1889. Certificate 279166. The pension file states that Standiford died Jan. 1, 1889.

and headaches between Jan. 7 and Feb. 15, 1864.[35] Pierce was discharged for disability by Paragraph 47, Special Order, No. 127, War Department, March 25, 1864.[36]

John Maguire, age 29, joined the regiment in June 1861 as a private. He was promoted to First Sergeant and Second Lieut. Co. C while sick in a hospital in Newark, New Jersey during October 1862, to First Lieut. January 19 and to Captain, Co. D on March 25, 1864 immediately after having been summoned to Washington D. C. to appear before a military commission to answer charges that he had been absent without leave. The charges were dropped.[37] Maguire was listed as commanding the Tammany regiment on May 31, 1864 just prior to the Battle of Cold Harbor and was mustered out with the regiment on July 13, 1864.

James Casey, age 22, a native of Ireland joined the regiment as a private in June 1861 and reached the rank of Sergeant in November 1861. At Gettysburg, as 2nd Sergeant, Co. K, Casey was wounded in the right arm requiring amputation. Casey recovered from his wound at hospitals in Fort Columbus, Fort Schuyler and David's Island, New York during which time he was promoted to Second Lieut. Co. K on Oct. 18, 1863. He returned to the regiment in March 1864 and was promoted to First Lieut. on June 10, 1864. Casey was captured at Weldon Railroad on June 22, 1864 and paroled December 17, 1864. He was mustered out of the service by Paragraph 48, Special Order No. 458, War Department, December 20, 1864.[38]

---

[35] Pierce had spent significant time in hospitals and under doctor's care for chronic stomach related problems. Between October and November 1862, Pierce was on leave and reported as suffering from Chronic Diarrhea and vomiting blood following being injured while on picket duty on Oct. 16 near Chancellorsville.

[36] Pierce had been dismissed from the service by Special Order 379, War Department, on Dec. 5, 1862 for being in Washington, D. C. without leave but was re-instated by Paragraph 24, Special Order 323, war Department July 21, 1863.

[37] Maguire had previously been fined 2 months pay in early 1863 for being away without leave. Maguire had family in Michigan and had been on leave visiting Detroit.

[38] Casey died on Thursday, November 22, 1900 at his home at 222 Fifty-third Street, Brooklyn, New York. He left a widow and two children. Brooklyn Eagle, Nov. 23, 1900, page 2 and New York Times Nov. 24, 1900.

Thomas H. Mallon, brother of Colonel James Mallon, was "discharged on account of physical disability from wounds received in action" on November 7, 1863. Mallon enrolled August 2, 1862, was wounded in the thigh at Gettysburg and was serving as regimental quartermaster when he was discharged.[39]

The most significant promotion to occur during the winter of 1864 was that of U. S. Grant to be Lieut. General in command of the entire Union Army. Nominated to the newly restored rank on March 1 and officially promoted on March 10, Grant put into action the Overland Campaign applying pressure on Robert E. Lee and placing the Tammany regiment and the rest of the Army of the Potomac in the middle of some of the most deadly fighting of the war. What would follow would be the Battles of the Wilderness (May 5-7), Spotsylvania Court House (May 8-21) and Cold Harbor (May 31-June 12). There was no way for Lieut. Colonel William A. Lynch, commanding the Tammany regiment,[40] to know just how badly his command would be depleted over the next two months.

---

[39] Paragraph 21, Special Orders No. 496, War Department, Nov. 7, 1863. Mallon married Mary Jane Theall and lived in Brooklyn until his death on October 26, 1910. He worked as a tax searcher. The 1875 New York Census list Mallon at 728 Lafayette Ave, Brooklyn with his wife, daughter Adelaide, age 8 and mother Ann age 68. The 1900 New York Census has Mallon, a widower, at the same address with his daughter and son-in-law Frank Powers and two grandchildren. Adelaide and Frank Powers were married in December 1889. Brooklyn Eagle, Dec. 8, 1889, page 4. Mallon's mother died Sunday July 1, 1888. Brooklyn Daily Standard.

[40] OR: S1, V29, 669 and S1, V33, 465. Lieut. Col. Lynch in command of Tammany regiment, Third Brigade (Col. Turner G. Morehead), Second Division (B. Gen. Webb), Second Corps. While Lynch was in command he was not with the regiment when the Overland Campaign started in May, he was in New York City on recruiting duty. For details on Lynch see Chapter 14.

Chapter Nineteen

BATTLE OF THE WILDERNESS

The Battle of the Wilderness, May 5-7, 1864 was the first of many actions that together are considered The Overland Campaign, although Grant never had any specific plan that would have selected the Wilderness as an objective. No sensible commander would have as it has been described as: "It was the Wilderness! This desolate region embraces a tract of country of many miles, stretching southward from the Rapidan, and westward beyond Mine Run, the whole face of it being covered with a dense undergrowth of low limbed trees and scraggy pines, stiff and bristling chinkapins, scrub oaks and hazel. It is a region of gloom and the shadow of death, such a darkling wood as that where through Dante passed into the inferno, savage and rough and strong, that in the thinking it reneweth fear."[1]

In fact, gaining terrain was not Grant's objective at all. The goal was the destruction of the Confederate army. To be sure the Overland Campaign included detailed plans for various parts of the Union Army to work together but, as was almost always the case, it fell to the Army of the Potomac to bear the brunt of the action. Grant's initial order to George Meade, a month before the battle was to start, simply said: "Lee's army will be your objective point. Wherever Lee goes, there you will go also. The only point upon which I am now in doubt is whether it will be better to cross the Rapidan above or below him. Each plan presents great advantages

---

[1] Swinton, William, Twelve Decisive Battles of the War, Dick and Fitzgerald, New York, 1867, page 370. The Chinkapin is a large multi-stemmed shrub, usually around 15 feet high, related to the Chestnut. It has small nuts covered in sharp spines.

over the other, with corresponding objections."[2] Union troops taking part in the battle included Second Corps, again under Hancock, Fifth Corps, under Warren, Sixth Corps under Sedgwick and a Cavalry Corps under Sheridan reporting to Meade. Additionally, the Ninth Corps under Burnside reported directly to Grant[3]. The action described in this chapter will be focused on Second Corps with details as they can be constructed on the likely movements of the Tammany regiment. Unfortunately, no direct accounts of the Tammany regiment's activities during the battle are available but a reasonable approximation of what happened can be put together through examination of the timeline and documented movements of the rest of their brigade commanded by General Alexander Webb.[4]

What does exist, thanks to Isaac Hadden, is a detailed description of what life was like for men of the Tammany regiment as they prepared for the battle they all knew was coming. In his letter dated April 22, Hadden says: "We had a corps review ... by General Grant ... There is a rumor that we cannot send any letters as soon as we move ... you must direct everything to Washington, DC to be forwarded to the regiment ... I enjoy this life first rate but it is not home. We drill three times a day, have plenty to eat at present but when we are on the march will not have time to cook it ... We have plenty fresh beef, salt pork, coffee, beans, potatoes, fresh bread, sugar and molasses, but on the move we will have nothing but salt pork and hard tack. We do not get any tea. There is three of us tents together. Our house is about 5 feet at the bottom square, coming to a peak at the top. We cook at our neighbor's tents ... Tell mother not to worry about me for I shall take as good care of myself here as if it was home, if not better, for I was going to the Devil fast home which was the cause of my joining the army. I hope to live to come home an altered man.

---

2   OR: S1, V33, 827-9: Grant to Meade, April 9, 1864.

3   Serving as commander of the Provost Guard of IX Corps was Captain Milton Cogswell, former Colonel of the Tammany regiment.

4   The brigade of General Webb (Gibbon's Division) contained the: 19ME (458 men), 7MI (293), 42NY (301), 59NY (160), 82NY (284), 19MA (221), 20MA (443), 15MA (269). Total strength: 2,429. Priest, Michael, *Victory Without Triumph*, Volume II, White Mane Publishing, Shippensburg, PA, 1996, page 233, citing RG 94, OAG, Volunteer Organizations, Civil War Returns, Second Corps, April 1864, Boxes 9, 19, 22, 24 and 126.

If I had stayed home with the company that I got going with, I would not have lived one year ..."[5]

Webb's brigade left their camp around 10 P. M. on Tuesday, May 3, moving to and crossing the Rapidan at Ely's Ford around 9 A. M. on May 4. Continuing in the direction of the Wilderness Tavern the brigade took a position at 3 P. M. on the Plank Road, three fourths of a mile in advance of the tavern. It was at this time that Captain Poinsett Cooper of the Tammany regiment, acting assistant inspector general on Webb's staff was wounded. The rest of the day was spent building breastworks.[6]

Webb's movements and those of the rest of Second Corps formed the left of the Union advance and were well beyond the right of Lee's defensive position. Grant had thought that Lee would be forced to move to positions more suitable to defending Richmond and that Union troops could move quickly through the Wilderness in the direction of Spotsylvania Court House. True to form, Lee reacted quite differently. He moved troops on the roads through the woods and attacked. On the morning of May 5 the opposing forces met. Second Corps was ordered at 9 A. M. to halt their advance about 2 miles beyond Todd's Tavern. Two hours later Hancock was ordered to move to the northwest taking a position at the intersection of the Brock and Orange Plank Roads. Between 4:30 and 8 P. M., the brigades of Carroll and Owen of Gibbon's Division engaged the enemy along the entire line on the right and left of the orange Plank Road. Webb's brigade was held in reserve. Night fell without any significant result for either side.[7]

Early on the morning of Friday, May 6, Hancock attacked leaving Webb's brigade and Barlow's division in the breastworks forming the left of the Union line. At 7 A. M. Webb's brigade was sent to the support

---

[5] American Historical Manuscripts Collection, NYHS, Hadden, Isaac. Letter of April 22 to friends from Camp near Brandy Station. Hadden's early letters are repetitive in describing his needs for food and comfort items that are not available. In particular short supply was postage stamps. Hadden makes repeated references to a man named Nick who is probably Nicholas Andrews who also enlisted on April 4 and is clearly a family member or friend. Andrews was discharged for disability on April 28, 1864.
[6] OR: S1, V36, 437-42. Report of General Webb. Also Nineteenth Massachusetts, page 303.
[7] Swinton, Supra, 365-373

of Getty's division of Sixth Corps. Webb described the action saying: "I received orders from General Gibbon to move to the right to the plank road and report to Major General Birney, which was promptly done. General Birney ordered my command to deploy on the right of the plank road, and move forward to join Brigadier General Getty, of the Sixth Corps. I deployed and advanced as ordered. I of course failed to find the line of General Getty. Since I do not know that any of our troops ever had been where I was ordered. We met the enemy in force across the plank road and engaged him. This fight opened without the employment of a line of skirmishers on my part, since I had been distinctly ordered to relieve General Getty with my brigade by General Birney in person. From this moment to the time my line was destroyed by the forcing in of the troops on my left, I was left totally unaware of any special object in disposing of my command and I am still at a loss to determine whether or not it was my duty to attack and attempt to drive the enemy on the plank road or to hold my position."[8]

Fighting continued for most of the rest of May 6 but neither side achieved victory. The forest had caught fire and men were caught in the smoke and flames and compelled to leave their positions. On Saturday morning, May 7 both sides were unwilling to continue the fight. The Battle of the Wilderness was described by Swinton: "As an action it was without brilliancy in its conduct. It was a mere collision of brute masses, or as an officer on the field pithily expressed it to me, "the bumping, bumping of two armies, to see which could bump the hardest." It might have been fought by any other commander. But the difference in the result was this: that while any other commander we had thus far seen would have fought the battle of the Wilderness and gone backward, Grant fought the battle of the Wilderness and went forward!"[9]

Looking more closely at the impact of the Battle of the Wilderness on the Tammany regiment, of the 301 men that took the field under the command of Major Patrick J. Downing a total of 22 became casualties.[10] Three were killed, four were captured and fifteen were wounded.

---

8   OR: S1, V36, 437-42
9   Swinton, Supra, 383
10   OR: S1, V36, 107. Not including Captain Pointsett Cooper, on General Webb's staff. See Chapter 17 for details on P. Cooper. Also not included is Robert Clare,

The three fatalities were: Stephen Mack, Co. D, who joined the regiment September 24, 1863, John Glendening, Co. C, who joined August 26, 1863 and Abram Goodwin, Co. D, who had been with the regiment about one month.[11]

Captured were two long time veterans: James Casey[12] and William Baxendale from Co. A. Also captured were John P. Lomasney[13], Co. E and William H. Lawrence, Co. F (also wounded), both had been with the regiment about seven months. Lawrence, age 46, and by trade a carpenter, had joined as a substitute for Robert M. Imlay. His record states he was also wounded and contains a letter from his wife Lavinia to Brig. General Wessells dated March 28, 1865 that reads: "Would you please be kind enough to give me a little information concerning my husband if you can. His name is Wm. Lawrence and he is a private in Co. F, 42nd New York Tammany regiment and was taken prisoner at the Battle of the Wilderness, May 6, 1864. I should be very thankful to you for the desired information if you could possibly give me any as it would greatly relieve the anxiety of my mind."[14] There is no record of a response to the letter but a widow's pension was filed on July 26, 1865.[15]

Co. I. Clare, 20, a native of Yorkshire, England stood five feet six inches, had hazel eyes and was a laborer. He mustered in March 15, 1864 and is listed as having deserted May 3, 1864 in the Wilderness. The records of the 59th NY list him as "transferred while a prisoner of war. What actually occurred is unclear.

[11] According to records in the Pension Office Glendening's widow was granted a pension filed for on Jan. 9, 1865. Application 78.409, Cert. 56.059.

[12] Private James Casey, Co. A should not be confused with Lieut. James Casey. Private Casey had been wounded and captured at Antietam, paroled in October 1862. He was paroled for the second time on Nov. 24, 1864 at Savannah.

[13] Lomasney had enrolled as a substitute in Brooklyn, NY. After his parole on December 16, 1864 at Charleston, S. C. he was seen suffering from Typhoid Fever by Doctor Henry Senff, 109 Clinton Place, New York City on January 26, 1865.

[14] General Henry W. Wessells had himself been a prisoner. Following his exchange he became commissary of prisoners.

[15] Pension application: 103.630, Certificate 83.466.

Wounded Tammany men were: Captain Robert C. Wright, Sergeant Edward W. Wilkinson, Co. G[16], Corporal Charles Brobest, Co. B[17], Corporal Joseph Edwards, Co. B[18], John Corcoran, Co. A,[19] Matthew Hillman, Co. F,[20] Andrew Hunter, Co. K,[21] John Hurst, Co. B,[22] James Johnson, Co. K,[23] Alexander Leeters (gunshot wound to the chest), Co.

---

[16] Wilkinson, age 31, joined the regiment September 12, 1863 as a private in Co. G. He was promoted to Sergeant and transferred to Co. B, October 1, 1863 having previously served as a First Sergeant with the 59th New York. He was discharged for disability in New York on October 11, 1864.

[17] Brobest, age 27, joined the regiment August 25, 1863 as Corporal.

[18] Edwards, age 20, joined the regiment in May 1861. Promoted to Corporal around September 1863. Sick in hospital at Ft. Monroe, VA, between March and June 1862. Sick at Hammond General Hospital, Point Lookout, MD, November 1862. Treated for his wound at General Hospital, Baltimore and Camp Parole General Hospital, Annapolis, MD, May and June 1864. Mustered out in New York July 13, 1864. Pension records show an invalid pension applied for Jan. 7, 1873 (Cert. 146.524) and a widow's pension applied for Feb. 11, 1911, Application 958.507 with a date of death of September 5, 1898 in New York.

[19] Corcoran, age 35, joined the regiment Feb. 12, 1864. He recovered from his wound and served with the 59th NY reaching the rank of First Sergeant on January 22, 1865. He was mustered out on June 30, 1865 at Munson'd Hill, VA with the 59th New York. Pension records show both invalid, filed Aug. 6, 1869, and widow's certificates 102.133 and 635.341.

[20] Hillman is discussed in Chapter 18. He had been convicted of selling rum.

[21] Hunter, age 29, joined the regiment in June 1861. Sometime in late 1863 he was transferred to the Veteran's Reserve but rejoined the regiment March 11, 1864. He was mustered out with the regiment in New York July 13, 1864.

[22] Hurst, age 21, joined the regiment August 25, 1863. He was at Central Park Hospital, New York when mustered out. Pension records show that his mother filed on Jan. 19, 1881. Application 280.045, Cert. 211.861.

[23] Johnson, age 22, joined the regiment September 17, 1863. He was discharged for disability from McClellan General Hospital, Philadelphia, July 15, 1865.

K,[24] Isaac Propper, Co. B,[25] John Scanlon, Co. F,[26] Frank Whalen, Co. F,[27] John Stewart (gunshot wound to right thigh, upper third), Co. I,[28] and Morand Young, Co. I[29].

Most significant was the wounding of Captain Robert C. Wright (gunshot wound of the left leg), one of the most senior officers of the regiment. On May 12, Wright was admitted to Third Division General Hospital, Alexandria, VA. The next day he was transferred to Seminary Hospital, Washington.[30] On February 15, 1865 Wright was appointed

---

[24] Leeters (aka Leaters), born in Ireland joined the regiment at age 19, August 25, 1863 as a substitute for George Pyatt. Recovered from his wound at Emory Hospital, Washington. Returned to duty July 10. Mustered out with the 59th New York at Munson's Hill, VA, June 30, 1865. Invalid pension filed Oct. 8, 1877. Cert. 199.340.

[25] Propper, age 22, joined the regiment August 26, 1863. Following his recovery Propper was mustered in as Second Lieut. Co. H, 39th NY on May 27, 1864 and was promoted to First Lieut. Nov. 20, 1864. He was mustered out on July 1, 1865 near Petersburg. Documents of the Assembly of the State of New York, Volume 33, page 2207. Invalid pension filed Aug. 25, 1879: Appl: 304.455, Cert. 190.483, widow pension application 436.493, Cert: 352.353. Listed as having died July 1, 1889.

[26] Scanlan, age 27, joined the regiment in June 1861and recovered from his wound at Patterson Park Hospital, Baltimore. Invalid Pension: filed Feb. 19, 1885, App: 532.865, Cert: 338.610. There is also a record of a John W. Scanlan who also joined Co. F of the regiment the same day at age 30. John W. was discharged for disability May 28, 1862 in Washington and is listed as having died March 22, 1916, in Denver, Colorado. Widow's Pension: App: 1.064.949a, Cert: 810.135. The two men were likely brothers.

[27] Whalen, age 32, enlisted at Buffalo, NY August 10, 1863. His record with the 59th NY lists him as "in arrest for desertion" at muster out of company.

[28] Stewart, age 21, joined the regiment August 2, 1863. He recovered from his wound at Finley Hospital, Washington and Mower Hospital, Philadelphia. Invalid pension application 681362 filed Dec. 10, 1888. Certificate 829671.

[29] Young, age 31, joined the regiment August 24, 1863. He is listed among the wounded received at Campbell hospital in Washington. New York Tribune, May 14, 1864, page 10, column 2-4. Young was mustered out at Stanton General Hospital, Washington, June 8, 1865.

[30] Wright had commanded the Tammany regiment at Bristoe Station and had been appointed Lieut. Colonel but never was mustered in at that rank. See Chapter 14. His parents were Robert and Martha Wright, both born in England in 1806 and 1819 respectively. New York State Census 1855, ED 1, Ward 12, New York City.

Captain in Hancock's First Army Corps of Veterans. Reaching the rank of Major, Wright resigned on March 18, 1865 stating that his wound received in the Wilderness had broken out again and made him so lame that he could no longer attend to his duties. Wright died on Dec. 14, 1876 in New York City. [31]

Families of soldiers anxiously awaited news reports from the battlefield and hospitals that filled with wounded hoping to learn what had happened to those they cared about. Numerous reports were filed and printed, many contained incorrect information and miss-spelled names.[32]

The action seen by the Tammany regiment during the Battle of the Wilderness was limited but at times intense. Tammany casualties were certainly not as bad as other Union regiments suffered but nevertheless amounted to almost 7% of those engaged. As the men moved south in pursuit of the Confederate army they had no way of knowing that within a week's time one out of every four survivors of the Wilderness would become a casualty of the Battle at Spotsylvania Court House.

Invalid Pension application 131058 dated Jan. 23, 1868, Cert. 90066. Widow's application 1025735 dated Apr. 8, 1914, Cert. 782966.

[31] New York Times, February 16, 1865. First Veteran Army Corps, created by General Orders, No. 287, Adjutant Generals Office, November 28, 1864.

[32] New York Times, May 12, 1864, page 8, column 7 listed Brobest and Edwards as wounded. New York Times, May 15, 1864 page 6, column 3 listed Scanlon at Emory Hospital and Whelan at Stanton Hospital. New York Tribune, May 13, 1864, page 7, Column 1-2 listed Hunter at Columbia Hospital. New York Tribune, May 16, 1864, page 6, column 1-3 listed Isaac Prosser as wounded at Washington Hospital. The Irish American May 21, 1864 page 2 listed Brobost, Edwards, Corcoran and Wilkeson as Wilderness casualties.

Chapter Twenty

BATTLE OF SPOTSYLVANIA
COURT HOUSE

The Tammany regiment remained in place with the rest of their brigade until 8 P. M. on May 8, when they moved into position on the right of the Plank Road. The next day they marched toward Spotsylvania Court House reaching Todd's Tavern at 10 A. M., continued down the road and into bivouac at eight in the evening about one mile in the rear of Fifth and Sixth Corps. On May 9, movement continued to and across the Po River, pickets were placed around 8 P. M. and the brigade settled in for the night.[1]

May 10 was to be an extremely active and long day. The morning was spent on the south side of the Po River skirmishing with the enemy. Early in the afternoon the brigade re-crossed the Po River and moved into position around 3 P. M. between Colonel Carroll's third brigade and General Crawford's division of Fifth Corps. Around 4:30 an attack was made that failed. General Webb described the action saying: "This could hardly be termed a charge. Orders were sent to the brigade to cheer when the division on my right, under General Crawford, did so, and to charge at once. The men had had time to examine the enemy's line. They had found it necessary to hug the ground very closely for some hours since the firing was severe. They had convinced themselves that the enemy was too strongly positioned to be driven out by assault, and this was evident in the attempt at a charge … At 5:45 another attempt was made to carry

---

[1]   OR: S1, V36, 439-440 Report of General A. S. Webb

the enemy's works, which likewise resulted in failure. At this time my rear line broke to the rear. I saw after the charge that but three regiments were to be found ..."[2]

Webb's description of the attack does not do justice to the situation. General Hancock described the same attack saying: "At 5:30 P. M ... I found the Fifth Corps and Gibbon's division of the Second Corps engaged in an assault on the enemy's line in front of Alsop's house. The enemy held the crest of a densely wooded hill, crowned by earthworks, his artillery and musketry sweeping his front. The approach to this position was rendered more difficult and hazardous by a heavy growth of low cedar trees, most of them dead, whose long, bayonet like branches interlaced and pointing in all directions presented an almost impassable barrier to the advance of our lines ... The men struggled on bravely for a time and even entered the enemy's breast works at one or two points, but soon wavered and fell back."[3] General Gibbon commented: "Webb's and Carroll's brigades made two ineffectual assaults on the enemy works, the first under orders from Warren the second, later in the afternoon, under orders from Hancock ... The only result of the two assaults was to kill and wound a large number of men, many of whom were burnt to death by the fierce conflagration which raged in the dry timber".[4]

Some historians have said that after Webb's brigade broke, staff officers found his missing regiments "gathered around their flags, brewing coffee and discussing their recent ordeal".[5] A corporal of the 20th MA, described the final attack saying: " ...the men were willing to face any hazardous undertaking if they imagined there was the slimmest possibility of success ... A large number were killed and wounded, mostly killed, as when they arose they were struck in the head ... We did not assault the works but we held our position which I considered doing well under the circumstances".[6]

---

[2] Ibid
[3] OR: S1, V36, 334 Report of General Hancock
[4] OR: S1, V36, 430 Report of General Gibbon
[5] Rhea, Gordon, C. The Battles of Spotsylvania Court House and the Road to Yellow Tavern, Louisiana State University Press, 1997, page 179.
[6] Miller, Richard, F. Harvard's Civil War, University Press of New England, 2005 page 354.

General Alexander S. Webb, Library of Congress

General John Gibbon, Library of Congress

Major Patrick Downing, USMHI

Webb's report very clearly expresses his anger with the Tammany regiment's commander. He says: "Major Downing, of the Forty-second New York, I arrested for his conduct in this affair". No other officer from any of Webb's regiments is listed as having been arrested or is specifically mentioned in a negative way. Captain McFadden, Major Rice and Major Hooper, commanding the 59th New York, 19th and 15th Massachusetts respectively, are favorably mentioned so it is reasonable to assume that Webb was satisfied with their performance and that it was these units that Webb was referring to in his report when he said: "I saw after the charge that but three regiments were to be found".[7] It also seems likely that these three regiments were in the front rank of Webb's formation as he comments " ...my rear line broke to the rear".[8]

---

[7] OR: S1, V36, 439-40 Webb's command consisted of the 19ME, 15MA, 19MA, 20MA, 7MI, 42NY, 59NY, 82NY (Battalion) and a company of MA Sharpshooters.

[8] This formation is supported by a comment in the Report of Captain Spaulding 19ME stating: "May 10, formed portion of a column, which twice assaulted the enemy's works." OR: S1, V36, 440-1.

Where did Major Downing fit in the command structure of the brigade on May 10, 1864? Was he in command of the rank that broke? There was only a single officer above the rank of major in command of any of Webb's units, Colonel Henry W. Hudson of the 82NY (Battalion). Where the 82NY was during the attack is unknown but if they were in the rear rank, Downing would not have been the senior officer present and not likely to be singled out for blame by Webb.[9] At the start of the Wilderness campaign the 19ME had been under the command of Colonel Conner but he had been seriously wounded with command going to Major Welch on May 8. All of Webb's other units were commanded by either a major or captain. Downing had been officially mustered in as major on April 14, 1864 but had been appointed major on March 17, 1863, so it is possible that he could have been the senior major in the second rank.

The date Webb's report was written is unknown. He was wounded on May 12 and was absent from the field until early 1865 so it is likely that the report was written during this period.[10] Gibbon's report was written November 7, 1864 and Hancock's on September 21, 1865, sixteen months after the events occurred. Neither the report of Gibbon nor that of Hancock mentions the arrest of Major Downing.

What is contained in the report of Gibbon is an addendum containing charges brought by Gibbon against General Joshua Owen, commanding his third brigade, for disobedience of orders between May 13 and June 3, 1864. Specification 1 of the charges reads: " ...Owen ... having been ordered ... to move his brigade up in support of the front line, then making an attack of the enemy's works, did fail to obey said order, and did fall back and occupy a line of rifle pits in his rear ..." Gibbon did not hesitate to bring charges against Owens. Hancock forwarded the charges stating on June 8 that "a proper court cannot at this time be convened in this command". On June 24, General Meade wrote: " ...Owen having been

---

9   Colonel Hudson was "Dismissed The Service" on May 20, 1864, just 10 days after the failed attack. Details of his dismissal are unknown to this author. Second Army Corps, page 554.

10 Webb's wound was a gunshot that "passed through the corner of his eye and came out behind his ear". While recovering, "he did court martial and recruiting duty until he rejoined his command". New York State Monuments Commission for the Battlefield of Gettysburg, J. B. Lyon Co., 1916, 93-106.

ordered to Fortress Monroe in arrest by Lieut. General Grant." Grant
recommended that "Owen be mustered out of the service" on June 27.
Within a month the recommendation had been approved by President
Lincoln.[11] So it is clear that senior commanders did not hesitate to pursue
charges against those that disobeyed orders.

What then happened following the arrest of Downing? Downing's
record has no mention of charges being brought against him and no
indication that he was disciplined in any way. There is no general or special
order of Second Corps or the Army of the Potomac detailing proceedings
against Downing. Reasonable explanations are: Webb did not pursue
further action against Downing, Gibbon or Hancock did not endorse
any action brought by Webb or that the matter was considered moot as
Downing had been mustered out of service prior to charges being filed.
Downing's file has a copy of a pass dated June 29, 1864, made out to "Maj.
Downing" providing passage for 5 officers and 62 men of the 42NY to
Washington for mustering out.[12] Exactly what Downing was doing and
where he was between May 10 and June 29 is unknown although thanks
to Isaac Hadden's letter of May 24 we do know that he was "under arrest
for cowardice since the second day of the fight".[13]

On May 12, the regiment took part in the massive attack described
later in this chapter that took the lives of three company commanders,
another officer and a large number of the rank and file. There is no official
report filed by any member of the Tammany regiment for the actions of
May 12. Reports of the attack printed in the Irish American, specifically
talking about the Tammany regiment, identify the officers killed but make

---

[11]   OR: S1, V36, 435-6: Addenda and 5 endorsements to General Gibbon's report.
General Owen was mustered out of service by Special Orders, No. 241, War
Department, Adjutant General's Office, July 18, 1864.

[12]   Pass number 124, written in accordance with S. O. 165, HQ, Second Corps.
Downing mustered out on July 13, 1864. Patrick Downing married Margaret
Jane Spillane and had 11 children between 1861 and 1882. He died July 25,
1885 in Washington, DC. Pension records show that he received an Invalid
pension filed for on May 25, 1869, Certificate 98777 and that his widow filed
for a pension on September 25, 1885, Application 331162, Certificate 264115.

[13]   American Historical Manuscripts Collection, NYHS, Hadden, Isaac. Letter to
his brother dated May 24, 1864. Hadden states: "Our Major is under arrest for
cowardice…"

no mention of Major Downing. If Downing had been present and survived the May 12 attack it would have been consistent with the way the Irish American handled news about top Fenian leaders to have somehow "talked up" Downing's participation.[14]

According to the report of General Meade detailing the organization of the Army of the Potomac on May 31, 1864, the Tammany regiment in the field was under the command of Lieut. John Maguire.[15] At Cold Harbor, June 2-12, Lieut. Colonel William A. Lynch was in command and was wounded on June 4.[16] No activities of Major Downing are reported during Cold Harbor or when on June 22 the Tammany regiment faced another disaster at the Battle of Jerusalem Plank Road, where, if present, he would have been in command following the wounding of Lieut. Colonel Lynch. Was Downing in arrest all this time? The answer to this question seems to clearly be yes.

It must be remembered that there was a history between General Webb and the Tammany regiment. On November 20, 1863, Webb wrote a letter requesting that Lieut. Colonel Lynch "be ordered to appear before the examining board, as I deem him inefficient and incompetent". Might Webb have formed an opinion of the command structure of the Tammany regiment that would have led to the arrest of Major Downing six months later? Could there have been a personal interaction between Webb and Downing following the attack on May 10 that led to the singling out of Downing for arrest? To understand if the answer to the preceding questions could be yes, it is worth looking deeply into the two men's backgrounds and personalities.

Alexander Stewart Webb was born in New York City, February 15, 1835 making him 29 years old on May 10, 1864. He had attended private schools and graduated from West Point in 1855. He served in the artillery

---

[14] Irish American newspaper, May 28, 1864, page 2 column 2.
[15] OR: S1, V36, 200: report of General Meade, November 1, 1864.
[16] NARA record of William Lynch. Gunshot wound to right leg. The wound is described as a flesh wound. Lynch had been in New York City on recruiting duty for several months. SO 41, 2 Div, 2 Corps, Feb. 10, 1864. He had reported to Rendezvous of Distribution, Alexandria, VA May 19 and was sent back to the regiment on May 23, 1864. He must have arrived after Meade's organizational listing was prepared. Lynch, like Downing was mustered out in July 1864. Second Corps, page 609.

in Florida and on the frontier until 1857 when he returned to West Point as an assistant professor of mathematics. In the early part of the Civil War Webb continued to serve as an artillery officer. At Chancellorsville, Lieut. Colonel Webb was on the staff of General Meade, commanding V Corps. Promoted to Brig. General on June 23, 1863, Webb was given command of the Philadelphia Brigade, in Hancock's Second Corps. At Gettysburg, Webb was awarded the Medal of Honor for his outstanding performance in repulsing Pickett's Charge. Following Gettysburg, Webb was given temporary command of Second Division, Second Corps, during General Gibbon's absence, serving in that capacity at the Battle of Bristoe Station.[17]

Webb came from a long established, wealthy and important family with a significant political and military background. The earliest Webb settler in the United States was Richard Webb, an English Protestant Puritan who arrived in Massachusetts in 1632 and was one of the original settlers of Hartford, CT in 1635. Some generations later, Samuel Blatchley Webb, Alexander's grandfather, was born on December 15, 1753, in Wethersfield, CT. He served as an officer in the Colonial army and Aide-de-Camp to General George Washington and was brevetted to the rank of Brig. General. Alexander Webb never knew his grandfather as he died in 1807, 28 years before Alexander's birth.

---

[17] One of the brigades under Webb's command at Bristoe Station was commanded by Colonel Mallon of the Tammany regiment. At Gettysburg the Tammany regiment was positioned just to the left of the Philadelphia Brigade and was one of the units that rushed the Copse of Trees at the end of Pickett's charge.

THE DEATH OF OLD TAMMANY AND HIS WIFE LOCO FOCO.

The death of old Tammany and his wife
Loco Foco, Library of Congress

Alexander's father, James Watson Webb was born in 1802. At the age of seventeen he went to Washington and obtained a commission as a Second Lieut. in the Fourth Artillery. In 1827 James resigned from the military, bought and ran the Courier and Enquirer, important New York newspapers, and became politically active in New York. It was in 1837, two years after Alexander's birth, that James Watson Webb and the Whig Party he supported, defeated Tammany Hall's candidate in New York City's municipal election. In a cartoon titled "The death of Tammany and his wife Loco Foco" published in 1837, James Watson Webb is depicted as firing an arrow into the heart of Tammany Hall.[18] How important were

---

[18] Webb's bow in the cartoon bears the names of the Courier and Enquirer newspapers emphasizing the role Webb had in defeating the Tammany Hall candidate in the 1837 election. Loco Foco also known as the Equal Rights Party, is depicted as the wife of Tammany Hall and a "crude Irish woman". A number of important Democrats, including Tammany Hall's Elijah F. Purdy, are depicted as fleeing the scene. H. R. Robinson, 1837, Library of Congress Call Number: PC/US-1837.C619, No. 3.

his father's conflicts with Tammany Hall in forming young Alexander character?[19]

James Watson Webb had an extreme sense of honor and reacted strongly to anyone he believed insulted him. Not long after the election of 1837, on February 24, 1838, Jonathan Cilley, a member of the House of Representatives from Maine was killed in a duel in Maryland with Congressman William Graves of Kentucky. Crilley, a Democrat, had considered Webb's coverage of Congress to be unfair and made comments to that effect in a speech on the floor of Congress. Webb was insulted and asked Graves, a Whig, to deliver a letter, expressing his outrage to Cilley. Cilley refused to accept the letter, an act taken by Graves as a direct insult to his character that resulted in a challenge to a duel. A second duel involving James Watson Webb occurred on July 2, 1842. This time Webb was a principle in the duel with Thomas Francis Marshall, a Whig Congressman from Kentucky who had accused him of bribery. Webb responded by strongly criticizing Marshall in print and Marshall issued a challenge. The duel took place in Delaware in an unsuccessful attempt to circumvent laws banning dueling. Webb was wounded and was brought before a grand jury in New York on a charge of "leaving the state with the intention of giving or receiving a challenge". Webb was convicted and sentenced to a term of two years in Sing Sing prison that he would never serve. The conviction was not a popular one, thousands of New Yorkers successfully petitioned the Governor of New York, William H. Seward, to pardon Webb.[20] At the time of the second duel and his father's trial Alexander was seven years old. It is no surprise that honor and the defense of honor in the extreme would become significant to Alexander S. Webb. During the Civil War James Watson Webb was Minister to

[19] Alexander Webb was the youngest child of James Watson Webb and his first wife Helen. Alexander's oldest brother Robert Stewart Webb was born in 1824, 13 years before the election of 1837. Robert's memory of the events and the relationship between his father and Tammany Hall could well have been shared with his younger brother.

[20] Byron, Matthew, A, Crime and Punishment: The Impotency of Dueling Laws in the United States, Pro Quest 2008, 86-8.

Brazil appointed by Lincoln, no doubt with the strong recommendation of Secretary of State Seward.[21]

Fortunately, there are a number of statements made by Alexander Webb that will help readers understand how he might have acted following the failure of the attacks on May 10. Soon after taking command of the Philadelphia Brigade in June 1863, Webb issued an officer's call where he said to his officers: "I presume you are all officers as you attend the call … There are few of you whom I am able to recognize as officers, as you have no insignia of office except your sword." The men were ordered "to prepare ourselves with insignia, as we were entitled to, so that when he met us he would know our rank". At Gettysburg on July 1, Webb's brigade broke camp with orders "that the officers should arrest any of the men found straggling, and to bring them to him and he would shoot them like dogs." On July 2, Webb warned "that any man found shirking his duty, even slightly, would be severely dealt with, and any man who fled the battle line would be shot". Webb once referred to his command as the "Straggling Brigade".

During the few months following Gettysburg, Webb ordered or approved a number of executions of enlisted men for desertion but wrote a letter recommending clemency for Captain Bernard J. McMahon of the 71st PA who had been convicted of murdering a fellow officer, Captain Andrew McManus of the 69th PA. McMahon had shot McManus in late May 1863 following accusations of cowardice toward him made in the presence of other officers. Webb's letter and others coupled with McMahon's performance in the Battle of Gettysburg under Webb, influenced Judge Advocate General Joseph Holt to recommend to President Lincoln that McMahon be given a full pardon. Holt said that McManus should "be regarded as having wantonly and wickedly thrown his life away" a clear reference to what the price was for challenging the "honor" of a fellow

---

[21]   James Watson Webb was a strong supporter of Seward in his 1860 campaign for the presidential nomination eventually won by Lincoln. He served in Brazil for eight years and returned to New York where he died on June 7, 1884. New York State Monuments Commission for the Battlefield of Gettysburg, J. B. Lyon Co., 1916, 93-106.

officer. There is little doubt that Alexander Webb's father James Watson Webb would have completely agreed with General Holt.[22]

Major Patrick Joseph Downing's background was about as different as it could be from that of Alexander Webb. He was born in Skibbereen, County Cork, Ireland on March 12, 1837, making him 27 years old at the time of the May 10, 1864 attacks. As a young man in Ireland and upon his arrival in the United States he was deeply involved with the Fenian movement that sought independence for Ireland from Great Britain. Downing's popularity with the Irishmen of the Tammany regiment and throughout the Army of the Potomac cannot be overstated. He was revered both by the men in the field and by the Irish press in New York because of his experiences in Ireland and his close friendship to top Fenian leaders, especially John O'Mahoney. Downing's promotion to Major came at the request of Colonel James Mallon, who in April 1863 considered Downing to be superior to another candidate saying that Downing "is much the superior in anything that makes the soldier".[23]

Downing's deep connection to the Fenian Brotherhood was not a secret. It is likely that most commanders knew that while Downing was frequently serving as a recruiting officer in New York he scheduled and held meetings of the Fenian Brotherhood at the Whitney House on the corner of Broadway and Twelfth Street. Notices for these meetings were published in the Irish American newspaper.[24]

Downing and Webb did share a common sense of honor. Both men considered their reputation to be their most precious possession and reacted immediately to any perceived attack on their character. For Downing that is best seen in his interaction with Captain O'Meara prior to Ball's Bluff. The failure of the attack on May 10 might well have been considered by

---

[22] Lash, Gary G., The History of Edward Baker's California Regiment, Butternut and Blue, 2001, 329-336, 356-60 citing a letter to Webb's wife, July 21, 1863, Webb Papers. General Orders No. 69, Army of the Potomac, July 16, 1863 (Conviction of McMahon) and General Orders No. 311, War Department, September 14, 1863 (McMahon's release from arrest. He was returned to duty.)

[23] See Chapters 2 and14.

[24] Irish American, Jan. 30, 1864, page 2, column 6. On this date in the column titled "Military News-Fenian Brotherhood-Army of the Potomac" appeared a notice of a meeting "by order of Patrick J. Downing".

Webb to be a reflection on his ability to command, especially after his highly acclaimed performance at Gettysburg.

Before moving away from what might have motivated the singling out of Major Downing for arrest on May 10 it is worth looking again at the three previous interactions of men from the Tammany regiment with Alexander Webb. In the months following Gettysburg, General Webb and Colonel Mallon of the Tammany regiment were recognized for their bravery in repulsing Pickett's Charge. Webb took command of Second Division, Second Corps and Mallon commanded Webb's third brigade. It is clear that Webb had great respect for Mallon. When Mallon was killed at Bristoe Station, Webb stated: "Colonel Mallon, commanding Third Brigade, was mortally wounded, rallying a few men of one of his regiments who were driven back from the most exposed position on his line. I lost in him an able commander and a brave, intelligent gentleman". [25] Webb's opinion of Lieut. Colonel Lynch, as mentioned earlier, was not the same. Webb doubted the efficiency and competency of Lynch sufficiently to request that he be brought before an examining board in November 1863, a month after the death of Colonel Mallon. Lynch had been on recruiting duty in New York at the time of Bristoe Station. Captain Poinsett Cooper of the Tammany regiment was wounded in the Wilderness while serving as acting assistant inspector general on Webb's staff. Cooper came from a prestigious military family, had served both in line and staff positions and was wounded four times during the war. [26] Taken together, it seems clear that Webb did not have a particular negative bias against officers from the Tammany regiment but rather judged his officers by the way they responded to the demands facing them in the field. This would explain why Major Downing might have been subject to arrest on May 10, but not why he would have been the only officer arrested. What actually happened between Webb and Downing after the events of May 10 has been lost to history but if Webb had found Downing and suggested that he had failed to follow orders to attack, it would have been likely that Downing would have responded in a way that resulted in his arrest.

Webb reported that on May 11 his brigade "threw up works, which was accompanied by much danger on account of the sharpshooters of the

---

[25] OR: S1, V29, 277-8. Report of Alexander Webb. Oct. 16, 1863
[26] See Chapter 17 for details on Captain Cooper.

enemy completely commanding our position". Major William G. Mitchell, Aide to General Hancock, reported that on May 11, "Sharp picket firing commenced at daybreak; also severe artillery fire ..."[27]

The major assault on Confederate positions at Spotsylvania aimed at the salient or "mule shoe", an outcrop of an elaborate entrenched defense line, was timed to commence just before dawn on May 12. Major Mitchell described the attack by Second Corps saying: " ...Before daylight the troops were formed as follows: Birney's division on the right in two lines of battle, but a few paces separated; Barlow's division in column of regiments, doubled on the center; Gibbon's and Mott's divisions ... in the rear of Barlow and Birney, in two lines of battle, each division with but very short intervals, this making almost a solid rectangular mass of nearly 20,000 men to hurl on the enemy's works as soon as it should be sufficiently light for our purpose. A dense fog fell before daylight, and we all stood shivering with cold and wet until 4:30 A.M. when the fog lifted somewhat and the command was given to advance. The whole corps stepped off at the same moment, and in about 300 yards marched over the enemy's pickets, who were so astounded at our appearance, marching on them out of the fog, that they never fired a shot, nor did we, but moved right over them. The first fire we received was from the picket reserve ... about halfway between the point at which we formed for the assault and the enemy's works ... our column kept on to capture the works, which we found to be about one-half mile from our point of formation. The ground was open and rolling ... to the works, and the troops dashed over it in fine style, not meeting a heavy fire until within about 300 yards ... the enemy opened a tremendous fire of musketry on us over the parapets with some artillery, but nothing could stop our men, who rushed up to the works, and, tearing the abatis way with their hands, poured in like a great wave, driving the enemy out pell-mell with clubbed muskets and bayonets, capturing twenty pieces of

---

[27] OR: S1, V36, 357. Report of General Hancock. William G. Mitchell reached the rank of Brevet Brig. General and remained a close friend of General Hancock. Mitchell died on Wed. May 30, 1883. He had taken ill on May 22, a day before he was to accompany Hancock at the ceremonies opening the Brooklyn Bridge in New York. OR: S1, V36, 439. Report of General Webb. Doc. Of the Assembly of the State of New York, 124th Session, 1901, Vol. VI, No. 30, Part 3, 952. New York Times May 31, 1883: Obituary for Gen. William G. Mitchell.

artillery and nearly 4,000 prisoners ... the prisoners got mixed up among our own men in the works, and were dodging in all directions from the bullets of their friends, who were firing on us as they fell back ... When we had carried the first line of works we continued to drive the enemy until about 5:30 A.M., when we came to a second line of entrenchments, when the enemy rallied their broken lines, and, being heavily reinforced, they compelled our troops to retire to the first line we had carried ..."[28]

General Gibbon's report fixes the formation and movement of his brigades as: "the division took up position in two lines in the rear of the First and Third divisions, Owen's and Carroll's brigades being in the front line, Webb's in the second ... shortly after daylight our troops moved to the assault, Owen's and Carroll's brigades were almost immediately started in support, and arrived in time to aid in carrying the enemy's works. Webb was soon after ordered up, and while rapidly moving forward on to the enemy's second line, the gallant general was severely wounded and left the field".[29]

Webb's report refines the actions of his brigade saying: " ...on the 12th, at about 1 a.m. we moved out of our works, leaving a skirmish line in front. We marched to the left, and about 4 a.m. the corps arrived on the extreme left flank of our army. At 5 a.m. an attack was made on the enemy's position, my command being the right of the line. We passed over the first line of the enemy's works, and when my brigade was about 30 yards from the second line, being with the Twentieth Massachusetts, I was wounded and carried to the rear".[30]

No specific report of the actions of the Tammany regiment exists however the following description of the attack on May 12 appears in the history of the Twentieth Massachusetts who were brigaded with them. "The rain was still pouring down in torrents, and the air was thick with mist and fog from the soaking earth. Whether through woods or open country, it was all the same. Objects great or small were alike invisible, and everywhere was deep and slippery mud through which the column floundered ... No officer was familiar with the location towards which they were moving, nor had ever seen, much less examined, the position

---

[28] OR: S1, V36, 358-9. Major Mitchell's attached comments to Hancock's Report.

[29] OR: S1, V36, 430-31: Report of General Gibbon.

[30] OR: S1, V36, 440: Report of General Webb

they were seeking to storm ... The difficulty of forming a column on such a night can only be imagined ... Hours were occupied in completing the formation. The first and fourth brigades were placed in the first line and the second and third in the second. A small space was left between the first and second lines and also between the brigade columns ... This attack was not to be heralded by a cannonade, but was to be performed by the infantry alone, in hope of taking the enemy unawares ... Twenty thousand men were standing still in a compact formation, silently awaiting the word to advance ... Seventy-two regiments ... stood arrayed in battle order ... For twenty four hours not one of these twenty thousand men had enjoyed a moment of sleep ... There was neither drum to beat the charge nor bugle to sound the call ... there were no officers on horseback, hurrying hither and thither, in front or on either flank, giving life, color and animation to the field with their clattering sabers, waving plumes and brilliant uniforms ... everyone was on foot, for all horses were left behind the lines ... at 4:30 the word was given for the movement to begin. Until the Salient was captured no other command was given. The great column became its own commander in chief, for brigade and division generals were buried in the mass. Still their presence was felt ... the enemy's pickets opened fire ... When ... the salient burst into view ... the troops rushed forward, broke down and burst through the abatis ... and for the first time were making quick and sharp use of the bayonet and clubbed musket ... The contest was quick, sharp and decisive. Many were killed and more were wounded ... Gibbon had been directed to remain in reserve; but ... the division followed close in the rear of Barlow and went over the works with his men ... Here in a small space in front of the captured works were twenty thousand men ... disordered ... now carried away by a sudden victory of un-looked for proportions and thrown into confusion that required the promptest action to disentangle ... At such times ... one might offer a kingdom for a horse, for he that is thus borne carries with him a dignity and authority that commands respect and wins obedience to his voice ... the great corps ... continued to follow its own impulse, which carried it forward in tumultuous pursuit of the enemy. Forward into the brush and woods the men went ... It was so bloody ... that it is well to leave its details to be filled in by the imagination ... It is ... hardly possible to describe the part taken by the Twentieth in this action. A little force of not much more than two hundred men is so lost in a mass of twenty thousand that it would be exaggeration to emphasize its influence or to give it special importance in such a battle. It moved with Webb's brigade, went over the works ... retired to its outer face by order, and remained there during the day and the following night."[31]

We do have Isaac Hadden's letter of May 15 where he conveyed to his wife some of his observations of the May 12 battle. After telling his wife Kate that he was "alive and well" he says: "I have no time to write much but know that one line now is worth a thousand some other time ... our officers is most all killed as well as the men. We have licked the rebs like hell since we commenced ... It has rained every day since we commenced and we are in mud up to our ass. The most of us threw the most of our clothes away on the first day ... I did not mind the fight after ten minutes but felt ticklish at first. Hard sights I tell you. We bury all the rebs dead and care for their wounded. They sent in for to bury their dead yesterday but Grant told them that he would do it for them ... Such is the General that, and is the kind we like for we want to fight and come home or die damn quick for this is no fun in these mud holes of Virginia."[32]

During the rest of May the Tammany regiment and their brigade, now under the command of Colonel H. B. McKeen[33], maneuvered to the southeast in a series of complex movements that eventually took them across the North Anna and Pamunkey rivers. Attacks against Confederate positions took place regularly resulting in further thinning of the ranks of all the units involved.

Isaac Hadden's letters fill in some of the details. He says on May 24: " ...on the 16th ... we had to go and guard our wounded about eight miles from here. The rebs made a dash and took the horses from the ambulances and let them, the wounded, on the road all day before we got word. We are near the North Anna River. The rebs have been routed across but have

---

[31] Twentieth Massachusetts, 369-78
[32] American Historical Manuscripts Collection, NYHS, Hadden, Isaac. May 15, 1864
[33] Colonel H. Boyd McKeen was a graduate of Princeton University and had commanded the 81st PA at Gettysburg. He assumed command of the brigade following the wounding of General Webb. McKeen would be killed in action on June 3 at Cold Harbor.

made a stand on the other side. We had to make a charge on their works on this side which we did in good style and drove them across the river last night with quite a loss on both sides ... We are 28 miles from Richmond and expect hard fighting before we get to it ... We only have the adjutant and three Lieutenants left and around 100 men in the whole regiment." On May 30 Hadden wrote to his brother from "On the field near the Pamunky" saying: "We have been building breastworks today and hope to sleep in them tonight ... The rebs have just commenced to shell our new works and their first shell burst about 100 feet from where I am scribbling this ... This is the 27th day of our campaign and the old vets say it is the hardest they have experienced, in the whole war, but I stand it like a brick and hope to be able to come home safe yet. We have some hard marches and hard fighting but have plenty to eat. Too much fresh meat which we throw away. It is hard to get salt pork to us at present but it is a great treat when we get it ... Grant is the man for me for he goes in to whip them at once and be done with it ... Tell Kate that I will be home by and by, and not to get stewing for a man for I am as good as ever yet ... Give my love to all and take a chunk yourself."[34]

When the battle for Spotsylvania Court House started the Tammany regiment numbered about 280 men. Total casualties during May 10-31 exceeded thirty percent with eleven killed, six mortally wounded, fifty-three wounded and seven captured. The officer ranks were especially hard hit with five killed, two wounded and one captured. Their loss was significant as they represented a core of experienced leaders that would never be replaced. Although some of the officers in the following paragraphs have been discussed previously, their records are partially repeated here.

Captain Patrick Henry Lennon, Co. H, was killed in action on May 12 by a gunshot to the thigh that cut his femoral artery. Uncle Pat, age 21, joined the regiment in June 1861 in Boston as a private, served as First Sergeant, Co. H at Ball's Bluff, was promoted to Second Lieut. Feb. 19, 1862, First Lieut. May 1, 1863 and Captain Feb. 11, 1864. On July 3, 1863

---

[34] American Historical Manuscripts Collection, NYHS, Hadden, Isaac. May 24 and May 30. The actual number of men still in the regiment was most likely closer to 200.

at Gettysburg, he was wounded by a gunshot to the right arm. Uncle Pat is buried in Fredericksburg National Cemetery, Grave 770.[35]

Captain Joseph Walter Tobin, Co. F, was killed in action on May 12. He is buried in Fredericksburg National Cemetery, Grave 899. Tobin, age 22, was mustered in as Captain, Co. F on June 1861. Captured on the Peninsula he was paroled in August 1862, resigned and rejoined the regiment in March 1863.[36]

Captain William O'Shea, Co. A, was killed in action on May 12. He is buried in Fredericksburg National Cemetery, Grave 3470. O'Shea, one of several Irish born Fenian heroes in the regiment, joined as a private in June 1861. He was promoted to Lieut. in Feb. 1862 and Captain in March 1863. O'Shea was wounded at Gettysburg on July 3, 1863 but is most remembered for his actions at the Grapevine Bridge during the Battle of Fair Oaks on the Peninsula in 1862.[37]

First Lieut. John Coffey, Co. K, was killed in action by a gunshot wound on May 12. Coffey had joined the regiment as a private in June 1861, was promoted to First Sergeant, Co. K in September 1862, to Second Lieut. in October 1863 and to First Lieut. in February 1864. At Gettysburg, he was wounded on July 3, 1863 and spent most of his recovery time at U. S. General Hospital, Fort Columbus, New York City.

---

[35] Following his wounding at Gettysburg Lennon was granted a thirty day leave on a Surgeon's Certificate of Disability by Paragraph 1, Special Orders No. 305, War Department, Adjutant General's Office, July 10, 1863. P. H. Lennon was originally buried at Laurel Hill, Spotsylvania, VA. Roll of Honor, Fredericksburg National Cemetery. He was one of over 700 identified men found in marked graves on the battlefields surrounding Spotsylvania Court House and moved to the National Cemetery in Fredericksburg. New York Times, July 4, 1865, "Burial of our Brave Dead". Uncle Pat never married. His mother applied for a pension on July 18, 1864 (Application 59103, Certificate 35880).

[36] Tobin was originally buried at Sanford's Farm, Spotsylvania, VA. Roll of Honor, Fredericksburg National Cemetery.

[37] O'Shea was originally buried at Brown's Farm, Spotsylvania, VA. Roll of Honor, Fredericksburg National Cemetery. O'Shea, born in Bantry, County Cork, Ireland, was one of the "Phoenix Prisoners" arrested and charged by the British in 1858. He, Patrick Downing and others were charged with treason. Downing was released before O'Shea who remained in prison for eight months. Savage, John, Fenian Heroes and Martyrs, Page 348

First Lieut. Emmet M. Faye, USMHI

Captain Francis F. Reynolds
Kreis, Philip. "Capt. Francis F. Reynolds," Under two flags, the
adventures of Philip Kreis; story of the Tammany Regiment
of New York ... John Shaw Pierson Civil War Collection
(W), Rare Book Division, Department of Rare Books and
Special Collections, Princeton University Library.

First Lieut. Emmet M. Faye (AKA Fay), Co. F was captured on May
12. Faye was born in Canastota, Madison County, New York in 1830.
He stood five feet six inches tall, had grey eyes and dark hair and listed
his profession as a clerk. At the age of thirty-three years and six months
he volunteered as a private to serve in the Tammany regiment on March

31, 1864 in New York City. At the start of the Civil War, Faye had been a private in Company F, 71st New York Militia and served sometime in the defenses of Washington. While the circumstances and motives surrounding Faye's enlistment in the Tammany regiment are less than perfectly clear there are some facts that paint a picture that can be interpreted in many ways. On Feb. 26, 1864 a letter was sent to Major General John Adams Dix, commanding Eastern Department by Daniel E. Delavan, a high Tammany Hall official, stating that Faye "is desirous of joining ... had rendered much service in recruiting for the regiment ... would like to be detailed on that duty after being mustered ..." The letter was forwarded on Feb. 27 to Brig. General William Hays "for such action as he may see fit". For some unknown period of time Faye had been employed as a clerk for recruiting purposes at Tammany Hall. What prompted Delavan's letter of recommendation for Faye is unknown but it is a reasonable conclusion that there was more than a casual relationship between Faye and Delavan.[38]

Following Faye's arrival at the camp of the Tammany regiment his commission as a First Lieut. was received by Major Downing. A pair of letters written on April 29 and 30 detail a complaint made by a drummer, Owen McManus that Faye had swindled him out of a $100 bill he had received as part of his enlistment bounty on March 15 in New York at Tammany Hall. McManus stated that Faye required the payment as a condition to allowing him to be enrolled. The complaint was forwarded to General Webb who on April 30, ordered that Faye be placed in the ranks and requested that his muster in as First Lieut. be delayed. Faye was mustered in as First Lieut. on May 2 just as the regiment was leaving camp, an act that would have not been received well by General Webb. Whether this was another possible reason for the subsequent actions taken

---

[38] General William Hays was serving as A. A. Provost Marshall General and Superintendent Volunteer Recruiting Service, Southern District of New York. New York Times, June 4, 1864. Faye's parents were Nahum Fay, born 1799 in Vermont and Lucy Fay born in New York State in 1805. The 1850 United States Census has the Fay family living in Lenox, Madison County, New York the birthplace of Emmet Faye. Nahum was a grocer and owned real estate valued at $2000. He had operated a grocery since at least 1831. Hammond, Luna, M., History of Madison County, State of New York, 1872, page 511.

by Webb against Downing is unknown.[39] What is known is that Faye never returned to recruiting duty. Following his capture he was confined near Columbia, South Carolina where he was listed on the rolls of sick and convalescent prisoners. First Lieut. Faye was paroled on December 10, 1864, reported to Camp Parole, MD on December 15 and was mustered out of service on April 3, 1865.[40]

Second Lieut. George Ruddy was born in Tyrone County Northern Ireland, stood 5 feet eight inches tall and had brown hair and eyes. Ruddy, age 26, had enrolled as a private in July 1861 and was promoted to Quartermaster Sergeant on Feb. 14, 1862. Following his re-enlistment as a veteran in Feb. 1864 he was promoted to Second Lieut. Co. C on April 24, 1864. Ruddy was wounded on May 12 but his wound must have been minor as he quickly returned to duty. Unfortunately, he was killed while on picket duty on May 31, 1864.[41]

First Lieut. Francis F. Reynolds was wounded May 12. Reynolds, age 26, had joined the regiment as a private in January 1862 and rose through

---

[39] See Chapter 6 for more details on the letters. The earliest $100 bill used in general circulation was printed in 1862 with subsequent printings in later years during the Civil War. Major Downing had served frequently on recruiting duty so it would have been known to him if it was commonplace for $100 bills to be used to pay enlistment bounties. Such a large denomination bill would have been quite unusual as it represented about a year's pay for a soldier.

[40] Paragraph 46, Special Order 171, War Department, Washington, DC, April 13, 1865. Pension records show two applications filed related to Faye. Invalid Application 540997 on June 1, 1882 and Minor Application on July 1, 1891. The New York State Census for 1875 lists Emmit Fay, age 45 living in Brooklyn, New York with his wife Isabella and 4 children ages 1-8. The US Census for 1880 lists Emmet M. Faye, a grocer, age 49, living in Brooklyn with his wife Isabella and their 5 children ages 1-12. Emmet M. Faye died in Brooklyn, New York January 4, 1885. The ages of the children suggest that the marriage of Emmet and Isabella took place after the Civil War. There is a record of a marriage at the Dutch Reformed Church, Greenwich Village, New York between Emmet M. Faye, age 26 and Harriet P. Hutchings, age 21 on June 18, 1857. This marriage produced at least one son, Charles born in Manhattan on March 30, 1859.

[41] Ruddy's record contains a note dated January 21, 1869 from the Treasury Department stating that Ruddy's mother had been issued certificate 203557 allowing her to receive her son's pay through May 31, 1864 based on an affidavit of First Lieut. John Maguire of the regiment.

the ranks being promoted to Second Lieut. in Jan. 1863 and First Lieut. in Oct. 1863. He was wounded at Antietam. His record contains a notation from the War Department dated Dec. 2, 1908 recognizing that he was promoted to the rank of Captain May 12, 1864, the same day he was wounded.[42]

First Lieut. Maurice Fitzharris, Co. E, wounded May 12, was born in Ireland and was one of the active Fenians in the regiment. Fitzharris, age 22, enrolled as a corporal in June 1861 and rose steadily through the ranks to Sergeant Major in August 1862, Second Lieut. in March 1863 and First Lieut. on October 22, 1863. He was wounded at Gettysburg on July 3. After the war Fitzharris returned to Ireland and was one of the Kilmainham Fenians arrested on February 17, 1866 and released in late March 1866.[43] Fitzharris returned to New York and worked as a merchant until his death on June 16, 1875.

---

[42] Notation Bookmark: 7822-US-1881, Adjutant's General Office, War Department reads: "Under the provisions of the act of Congress, approved February 24, 1897, this officer is held and considered by this department to have been mustered into the service of the United States in the grade of Captain, Co. F to take effect from May 12, 1864 vice Joseph W. Tobin, deceased…". Therefore it seems clear that Reynolds took part in the attack on May 12 as a First Lieut. since Captain Tobin was killed that same day. Reynolds spent the rest of the war at Carver General Hospital. He died March 7, 1894 at his home 517 West 159th St. New York City at age 58. New York Herald, March 8, 1894.

[43] O'Sullivan, N., Every Dark Hour, A History of Kilmainham Jail, The 1866 Kilmainham Fenians, 2007. Also US Printing Office, 1868, Congressional Series of United States public documents, American Citizens in Great Britain, page 167, No. 22, Mr. M. Fitzharris to Mr. William B. West (American Consul), Kilmainham Jail, March 6, 1866. Letter reads: "Sir: I came to this country in October 1865 for the restoration of my health, which was much impaired at that time. I stopped in the County Carlow until the 13th of Feb., when I came to Dublin for the purpose of returning to the States. On the morning of the 17th of Feb., I was arrested at my hotel and brought to this jail. Since my confinement here I have been suffering from wounds received in the service of the United States. I have papers of Citizenship with me. I am yours obediently, Maurice Fitzharris". It is likely that the statements made in this letter were self serving more than truthful and designed to provide a basis for pressure to be placed on the authorities for the release of the prisoners. Numerous letters were sent to the American Consul on the behalf of various Fenian prisoners. Citizenship

Three enlisted men, Stephen Endrest, Patrick Fitzgerald and Wesley O'Brien are listed as having been killed in action on May 11. Nicholas Fitzpatrick, John Quirk and William Shultz died in the attack on May 12.[44] Six men were mortally wounded: Thomas Duffney, Edward Long, Corporal Thomas Burnham, Thomas Lancaster, Patrick Geggin and Henry Merstine.[45] John Kemp, Co. I was captured May 10.[46] Enlisted men taken

---

granted to Fitzharris: October 28, 1864, County Court, Kings County, New York, record 499.

[44] Nicholas Fitzpatrick was originally buried at Laurel Hill and then moved to the National Cemetery at Fredericksburg (Grave 1972). Fitzgerald and Quirk had been with the regiment since 1861, the other men had joined after Gettysburg. Shultz is listed as "Buried on Battlefield", New York Times, May 18, 1864, page 1, column 3-5.

[45] Duffney was wounded May 12 and died May 21 at a hospital in Fredericksburg. Long was wounded on May 12 and died on May 13. He was originally buried at Laurel Hill and then moved to the National Cemetery at Fredericksburg (Grave 1976). Burnham was wounded May 10 by a rifle ball and was admitted to Armory Hospital on May 28. He died June 4 from complications of the amputation of his left arm at Armory Square Hospital, Washington. Lancaster, born in England was wounded May 12 by a Minnie ball. He was admitted to Douglas Hospital, Washington on May 26 and transferred to DeCamp Hospital, David's Island, New York on July 21 with an amputated right leg and to Central Park Hospital, New York in 1865. He died March 8, 1865, at age 45, from his wound at the New York State Soldier's Home at 52 Howard Street, New York City. Geggin, born in Ireland was a shoemaker and stood five foot six. Initially taken to Ft. Wood hospital on May 14, he died June 5 from a gunshot wound to the left thigh received on May 12, at Armory Hospital, Washington. The record of Merstine is somewhat confusing as he is listed as having been transferred to the musters of the 82nd and 59th NY while a prisoner of war and as having died of disease on July 5, 1864 while at Second Army Corps Hospital. H. Merstine, spelled Mearstine, is listed as wounded at Carver Hospital, Washington, New York Tribune Friday, June 3, 1864, page 6, column 3-4, "Roll of Honor, Names of New York Wounded at Washington Hospitals". Merstine is buried at City Point National Cemetery, Hopewell City, Virginia, plot 1646. Perhaps future research will clarify the events surrounding Merstine. For now he is included as "mortally wounded" as the most likely scenario.

[46] Kemp, born in Germany stood five feet six inches, had blue eyes and brown hair and was a tailor by trade. He had been wounded at Glendale in 1862 and re-enlisted as a veteran on Feb. 25, 1864. He was confined at Goldsboro, NC through Feb. 23, 1865 when he was admitted to the prison hospital with

prisoner on May 12 were Sergeant Thomas Ramsdell,[47] Corporal Thomas M.C.G. Somerville[48], James Lynch[49], Jacques Brusquer[50] and Joseph Murphy[51].

New York newspapers printed numerous lists of wounded men arriving at Washington hospitals. Included on those lists were thirty seven Tammany men. Carver Hospital: Corporal John Nagle, Moses M. Kerr, Michael Flood, James Murphy, Sgt. Arthur Kenny, Henry Mason, Michael O'Brien, Michael Murphy, Andrew Steinbeck. Harewood Hospital: Otto Speil, Thomas Kelly, Edward Keating, Philip Kennedy, Paul Rooney. Campbell

---

Debilitas. Paroled on March 4, 1865 at N. E. Ferry, NC, Kemp reported to Camp Parole April 2, 1865.

[47] Ramsdell, born in Yorkshire, England was a machinist by trade, stood five foot three, had grey eyes and brown hair. He enrolled in the regiment in July 1861 and rose to the rank of sergeant. Wounded at Antietam and Gettysburg he re-enlisted as a veteran in February 1864. He escaped and reached Union lines at Fayetteville, N. C. March 16, 1865. He reported to New Bern, N. C. March 30, 1865. His record contains passes for him to travel as an "escaped prisoner" to Brandy Station in April 1865. He was officially mustered out June 30, 1865 as a member of the 59th NY.

[48] Somerville, age 21, was mustered into the regiment as a corporal, Co. C, in June 1861. He was captured at Ball's Bluff. On May 12 he was wounded and captured. Records show him mustered out in New York City August 12, 1864 although it is likely that he was still a prisoner at that time. Pension records show an entry dated Feb. 27, 1865.

[49] Lynch, 31, was mustered into the regiment June 22, 1861. He spent some time in a hospital for sickness during the Peninsula Campaign. He was confined in a hospital in Richmond on May 21. Paroled at Aiken's Landing August 13, 1864 and admitted to hospital, Annapolis, MD August 14. His record has a letter dated September 3, 1864 authorizing his travel to New York City to be mustered out of service. Pension files have a record dated October 5, 1874.

[50] Brusquer had joined the regiment in August 1863. He was mustered out with the 59th NY on June 20, 1865. Where he was at that time is unclear.

[51] Joseph Murphy, age 27, was mustered into Co. G as a corporal in July 1861. He was promoted to sergeant Nov. 1, 1861and served at that rank until May 13, 1863 when he was assigned as a private as brigade Blacksmith. His record shows him on detached service as a blacksmith through March 1864. He was mustered out July 15, 1864 in New York City although where he was on that date is unclear. There is another Joseph Murphy, eight years younger who served in Co. D and was wounded at Cold Harbor.

Hospital: John H. Moly. Finley Hospital: James Coughlin, Michael Quirk, John Guisal. Columbian Hospital: James Reilly, John Kennedy, Sgt. John Gillen. Douglas Hospital: Christian Bodi. Mt. Pleasant Hospital: George Dellery, Charles Ashdown, Marcus Puffer, Corporal Francis Campbell, Musician Michael Donovan. Second Division, III Corp Hospital: James Smith. Lincoln Hospital: Michael Burgessey, Corporal Edward Kelly. No hospital specified: James Bergen, William B. May, James Sheeran, Austin W. Simons, Arthur Cosgrove, Sgt. Michael Lahy, and William Gottenbach.[52] The following fourteen additional Tammany men have been identified as having been wounded at Spotsylvania either through their service records or other government documents: Sgt. William Cook, Corporal George Costello, Corporal Joseph Graham, John Peters, James McGeever, Edward Flaherty, Antone Frank, Walter Haw, Adam Hydenoff, Sgt. James Kean, Joseph O'Neil, Dudley Byrnes, Patrick Connelly and Peter Lewis. The majority of the men wounded at Spotsylvania would never rejoin the regiment. They would spend the rest of the war moving through various hospitals. Many were mustered out while still recovering from their wounds. The extensive notes in this chapter are presented to give the reader a sense of the magnitude of what happened in the three weeks at Spotsylvania.[53]

---

[52] The lists published contained misspelled names and incorrect regimental identifications. Soldiers were not identified by whether they had been wounded in the Wilderness or at Spotsylvania. Daily Tribune, Friday, June 3, 1864, pages 1 and 6. Daily Tribune, Friday May 27, 1864, page 6, column 3-6. Daily Tribune, May 21, 1864, page 4, column 3-4. Daily Tribune, May 19, 1864, page 1, column 5-6. New York Times, May 18, 1864, page 1, column 3-5. Author's note: It is quite possible that names included as having been wounded at Spotsylvania or in the Wilderness can be associated with the incorrect battle as records of the period are extremely difficult to sort through and knowing the day a soldier was wounded is rarely able to be determined.

[53] C. Ahston, wounded May 17, mustered out from Finley Hospital. J. Bergen was mustered out June 13, 1865 from Whitehall Hospital, Philadelphia. C. Bodi was discharged for disability at Douglas Hospital May 18, 1865. J. Burgessey was listed as sick in Judiciary Square Hospital, June 30, 1865. D. Byrnes was discharged for disability Feb. 18, 1865 at Fairfax Seminary. F. Cambell was mustered out with the Tammany regiment on July 13, 1864. He subsequently served in the Twentieth Independent Battery. P. Connelly spent

several months between June and November 1864 at Mower Hospital Chestnut Hill, Philadelphia and is listed as being at Jarvis Hospital, Baltimore on June 30, 1865. J. Coughlin is listed as recovering from his wounds on June 30, 1865 at Chestnut Hill Hospital, Philadelphia. Sgt. W. Cook was admitted to DeCamp Hospital, David Island New York Harbor June 2, 1864 with a wound to the right shoulder. He was mustered out Oct. 18, 1864 near Petersburg, VA as a supernumerary. A. Cosgrove was mustered out with the Tammany regiment in July 1864. Corporal G. Costello was admitted to Ward Hospital, Newark New Jersey with a wound to the hand and hip on June 3, 1864 and is mentioned in documents from that hospital through December 1864. He was transferred to the Veterans Reserve Corps from the 59th NY on March 20, 1865. Musician M. Donovan was mustered out with the Tammany regiment July 13, 1864. G. Dallery was discharged for disability Aug. 28, 1865 in Washington. E. Flaherty is listed on the muster sheets of Fairfax Seminary for June through August 1864. A. Frank was wounded on May 13 and admitted to Third Division General Hospital on May 16 with a gunshot wound of the left leg. He is on the muster rolls of Mower Hospital, Philadelphia from May through December 1864. M. Flood recovered from his wound and returned to duty September 10, 1864. He was wounded again on October 27, 1864. Corporal J. Graham was wounded May 11 and was at an unknown hospital in July 1864. Sgt. J. Gillen is listed as having spent time at Howard Hospital Washington. He died June 3, 1902, New York Times, June 8, 1902. W. Grottenbock was mustered out while at Harwood Hospital, June 6, 1865. W. Haw was wounded May 11. He was discharged July 15, 1864. A. Hydendorf was mustered out with the Tammany regiment July 13, 1864. J. Kean was wounded May 12 and was discharged for disability at Judiciary Square Hospital Feb. 16, 1865. E. Keating was discharged May 16, 1865 at Satterlee Hospital, Philadelphia. E. Kelly was mustered out with the Tammany regiment July 1864. T. Kelly is listed at Central Park Hospital, New York, June 1865. P. Kenedy is listed as being at Hart's Island, New York Harbor September 15, 1864. J. Kennedy was discharged for disability at David's Island, New York Harbor Oct. 5, 1865. Sgt. A. Kenny was transferred to Third Company, Second Battalion Veteran's Reserves April 25, 1865 and discharged September 25, 1865. M. Kerr is listed at Mower Hospital, Philadelphia, December 1864. Sgt. M. Lahy was mustered out with the Tammany regiment July 1864. H. Mason was wounded May 12. At U. S. Hospital, Washington, June 1865. W. May was discharged June 19, 1864 in New York City. J. McGeever was wounded May 10 and admitted to Emory Hospital with a gunshot to the right foot. He mustered out with the Tammany regiment July 1864. J. H. Moly was mustered out with the 59th NY at Munson's Hill, VA, June 30, 1865. J. Murphy is listed at Harewood Hospital

As the Tammany regiment now numbering barely two hundred men and the rest of the Army of the Potomac tried to mend their wounds and reform into units that could once again face the enemy, General Grant had no intention of losing contact with the Confederate army. His goal was to go wherever Robert E. Lee went and as he and his staff looked over their maps on May 31, 1864 they focused on ground that had been fought over two years earlier during the Peninsula Campaign. In 1862 the ground had been referred to as Gaines Mills and the action there was part of the Seven Days Battles that forced General McClellan to retreat from his attack targeted at Richmond. In 1864 the attacks ordered by Grant would be known as the Battle of Cold Harbor.

March 1865. M. Murphy was transferred to the 59th NY and mustered out with them at Munson's Hill, VA June 30, 1865. J. Nagle was mustered out with the 59th NY at Munson's Hill, June 1865. M. O'Brien was wounded May 12 and is listed as having been in New York City Feb. 23, 1865. J. O'Neil was captured while with the 59th NY November 6, 1864 at Petersburg. VA. J. Peters was discharged for disability Feb. 24, 1865. L. Peters was mustered out with the Tammany regiment while wounded July 1864. M. Puffer, M. Quirk and J. Sheeran were mustered out with the Tammany regiment July 1864. J. Reilly was discharged for disability March 15, 1865 in New York City. P. Rooney was discharged May 18, 1865. A. Simons is listed as mustered out near Petersburg September 23, 1864. In some records he is listed as having been captured on May 12 but he was reported as wounded in a Washington hospital in the New York Times on May 18. J. Smith was mustered out with the 59th NY June 1865 at Munson's Hill. A. Steinbeck recovered from his wound and was wounded again while with the 59th NY at Deep Bottom, VA on August 14, 1864. He was discharged July 25, 1865 in Philadelphia.

Chapter Twenty-One

BATTLE OF COLD HARBOR

The end of May and the early part of June 1864 saw the Tammany regiment and the rest of the Army of the Potomac continuing their pursuit of the Confederate army. Gibbon's division of Second Corps reached Cold Harbor at six o'clock in the morning of June 2. Early the next morning, June 3, the division was ordered to assault the enemy's works with the brigade commanded by Colonel McKeen, including the Tammany regiment, in the second line and on the right of Owen's brigade with orders to "push rapidly forward and over the front line in column and effect a lodgment, if possible, on the enemy's works, and not to deploy until they got there ... The country was rolling, in places intersected by ravines and marshes, and my line was cut in two by a deep, impassable swamp, which widened as we advanced toward the enemy. The troops pushed gallantly forward under a most terrific fire of cannon and musketry until close up to the enemy's works ... McKeen, who, following his orders ... lay dead on the field, and his ranks were much thinned and scattered."[1]

Major William G. Mitchell, aide to General Hancock described the action of June 3 saying: " ...the Second Corps assaulted the enemy's position at 4:45 this a.m.; the enemy in entrenchments. Barlow and Gibbon attacked in two lines, Birney in support. After a desperate and bloody fight Barlow and Gibbon both penetrated the enemy's works ... The enemy, however, rapidly threw fresh troops ... upon our forces and compelled them to return with terrible slaughter. The musketry was infernally hot ... When our troops were driven out of the enemy's works they did not

---

[1]   OR: S1, V36, 432-3. Report of General Gibbon, November 7, 1864

retreat in any disorder, but gallantly held on and entrenched themselves by throwing up the sand with their bayonets and hands, under a scathing fire of musketry. By 6 a.m. the battle on our front was over and the brave old Second Corps had lost over 3,000 of its bravest and best ... Altogether this has been one of the most disastrous days the Army of the Potomac has ever seen, and the old Second Corps has especially suffered ..."[2] Orders were sent by General Meade at 1:30 p.m. calling for an end to the assault and saying: "For the present all further offensive operation will be suspended. Corps commanders will at once intrench the positions they now hold, including their advance positions, and will cause reconnaissance to be made with a view to moving against the enemy's works by regular approaches from the advanced positions now held."[3]

The month of June 1864 represented a significant milestone in the history of the Tammany regiment. It was on June 22, 1861 that the regiment was mustered into federal service and for those men that had been active from the beginning and had chosen not to re-enlist, the end of their three year term of service was rapidly approaching. Unfortunately, because of battle and sickness not many men remained that could look forward to going home but for those that did it must have been a time where nothing else occupied their minds.

On June 5, two days after the battle described above, Isaac Hadden wrote: " ...We came on the rebs on the 3rd of June at this place and have drove them into their strong works and are digging up to them very fast and hope to drive them out soon. The boys are all fighting except a few whose time is out this month and they hang back so we will be glad when they go for they are a nuisance" ... Our brigade has lost a good many men in this last encounter. There is a lot of men in our front between us and the rebs and dare not move one way or the other. They have been there two days but we are digging close to them and hope to get them out tonight ... The rebs gave us a dose of grape canister when we first made the charge on the 3rd, which made quite a gap in our regiment. Our Adjutant and Colonel were both wounded on that day. The Colonel had not been in command two hours before he was carried out ... Our regiment is commanded by

2   OR: S1, V36, 366-7. Comments by Major Mitchell in the Report of General Hancock.
3   OR: S1, V36, 528-9. Orders, Headquarters Army of the Potomac, June 3, 1864

one of our Lieutenants and we have but one more Lieut. left ... There was a man shot in the belly 20 feet from me which is nothing unusual in this country. It is worth a man's life to go to shit here. I have had the diarrhea two weeks which so much fresh meat is not very good for, but I must eat something ..."[4]

In letters dated June 7 and 12, Hadden says: " ...We have had rather hard marching and fighting since we left camp and expect a big fight every day where we are, which I think will be the last of this summer's campaign, let it go which way it will ... The sharpshooters is picking off our men one by one all the time ... We was relieved yesterday (June 11) from the front, the first time since the third of May ... There damned little rest for us this summer but I don't care if we can only whip hell out of the damned rebs which I hope we will for I hate them worse every day ... One of our boys was shot on Thursday through the heart by one of the rebs sharpshooters while I was eating my supper. We finished our supper and waited till dark and buried him ... I have not had my shoes off but twice since I left camp ... We have to dig holes alongside of the swamp to wash in and once in a while we find a spring and you can bet there is a rush for drinking water. I boil most all that I use for I make two or three quarts of coffee a day. We have plenty to eat if we can get time to cook it ... I hope to get furlough this winter to come home and see you all. You can send the likeness in a letter and if we get anywhere where I can get mine I will send my own ugly mug to you." Unfortunately, ten days after writing for the last time to his wife, Isaac Hadden was captured at the Battle of Jerusalem Plank Road. He would not survive imprisonment.

What Hadden is describing is the plight of many men that were wounded on June 3 and remained on the field beyond the reach of friendly troops and medical teams, coupled with the strategy of digging entrenchments to reach the wounded. Gibbon reported: " ...The wounded could be recovered and the dead buried only by a means of a flag of truce, arrangements for which were made four days afterward ... From the 3rd to the 12th the division was occupied in perfecting its position and pushing forward works toward the enemy, constantly under fire, both cannon and musketry, day and night ... confined for ten days in narrow trenches with

---

4   American Historical Manuscripts Collection, NYHS, Hadden, Isaac. June 5 letter to his brother and wife.

no water to wash with and none to drink except that obtained at the risk of loss of life. Unable to obey a call of nature or to stand erect without forming targets for hostile bullets ..."[5]

New York newspapers carried daily articles from the field describing for relatives of soldiers the events surrounding the aftermath of the June 3 battle. A June 6 report read: "No battle yesterday, but constant firing across from one line of works to the other as soon as any portion of a man's body could be seen. The casualties of the day, all from sharpshooters and intermittent artillery, are not less than 400. To these must be added between 100 and 200 during the night".[6] A June 8 report read: " ... Today has been one of comparable quiet, scarcely a shot having disturbed the vigil of our men in the picket line. The short interval of last night, enjoyed by both sides in the humane occupation of removing the wounded and interring the dead between the lines seems to have visibly diminished the hostility of the pickets, and led to a tacit agreement on the subject of picket firing at certain points along our front ... The truce lasted from six to eight o'clock ... But few wounded were found by either party. As several days had elapsed since the battle, many had probably died from the exposure alone. The bloated form of many a poor fellow whose name had been enrolled among the missing was found lying between the lines and buried where it fell. Blue jackets and gray lay side by side in the embrace of death and in many cases were found within a few feet of each other's works. Decomposition had already commenced, and in many cases identification was impossible ... A detail from every brigade, consisting of a surgeon, accompanied by the pioneers and stretcher bearers mounted the works, preceded by a white flag, and advanced halfway between the works, where it was met by a similar detail from the other side. A few moments of conversation on the object of the truce, and both parties proceeded to explore the intervening space for their dead and wounded."[7]

From June 2-19, the Tammany regiment had five men killed in action, one mortally wounded, three taken prisoner and fifteen wounded, a total

5   OR: S1, V36, 433-4
6   New York Tribune, June 8, 1864, page 1, column 2. Dispatch from Special Correspondent C. A. P. Headquarters Army of the Potomac, June 8, 8 a.m.
7   New York Tribune, June 11, page 1, column 2. Dispatch from T. C. Gray, HQ Army of the Potomac, June 10, 1864.

of twenty-four casualties. Although there are different estimates of the strength of the regiment at the start of the action at Cold Harbor, a reasonable number would be two hundred meaning that the regiment would have lost twelve percent of its strength.

Two officers were wounded, Lieut. Colonel William Lynch and First Lieut. and Adjutant, Julian Ellendorf. Both suffered minor wounds on June 3 and would recover but never return to active service with the regiment.[8]

The story of Sgt. James McNamara, Co. H, killed on June 9 is one of the saddest given the circumstances of his death. McNamara, 21, joined the regiment in July 1861. He stood five feet seven inches, had blue eyes, was born in Limerick, Ireland and was a butcher by trade. From his record it seems certain that he had served most of his time as a clerk, including an assignment as Brigade Clerk from November 1862-April 1863. Promoted to Fifth Sergeant on August 31, 1863 he was mustered out at that rank March 17, 1864 and re-enlisted as a veteran and private the following day in Stevensburg, VA in the presence of Captain Robert Wright of the regiment. Why his rank was reduced is unclear. In his record is a statement from the Adjutant General's Office dated November 13, 1878 that reads: "This man, while the regiment lay entrenched before the enemy at Cold Harbor, VA, June 9, 1864 was ordered to proceed to the rear to make out the discharge papers of those men whose term of service had expired, and in the act of procuring the necessary papers from the officers of the regiment, was killed instantly by a rifle ball from the enemy, striking him in the heart." Clearly, his experience as a clerk was why he had been selected to perform the paperwork and although in most cases serving as a clerk provides a degree of safety form becoming a casualty, in this case just the opposite was true. His certification of death was signed on June 26, near Petersburg by First Lieut. John Maguire, commanding the Tammany regiment. It is also clear that McNamara is the man Isaac Hadden mentioned as having been shot through the heart on "Thursday by sharpshooters". June 9 was a Thursday. Lieut. Maguire also must be the officer mentioned by Hadden as in command.[9]

---

[8] Details on Lynch and Ellendorf can be found in Chapter 14.
[9] James McNamara is buried at Cold Harbor National Cemetery, Route 156 North near Mechanicsville, VA. Grave B29.

Theodore Holderman, Co. F, killed on June 2, John Johnston, Co. G, killed on June 3 and Peter McGinnis, Co. D, killed on June 16 enrolled between July 11 and September 12, 1863. Sgt. Owen Keefe, Co. B, killed on June 3 had been with the regiment since the start of the war.[10]

Tim McCarty, Co. E, had been with the regiment from the beginning. In the summer of 1863 he spent a month in Fairfax hospital suffering from sunstroke. During the last six weeks of 1863 he was on temporary duty as a guard at brigade headquarters. Wounded on June 16, he died in Annapolis, MD on July 30, 1864.[11]

James Turner 42, enrolled as a substitute for Frederick A. Whitney in Brooklyn, New York on August 31, 1863. He was born in Great Britain, stood five foot three inches, had blue eyes, light grey hair and was a shoemaker by trade. His was captured on June 3. Turner died in November 1864 from disease at Andersonville, GA.[12]

Cpl. Henry Peters, 20, joined the regiment on August 24, 1863. He was captured June 13 and sent to Andersonville on June 21 where he enlisted in the Confederate 10th TN Infantry. Peters was captured by Union troops December 28, 1864 at Egypt Station, Mississippi and was confined at Alton, IL where he enlisted in the 5th U.S. Vol. Infantry.

Sgt. John Cunningham, Co. D, is recorded in records of Andersonville Prison as having been captured at Cold Harbor on June 3, having died of disease (Debilitas) on August 24, 1864 and being buried in Grave 6721.[13]

---

[10] John Johnston, age 23, is buried at the Cold Harbor National Cemetery, Route 156 North, near Mechanicsville, VA, Grave C433. McGinnis was 24 years old. Sgt. Keefe was 36.

[11] McCarty was wounded by a gunshot to the thigh. He is buried in Ashgrove National Cemetery, Annapolis, MD. His record of death and interment lists him as being born in London, married with a residence at 65 Mulberry Street, New York City and having died in hospital 16221, Ward 6, Section 5. There is some question as to how old McCarty was when he died. One document has his age at 52, another document says he was 37 when he enlisted, which would have him around 40 in 1864. Regardless of which is correct he was certainly one of the oldest members of the regiment. Reported admitted to Second Corps hospital June 18: New York Tribune, June 24, 1864.

[12] Turner's death is reported in the records of the 59th New York Infantry, report of the Adjutant General of New York.

[13] There is some confusion in the various records of the Adjutant General of New York regarding John Cunningham. The record of the 42nd NY has two men

Orderly Sgt. James P. Daly (sometimes spelled Daley), Co. G, was wounded on June 3. Born in Ireland he stood five feet six inches, had grey eyes and was a clerk. He had enrolled at age 24 in June 1861and rose through the ranks reaching the grade of First or Orderly Sergeant, Co. G, on December 22, 1863. In June 1862, Daly had been one of the Tammany men captured at Tunstall's Station on the Peninsula by Jeb Stuart's ride around McClellan. He was paroled at Aiken's Landing, August 5, 1862. At Antietam, Daly was wounded, captured and paroled at City Point, VA on Oct. 6, 1862. He re-enlisted as a veteran on March 30, 1864. On June 23, Daly was commissioned as a Second Lieut. but was never mustered in at that rank.[14]

---

named John Cunningham. One man enlisted at age 44 as a private in Co. F in September 1863 and was transferred to Co. C, 82nd NY in June 1864. That man is listed in the record of the 82nd NY as being "absent wounded" at the time he was transferred and that he was subsequently transferred to Co. D, 59th NY on July 10. The record of the 59th NY has Private John Cunningham, Co. D, "captured, no date; died of disease, August 24, 1864, at Andersonville, GA." The second man named John Cunningham is listed in the record of the 42nd NY as having enlisted, at age 21, as a private in Co. B on August 25, 1863, being promoted to Sergeant, wounded at Cold Harbor on June 3 and transferred to Co. B, 82nd NY. The record of the 82nd NY has Sgt. John Cunningham, Co. B, as transferred to Co. A, 59th NY. The record of the 59th NY has Sgt. John Cunningham, Co. A, transferred to 170th NY and promoted to Second Lieut. in September or October 1864. The record of the 170th NY has only one man named John Cunningham, who enrolled October 27, 1863 and was mustered in as a Second Lieut. on August 28, 1864. If the enrollment date of October 27, 1863 is correct the man listed in the record of the 170th NY cannot be one of the men listed in the record of the 42nd NY. A record obtained from the National Archives for John Cunningham, Co. F shows him enrolled as a substitute on Sept. 1, 1863 and has no mention of his being wounded or captured. There is therefore a chance that the information reported referring to John Cunningham could be incorrect. It is hoped that at some time in the future information will surface that clarifies exactly what the record should be. Until that happens, it is being assumed that the records of the Adjutant General of New York are in error and that those at Andersonville are correct, and that Sgt. John Cunningham, Co. D, was both wounded and captured on June 3. It is also being assumed that the other John Cunningham was not wounded or captured.

[14] See Chapter Eight for details on what happened at Tunstall's Station. Daly's record shows him arriving at Finley General Hospital, Washington on June 8,

Sergeant James Lanagan was wounded on June 5. Born in Albany, New York he stood five feet four inches, had blue eyes, brown hair and was a railroad brakeman. Lanagan, 23, enrolled on August 28, 1861, was sick and detailed as a guard at Lincoln Hospital, Washington between April and July 1863, was promoted to Fifth Sergeant September 1, 1863, re-enlisted as a veteran Feb. 22, 1864 and recovered from his wound at McClellan General Hospital, Philadelphia, PA.[15]

Sergeant James H. Dougherty was wounded on June 3 by a gunshot of the scalp. Born in Donegal, Ireland he stood five feet seven inches and was a stonecutter. He enrolled in Co. C at age 26 on July 2, 1861, was captured at Ball's Bluff, paroled in February 1862, wounded at Gettysburg on July 3, recovered from his wound at Mower Hospital, Philadelphia, was promoted to Sgt. September 29, 1863 and re-enlisted as a veteran Feb. 12, 1864. Dougherty recovered from his wound at Finley Hospital, Washington, arriving there the same day as Orderly Sgt. Daly, June 8. The two men were next to each other in beds 20 and 21.[16]

Sergeant Mark R. Thomas was wounded on June 5. He enrolled at age 39 in September 1861, was promoted to Sgt. August 4, 1862, spent two months sick in the hospital between May and July 1863 and was commissioned a Second Lieut. with a date of rank of June 20, 1863 but not mustered in at that rank due to a shortage of men in the regiment.[17]

---

with a gunshot wound of the left thigh in bed 21. He likely made a quick recovery as the record of the 59th NY shows Daly as "captured August 25, 1864...paroled April 30, 1865" and "Commissioned, not mustered, Second Lieut., September 16, 1864". There is a record of a James P. Daly having enlisted in the 22nd U.S. Infantry on October 16, 1869. That record states that the enlistee was born in Ireland, was a clerk by profession and was 31 years old. It seems reasonable to believe that this is the same man that served in the Tammany regiment.

[15] Records of the 59th NY lists Lanagan as having been returned to the ranks after September 1, 1864 and mustered out at Munson's Hill, VA on June 30, 1865.

[16] Records of the 59th NY have a Sergeant James H. Daugherty "captured August 24, 1864 at Reams Station, VA...killed in action, April 7, 1865 at Farmville, VA". The action at Farmville would have been the Battle of High Bridge during the Appomattox Campaign.

[17] Records of the 59th NY show Thomas as being mustered out September 6, 1864, near Petersburg, VA.

Wounded on June 16 were: Charles Hoose, Co. H, (shoulder), Peter Lopez, Co. F, (shoulder), Thomas O'Brien, Co. I, (thigh) and George F. Taylor, Co. C, (breast). John Pearing, Peter Dwyer (gunshot of left leg) and David McKinley (gunshot wound to fleshy portion of left leg-ball passing through) were wounded on June 6, 8 and 3 respectively. All seven had enrolled between August 1863 and March 1864.[18]

Patrick O'Neill, Co. A, wounded June 3 and Joseph Murphy, Co. D, were both with the regiment from the beginning of the war and would have been names entered on the paperwork Sgt. James McNamara was in the process of preparing for the discharge of men whose term of service was soon to expire on June 22. Both men were mustered out on July 13, 1864 while recovering from their wounds.

Subtracting the twenty four casualties from the number of available fighting men reported previously establishes the strength of the Tammany regiment at roughly one hundred and seventy five. It is worth repeating that there are numerous reports that list strength numbers that are less likely to be accurate for the Tammany regiment between May and June 1864. One report published in the New York Leader said: "The gallant regiment suffered severely in officers and men during the recent battles. A letter has been received from Lt. Walsh ... The regiment left camp

---

[18] New York Tribune, June 24, 1864, page 6, column 5-6, New York Times, June 21, 1864, page 3, column 4. Hoose was treated and served as a guard at Division 1, US General Hospital, Annapolis, MD through Oct. 1864 and was mustered out June 30, 1865 at Munson's Hill, VA. The record of O'Brien is a bit unclear as he was listed as being transferred to the 82nd NY "while absent wounded". Records of the 59th NY have him transferred to that regiment "while a prisoner of war" and "absent at Jarvis General Hospital, March 16, 1865". Taylor was discharged June 28, 1865 at Lovell General Hospital, Portsmouth Grove, Rhode Island. Pearing was treated at Harewood Hospital, June 28, Mower Hospital, Philadelphia in July and is listed at Central Park Hospital, New York City in 1865. Dwyer was treated at Patterson Park Hospital, Baltimore and was returned to duty September 20, 1864. McKinley, born in Ireland and a cabinet maker was treated at Emory Hospital, Washington, Patterson Hospital, Baltimore and Ladies Home Hospital, New York City between June 7, 1864 and Feb. 28, 1865. He was discharged for disability at Fort Schuyler, New York Harbor, June 16, 1865.

numbering 340 men but 45 are now fit for duty. Lt. Walsh is the son of Mike Walsh …"[19]

George Speers Walsh, 24, born in New York, stood five feet 10 inches, had blue eyes, brown hair, was a clerk by profession and was commissioned a Second Lieut. in the regiment March 16, 1864. On June 18, Walsh was ordered to Washington to receive treatment with illness symptoms similar to Typhoid Fever. He would not return to the regiment and was mustered out on July 13, 1864.[20]

Between June 16 and 21 the Army of the Potomac, along with the Army of the James under General Butler, repositioned itself in front of Petersburg and started what would amount to one of the biggest sieges of the Civil War. June 21 found the remaining one hundred and seventy five men of the Tammany regiment and the rest of Second Corps prepared to achieve an objective of cutting the Weldon Railroad. No one from the most senior commanders in the field to the newest privates in the front line had any idea of what was going to happen on the morning of June 22.

---

[19] New York Leader, May 21, 1864, page 4, column 2. "Tammany Regiment". George's father was Michael Angelo Walsh. His mother was Katherine Wiley Van Valkenburg. Although some of the available data is confusing it seems most probable that George's father was a Tammany politician who served in the U. S. Congress from 1853-1855. He was born in Ireland in 1810 and settled first in Baltimore before moving to New York. To say that he was controversial would be an understatement. He started a newspaper called the Subterranean in 1843 but ended its run two years later after being sued for libel. Mike Walsh died on St. Patrick's Day, 1859 in New York City. His death was reported saying: "Mr. Mike Walsh, a well known Democratic man about town, met with a violent death yesterday morning, in the upper part of the city. He had apparently fallen down the stone steps of a cellar; but he had been robbed, and there are suspicions of foul work. Mr. Walsh was once a member of the Legislature and of Congress; he edited several short-lived newspapers in this city, the chief of which was a radical print called "The Subterranean". He was a radical opponent of teetotalism, and looked upon grog-shops as "the nurseries of Democracy." He was intoxicated when last seen alive." New York Daily Tribune, March 18, 1859, page 4.

[20] George Speers Walsh died December 16, 1915 at his home at 226 West Seventy-fifth Street, New York City. After the war he was a produce merchant. New York Times, Dec. 16, 1915. Pension and New York City Municipal records list his date of death as December 24, 1915. His wife Sarah was granted a pension. Application 1059969 filed Jan. 31, 1916, Certificate 807745. An Invalid Pension was also granted. Application 1188863, Certificate 941270 filed Apr. 2, 1897.

Chapter Twenty-Two

JERUSALEM PLANK ROAD
WELDON RAILROAD

The siege around Petersburg was designed to strangle the ability of the Confederacy to supply Richmond. Petersburg was the center of a complex series of railroad connections linking Richmond, roughly twenty miles away, with sources of supply in North and South Carolina. The railroad that would impact the Tammany regiment ran from Petersburg to Weldon, North Carolina with connections to Wilmington and Charleston. This line was sometimes referred to as the Weldon or the Petersburg-Weldon Railroad. It ran north and south and was generally to the west of the Jerusalem Plank Road connecting Petersburg with Jerusalem, Virginia.[1]

As the sun rose on the morning of June 22, Second Corps, under the temporary command of General Birney, was, together with Sixth Corps, continuing a series of maneuvers designed to cut the Weldon rail line several miles below Petersburg and envelop Confederate troops in the area. Someone once said: "No plan survives contact with the enemy". As it turned out the Union advance turned into a disaster described as: " … the most humiliating episode in the experience of the Second Corps …" What had been planned was for the two corps to move while maintaining close connection with each other. During the advance a significant gap was

---

[1] Jerusalem, Virginia is currently known as the town of Courtland and was the location of the trials and executions associated with the Nat Turner Slave Rebellion of 1831. It was also the home of General William Mahone who would play a critical role in what would happen to the Tammany regiment on June 22, 1864.

created that allowed Confederate troops under the command of General Mahone to slip behind the positions of Second Corps and capture a significant part of a brigade of Gibbon's division.[2]

William Mahone, had grown up in Jerusalem, Virginia where his father ran a tavern. He had graduated from the Virginia Military Institute in 1847 with a degree in civil engineering and had played a significant role in the building of the rail lines between Petersburg and Norfolk. He was very familiar with the area between Petersburg and Weldon, N. C. and this knowledge, no doubt, aided him in his defense against the attack by Union troops on June 22.[3]

Although there are numerous accounts of what happened on June 22, many designed to cover the unsuccessful actions of various Union officers, what is clear is that for the men of the Tammany regiment and many of their comrades the war was coming to an end except for the difficulties associated with being a prisoner of war under some of the worst conditions imaginable. Perhaps the simplest of descriptions appears in Chapter XXXIX of the History of the Nineteenth Massachusetts. The chapter is called simply "Capture of the Regiment" and says: " ...Gibbon's men stood their ground and before they were aware of the fact, the bayonets of the enemy were at their back. In a moment the rebels had captured the majority of the Nineteenth Massachusetts, together with the Fifteenth Massachusetts, the Forty-Second and Fifty-Ninth New York, part of the Eighty-Second New York and a few men from the Twentieth Massachusetts."[4] Second Corps historians said: "The whole affair was over in a very short time ... The Second Corps had been defeated almost without being engaged. There had been very little fighting, and comparatively small loss, except in prisoners. Of these the Second Corps had lost seventeen hundred, more than it had lost on the Peninsula, more than it had lost at Antietam, Fredericksburg and Chancellorsville combined ... The whole operation had been like that of an expert mechanician who touches some critical point with a

---

[2]   Second Army Corps, page 544
[3]   Mahone would survive the war and serve as a United States Senator from Virginia 1881-87.
[4]   History of the Nineteenth Massachusetts, page 326-7.

fine instrument, in exactly the right way, producing an effect seemingly altogether out of proportion to the force exerted."[5]

We are fortunate to have an account of what happened on June 22 written in a letter by Morgan Doheny to his mother dated June 23 in which he says: " ...The whole Tammany regiment was captured in the fight yesterday. Your obedient servant is the last of the race and will go home in his glory on the 23rd. Our time was up at 12 o'clock yesterday, and at two the whole regiment was on their way to Richmond. The brigade was flanked in the morning but the 42d refused to leave the works and nobly held the position until surrounded and ordered to surrender ..." James Fennessy also filed a report dated June 24 that reads: " ...The Tammany regiment, 4 officers and 164 men, whose three years term of service had expired ... was captured ... The Tammany regiment was to have been sent home on the 27th of the month."[6]

Robert E. Lee reported what had happened saying: "June 22, 1864: The enemy's infantry was attacked this p. m. on the west side of the Jerusalem Plank Road and driven from his first line of works to his second, on that road, by General Mahone, with a portion of his division. About 1600 prisoners, 4 pieces of artillery, 8 stands of colors and a large number of small arms were captured."[7]

---

[5]   Second Army Corps 545-6

[6]   Irish American, July 9, 1864, "In Front of Petersburg, June 24, 1864". Some of the numbers are inconsistent throughout the different accounts.

[7]   OR: S1, V40, 749-50. 12th New York Independent Battery, aka McKnight's Battery, of 4 guns was captured. Captured colors included those of the Tammany regiment, 15th MA, 19th MA, 7th NJ, two stands of colors of the First Maine Heavy Artillery and most likely those of the 59th NY and 82nd NY. OR: S1, V40, 411-: Report of Col. Robert McAllister. Also, Ford, Andrew Elmer, Story of the Fifteenth Regiment Massachusetts Volunteer Infantry in the Civil War, Coulter Press, 1898, page 334. Also, OR: S1, V40, 371 Report of Gen. Byron Pierce saying "...the regiments captured were the Nineteenth Massachusetts, Forty-second New York, Eighty-second New York, Fifteenth Massachusetts and Fifty-ninth New York. Officers and men who escaped informed me that the first they knew of the close proximity of the enemy (he) was in their rear in force, ordering them to surrender, which they did, colors and all." Also, Captured Battle Flags, House of Representatives, 50th Congress, Ex. Doc. No. 163, Feb. 16, 1888, page 12, Recaptured Union Flags, Items 82 and 91 states that the flag

Libby Prison, Richmond, VA. 1865 Library of Congress

Andersonville Prison, GA, August 1864, Library of Congress

of the 19th MA was taken by the 11th Alabama and the flag of the 15th MA was captured by 3rd GA, both on June 22, 1864.

Parole Camp, Annapolis, MD, Library of Congress

The residents of Richmond quickly saw the result of what had happened on June 22. A local newspaper reported on June 25: "PRISONERS FROM RICHMOND: Yesterday morning six hundred and seventy-six non-commissioned officers and Yankee privates and sixty seven commissioned officers, captured in the fighting around the "Cockade City", were received in Richmond by the Petersburg railroad and quartered at Libby".[8] Another report on June 27 read: "During Friday, Saturday and yesterday, over three thousand prisoners, including one hundred officers, were received in Richmond from Petersburg, and sixteen hundred more were announced as on their winding way, or ready to come. On Friday seven hundred and fifty six were registered; on Saturday morning one thousand and eighty eight were added, and during the afternoon, three hundred and forty-eight with thirty officers, poured in a dusty, dirty blue stream through the streets. None of the officers were above the rank of Major. The Libby and prisons contiguous are again filled to overflowing. Yesterday the cry was "still they come", and the shady retreat on Belle Isle had to be thrown open for their accommodation. The appearance of the above two or three

---

8   Richmond Examiner, June 25, 1864. Petersburg was known as the "Cockade City" since being referred to as the "Cockade of the Union" by President Madison during the War of 1812 because of the decoration worn on the hats of Petersburg Volunteers.

thousand impudent wretches on our streets, demonstrates one fact ... too many prisoners are taken, and the facility with which Yankee thieves, murderers, woman ravishers and desolators generally, convert themselves into prisoners of war, covering their craven heads with a shield of mercy is working abominations, and bodes no good for the cause. Who knows but that it is part of Grant's great, comprehensive plan to send a Trojan horse into the city of Richmond in the shape of prisoners of war, who shall consume our food in the time of our necessity, and require strong guards to keep them in subjection when the need of men is sorest at the front."[9]

Two Tammany non-commissioned officers were wounded, one mortally, on June 22. Three First Lieut., a Second Lieut., the regimental Sergeant Major, three Orderly (First) Sergeants, eighteen other non-commissioned officers and seventy six Privates, a total of 102 men, were captured bringing the number of casualties to 104.

Mortally wounded was Corporal Michael Lynch, a Boston man. He had been taken prisoner at Ball's Bluff October 21, 1861 and paroled in February 1862. Between September 1862 and February 4, 1863, Lynch was sick at Harewood, Mount Pleasant and Satterlee hospitals. He was wounded at Gettysburg on July 3 and promoted to Corporal in September 1863. Lynch died from cerebral inflammation at Stanton hospital on July 14, 1864.

Orderly Sergeant Andrew Cline (aka Kline, Klein, Clines) was injured slightly by a gunshot wound to the left thigh. Cline, born in Ireland, joined the regiment in June 1861 at age 22. He was promoted to Sergeant March 3, 1863 and wounded slightly at Fredericksburg during the Battle of Chancellorsville in May 1863. From July 1863 through April 1864, Cline was on recruiting duty at Riker's Island, New York with the rank of 2nd Sgt. Two muster rolls list the mustering out of Andrew Cline and Andrew Kline at New York City on July 23 and August 16, 1864, both with a rank of 1st Sgt. Co. K.[10]

---

[9] Richmond Examiner, June 27, 1864. The number of prisoners reported includes those taken on June 22 as well as on June 23, when another attack on the Weldon Railroad resulted in the capture of large numbers of Union troops from Sixth Corps including 400 from the Vermont Brigade.

[10] Cline's record lists him as single with a residence at 188 East 11th Street, New York City where his relative Margaret Cline lived. The regimental muster sheet

The officers and men that were captured remained near each other but were not allowed to intermingle. Traveling by foot and rail the prisoners reached Macon, GA, where the officers were separated and sent to Charleston, S. C. Enlisted men were sent to Andersonville, arriving there on July 12.[11] Andersonville was built in late 1863 and approximately 20,000 prisoners had been interned there by June 1864. Union advances in Georgia prompted the evacuation of Andersonville with the majority of men that survived their time in Andersonville being moved to other camps in Georgia and South Carolina by early 1865. Documents vary significantly, so where specific records exist; details are provided to better describe a specific soldier's experiences.[12]

First Lieut. Stuart A. Staniford, Co. G, was the most senior officer captured June 22. It wasn't until December 30, 1908 that he was considered by the War Department to have been mustered in at the rank of Captain in April 1864 as part of what are called "Pension Department Remuster Cases". Regardless of whether he wore the insignia of a Captain or that of a First Lieut. on June 22, it would be certain that he would have been considered by the rank and file as one of the most experienced leaders present on the field of battle having risen through the ranks since 1861. Staniford was paroled March 1, 1865.[13]

---

for April 10, 1863 lists Cline as 4th Sgt. Co. K. Pass number 491, Headquarters, Department of Washington, Aug. 8, 1864, gave Sgt. Cline, safe passage to New York to be mustered out.

[11] Nineteenth Massachusetts, Chapter XL, Prison Experiences, 336-40.

[12] There are several databases available that list men that died or were imprisoned at Andersonville. To say that there are inconsistencies in what is available would be an understatement. Record numbers, spelling of names, ranks, dates captured and units served in are sometimes unclear. Deaths at Andersonville were listed in: Goss, Warren Lee, The Soldier's Story, Appendix, I. N. Richardson and Co., Boston, 1872 hereinafter referred to as 'Soldier's Story". Men from New York are listed in pages 307-323. Most men that survived Andersonville are listed as "Sent to Millen" between October and November 1864. Camp Lawton, located in Millen, GA, was a large camp built a few miles from a rail line. It operated for only a few months with the last prisoners being moved to Savannah and other places by the end of November 1864.

[13] Details on Staniford are presented in Chapter 18. Remuster Cases were handled by the Pension Department for many years as pension applicants petitioned the War Department for "recognition of rank" under the provisions of an Act of

James Casey, Co. K, had been promoted to First Lieut. on June 10, 1864. Like Staniford, he had enrolled as a private and risen through the ranks. Casey was paroled December 17, 1864.[14]

Michael Cunningham, 20, a stonecutter from Ireland, stood five feet eight inches, had blue eyes and joined the regiment as a private in 1861. He was captured at Ball's Bluff and paroled in Feb. 1862. Following Antietam, Cunningham was promoted to Orderly Sergeant, Co. E, spent time in New York on recruiting duty, re-enlisted as a veteran and was promoted to Second Lieut. May 2, 1864 and then to First Lieut. Co. B, ten days later on May 12, 1864 after the action at Spotsylvania. Following his capture he was sent to Macon, GA, June 29, paroled at N. E. Ferry, N. C., March 1, 1865 and was mustered out and discharged March 10, 1865.[15]

Second Lieut. Mortimer Brinkerhoff, 29, enrolled in the regiment on March 4, 1864 in New York City. He was mustered in at Cold Harbor on June 10, less than two weeks before his capture. He was sent to Macon, GA June 29, confined for a time at Camp Asylum, S. C., paroled at N. E. Ferry, N. C. March 1, 1865 and mustered out of the service by paragraph 14, Special Orders, No. 121, War Department, March 12, 1865.

Sergeant Major Patrick Nilan, 26, joined the regiment as 5th Sgt. Co. F in June 1861. He was promoted to Orderly Sgt. July 1, 1862 and to Sgt. Major just before Chancellorsville. Nilan was sent to Lynchburg, June 29 and paroled at Savannah, November 26, 1864.[16]

Congress dated February 24, 1897, that provided "for the relief of certain officers and enlisted men of the volunteer forces". The War department made rulings and in some cases actions were brought in the Court of Claims. Similar actions were made on the behalf of men seeking to have charges of desertion removed from their records based on an Act of Congress approved March 2, 1889. Annual Report of the War Department 1903, Report of the Chief of the Record and Pension Department, 198-9.

[14] Details on Casey are presented in Chapter 18.

[15] Cunningham's Pension records show an Invalid Pension Application 221432, Certificate 362765 dated June 23, 1876 and a Widow's Application 442886, Certificate 343873. Pension records list his death on November 22, 1888. His rank of First Lieut. was established as a "Remuster case" under the provisions of the Act of Congress of Feb. 24, 1897 and is reported in his file by a notation from the War Department dated September 2, 1910.

[16] Some records list Nilan's promotion date to Sgt. Major as Feb. 1, 1863 and others have it as March 1, 1863. Nilan was sent to New York City to be mustered out

Albert Brandt, born in Rudolstadt, Prussia, stood five feet three inches tall, had hazel eyes and brown hair and was a gun maker by trade. At age 20, he enrolled July 7, 1861and rose through the ranks being promoted to Sgt. December 19, 1862 and to Orderly Sergeant, Co. I, May 1, 1863. Brandt re-enlisted as a veteran in December 1863. Records have Brandt commissioned as a Second Lieut. but never mustered in at that rank while with the Tammany regiment. Sent to Lynchburg on June 29, Brandt was paroled at Charleston December 13, 1864 and was carried on the February 1865 muster roll of the 2nd Battalion, Paroled Prisoners, near Annapolis. On April 2, 1865, Brandt was sent to City Point, VA enroute to join the 59th NY.[17]

Charles Wiegard, 32, enrolled in the regiment in June 1861. He was captured at Ball's Bluff in 1861, paroled Feb. 1862, promoted Sgt. Co. C, January 24, 1863 and Orderly Sgt. April 18, 1863. Wiegard was sent to Lynchburg June 29, to Andersonville and then to Millen on October 31, 1864.[18]

John McDonogh, a native of Troy, New York, stood five feet nine inches, had blue eyes, brown hair and had been a sailor. At age 29 he had enrolled in the regiment in June 1861and was promoted to Sgt. March 3, 1863. He re-enlisted as a veteran March 26, 1864. McDonogh was paroled at Charleston, December 13, 1864 and was admitted to General

---

by Special Orders. No 24, Headquarters, Camp Parole, near Annapolis, MD, January 25, 1865. There is a record of Nilan being at Andersonville listing him as "Private, Co. F" captured June 22, 1864. The "Memorandum from Prisoner of War Records" in Nilan's file has him as Sergeant Major. Sergeant Major is also the rank on the "Field and Staff Muster-out Roll" of the regiment dated July 13, 1864 and Nilan's "Individual Muster-Out" entry dated New York City, January 30, 1865.

[17] The 2nd Battalion Paroled Prisoners was a unit formed to process released prisoners that was compatible with the conditions of their parole until they were able to be returned to their active commands. General Orders No. 72, Adjutant's General Office, June 28, 1862, and G. O. No. 10, AGO, Jan. 10, 1863. Records of the 59th NY have Brandt mustered in as Second Lieut., Co. B, June 30, 1864 and promoted to First Lieut. but not mustered June 30, 1865, the same day he was mustered out at Munson's Hill, VA. A notation in Brandt's record says: "Remuster case returned May 27, 1889" but no details are listed.

[18] There are records for Charles Wiegard and Charles Wickard at Andersonville. Both of these records appear to be for the same man.

Hospital No. 1, Annapolis, MD on December 19 where he was listed as "1ˢᵗ Sergeant, doing duty as a nurse" and furloughed January 16, 1865.[19]

Eighteen other non-commissioned officers were taken prisoner: Sergeants: William P. Church, Co. C, John Caren, James Moran, Co. D, Patrick Butler, George Dixon, James McRay, Co. F, Andrew Galvin, William O'Neil, Co. H, Joseph Schneider, Co. I, Luke Burns, John Seymour Ritter, Eugene Sullivan, Co. K and Corporals: James Irvin, Co. B, Augustus Cronier, William Stripp, William Smith, Co. C, Thomas Sylvanus, Co. D and James Byron, Co. H.

Co. B Corporal Irvin mustered into the regiment on Feb. 29, 1864 at age 23. Information exists that has Irvin being transferred to Millen October 31, 1864, where he died.[20]

Co. C Sergeant Church and Corporals Smith (aka Michael Kenny), Cronier and Stripp had all been previously captured at either Balls Bluff or Antietam. Smith died in Andersonville October 27, 1864 from Scorbutus. Cronier had been wounded at Gettysburg. His record has a muster sheet entry that reads: "Missing in action near Petersburg, VA June 22, 1864." Stripp, sometimes spelled Strip or Strup, died in Andersonville on November 10, 1864.[21]

---

[19] McDonogh's record has a note dated Feb. 21, 1865 and signed by an officer taken prisoner on June 22, James Casey, First Lieut, Late 42d New York saying: "I certify that John McDonogh, First Sergeant, K Co. 42d New York was furloughed at Annapolis, Maryland…and having lost his furlough I ask his transportation to Annapolis". While the date of McDonogh's promotion to Orderly Sergeant is unknown it is clear that he held that rank as Lieut. Casey was the senior officer of Co. K on June 22 and certainly would have known who his Orderly Sergeant was. There is a conflict with the record of Andrew Cline who is also documented as having the rank of Orderly Sergeant, Co. K at roughly the same time as McDonough.

[20] Records of the 82ⁿᵈ and 59ᵗʰ NY list Irvin as being transferred while a prisoner with "no further record". Record ID 18701 on civilwarprisoners.com lists Irvin's death at Camp Lawton, date unknown.

[21] The only record located for William P. Church was a pension filed by his mother June 10, 1865: Application 98,259, Certificate 163,175 suggesting that he had died before that date. Smith aka Kenny is buried in Grave 11558 at Andersonville under the name M. Kinney: Soldier's Story Appendix page 315. Exactly what happened to Cronier is unclear. No record of him was located at Andersonville. His service record has several entries dated November 1866 that appear to be

Co. D Sergeants Caren and Moran mustered into the regiment in June 1861. Caren was paroled November 21, 1864 and mustered out in New York City January 9, 1865. Moran was promoted to Sergeant Nov. 1, 1862 and re-enlisted as a veteran March 30, 1864. He was paroled at Savannah, November 21, 1864, reported to Camp Parole Nov. 28 and was sent to New York to be mustered out Feb. 10, 1865.[22]

Corporal Thomas Sylvanus, Co. D, (aka Ching Lee, aka Ye Way Lee) was a native of Hong Kong and the only man of Chinese ethnicity known to have served in the ranks of the Tammany regiment. Sylvanus joined the regiment in July 1863, having served previously in Co. D, 81st PA Infantry. At Cold Harbor he was corporal of the regimental color guard and it is likely that he served in that position when he was captured on June 22. He was released at Jacksonville April 28, 1865. Returning to Pennsylvania in 1870 he received a pension related to issues with his eyesight. Of particular interest is an affidavit in his pension file dated January 16, 1889 that reads in part: " …At Cold Harbor, while making an advance, June 2, 1864, in the face of the enemy's fire, our lines were broken and forced to fall back. In making the advance, Sylvanus received a fall, sustained a slight cut upon the tibia of one of his legs … not so bad, however to require treatment, nor to keep him off duty. The only person present at the time of receiving the fall, with whom Sylvanus had acquainted, as far as he knows or is able to recall, was one Peter McGinley or McGiniss or McGinnies and who was killed a few days later, in the rifle pits at Cold Harbor by a shot from a rebel sharpshooter …" The man referred to was Peter McGinnis, Co. D, killed at Cold Harbor on June 16. The two men had joined Co. D in New York the same day, July 11, 1863 and travelled together to Virginia. Sylvanus was a member of Indiana, PA Post No. 28, GAR. He died June 15, 1891 and is buried in Oakland Cemetery, Indiana, PA.[23]

---

unsuccessful searches for information on him at Camp Chase, Ohio, Benton Barracks, MO and Camp Parole, MD. Strip's file has a reference to his death recorded on Nov. 10, 1864. Andersonville Hospital Records, page 26-S and 50. His Andersonville record has him buried in Grave 11967 and the date of his death as Nov. 11 from Scorbutus (Scurvy), Soldier's Story Appendix page 321.

[22] Moran's file contains a pension case reference 607165. Moran was present at the dedication of the Tammany Monument at Gettysburg in September 1891.

[23] A special thank you to Gordon Kwok and the Association to Commemorate the Chinese Serving in the American Civil War for providing details on the life of

Co. F Sergeants Butler (aka Buttes) and McRay (aka McCrea) had been with the regiment since 1861. Butler was paroled at Savannah, November 25, 1864, admitted to Division No. 1, General Hospital at Annapolis, Dec. 10 and sent to New York City to be mustered out January 30, 1865. McRay, born in Ireland, stood five feet six inches had blue eyes, brown hair and was a tailor. Promoted to Sergeant on March 1, 1863, McRay re-enlisted as a veteran March 18, 1864. He was paroled at Charleston, December 16, 1864, reported to Camp Parole Dec. 24, received a thirty day furlough ending January 24, 1865, was transferred to City Point, VA, April 2, 1865 and sent to Camp Distribution April 4.[24]

Sergeant Dixon, also from Co. F, a native of Ireland stood five feet eight inches, was promoted to Sergeant, September 10, 1863 by Regimental Order No. 39 and re-enlisted as a veteran March 28, 1864. Paroled on November 26, 1864 at Savannah, Dixon reported to Camp Parole Dec. 3. Dixon's file contains a letter written by his wife to President Lincoln dated New York, November 17, 1864 just eight days before Dixon was paroled. It is impossible to read the letter without coming to tears and the pain is worsened when the response is read. The letter reads: "Mr. President:

Thomas Sylvanus. Much of what was learned came from a presentation made to the Cape Cod Civil War Roundtable on the subject of the contributions of Civil War soldiers of Chinese ethnicity. Numerous newspaper articles were written on the life of Thomas Sylvanus. Some of the details in the articles are inconsistent. It is this author's opinion that the above mentioned work done by Gordon Kwok should be consulted for the most complete understanding of the details of the life of T. Sylvanus. New York Times, June 21, 1891: "Our Chinese Soldier Buried-The Singular Career of Thomas Sylvanus Ended". Gettysburg Compiler, April 5, 1882, Madison Observer, Morrisville, New York, December 24, 1884, The National Tribune, Washington, DC, May 24, 1888, Saginaw News (Michigan), April 2, 1891, The Patriot, Harrisburg, PA, June 18, 1891, Buffalo Courier, June 19, 1891.

[24] Butler had enrolled on September 5, 1861 and did not re-enlist as a veteran. He was transferred to the 82nd and 59th NY while a prisoner as he still had time left on his 3 year enlistment in July 1864. McRay's record has a notation that he was reduced to the ranks September 30, 1863, GO No. 140, Second Division, Second Corps and promoted back to Sergeant January 1, 1864. From Camp Distribution McRay joined the 59th NY and was mustered out with that unit at Munson's Hill, June 30, 1865. McRay was present at the dedication of the Tammany Monument at Gettysburg in September 1891.

I write you these lines hoping that you will be kind enough to spend so much time as to read them. Dear President. My husband was captured on the 22 of June 1864. He belonged to the 42nd New York Volunteers. He re-enlisted and was after joining his regiment. Dear President, I have two children and not one friend in the country where I could stop one night belonging to me or my husband. I receive 10 dollars a month from the relief committee and I pay 5 and a half rent. All I have left is 4 and a half to support me Dear Sir, I have all my clothes in pledge and I owe to the landlord about 20 dollars for rent and groceries. He will now put me out when I can't pay him and God help me. My oldest girl is sick for 10 days with sore eyes. I have offered to pay to anyone whatever they would charge me for the loan of the money to I would get it from my husband but I had no one to help me. Dear sir, it is too hard to have me and my children in a starving condition and can't get my husband's hard earnings. Dear Sir: you are a father of a noble and respected family and if your noble and generous hearted kind lady would see the two dear little girls I got she or any mother would feel for me to see them at want in this season of the year. I can't live if I have to part them. Dear President, can I ask you for God's sake, to do something for me to I get his pay and by so doing you will relieve the broken hearted wife of Sergeant George Dixon, Company F, 42nd New York Volunteers captured 22 of June 1864. Your humble servant, Mary Ann Dixon, 66 East Broadway, New York City." On November 23, three days before Dixon was paroled, a letter was sent from the War Department to Mary Dixon that reads: "Your letter of the 17th instant addressed to the President has been received and in reply thereto I am instructed to enclose a copy of General Order No. 90, for 1861, showing the way in which you may draw the pay due to your husband Sergeant George Dixon, of the 42nd Regiment New York Volunteers, now held in confinement by the rebels as a prisoner of war." One can only imagine the pain of Mary Ann Dixon when she read General Orders No. 90 that gave her the following instructions: " ...Payment will be made to persons presenting a written authority from a prisoner to draw his pay; or without such authority to his wife, the guardian of his minor children or his widowed mother in the order named. Application for such pay must be made to the senior paymaster of the district in which the regiment of the prisoner is serving, and must be accompanied by the certificate of a judge of a court of the United States, of a district attorney of the United States or of some other party under the seal of a court of record of the State in which the applicant is a resident setting forth that the said applicant is the wife of the prisoner, the guardian of his children or his widowed mother, and if occupying either of the last two relationships toward him that there is no one in existence who is more nearly related according to the above classification. Payments will be made to parties thus authorized and identified on their receipts made out in the manner that would be required of the prisoner himself, at least one month's pay being in all cases retained by the United States ..." Exactly what happened to George Dixon and his family is unclear although it appears that the family fared better than might have been expected. It is quite possible that Mary Dixon received both the response letter from the War Department and the news of her husband's release from prison the same day. Following his parole Dixon was furloughed Dec. 12, 1864 for thirty days. A pension application 407815 (194891) dated May 4, 1890 is referenced in Dixon's file.[25]

Co. H Sergeants Galvin and O'Neil and Corporal Byron were Boston men that had enlisted with Uncle Pat in July 1861. Galvin had family in Holliston, Massachusetts. He spent periods of time sick in hospitals between 1862 and 1863 and was promoted to Sgt. July 3, 1863. Galvin died around December 1, 1864 at Camp Lawton. O'Niel had recently been promoted to Sgt. On May 1, 1864. He was paroled at Savannah, November 20, 1864 and was mustered out in New York City January 9, 1865. Byron had previously been taken prisoner at Ball's Bluff in 1861 and was wounded at Antietam and Fredericksburg.[26]

---

[25] While Dixon was at Camp Parole he was confined for a short time for disorderly conduct. He joined the 59th NY in the field in April 1865 and was mustered out with the 59th NY at Munson's Hill, VA June 30, 1865. The records of the 59th NY incorrectly list Dixon's parole after his capture on June 22 as April 30, 1865.

[26] Galvin's record has a letter written January 16, 1865 by John M. Batchelder the Town Clerk of Holliston, MA, requesting a Certificate of Death to aid his family in their application for support. The letter says that Galvin died at Andersonville, however there is a notation from the War Department in the record dated March 21, 1867 that reads: "Died at Camp Lawton, GA. while a prisoner of war about Dec. 1, 1864. O'Neil was present at the dedication of the Tammany monument at Gettysburg in September 1891. No record at Andersonville was located for Byron.

Sergeant Joseph Schneider (aka Snyder) had joined the regiment at age 34 as 3rd Corporal, Co. I, June 22, 1861. He was promoted to 2nd Sergeant April 1, 1862 and served as Color Sergeant while on the Peninsula. He was carried on the rolls at Fort Hamilton, New York Harbor between Dec. 1862 and August 1863 where he drilled recruits. On October 20, 1864 Schneider was admitted to the hospital at Andersonville suffering from Scurvy. Paroled at Savannah, November 20, he died Nov. 23, while on board a steamer enroute to New York.

Co. K Sergeants L. Burns, J. Ritter and E. Sullivan were all long time original members of the regiment. Burns was released April 25, 1865 and mustered out in New York City May 16. Ritter, a native of Aargua, Switzerland, stood five feet five inches, had grey eyes, brown hair and had been a sailor prior to joining the regiment at age 20. Wounded at Gettysburg, Ritter was promoted to Corporal and then to Sergeant between September 1863 and April 1864. Paroled at North East Ferry Feb. 27, 1865, Ritter was sent to USA General Hospital in New York City March 21. He was discharged June 7, 1865. Eugene Sullivan had been captured at Ball's Bluff and spent significant time in New York on recruiting duty. He was released at Jacksonville, April 28, 1865.[27]

Of the seventy-six privates captured on June 22, twenty-one died either at Andersonville or during their transfer to other prisons. Five had been with the regiment since 1861, four had served less than six months and twelve were men that had joined in 1863 after Gettysburg.

William Curran (aka Carroll), Co. B, a native of Ireland, stood five feet ten inches, had brown hair and eyes and was a shoemaker. He joined

---

[27] Aargua is located in German speaking north central Switzerland. Pension records show an invalid application 696021, March 27, 1889, Certificate 756092. An application 779239 for a minor child named Magdalena was filed Feb. 26, 1903. On March 11, 1865, Ritter sent a letter from Camp Parole, Annapolis regarding the death of Private Isaac Hadden to his wife at 272 Sixth Street New York City. American Historic Manuscripts Collection, NYHS, Hadden, Isaac. Statement of Emeline Cornell and Caroline Moeschen in relation to the claim of Catherine Hadden, widow of Isaac Hadden. May 16, 1866. In this letter a reference is made that Ritter was currently in Europe. For the writings of Eugene Sullivan see Chapter 8. Sullivan was a senior official of the regiment's veteran's association and was present at the dedication of the Tammany Monument at Gettysburg in September 1891.

the regiment June 10, 1861 at age 35 and re-enlisted as a veteran February 22, 1864 at age 41. Curran died at Andersonville November 15, 1864 from Scurvy.[28]

Garrett Hyde, Co. C, joined the regiment June 19, 1861 at age 23, was captured at Ball's Bluff in October 1861 and paroled in February 1862. He died October 18, 1864 at Andersonville from Scurvy.[29]

William Mulcahy, Co. E, joined the regiment September 18, 1861 at age 26. He died in Andersonville October 26 from Diarrhea.[30]

Jeremiah Gearin, Co. E, joined the regiment June 2, 1861 at age 21, was taken prisoner at Ball's Bluff and paroled in Feb. 1862. He died in Andersonville August 26, 1864 from Diarrhea. Gearin's file contains a letter that reads: "New York City, December 28. Col. will you please to send me word whether you have received any word from Jerrymire Gearen who was taken prisoner in front of Petersburg on or about the 22nd of June 1864, he belong to the 42nd Tammany Regiment, New York Vol. whose time of service is out on the 22nd of June. I have seen two young men who was prisoner with him and they told me he was dead. Will you be so kind as to let me know whether it is so or not ... Direct your answer to Mary Ann Gearren in care of John Short, 154 Cherry Street, New York". The record indicates that the letter was received on Dec. 30 and a response was written Jan. 11, 1865. The record does not identify who the letter was sent to or what the response was. The record of the Tammany regiment included in the Report of the Adjutant General of New York, states that Gearin was mustered out with the regiment on July 13, 1864. However, Gearin's file contains a War Department Notation dated July 19, 1872,

---

[28] Curran is buried at Andersonville in Grave 12015 under the name of Carroll. Soldier's Story page 310. There is another William Curran that served with the regiment who was wounded at Antietam and discharged April 1, 1863.

[29] Hyde is buried in Grave 11083 at Andersonville, Soldier's Story page 314. Hyde was not carried on the rolls of the 82nd and 59th NY regiments indicating that he had not re-enlisted as a veteran and would have been mustered out with the regiment in July had he not been captured.

[30] Mulcahy is buried in Grave 11466 under the name Mulcaby, Soldier's Story page 317. As his original enlistment had not run out Mulcahy was transferred to the 82nd and 59th NY. His record with the 82nd NY has him promoted to Sergeant. It is quite possible that Mulcahy should have been included in this chapter as a non-commissioned officer.

Bookmark 3444B1872, that reads: "The charge of desertion against this man is removed. He was captured June 22, 1864 near Petersburg, VA and died at Andersonville, GA August, 26, 1864 of Diarrhea while a prisoner of war."[31]

Andrew Caldwell, Co. A joined the regiment March 31, 1864 at age 36. He died in Andersonville November 4, 1864 from Scurvy.[32]

Henry C. Black, Co. H joined the regiment February 20, 1864 at age 22. He died in Andersonville November 12, 1864 from Scurvy.[33]

Isaac Hadden's letters were referred to in some detail above and in Chapter 23. He stood five feet eight inches, had blue eyes, was a ship fastener and joined Co. K of the regiment April 4, 1864 at age 33. He died February 16, 1865 at Florence, South Carolina. His record contains two letters written by M. F. Hadden dated September 18, 1864 and January 2, 1865 from Green Point, NY directed to Colonel W. Hoffman inquiring about information on Isaac and stating that the last time they had heard from him was June 27 when he was in Richmond. The record only states that the letters were received and answered.[34]

---

[31] The charge of desertion mentioned in the War Department Notation most likely referred to charges that had been placed on Gearin's record related to his parole after his capture at Ball's Bluff in 1861. No record of where Gearin is buried has been located.

[32] Caldwell is buried in Grave 11807 at Andersonville. Soldier's Story page 309.

[33] Black, Henry C. is buried in Grave 11971 at Andersonville. Soldier's Story page 308

[34] The letters were written by Isaac's brother Melancthon F. Hadden (1824-1903). Letters were written by Martin V. B. Phillips, a veteran of the 26th Illinois Infantry during 1866 in support of claims for assistance by Isaac's wife Catherine stating that he had seen Isaac "dead on the bank of the RR on or about the 16th of February 1865. His body... was being transferred from Florence, South Carolina, for some point north...believes that said Hadden died of starvation and scurvy and that... his death was caused by exposure and hardship while a prisoner of war." American Historical Manuscripts Collection, NYHS, Hadden, Isaac. Letters by M. V. B. Phillips. There is a record of a Private Martin V. B. Phillips, 26 IL, having been captured at Missionary Ridge, TN, Nov. 25, 1863 and being at Andersonville.

John N. Wilkinson, Co. A joined the regiment July 11, 1863 at age 34. He died in Andersonville October 15, 1864 of Scurvy.[35]

Michael Corcoran, Co. A joined the regiment at age 34 as a substitute August 26, 1863 and was absent sick between October 17, 1863 and March 1864. He died in Andersonville November 3, 1864 of Scurvy.[36]

William Rapp, Co. B joined the regiment in Brooklyn, New York August 31, 1863 at age 23 as a substitute. A native of Germany, he stood 5 feet seven inches, had blue eyes and light brown hair and was a butcher. His record contains muster sheets that list him as "deserted on the march to Bristoe Station, Oct. 14, 1863". He was actually taken prisoner and paroled arriving at College Green Barracks, Camp Parole where he was assigned to 2nd Battalion, Paroled Prisoners awaiting exchange and orders for returning to his regiment. New York Times, December 29, 1863, listed as W. Repp, Co. C, 42 NY. Following his recapture he died in Andersonville November 3, 1864 from Scurvy.[37]

William Taylor, Co. B joined the regiment August 31, 1863 at age 32. He died at Andersonville January 17, 1865 from Scurvy.[38]

Joseph Abbinson, Co. C joined the regiment December 24, 1863 at age 19. He died at Andersonville August 28, 1864 from Diarrhea.[39]

Robert McLean, Co. F joined the regiment September 12, 1863 at age 19. He died at Andersonville October 6, 1864 from Scurvy.[40]

James Connell, Co. G joined the regiment July 7, 1861. He died at Andersonville, Nov. 1, 1864.

Charles Martin, Co. G joined the regiment August 23, 1863 at age 43. He died at Andersonville a year later on August 32, 1864 from Diarrhea.[41]

---

[35] Wilkinson is buried in Grave 10977 at Andersonville. Soldier's Story page 323. Some records list his date of death as Oct. 14 and his rank as Corporal.

[36] Corcoran is buried in Grave 11775 at Andersonville as M. Cochran. Soldier's Story page 310.

[37] Rapp is buried in Grave 11760 as W. Ripp. Soldier's Story, page 319.

[38] Taylor is buried in Grave 12480 at Andersonville. Soldier's Story page 321. His record with the 59th NY lists his date of death as Jan. 19.

[39] Abbinson is buried in Grave 7062 at Andersonville as J. Albarson. Soldiers Story, page 307.

[40] McLean s buried in Grave 10393 at Andersonville as R. McLain. Soldier's Story page 317.

[41] Martin is buried in Grave 6543 at Andersonville. Soldier's Story page 316.

John Black, Co. G joined the regiment August 26, 1863 at age 22. He died at Andersonville October 16, 1864 from Scurvy.[42]

David G. Moran, Co. G joined the regiment August 28, 1863 at age 35. He died at Andersonville October 30, 1864 from Diarrhea.[43]

Thomas H. Bailey, Co. I joined the regiment August 24, 1863 at age 25. He died at Andersonville September 13, 1864 from Pneumonia.[44]

Henry Meyer, Co. I joined the regiment on August 24, 1863 at age19. He died at Andersonville September 15, 1864 from Scurvy.[45]

---

[42] Black, John is buried in Grave 11018 at Andersonville. Soldier's Story page 308.

[43] Moran is buried in Grave 11650 incorrectly identified in Soldier's Story page 317 as from the 40th NY. NARA record of David G. Moran confirms date and cause of death and burial in Grave 11650 at Andersonville. Andersonville records updated July 2015.

[44] Bailey is buried in Grave 8650 at Andersonville as T. Daley, Soldier's Story, page 311.

[45] The records of the Adjutant General of New York show two men named Henry Meyer as members of the Tammany regiment. Both joined at age 19. One was mustered into Co. I, August 24, 1863 the other into Co. F on September 12 or 14, following his enlistment on August 25 in New York's Fourth District. NARA records have a notation from the War Department dated Aug. 9, 1866 (538-1866) stating the man that died at Andersonville was the one that had been mustered into Co. I. NARA records are confusing in that they contain a record of a Henry Meyer, a native of Germany who had joined as a substitute for John O'Hollan in New York's Fourth Congressional District and stood five feet three inches, had grey eyes and was a baker by trade. This man is listed as assigned to Co. I, which is in conflict with the records of the Adjutant General of New York that has the man joining from the Fourth District in Co. F. Both men are listed as having been transferred to Co. C 82nd NY on June 28, 1864. Records of the 82nd NY have the man from Co. I "transferred…while a prisoner of war" and subsequently transferred to Co. D 59th NY July 10. The other man is listed only as transferred to Co. F 59th NY July 10. The records of the 59th NY states: "Meyers, Henry, Private, transferred from Eighty-second Infantry to Co. D, this regiment, July 10, 1864 while a prisoner of war; died September 15, 1864, at Andersonville, GA, also borne as Myers". There is no listing of another Henry Meyers in the records of the 59th NY but there is a record of a Henry Myer that was transferred to Co. F of the 59th while a prisoner of war. That record lists the man as "absent at Camp Parole, Annapolis, MD, at muster out of company" suggesting only that the man's whereabouts were unknown. A note on the "Memorandum from Prisoner of War Records" for Henry Meyers, in his NARA file, says that he "died in quarters, Sep. 15" however no record of

Dennis Laheff, Co. K joined the regiment March 10, 1864. He died at Andersonville March 14, 1865 from Diahhrea.[46]

James Larkins, Co. K joined the regiment as a substitute for John Barrett on September 14, 1863 at age 23. A native of Ireland he stood 5 feet 5 inches tall, had blue eyes, light hair and a light complexion and was a clerk. He died at Millen, GA, November 15, 1864.[47]

What is remarkable is that the following fifty-five privates captured on June 22 survived their imprisonment at Andersonville.

Company A: Thomas Clairmount, Thomas Griffin, David Mehon, Patrick O'Shea and Benjamin Solomon.[48]

Company B: Richard Fitzpatrick, William Kongezer, John McKenna and Brice Moore.[49]

---

a grave for a Tammany man named Henry Meyer, or any other spelling of the name, appears in Soldier's Story. Further confusing the issue is a NARA record with regimental muster sheets for Henry Meyers of Co. F that shows him sick in hospital between October 1863 and April 1864. That record also shows him on a list of deserters from Convalescent Camp, VA as of November 13, 1863. The man on that list is said to be 27 years old and five feet 1 inch tall. Hopefully information located in the future will clarify exactly what is correct.

46 Laheff is buried at Andersonville in Grave 12775. Soldier's Story page 315.

47 Documents of the Assembly of the State of New York, 124th Session, 1901, Vol. 6, 59th NY, page 511.

48 Clairmount, 24, a native of England stood five feet two, had blue eyes, brown hair and was a mason. He joined March 25, 1864. Pension records show an invalid application 1063436 dated Oct. 10, 1891. Griffin joined June 22, 1861. He was mustered out in New York January 27, 1865. He was not transferred to the 59th NY indicating that he had not re-enlisted and would have been one of the men whose enlistment had run out the day he was captured. Mehon, aka Meehan, joined April 1, 1864, was paroled April 19, 1865. O'Shea joined Jan. 23, 1864 and had previously served in the 176th NY and was paroled April 19, 1865. Solomon, 20, a native New Yorker, stood five feet eight, had black eyes and dark hair and was a cigar maker. He was mustered in March 29, 1864. Paroled at Goldsboro, NC March 15, 1865 he was on furlough from 2nd Battalion Paroled Prisoners Annapolis from May 4, 1864 until May 27 and mustered out June 17 at Camp Parole.

49 Fitzpatrick, 30, joined the regiment April 12, 1864. He was paroled April 28, 1865 and mustered out July 21 in New York. Kongezer (aka Ningeser), 27, mustered in on June 22, 1861 and re-enlisted as a veteran Feb. 22, 1864. Records of the 59th NY list him as paroled, promoted First Sergeant April 26, 1865 and

Company C: August Kehrweider, William Liese, Alanson Warner and Percival Werner.[50]

Company D: Dennis Collins, Cornelius Blackburn, Patrick Cain, Archibald Hayes, James Maher, David McGarrell, John Ray, Antone Schrodio and Dedrick Schultz.[51]

---

commissioned but not mustered as Second Lieut. June 30, 1865 when mustered out with that regiment at Munson's Hill. McKenna, 26, mustered in June 22, 1861 and did not re-enlist as a veteran. He was released November 27, 1864 and mustered out Feb. 3, 1865 in NY. Moore, 21, mustered in June 22, 1861 and did not re-enlist as a veteran. He was sent to Millen Oct. 31, 1864 and mustered out Jan. 28, 1865 in NY.

[50] Kehrweider, 25, mustered in July 6, 1861. He was wounded slightly at Chancellorsville (Second Fredericksburg) May 1863, paroled November 30, 1864 at Savannah and mustered out in New York March 1, 1865. Liese, 28, mustered in August 24, 1863, was paroled May 17, 1865 and mustered out with the 59th NY June 30. A. Warner, 18, enlisted in Schenectady New York, mustered in on September 14, 1863, was exchanged Nov. 14, 1864 at Savannah and mustered out with the 59th NY June 30, 1865. P. Werner, 20, mustered in August 26, 1863 and was exchanged April 1, 1865.

[51] Collins, 24, a native of Clare, Ireland, stood five feet four, had brown eyes and hair, was a blacksmith by trade and mustered in June 22, 1861. He was wounded at Fredericksburg, Dec. 1862, hospitalized until Nov. 29, 1863 at Hammond General Hospital, Point Lookout, MD and re-enlisted as a veteran March 25, 1864. His record is completely silent on when he was captured or the date he was released. There is a muster sheet that places him with the 2nd Battalion, Paroled Prisoners Annapolis, MD for Jan.-Feb. 1865. He would then have been sent to his unit to finish his enlistment. The rosters of the 82nd and 59th NY state that he was transferred to them "while a prisoner of war" and mustered out with the 59th on June 30, 1865. It is possible that Collins was captured in the Wilderness, at Spotsylvania or Cold Harbor rather than on the Jerusalem Plank Road. He is included here since that is the most likely place given the number of men captured at the different battles. Blackburn, 24, a native of Tipperary, Ireland, stood five feet five inches, had brown eyes and dark hair and was a laborer. He was mustered in July 6, 1861, was wounded at Antietam, was hospitalized for most of 1863 and re-enlisted as a veteran March 25, 1864. He was paroled at Savannah, Nov. 27, 1864 and mustered out with the 59th NY June 30, 1865. Cain, 28, a native of Sligo, Ireland stood five feet eleven inches, had brown hair and eyes and was a laborer. He mustered in July 5, 1861, was wounded at Gettysburg and re-enlisted as a veteran March 25, 1864. He was paroled at N. E. Ferry, Feb. 28, 1865 was admitted to the hospital in Annapolis March 5, returned

Company E: Francis Crilly, William Carey, James MacDonald, John Mitchell, James Ostrander, Henry Roach and Michael Walsh.[52]

to duty May 11 and was mustered out with the 59th NY on June 30. Hays, 35, mustered in July 11, 1863. He was paroled Dec. 16, 1864 at Charleston, returned to duty May 5, 1865 and mustered out with the 59th NY on June 30. Maher, 26, mustered in June 22, 1861 and did not re-enlist as a veteran. He was released November 26, 1864 at Savannah and mustered out in New York Feb. 10, 1865. McGarrel, 26, mustered in June 22, 1861 and did not re-enlist as a veteran. He was released Nov. 27, 1864 at Savannah and mustered out in New York Feb. 3, 1865. Ray, 18 mustered in July 11, 1863. Details of his release are not known. He was mustered out June 22, 1865 in New York. Schrodio (aka Schrade), 25, a native of Germany, joined the regiment as a substitute for John W. Hanna living at 186 West 41st St. in the 22nd Ward of New York City and was mustered in July 11, 1863. He stood 5 feet four, had dark hair and eyes and was a blacksmith. He was sent to Millen Nov. 11, 1864. Schultz, 28, enrolled as a substitute and was mustered in July 11, 1863, was transferred to the 59th NY as a prisoner of war, paroled on an unknown date and mustered out July 28, 1865 at Hicks General Hospital, Baltimore.

[52] Crilly (aka Cully), 34, a native of Ireland, a laborer, stood five feet six, had blue eyes and dark hair, mustered in June 22, 1861, was captured previously at Ball's Bluff and did not re-enlist as a veteran. He was paroled Nov. 30, 1864 at Savannah, reported at Camp Parole Dec. 10, was on leave until Jan. 10 and was sent to New York to be mustered out Jan. 27, 1865. Crilly's record contains a letter dated September 22, 1864 from his wife Ann at E48[th] St and 1st Ave. NY City to General Hoffman inquiring about the status of her husband that is very similar to the letter by the wife of Sgt. Dixon presented previously. Ann Crilly's letter says: "…his time of service expiring…relief is stopped from me on yesterday, I am a poor woman and have a child to support…will not give me any until you inform me". Carey, 18, a native of Ireland, a laborer, stood five feet seven, had hazel eyes and dark hair mustered in June 22, 1861. He re-enlisted as a veteran Feb. 25, 1864. Carey was detailed on recruitment duty at Riker's Island, NY, July 27, 1863 and then at the regimental recruiting office on Centre St, NY City until March 1864. He was taken ill and went home to Norwich, CT until the end of April when he reported to Tammany Hall. On May 4, on the way back to the regiment he was arrested while in uniform but without a pass as a deserter in Washington. A letter sent by Lieut. Cunningham, commanding Co. E to the Provost Marshal of Washington dated June 7 from the regiment camp near Cold Harbor stating that Carey "…is not by any means, considered a deserter". Carey was admitted to the hospital at Andersonville Aug. 17, 1864 suffering from Diarrhea, was at Camp Lawton Nov. 20, 1864, paroled at Savannah Nov. 21 and was sent to Camp Distribution Jan. 7, 1865, was promoted to Sgt. June 4,

Company F: Herbert Stout, Charles Bach, John Brown, Lewis Dupray, William Hughes and Gottlieb Scifang.[53]

Company G: Thomas Dough, Jacob Krabs, Matthew Walsh and Edward Yaw.[54]

1865 and mustered out with the 59th NY on June 30. MacDonald, 34, mustered in September 4, 1863. The exact date of his capture is unclear. He could have been captured in the Wilderness, Spotsylvania or at Cold Harbor but is listed here as this is the most probable location. His parole date is also unknown. He was discharged July 6, 1865 at Rochester, NY. Pension records show an Invalid Application 76742 filed July 10, 1865: Certificate 163947. Mitchell, 24, mustered in June 22, 1861 and did not re-enlist as a veteran. He was mustered out May 15, 1865 in New York. Ostander mustered in September 2, 1863, was assigned for several months to recruiting duty (see chapter 17), paroled at Charleston Dec. 10, 1864 and mustered out with the 59th NY. Roach, 32, mustered in June 21, 1861, was wounded in the leg at Savage Station in 1862 and did not re-enlist as a veteran. He was released Nov. 21, 1864 and mustered out in New York Jan. 9, 1865. Walsh, 19, mustered in June 22, 1861, spent significant time as a pioneer and regimental cook, was paroled at Savannah, Nov. 21, 1864, reported to Camp Parole, was on furlough from Dec. 6 to Jan. 5, 1865. Regimental records include another Michael Walsh, 27, who is listed as having deserted June 30, 1861.

[53] Stout, 26, mustered in June 22, 1861. A native of Germany he stood five feet three, had blue eyes, dark hair, was a tarnisher by trade, had been previously captured at Fredericksburg in Dec. 1862 and did not re-enlist as a veteran. He was paroled at Charleston Dec. 6, 1864, arrived at Camp Parole Dec. 15, on furlough until Jan. 18, 1865 and sent to New York to be mustered out March 1. Bach, 29, mustered in June 22, 1861, was wounded at Gettysburg and did not re-enlist as a veteran. He was released April, 28, 1865 and was mustered out in New York July 11. Brown, 24, a native of Ireland, mustered in June 22, 1861 and did not re-enlist as a veteran (See Chapter 18). He was paroled at Savannah, Nov. 24, 1864, reported to Camp Parole Nov. 28 and was mustered out in New York, Jan. 12, 1865. Dupray mustered in September 12, 1863. Records of the 59th NY show him at Camp Parole on the muster out date of that regiment in June 1865. Hughes mustered in September 12, 1863. Details of his release are unclear. He was mustered out June 15, 1865 in New York. Scifang, 35, mustered in June 22, 1861 and did not re-enlist as a veteran. He was released Feb. 26, 1865 and mustered out in New York April 10.

[54] Dough (aka Dow, Daw), 21, a native of Oswego New York, stood five feet nine, a boatman mustered in August 26, 1863 as a substitute for William Readon. While a prisoner at Andersonville he and other prisoners joined the 10th TN, C.S.A. Further details will be presented later in this chapter. Krabs (aka Krebs),

Company H: John Smithwick, William Gunther, Bernard Minturn and James Ward.[55]

Company I: Matthew Killeavy, Daniel Kelly, William Kraser, William Montgomery, John Pett, Thomas Ryan and John Vilbert.[56]

21, a native of Germany, stood five feet 3 inches, had grey eyes and light hair and had been a farmer. He mustered in August 26, 1863 as a substitute for William Grotucloss who had been drafted August 19 in the 6th District of New York. The roster of the 59th NY list Krebs as a prisoner of war and his service record reads: "no record subsequent to June 21, 1864" although there are references to unclear activity in 1884, 1885 and 1903 that might be related to pension applications. Walsh, 19, a native New Yorker, stood five feet five, had blue eyes, brown hair and was a laborer. He mustered in August 26, 1863 as a substitute for W. W. Richardson. Records of the 59th NY list him as "absent prisoner of war since June 22, 1864 and at muster out of company". Yaw mustered in August 27, 1863. His Memorandum from Prisoner of War Records shows him as "escaped at Charleston, March 1, 1865". On March 17 he was sent from Fort Columbus, New York Harbor to Annapolis and was carried on the muster roll of escaped prisoners, 2d Battalion Paroled Prisoners. He was mustered out with the 59th NY June 30, 1865.

[55] Smithwick, 19, a Boston man, enlisted with Uncle Pat in June 1861. A native of Kilkenny, Ireland, he stood five feet six, had blue eyes and was a baker. He had been captured previously on the James River in July 1862, wounded at Antietam and Gettysburg, had served as the regimental baker and had not re-enlisted as a veteran. He was paroled Nov. 19, 1864 at Savannah, admitted to hospital in Annapolis Nov. 25, sent to Baltimore Nov. 27 and mustered out in New York January 30, 1865. Gunther (aka Graser), 24, mustered in Feb. 23, 1864. A record exists stating that he was exchanged April 1, 1865 and mustered out May 29, 1865 at Fort Snelling, MN. Minturn, 19, another Boston man, had been wounded at Antietam and did not re-enlist as a veteran. He was paroled April 28, 1865 near Petersburg. Ward, 24, a native New Yorker, stood five feet seven, had hazel eyes and was a seaman. He agreed to serve as a substitute for John H. Dally of Brooklyn on September 12, 1863. He was paroled Nov. 20, 1864 at Savannah, reported to Camp Parole Nov. 29 and was sent to Camp Distribution Dec. 3. Records of the 59th NY show him promoted to Sgt. In May or June 1865 and mustered out with that regiment on June 30.

[56] Killeavy, 25, mustered in September 16, 1863. Specifics on his capture and release are sketchy. He was carried on the roll of 2nd Battalion, Paroled Prisoners, Camp Parole, Annapolis as "absent on furlough starting Dec. 10, 1864 for thirty days". Records of the 59th NY have him absent at Camp Parole at the muster out of that regiment. It is possible that he was captured somewhere other than at

Company K: John Fisher, Charles Hartman, John McGowan and Patrick McNamee.[57]

the Jerusalem Plank Road but that is the most likely place given the number of men taken prisoner there. Kelly, 25, a native of Donegal, Ireland, stood five feet six inches, had grey eyes and brown hair and was a machinist. He mustered in June 21, 1861 and re-enlisted as a veteran March 25, 1864. His rank is unclear as some records have him as a private and others as a sergeant. He was paroled Nov. 26, 1864 at Savannah and was carried on the rolls of Camp Parole Hospital in Dec. and 2nd Battalion, Paroled Prisoners, Camp Parole in January and February 1865. He mustered out with the 59th NY, June 30, 1865. Kraser, 33, a native of Germany, stood five feet six, had blue eyes and brown hair and was a mason. He mustered in July 6, 1861 and re-enlisted as a veteran March 26, 1864. He was exchanged April 1, 1865 and mustered out in New York City August 16, 1865. Montgomery, 25, a native of Canada had blue eyes, brown hair, stood five feet five inches and mustered in August 10, 1863 as a substitute for Valantine Wolf of Buffalo, NY. Details on his release are not known. His record has a reference to a pension case 674608, April 11, 1889 and a notation "claims escape". He was mustered out with the 59th NY June 30, 1865. Pett (aka Bett), 21, a native of Germany, stood five feet ten inches, had blue eyes, light hair and was a steward. He mustered in August 26, 1863 as a substitute for William H. Ritch. He was sent to Millen, Nov. 11, 1864 and mustered out at Howard General Hospital in June 1865. Ryan, 31, mustered in June 22, 1861. He had been wounded at Antietam and did not re-enlist as a veteran. He escaped from Wilmington, N. C. February 22, 1865, arrived at Camp Parole March 7 and was mustered out in New York April 4, 1865. Vilbert, 23, mustered in July 6, 1861, was wounded at Antietam and Gettysburg. He was confined at Florence, S. C. Nov. 29, 1864. His record has a reference to pension cases 749068 and 141533 dated March 5, 1890. He was mustered out June 7, 1865 at Munson's Hill.

[57] Fisher, 27, mustered in July 11, 1863. Details on his release are unknown. He was mustered out with the 59th NY June 30, 1865. Hartman, 20, mustered in July 11, 1863. He was paroled Nov. 30, 1864 at Savannah and was on leave from Dec. 16, 1864 until January 27, 1865 from 2nd Battalion, Paroled Prisoners Annapolis, MD. His record with the 59th NY shows him paroled in March or April 1865 raising the question of whether he was recaptured. He was mustered out June 30, 1865 at Munson's Hill. McGowan, 32, a native of Ireland, stood five feet seven, had blue eyes, dark hair and was a machinist. He mustered in April 6, 1864. Details on his release are unknown. His record shows him on the rolls of 2nd Battalion Paroled Prisoners Annapolis and absent on furlough from December 25, 1864 until January 25, 1865. He was arrested April 3, 1865 in New York City by Special Officer E. M. Davis at 23 Chatham Street and sent to Fort Columbus. He was mustered out with the 59th NY June 30, 1865. McNamee, 19, mustered

Lafayette Clarke, 28, mustered in March 22, 1864 but was not assigned to a specific company. He was paroled in Feb. 1865 at N. E. Ferry, N. C. and mustered out August 14, 1865 at Elmira, New York.

The record is unclear for Oliver Adams (aka Adam Oliver), Co. I. He was mustered in August 24, 1863. Although his record does not have a reference to his being captured the records of the 59th NY state that he was transferred to that regiment as Adam Oliver, a prisoner of war. Two Tammany men George Schwab, Co. F and John Myers, Co. G were captured in the area of the Weldon Railroad but not on June 22.[58]

Looking at the men that were captured it is clear that the entire regiment, all ten companies, were taken prisoner. It is also clear that men that were due to be discharged, their terms of enlistment having expired on June 22, were not "held back". There were however, at least thirty-four Tammany men that were fortunate enough to have been on special duty that allowed them to avoid capture.[59]

---

in July 11, 1863. He was admitted to Andersonville hospital September 15, 1864 suffering from Scurvy. He returned north January 6, 1865 and was mustered out June 30 in New York.

[58] Adams would most likely have been captured at Jerusalem Plank Road. Myers was captured August 25, 1864 at Ream's Station after he had been transferred to the 59th NY. He escaped March 13, 1865 at Fayetteville, NC, was at Newbern, NC March 30, 1865 and passed through Washington April 17. He was mustered out with the 59th NY at Munson's Hill. Schwab, 20, mustered in September 12, 1863. His record states that he was captured at the Weldon Railroad July 9, 1864, sent to Richmond July 10 and to Salisbury, N. C. October 9, 1864. His POW record has a notation stating he was sick and admitted to a hospital in Richmond and that he was a baker, age 17.

[59] Men on special assignments were: Patrick Boyle, division butcher, William Desmond, blacksmith, Hiram Manton, cook at regimental hospital, Thomas Coleman, Charles Carr and Hugh Riley, nurses at regimental hospital, Patrick McHale, quartermaster duty, Charles Miller, ambulance trains, Amasa Soper, carpentry, William Vaneaver, wagon driver, Ezra Webb, corps clerk, Charles Wilson, QM clerk, John Deaveson, brigade QM duty, James H. Welch, Quartermaster Sgt., Michael Spellman, brigade QM wagon driver, Alexander Smith, brigade blacksmith, John Sands, Edward Kelly, William Lynch and John Boyd, pioneers, Daniel Leddy, brigade QM duty, Geradus Mabie, Asst. wagon master, 3rd Brigade, Frank Kennedy, brigade QM teamster, Patrick Kehoe, division provost guard, John Elliot, regimental servant and wood cutter, William Desmond, blacksmith, Thomas Dennis, brigade QM teamster, William Davis,

Captain Ed Cauvet, Co. C, serving as Provost Commander, Second Corps and First Lieut. Morgan Doheny, Regimental Quartermaster also avoided capture. Major Patrick Downing was still "under arrest". First Lieut. John Maguire who had been in command of the regiment before Cold Harbor was not captured. Why he was not with the regiment on June 22 is unclear.[60]

Some further comments are necessary on the case of Thomas Dough, Co. G. He and another man Henry Peters, Co. K who had been captured at Cold Harbor, joined the 10th TN of the Confederate army while prisoners at Andersonville. This was made possible by authority of Confederate General John Blair Hoge and others that authorized enlistment of prisoners of foreign descent at Andersonville and other prisons.[61] On December 28, 1864 both men were captured, along with the rest of their unit, by Union forces at Egypt Station on the Mobile and Ohio rail line. On January 23, 1865 both men were confined at Alton, Illinois and enlisted in the 5th US Volunteer Infantry (Galvanized Yankees) on April 14.[62] The efforts of General Grenville M. Dodge set in motion the transfer of the men of the

---

QM teamster, Peter Reilly, regimental commissary, Joseph Crumbs, brigade commissary, William Cheeseman, mail carrier and drummer, Joseph Carr, Patrick Condon and Christopher Allen ambulance drivers.

[60] For details on E. Cauvet see Chapter 14, M. Doheny, Chapters 10 and 12. Doheny and Maguire (see Chapter 18) were mustered out with the regiment in July 1864. Details on the arrest of Major Downing are in Chapter 20.

[61] OR: S4, V3, 821: John Blair Hoge to Maj. Garnett Andrews, Gen. Gardner's HQ, November 10, 1864 reads: ...I am instructed by the Hon. Secretary of War to say that your original authority "to enlist a battalion of infantry from among the foreigners now prisoners of war at Millen, Andersonville, and other points in Georgia is enlarged ...to effect such enlistments...in any of the military prisons...". Also, OR: S4, V3, 1011-12. John Blair Hoge to Maj. Gen. Maury, Jan. 10, 1865 stating: "...that by recruiting chiefly among Catholic Irish and other foreigners and obtaining the influence of the Catholic priesthood they may secure faithful soldiers...Men born in the United States should not be received unless known to have sincere and positive predilections for the South..."

[62] What happened to Henry Peters is unclear but it is known that Thomas Dough (aka Doe) was listed as having deserted September 16, 1865 at Cottonwood, Nebraska Territory. Pension records show applications 446626 and 1089049 filed in 1882 and 1916 related to service of Doe but no indication that either application was approved. Generally, pensions were denied to men that had joined

5th US Volunteers and other Galvanized Yankees to the Department of the Missouri.[63]

As early as November 1862 various Union commanders had raised questions on how former soldiers of the Confederacy that had deserted should be handled. Instructions issued to all commands were initially to send such men to Camp Chase in Ohio.[64] Six other Tammany men had previously served in the Confederacy.

Patrick Williams, a native of Canada, stood five feet six, had blue eyes and brown hair and was a blacksmith. He mustered in September 2, 1863 and was placed on detached service October 23. He is listed as having deserted from Camp Chase, Ohio November 1, 1863.

Thomas Clark, 23, mustered in September 25, 1863. He was transferred to 30th Wisconsin Infantry April 4, 1864 by S. O. No. 36, 30th Wisconsin Volunteers, Camp Reno, Milwaukee, WI. For most of 1864 the 30th WI served in the Dakota Territory.

James Kelly, 30, a native of Scotland, stood five feet five, had blue eyes and dark hair and was a tailor. He deserted from the Confederate army March 26, 1864 and enrolled in the Tammany regiment March 29 at Stevensville, VA. On April 27, Major Downing wrote a letter requesting

---

the Confederacy while in captivity on the basis that they joined voluntarily. Doe is reported to have died Oct. 12, 1909.

[63] OR: S1, V48, 835: G. M. Dodge to Maj. Gen. Pope, Feb. 13, 1865 reads: "I recommend that the 200 men in Alton waiting decision of case in Washington, known as galvanized Yankees…be formed into a battalion and sent to me…" OR: S2, V8, 358-9: G.M. Dodge to Captain Joseph McBell: March 5, 1865 reads: "…there are 250 men in confinement at Alton, ILL, known as the "galvanized Yankees" i.e. men who were taken prisoners by the enemy during the last year, and who, to avoid starvation and death…and who in the recent raid deserted on the approach of our forces to us. These men have already applied to be sent back to their regiments, but it is not considered safe to send them where they will be in danger of capture by the enemy…These men have applied to enlist in our army…I have 3,000 miles of overland mail and telegraph route to guard, and every regiment of infantry that I can put along it will relieve that number of cavalry to use in offensive operations…". Also: OR: S1, V48, 1152. Pope to Halleck: March 11, 1865: "General Dodge informs me that a regiment can be recruited from prisoners of war at Alton. By doing so we get rid of the whole question of "galvanized Yankees"…".

[64] OR: S2, V5, 27, OR: S2, V5, 28 and OR: S2, V6, 627.

that Kelly be transferred as he had served in the Confederate army.[65] It wasn't until July 13, 1864 that Kelly was ordered by S. O. 186, Army of the Potomac to be sent to Camp Chase, Ohio for "transfer to some regiment serving with the Department of the North West".

John Price, 36, mustered in August 27, 1863. Almost immediately he was detached to Battery A, 1st RI Artillery and was transferred to the Navy April 12, 1864.

William Stewart, 35, a native of Canada, stood five feet five, had blue eyes and brown hair and was a sailor. He mustered in Aug. 26, 1863 and is listed as having deserted from Camp Chase November 1, 1863.

John Vaze mustered in August 26, 1863 and was sent to Alexandria on detached service as a former rebel October 28, 1863. Records of the 59th NY show him as sick in Carver Hospital, Washington. See chapter 17 for detailed discussion as to why it is possible that Vase was actually P. Kreis serving under an assumed name. Vaze and Kreis are the only Tammany men known to have served the Confederacy that were not transferred to units in the west, adding another fact that is consistent with them being the same person.

On June 27, General Hancock resumed command of Second Corps and immediately took steps to distance himself from the disaster of June 22. General Orders, No. 22, Headquarters, Second Army Corps announced the return of Hancock saying: " ...he desires to express his regret that during his absence from the command it suffered a disaster from the hands of the enemy which ... seriously damaged its fame. The abandonment of the line by brigades and regiments without orders and without firing a shot, and the surrender to the enemy of entire regiments by commanders without resistance was disgraceful ... the guilty will not be allowed to go unpunished, and those officers that surrendered their commands to the enemy without fighting will be brought to trial when opportunity offers ... Hereafter those skulkers who abandon the field ... will be shot down by

---

[65] The letter by Downing reads: "I most respectfully apply for the transfer of... Private James Kelly...entered the rebel army, according to his statement, nearly three years ago in South Carolina, was present at the Battles of Manassas, the siege of Sumter, Fredericksburg, Gettysburg, and Chancellorsville and served in General McLaw's division of Longstreet's corps. He deserted about 7 weeks ago, swam the Rapidan and came into our lines near Morton's Ford."

the provost guard, who are required to execute this order. This order will be read at the head of every regiment or battalion, and will not be given to the press for publication."[66]

Hancock's order was immediately followed by General Gibbon who issued General Orders, No. 51, Second Division, Second Corps, June 28 stating: " ...The disgraceful conduct of the Second Brigade, and a portion of the first ... was not to be expected from troops which gained such high reputation at Gettysburg ... Brigade commanders will at once make investigation, and report the names of the officers in the Second Brigade who first gave the order to retreat, and the names of the regimental commanders in the First Brigade who surrendered their regiments without resistance ..."[67]

Were officers placed under arrest and tried for their part in what happened on June 22 or were the orders of Hancock and Gibbon simply intended to demonstrate that they were not personally to blame for the disaster? From the perspective of the Tammany regiment it really didn't matter. The officers and men in Confederate prisons had more important issues to deal with.

Do all the numbers come close to making sense? Following Cold Harbor the strength of the Tammany regiment was estimated at 175. Subtracting the 104 casualties detailed above leaves 71. The thirty-four men known to have been on temporary duty and the four officers bring the unaccounted for to thirty three, many of whom could well have been on special detail that day or sick. Close enough! We know from the record of Major Patrick Downing that on June 29 he was in charge of a group of five officers and sixty-two men of the Tammany regiment that were authorized by pass No. 124 to travel to Washington for the purpose of being mustered out per Special Order No. 165, Headquarters, Second Army Corps.[68] Men who had time remaining on their original enlistments, or had re-enlisted, were transferred to the 82nd NY on June 28 and then to the 59th NY on July 10. The Tammany regiment disappeared from the rolls of the Second Corps.[69] On July 2, 1865 the 59th

---

[66] OR: S1, V40, 468

[67] OR: S1, V40, 480

[68] Exactly who the men were that traveled with Major Downing is unclear although the details presented above should provide a good starting point.

[69] The process of consolidation actually started on June 26 with the issuance of Special Orders No. 165, Headquarters Second Army Corps that authorized

NY arrived in New York and prepared to march in the July 4 parade. Of the 6,000 men that had been mustered into the three regiments comprising the 59th only 260 returned to be in the parade.[70]

What happened to the colors of the Tammany regiment? Not an easy question to answer as there were numerous flags carried during the three years the regiment served. Several of the original flags were described in Chapter 1. On December 4, 1862 in an article written by James Fennessy for the Irish American he said: "Many of the old regiments have lately sent their tattered banners North, and among these war torn banners will be seen, in "all its torn beauty" the flag of the Tammany Regiment (42d N.Y.V.), taken to New York by Captain Patrick J. Downing." On Monday, December 15, the colors were turned over to the Tammany Society by P. Downing accompanied by J. McGrath, J. Tobin and M. Doheny. At that meeting it was said: " ...this flag has been borne throughout the campaign, and never yet been suffered to go down before the enemy. Very properly, therefore, the society has voted to place it in a safe keeping with other ancient relics of Old Tammany".[71] It is clear that colors were captured on June 22. On April 23, 1880 a "United States flag, inscribed "Tammany" belonging to the Forty-second Regiment New York Volunteers (Tammany Regiment)" was sent to Captain James Casey by authority of Secretary of War Alexander Ramsey.[72] Exactly when the colors were returned north is unclear. There are several references to the presence of the regiment's colors over the years. In 1878 the Veteran Association of the Tammany regiment celebrated the "seventeenth anniversary of their departure for the scene of the conflict". Members met at Terrace Garden, 58th Street, enjoyed a concert and dancing. "The tattered colors of the regiment, borne through

---

division commanders to make temporary changes if they felt it would improve efficiency. Special Orders, No. 91, Second Division issued the same day consolidated the Tammany regiment for service in the field with the 59th and 82nd NY. OR: S1, V40, 444-445

[70] New York Times, July 3, 1865.

[71] Irish American, Dec. 13, 1862, page 4, column 8 and Irish American Dec. 20, 1862, page 4, column 1-2.

[72] Item No. 115, Exhibit B, Page 7: List of recaptured Union flags delivered by War Department to governors of States and others. Captured Battle Flags, House of Representatives, 50th Congress, Ex. Doc. 163, February 16, 1888.

the war, were displayed in the hall."[73] Timing and the description suggests that these colors were the ones presented in Dec. 1862. An account of the 1895 Decoration Day parade in New York reads: "Among the battle flags carried in the parade were the four belonging to the Tammany Regiment".[74] The last known display of the colors was reported on June 27, 1943, describing their presence as part of the 157th anniversary of the founding of the Columbian Order on East Seventeenth Street outside Tammany Hall on Union Square.[75]

As a final look at the numbers it helps to reference an article dated April 24, 1914. Written in response to the United States invasion of Veracruz on April 21, the article touts the Tammany Society as having actively raised troops a number of times over the years and states that in the Civil War the Tammany regiment had a total enrollment of 1210, 152 officers and men were killed, 69 died from disease or accidents and 35 died in Confederate prisons bringing the total number of men that lost their lives to 256.[76] In researching this book 1709 men were identified as having at some point been enrolled in the Tammany regiment. Requests were sent to the National Archives for the records of 529 men and 495 records were obtained. All together 225 Tammany men were identified as having lost their lives from various causes, 311 had been wounded at least once and 283 had been taken prisoner at some point during the war resulting in a final casualty rate of just short of 50%! There is little doubt in this author's mind that additional research could have done a more complete job in detailing everything that happened during the three years the Tammany regiment served. It is hoped that others will fill in the gaps.

[73] New York Times, July 19, 1878.
[74] New York Tribune, May 31, 1895, page 2. The article has the flags carried by "Stephen Wolfer, Henry Bird, John McCloughlin and John Ferguson marching under command of Captain Philip Kreis". This is further evidence of the legitimacy of the service of Philip Kreis. His status as "Captain", which was also used at the dedication of the regiment's monument at Gettysburg, was likely a rank granted through service in the Veteran Association.
[75] New York Times, June 27, 1943.
[76] New York Times, April 24, 1914. "Tammany Prepares to Recruit Troops". This article was written to detail the resolutions of the Tammany Society to raise troops in response to the invasion of Veracruz on April 21, 1914.

BIBLIOGRAPHY

Books

Alden, Ebenezer. Memorial of the Descendants of the Honorable John Alden. Printed 1867 by S. P. Brown for the family, Randolph, MA.

Armstrong, Marion V. Unfurl Those Colors, McClellan, Sumner and the Second Army Corps in the Antietam Campaign, University of Alabama Press. 2008.

Basler, Roy. Collected Works of Abraham Lincoln, Abraham Lincoln Association, Rutgers University Press, Volume 5, 1953.

Brown, Joseph Willard, The Signal Corps in the War of the Rebellion, U. S. Veteran Signal Corps Association, Boston, 1896.

Bruce, George A. The Twentieth Regiment of Massachusetts Volunteers, Houghton, Mifflin and Company, The Riverside Press, Cambridge, MA. 1906.

Busey, John W. These Honored Dead, Union Casualties at Gettysburg, Longstreet House, Hightstown, New Jersey, 1996.

Byron, Matthew, A. Crime and Punishment, The Impotency of Dueling Laws in the United States, Pro Quest, 2008.

Coco, Gregory A. From Ball's Bluff to Gettysburg and Beyond, The Civil War Letters of Private Roland E. Bowen, 15th Massachusetts Infantry, 1861-1864, Thomas Publications, Gettysburg, PA 1994.

Cogswell, Donald James. Descendants of John Cogswell, The Cogswell Family: 1635-1996. Family Line Publications, 65 Main Street, Westminster, Maryland, 1998.

Correspondence of John Sedgwick, Butternut and Blue, 1999 Baltimore, MD.

Cozzens, Peter. The Shipwreck of Their Hopes, The Battles for Chattanooga. University of Illinois Press, Chicago 1957.

Craighill, William P. The 1862 Army Officer's Pocket Companion, A Manual for Staff Officers in the Field, Stockpole Books, Mechanicsburg, PA 2002.

Dershowitz, A. M. Trial of the Officers and Crew of the Schooner Savannah, The Notable Trials Library, Special Edition, 1997, New York.

Dowdy, Clifford. The Seven Days Battles, Fairfax Press, New York, 1964.

Farwell, Byron. Ball's Bluff, A Small Battle and Its Long Shadow. EPM Publications, Inc. McLean, VA, 1990.

Ford, Andrew Elmer. Story of the Fifteenth Regiment Massachusetts Volunteer Infantry in the Civil War, Coulter Press, 1898.

Fowler, Marsha. Religion, Religious Ethics and Nursing, Springer Publishing, New York, 2012.

Gibson, Charles Dana and Gibson, E. Kay. Dictionary of Transports and Combatant Vessels Steam and Sail Employed by the Union Army 1861-1868. The Army's Navy Series, Ensign Press, Camden, Maine, 1995.

Gross, Warren Lee. The Soldier's Story, Appendix I: Deaths at Andersonville, Richardson and Company, Boston, 1872.

Hammond, Luna M. History of Madison County, State of New York, 1872.

Holien, Kim Bernard. Battle of Ball's Bluff, Publishers Press, 1985.

Johnson, Curt and Anderson, Richard C. Jr. Artillery Hell, The Employment of Artillery at Antietam, Texas A and M University Press, College Station, Texas, 1995.

Kreis, Philip. Under Two Flags, The Adventures of Philip Kreis, Story of the Tammany Regiment of New York, John Shaw Pierson Civil War Collection, Rare Book Division, Department of Rare Books and Special Collections, Princeton University Library, 1895.

Ladd, David L and Audrey J. The Bachelder Papers: Gettysburg in Their Own Words, Morningside Press, Dayton, Ohio, 1994.

Lash, Cary C. The History of Edward Baker's California Regiment, Butternut and Blue, Baltimore, MD, 2001.

Miles, Ed. Bridge Building in Wartime, Colonel Wesley Brainerd's Memoir of the Fiftieth New York Engineers, University of Tennessee Press, Knoxville, 1997.

Miller, Richard F. Harvard's Civil War, A History of the Twentieth Massachusetts Volunteer Infantry, University Press of New England, Hanover and London, 2005.

Myers, Gustavus. The History of Tammany Hall, Second edition, originally published 1917, reprinted 1968. Burt Franklin, New York.

Nofi, Albert A. A Civil War Treasury, Combined Books, Inc., Conshohocken, PA, 1992.

O'Sullivan, N. Every Dark Hour. A History of Kilmainham Jail, The 1866 Kilmainham Fenians, 2007.

Palfray, Francis W. Memoirs of William Francis Bartlett, Houghton, Osgood and Company, Boston, 1878.

Parker, John L. History of the Twenty-second Massachusetts Infantry, Published by the Regimental Association, Press of Rand Avery Company, 1887. Reprinted as Vol. 17, Army of the Potomac Series, Butternut and Blue, Baltimore, MD 1996.

Patch, Joseph D. The Battle at Ball's Bluff, Potomac Press, Leesburg, VA 1958.

Penniman. The Tanner Boy and How he Became Lieutenant General, Robert Brothers Publishers, Boston, 1864.

Priest, John Michael. Antietam: A Soldier's Battle, White Mane Publishing Company, Shippensburg, PA, 1989.

Priest, John Michael. Victory Without Triumph, Volume II, White Mane Publishing Company, Shippensburg, PA, 1996.

Rhea, Gordon, C. The Battles of Spotsylvania Court House and the Road to Yellow Tavern, Louisiana State University Press, 1997.

Rhodes, John H. The History of Battery B. First Regiment Rhode Island Light Artillery, Snow and Farnham, Providence, R. I., 1894.

Robertson, James I. Jr. The Civil War Letters of General Robert McAllister. Published for the New Jersey Civil War Centennial Commission, Rutgers University Press, 1997.

Savage, John. Fenian Heroes and Martyrs, Gertrude Kistler Memorial Library, Boston, Patrick Donahoe, Franklin Street, 1868.

Scott, Robert Garth. Fallen Leaves, The Civil War Letters of Major Henry Livermore, Kent State University Press, Kent Ohio, 1991.

Sears, Stephen W. To the Gates of Richmond, The Peninsula Campaign, Ticknor and Fields, New York, 1992.

Shea, John Gilmary. The Fallen Brave, Charles B. Richardson Co. New York, 1861.

Swan, James B. Chicago's Irish Legion, the 90th Illinois Volunteers in the Civil War. SIU Press, 2009.

Swinton, William. Campaigns of the Army of the Potomac, Blue and Grey Press, Secaucus, New Jersey, 1988.

Swinton, William. Twelve Decisive Battles of the War, Dick and Fitzgerald, New York, 1867.

Townsend, David. The Seventh Michigan Volunteer Infantry, Southeast Publications, Fort Lauderdale, FL, 1993.

Waitt, Ernest Linden. History of the Nineteenth Regiment Massachusetts Volunteers, Salem Press, 1906.

Walker, Francis A. History of the Second Army Corps, Charles Scribner's Sons, New York, 1887.

White, Colonel E. V. History of the Battle of Ball's Bluff, The Washington Press, Leesburg, VA 1904.

Wilt, Richard A. New York Soldiers in the Civil War. A Roster of Military Officers and Soldiers who Served in New York Regiments in the Civil War as Listed in the Annual Reports of the Adjutant General of the State of New York. Heritage Books, Bowie MD 1999.

Wise, Jennings Cropper. The Long Arm of Lee, The History of the Artillery of the Army of Northern Virginia, University of Nebraska Press, Lincoln Nebraska, 1991.

Newspapers

Boston Herald
Boston Journal
Boston Saturday Evening Gazette
Brooklyn Daily Standard
Brooklyn Eagle
Brooklyn Standard Union
Buffalo Courier
Democratic Mirror
Gettysburg Compiler
Madison Observer, Morrisville, New York
National Republican
National Tribune
New York Daily Tribune
New York Irish American
New York Herald
New York Leader
New York Sun
New York Times
New York Tribune
Pittsburgh Gazette Times
Richmond Dispatch
Richmond Enquirer
Richmond Examiner
Roxbury City Gazette
Saginaw (Michigan) News
The Evening Star
The Patriot, Harrisburg, PA

Other

Account of Pickett's Charge by Lieut. Colonel Rice, 19th MA, April 19, 1887, written at Ft. Totten, Dakota Territory. Vol. 1, Gettysburg Volume, Abner Doubleday Papers, NY Historical Society, New York, Gettysburg National Military Park Library, Box B-46.

American Historical Auctions, Auction Catalog, Battles and Leaders, Collection of Civil War Letters, February 24, 1996, Boston Massachusetts. Item 686.

American Quarterly Church Review, Ecclesiastical Register, Volume XVII, 1865-6, Bible House, Astor Place, New York, 1866.

Ancestry.com Message Boards, UN64B0, April 25, 2007.

Appeal of the Gettysburg Battlefield Memorial Association from the Decree of the Court of Common Pleas of Adams County, Supreme Court of Pennsylvania, May Term 1891.

Association to Commemorate the Chinese Serving in the American Civil War, Work of Gordon Kwok and others.

Congressional Record, 37th Congress, 3d Session, Chapter 74-75, 1863.

Congressional Series of United States Public Documents, American Citizens in Great Britain, United States Printing Office, 1868.

Documents of the Assembly of the State of New York, 124th Session, 1901. Volume VI, No. 30-32, Part 3, Albany.

Documents of the 50th Congress of the United States, House of Representatives, Document 163, Captured Battle Flags, 1888.

Episcopal Church, Glossary of terminology.

Farrington, William G. The Protestant Episcopal Tract Society Church Almanac, Cooper Union, New York, 1873.

Fourth Annual Report of the Bureau of Military Statistics, State of New York, Albany, 1867.

Grolier Multimedia Encyclopedia, Grolier Company, New York.

Journal of the 53rd Annual Convention of the Episcopal Church in Ohio, Trinity Church, Columbus, 1870.

Journal of the Executive Proceedings of the Senate of the United States.

Journal of the House of Representatives of the United States.

Journal of the Proceedings of the Bishops, the Clergy and the Laity of the Protestant Episcopal Church of the United States of America, General Convention, 1859, St. Paul's Church, Richmond, VA, King and Baird Printers, Philadelphia, 1860.

Longacre, Edward G. All the Way Around, Civil War Times, June 2002.

Magazine of History, Volume X, No. 3.

Mewborn, Horace. A Wonderful Exploit, Jeb Stuart's Ride Around the Army of the Potomac, Blue and Gray Magazine, Summer 1998.

National Archives, Record Group 94, records of the Adjutant General.

New York Adjutant General's Office, Records of Officers and Privates of regiments organized in New York, Volume II, Comstock and Cassidy, Albany, New York, 1864.

New York Historical Society, Manuscript Collection, Letters relating to Hadden, Issac.

New York State Archives, Albany, New York. Series BO4-62-84. Adjutant General Correspondence and Petitions, Boxes 33, 39-43, 45.

Ninety-eighth Convention of the Episcopal Church in Pennsylvania, 1882.

North Adams Massachusetts Historical Society, Records relating to John Brown.

Official Army Register of the Volunteer Force of the United States, Volume 2, 1865.

Proceedings at the Dedication of the Monument to the Tammany Regiment erected on the battlefield of Gettysburg, September 24, 1891. Tammany Society 1892.

Report of the New York State Monuments Commission for the Battlefield of Gettysburg, J. B. Lyon Company, 1916.

The Abraham Lincoln Papers at the Library of Congress, Series 1, General Correspondence, 1833-1916.

The Churchman, Volume 99, 1909, New York.

Towers, John H. Journal of the 56th Annual Convention of the Protestant Episcopal Church in Virginia, Convention held at Trinity Church, May 21-24, 1851. Volume 56-63.

U. S. War Department, The War of the Rebellion: A Compilation of the Official Records of the Union and Confederate Armies, 127 volumes, Washington, D. C. GPO, 1880-1901.

Printed in the United States
By Bookmasters